COUNTRY LIVING
M A G A Z I N E

GUIDE TO
RURAL
ENGLAND

EAST ANGLIA

By Peter Long

Published by:
Travel Publishing Ltd
7a Apollo House, Calleva Park
Aldermaston, Berks, RG7 8TN
ISBN 1-902-00769-7
© Travel Publishing Ltd

Country Living is a registered trademark of The National Magazine
Company Limited.

First Published: *2001*

COUNTRY LIVING GUIDES TO RURAL ENGLAND:

East Anglia
The South East
The South
The West Country

PLEASE NOTE:

All advertisements in this publication have been accepted in good faith
by Travel Publishing and they have not necessarily been endorsed by
Country Living Magazine.

All information is included by the publishers in good faith and is believed
to be correct at the time of going to press. No responsibility can be
accepted for errors.

Editor: Peter Long

Printing by: Scotprint, Haddington

Location Maps: © Maps in Minutes ™ (2000)   © Crown Copyright, Ordnance Survey 2001

Walk Maps: Reproduced from the 2001 Pathfinder 1:25,000 Ordnance Survey Maps by
                permission of Ordnance Survey on behalf of the Controller of Her Majesty's
                Stationery Office, © Crown Copyright MC 100035812

Cover Design: Lines & Words, Aldermaston

Cover Photo: "The Restored Windpump in Wicken Fen" © The National Trust Photographic
                Library - Photographer: Rod J Edward

Text Photos: © www.britainonview.com

Foreword

Photograph by Hugo Burnand

From a bracing walk across the hills and tarns of The Lake District to a relaxing weekend spent discovering the unspoilt hamlets of East Anglia, nothing quite matches getting off the beaten track and exploring Britain's areas of outstanding beauty.

Each month, *Country Living Magazine* celebrates the richness and diversity of our countryside with features on rural Britain and the traditions that have their roots there. So it is with great pleasure that I introduce you to the *Country Living Magazine Guide to Rural England* series. Packed with information about unusual and unique aspects of our countryside, the guides will point both fair-weather and intrepid travellers in the right direction.

Each chapter provides a fascinating tour of the East Anglia area, with insights into local heritage and history and easy-to-read facts on a wealth of places to visit, stay, eat, drink and shop.

I hope that this guide will help make your visit a rewarding and stimulating experience and that you will return inspired, refreshed and ready to head off on your next countryside adventure.

Susy Smith

Susy Smith, Editor of Country Living *Magazine*

P.S. To subscribe to Country Living Magazine every month, call 01858 438844.

Introduction

Peter Long, the editor of this guide, is an experienced travel writer who spent many years with Egon Ronay's Hotels and Restaurant Guides before joining the Travel Publishing team. He has used this experience to ensure that this East Anglian edition of **The *Country Living* Magazine Guide to England** is packed with vivid descriptions, historical stories, amusing anecdotes and interesting facts on hundreds of places in Norfolk, Suffolk, Essex and Cambridgeshire.

The coloured advertising panels within each chapter provide even more information on places to see, stay, eat, drink, shop and even exercise! We have also selected a number of walks from Jarrold's *Pathfinder Guides* which we highly recommend if you wish to appreciate fully the beauty and charm of East Anglia's rural landscape.

The guide however is not simply an "armchair tour". Its prime aim is to encourage the reader to visit the places described and discover much more about the wonderful towns, villages and countryside of East Anglia. Whether you decide to explore this region by wheeled transport or by foot we are sure you will find it a very uplifting experience.

We are always interested in receiving comments on places covered (or not covered) in our guides so please do not hesitate to use the reader reaction form provided at the rear of this guide to give us your considered comments. This will help us refine and improve the content of the next edition. We also welcome any general comments which will help improve the overall presentation of the guides themselves.

Finally, for more information on the full range of travel guides published by Travel Publishing please refer to the details and order form at the rear of this guide or log on to our website at www.travelpublishing.co.uk

Travel Publishing

Locator Map

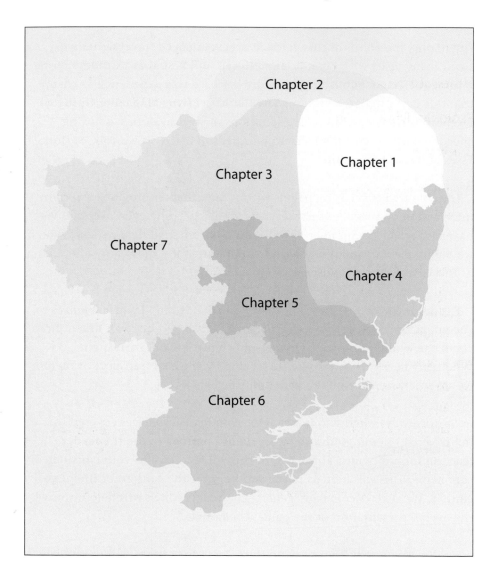

Contents

The area of Norfolk between the border with Suffolk and the county capital of Norwich is mainly flat farmland, with quiet villages, handsome old

farmhouses and the charming spires and towers of churches. The major centres of population include Diss, an old market town with a mix of Tudor, Georgian and Victorian houses and Wymondham, with timber-framed houses, a picturesque market place and an Abbey church that bears comparison even with the majestic Norwich Cathedral. Norwich, once an important centre of the worsted trade, retains many medieval buildings, a number of which now serve as museums relating the fascinating history of the region. The area to the east of this fine city contains the unique Norfolk Broads,

Norwich Cathedral

beautiful stretches of shallow water, most of them linked by navigable rivers and canals. Visitors who want to experience a bird's-eye view that encompasses the essence of the Broads should climb the tower of the 'Cathedral of the Broads', the Church of St Helen's at Ranworth. Spread out below lies a vast panorama of glittering waterways, acres of marshland dotted with windmills, reed beds which are still harvested for thatch, grand medieval churches, and farmhouses of warm, red brick.

This is Britain's finest wetland area, a National Park in all but name. Broadland covers some 220 square miles, and three main rivers, the Ant, the Thurne and the Bure, thread their way through the marshes, providing some 120 miles of navigable waterways. The Broads, long popular for restful, relaxing holidays, are also a refuge for many species of endangered birds and

plants, and during the spring and autumn they are a favourite stopping-off place for migrating birds. On the coast due east of Norwich is the old port and modern holiday resort of Great Yarmouth, where the visitor will find miles of sandy beaches, a breezy promenade, two grand old traditional piers and all the fun of the fair as well as a rich maritime heritage that lives on to this day.

Thurne, Norfolk

LOCATOR MAP

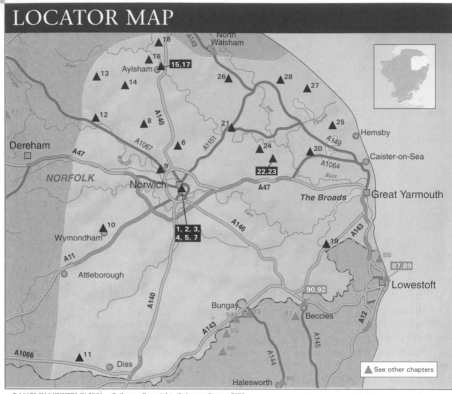

North Walsham

18

16

Aylsham **15,17**

13

14

26

28

27

12

8

21

25

Hemsby

Dereham

6

24

20

Caister-on-Sea

A1064

NORFOLK

9

Norwich

A47

The Broads Great Yarmouth

10

1, 2, 3, 4, 5, 7

Wymondham

19

87,89

Attleborough

90,92

Lowestoft

Bungay

Beccles

11

Diss

Halesworth

▲ See other chapters

© MAPS IN MINUTES ™ 2001   © Crown Copyright, Ordnance Survey 2001

Advertisers and Places of Interest

NORWICH

"Norwich has the most Dickensian atmosphere of any city I know" declared JB Priestley in his English Journey of 1933. "What a grand, higgledy-piggledy, sensible old place Norwich is!" More than half-a-century later, in a European Commission study of most habitable cities, Norwich topped the list of British contenders, well ahead of more likely

Elm Hill, Norwich

candidates such as Bath and York. The political, social and cultural capital of Norfolk, Norwich has an individual charm that is difficult to define, a beguiling atmosphere created in partly by its prodigal wealth of wonderful old buildings, partly by its intriguing dual personality as both an old-fashioned Cathedral town and a vibrant, modern metropolis. In prehistoric times, there were several settlements around the confluence of the Rivers Wensum and Yare and by the time of the Domesday Book Northwic/Norwich had become the third most populous city in England, outnumbered only by London and York. To the Norman conquerors such a major centre of population (about 5,500 residents) needed a castle to make sure its

Saxon inhabitants were kept in order.

The first **Norwich Castle**, a wooden structure, was replaced in the late 1100s by a mighty fortress in stone which, unlike most blank-walled castles of the period, is decorated with a rich façade of blind arcades and ornamental pilasters. The great fort never saw any military action and as early as the 13th century it was being used as the county gaol, a role it continued to fill until 1889. The castle is now a lively museum where the old dungeons house a forbidding display of instruments of torture, along with the death masks of some of the prisoners who were executed here. Among the countless other fascinating exhibits are the Bulwer and Miller collection of more than 2,600 English china teapots; the Langton

THE JADE TREE

39 Elm Hill, Norwich, Norfolk NR3 1HG
Tel/Fax: 01603 664615
e-mail: thejadetree@aol.com

The Jade Tree is a fine art and contemporary craft shop with its own studios where five artists work and sell. Choose an unusual gift from the range of handmade cards, embroidered textiles, contemporary jewellery, handbuilt ceramics, sculpture and more. Visitors can meet the artists and discuss commissions. All work is beautifully showcased in a 17th century merchant's house in the heart of Norwich's historic centre.

collection of around 100 cats, fashioned in porcelain, ivory, bronze, glass, and wood, and originating from anywhere between Derbyshire and China; and Margaret Elizabeth Fountaine's mind-boggling accumulation of 22,000 butterflies which she had personally netted during her travels around the world. Pride of place must go, however, to the museum's incomparable collection of paintings by the celebrated artists of the group known as the **Norwich School**. Their subjects were mostly landscape scenes, and quite apart from the artistic quality of their works, they have left a fascinating pictorial record of early 19th century Norfolk.

The Castle's function has changed over the years, but **Norwich Cathedral** is still the focus of ecclesiastical life in the county. It's even older than the castle, its service of consecration taking place 900

years ago, in 1101. This peerless building, its flint walls clad in creamy-white stone from Caen is, after Durham, the most authentic Norman cathedral in England, its appeal enhanced by later Gothic features such as the flying buttresses. The Norman cloisters are the largest in the country and notable for the 400 coloured and gilded bosses depicting scenes from medieval life. Another 1600 of these wondrous carvings decorate the glorious vaulted roof of the nave. Its treasures are too numerous to list in full, but among those not to be missed are the Saxon Bishop's Throne in the Presbytery; the lovely 14th century altar painting in St Luke's Chapel; and the richly carved canopies in the Choir.

Outside, beneath the slender 315 foot high spire soaring heavenwards, the Cathedral Close is timeless in its sense of peace. There are some 80 houses inside

---

Sun Essences

PO Box 728, Norwich NR6 6EX
Tel: 07000 785337 e-mail: sunessence@aol.com
Fax: 01603 861317 website: www.sun-essence.co.uk

Sun Essences produce a range of hand-prepared Flower Essence Blends using fresh blooms gathered from wild countryside locations. These are a safe, natural solution for stress and the daily ups and downs of family life. Pets in particular seem to benefit greatly from flower essences. They are helpful for sensitive 'show' animals and effective in calming personality extremes. Just add to their food and water. Phone or view the website for more information. Orders supplied by mail order.

Montage

4 Royal Arcade, Norwich, Norfolk NR2 1NQ
Tel: 01603 633313
e-mail: montage@onetel.co.uk

An eclectic and fascinating collection of high-quality, primarily hand-crafted English pewter, glassware, lighting and furnishings awaits visitors to **Montage**, situated in the prestigious Art Deco Royal Arcade in Norwich, built in 1899 by renowned architect George Skipper. Beautifully laid out, this spacious shop showcases a range of unique pieces including hand-blown perfume bottles and wine glasses, small ornaments, picture frames case in pewter and much more.

Norwich Cathedral

resonant epitaph: "Standing as I do, in the view of God and eternity, I realise that patriotism is not enough. I must have no hatred or bitterness towards anyone."

Every weekday in the great open **Market Square** a colourful jumble of traders' stalls offers just about every conceivable item for sale. Dominating the western side of the market square is **City Hall**, modelled on Stockholm City Hall and opened by George VI in 1938. Opinions differ about its architectural merits, but there are no such doubts about its predecessor as Civic Centre, the nearby Guildhall, a fine example of 15th century flintwork which now houses the Tourist Information Centre and a small museum.

Around the corner from London Street, in Bridewell Alley, is the **Bridewell Museum**, a late 14th century merchant's house now dedicated to Norfolk's crafts and industries. And right next door another museum/shop celebrates the county's great contribution to world cuisine, mustard. Back in the early 1800s, Jeremiah Colman perfected his blend of mustard flours and spice to produce a condiment that was smooth in texture and tart in flavour. Together with his nephew James he founded J & J Colman

the Close, some medieval, many Georgian, their residents enjoying an idyllic refuge free from cars. In this peaceful spot lie the remains of Nurse Edith Cavell. A daughter of the rector of Swardeston, a few miles south of Norwich, Nurse Cavell worked at a Red Cross hospital in occupied Brussels during the First World War. She helped some 200 Allied soldiers to escape to neutral Holland before being detected and court-martialed by the Germans. As she faced execution by firing squad on 12th October 1915, she spoke her own

COLMANS MUSTARD SHOP

15 The Royal Arcade, Norwich, Norfolk NR2 1NQ
Tel: 01603 627889 Fax: 01603 762142

For nearly 200 years, Colmans has produced fine mustards. At the **Colmans Mustard Shop** there are 15 different varieties of mustard as well as a selection of speciality gifts and original memorabilia, including books, mustard pots, cross-stitch kits and much more. The integrated museum charts the history of Jeremiah Colman, who founded the firm and improved Norwich society. Mail order catalogue available.

in 1823 and, a century and a half later, **The Mustard Shop** (see below) was established to commemorate the company's history. It also serves as a showcase for the range of Colman products which nowadays includes a variety of drinks and foods. The shop has an appropriately Victorian atmosphere with lots of mahogany and marble, and a lip-smacking display of vintage containers and advertisements.

There are still 32 churches in Norwich, all worth attention, although many are now used for purposes other than worship. Outstanding among them are **St Peter Mancroft**, a masterpiece of Gothic architecture built between 1430-55, and **St Peter Hungate**, a handsome 15th century church which, since 1933, has been a museum illustrating all aspects of the arts and crafts involved in ecclesiastical decoration and ritual. **St Gregory's Church**, now a vibrant,

go-ahead centre for the arts, takes it name from Gregory the Great, the 6th century Pope best known for his campaign to convert the heathen Anglo-Saxons of Angle-land to Christianity. His enthusiasm for this mission, it is said, was fired by the sight of fair-haired youths from that distant country being paraded for sale in the Roman slave market. On being told that the captives were "Angles", he remarked that they were well named, for they resembled angels. Impressed by their physical beauty, and pitying their ignorance of Christ's redemption, the Pope sent a party of 40 monks to Angle-land in AD596, led by Augustine, whom he consecrated as the first Archbishop of Canterbury. The **Church of St Julian** has a small cell built on one side that is the reconstructed shrine to Mother Julian, a 14th century anchoress and author of the first book known to have been written by

WORLDWIDE POTS

12-14 Ber Street, Norwich, Norfolk NR1 3EJ
Tel: 01603 625180
website: www.worldwidepots.com

Worldwide Pots offers what is undoubtedly one of the widest ranges of pots in East Anglia, with garden pots from all over the world. Selling retail and wholesale, the majority of the pots sold at this

vast emporium are handmade. All are guaranteed frost-proof.

Established in 1998 by Andrew Sloan and Stewart Piggot they are always on the search for new ranges from across the globe. A few examples of the many fabulous pots on offer here include items made of cast iron, terracotta, stoneware, glazed in a rainbow of colours, antique pots from Turkey, a range of chimeneas from Mexico, and earthenware from Vietnam, Malaysia, the Philippines and Tunisia.

Pots in every size, shape, colour and style can be found here. The large, open site in Ber Street right in the centre of Norwich is the perfect place to browse for the perfect example for any garden, from simple to ornate, delicately crafted to sturdy and practical. Whether you're seeking the right pot for any place in the garden or home, or a uniquely beautiful gift, look no further. Parking available.

CITY OF NORWICH AVIATION MUSEUM

Old Norwich Road, Horsham St Faiths, Norwich,
Norfolk NR10 3JF   Tel: 01603 893080

Follow the brown tourist signs from the A140 Norwich-Cromer road to find the **City of Norwich Aviation Museum**, a museum dedicated to keeping Norfolk's aviation heritage alive. Dominating the museum's collection is a massive Avro Vulcan bomber, a veteran of the Falklands War of 1982.

Eight other military and civilian aircraft are on show, and although they are the main attraction for many visitors, the most fascinating feature is the display within the main exhibition building showing the development of aviation in Norfolk. From the

pioneering days of aviation to present-day civilian and military operations, every aspect is covered in a number of displays that are constantly being revised and expanded. The major roles played by Norfolk-based aircraft during the great air battles of World War II are remembered by exhibitions on the USAAF 8th Air Force and the role of the Royal Air Force in this conflict.

A special section is dedicated to the operations of RAF Bomber Command's 100 Group which flew on electronic counter measure, deception and night intruder missions from a number of Norfolk airfields.

a woman. In the churchyard of **St Clement's** is the tomb of a 16th century Archbishop, Matthew Parker, whose notoriety for prying into the affairs of others is said to be the origin of the expression 'Nosey Parker'.

On the western edge of the city stands the University of East Anglia, where the **Sainsbury Centre for Visual Arts**, housed in a huge hall of aluminium and glass designed by Norman Foster, contains the eclectic collection of a the passionate art connoisseur Sir Robert Sainsbury. For more than 50 years, Sir Robert purchased whatever works of art took his fancy, ignoring fashionable trends and 'correct' choices. Sculptures and pictures by Henry Moore, Bacon and Giacometti share space with African and pre-Columbus artefacts; Egyptian, Etruscan and Roman bronzes; works by Indians and Inuits; sculptures from the

Cyclades, the South Seas, the Orient and medieval Europe.

A few miles to the north of lies the **City of Norwich Aviation Museum** (see panel above) whilst to the south of

Pull's Ferry, Norwich

BEAUFORT LODGE

62 Earlham Road, Norwich, Norfolk NR2 3DF
Tel: 01603 627928 e-mail: beaufort-lodge@faxvia.net
Fax: 01603 440712 web: www.accomodata.co.uk/beaufort.htm

Beaufort Lodge offers excellent non-smoking bed and breakfast accommodation in congenial and attractive surroundings. This charming and spacious family home dates back to Victorian times and has been thoughtfully refurbished to provide the highest standard of comfort and quality. It is ideally placed for exploring Norwich, as it is just a few minutes' walk from the city centre. There are four comfortable and well-appointed guest bedrooms (two singles, two doubles) with either ensuite facilities or private bathroom.

FELTHORPE FOREST NURSERY

Felthorpe, Norwich, Norfolk NR10 4DF
Tel: 01603 754553

Felthorpe Forest Nursery offers a comprehensive range of on-site-grown trees sold bare root or in containers. Established in 1997, this fine nursery covers 10 acres of primarily native species of trees and traditional old English hedging.

There are 150 varieties of bamboo, as well as native species of hawthorn, blackthorn, field maple and hazel trees to provide excellent hedging.

GRACIES THE DOLLY AND MINIATURES SHOP

189-191 Reepham Road, Hellesdon,
Norwich, Norfolk NR6 5NZ
Tel: 01603 429135 Fax: 01603 419496
e-mail: gracies@btclick.com website: www.gracies.co.uk

Prepare to be transported with delight by a visit to **Gracies The Dolly and Miniatures Shop** in Hellesdon. This wonderfully comprehensive shop offers a treasure trove of dolls, soft toys, collectibles and exquisite dollhouses and accessories. Run by sisters Susan Fisk and Janet Jones, this fascinating shop stocks a vast selection of teddy bears in all shapes and sizes, including a range of Steiff teddy bears, gorgeous, beautifully dressed porcelain dolls, decorative eggs, doll-making supplies, hand-made dollhouses and a wide choice of 1/12th scale miniatures. Opened in 1998, this shop must be seen to be appreciated. Many happy hours can be spent here by any enthusiast or newcomer to the joys of collecting.

The shop also features baby gifts, ornamental prams, resin gifts, porcelain clowns and a variety of cuddly toys and rag dolls. Large, bright and well-lit, this Aladdin's Cave of beautiful and finely made dolls and toys displays all its wares to their best advantage. Susan, Janet and their friendly staff offer expert advice, information and service, and also run doll-making classes for small groups. Open: Monday 10.00am- 4.00pm; Tuesday to Saturday 9.30am - 5.00pm

Norwich are the remains of *Venta Icenorum*, the Roman town established here after Boadicea's rebellion in AD 61. Unusually, this extensive site has not been disturbed by later developments, so archaeologists have been able to identify the full scale of the original settlement. Sadly, very little remains above ground, although in dry summers the grid

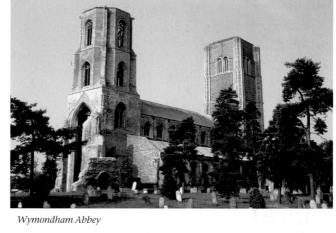

Wymondham Abbey

pattern of the streets show up as brown lines in the grass. Most of the finds discovered during excavations in 1920s and 1930s are now in Norwich Castle Museum, but the riverside site is still worth visiting, especially by those with a vivid imagination. On the southeastern outskirts of Norwich lies **Whitlingham Country Park**, with nature trails and cycle trails through woods and meadows by the River Yare.

AROUND NORWICH

PORINGLAND
6 miles SE of Norwich on the B1332

This sizeable village is surrounded by mustard fields, a dazzling sight in June when the custard-coloured blooms create a cloth of gold and, according to old folk lore, their glow shines all the way up to the moon. The name of the village will be familiar to those who love the paintings of the Norwich artist John Crome (1794-1842) whose arcadian painting of *The Poringland Oak* hangs in the Tate Gallery.

WYMONDHAM
9 miles SW of Norwich off the A11

The exterior of **Wymondham Abbey** presents one of the oddest ecclesiastical buildings in the county, while the interior reveals one of the most glorious. The Abbey was founded in 1107 by the Benedictines, or Black Monks, as they were known from the colour of their habits. The richest and most aristocratic of the monastic orders, the Black Monks apparently experienced some difficulty in respecting their solemn vows of poverty and humility. Especially the latter. The monks were constantly in conflict with the people of Wymondham. In 1249, the dissension between them was so bitter that Pope Innocent IV himself attempted to reconcile their differences. When his efforts failed, a wall was then built across the interior of the Abbey, dividing it into an area for the monks and another for the parishioners. Even that drastic measure failed to bring peace. Both parties wanted to ring their own bells, so each built a tower. The villagers erected a stately rectangular tower at the west end; the monks an octagonal one over the crossing, thus creating the Abbey's

WYMONDHAM GALLERY AND ALL THAT JAZZ

8 Market Place, Wymondham, Norfolk NR18 0AQ
Tel: 01953 602290

Established since 1993, **Wymondham Gallery and All That Jazz** is, as its names tell us, a showcase for both the fine arts and music. Set in the market square of this lovely town, it is housed in two floors of a distinguished 17th century building that has undergone various changes over the years. The ground floor features an excellent selection of artists' cards, sheet music and instruments including guitars, flutes, saxophones, keyboards and percussion instruments. Up a spiral staircase to the first floor, visitors will find a collection of artwork such as paintings, sculpture, photographs, woodcarvings and jewellery, all made by local artists and craftspeople. There are changing exhibitions featuring the work of East Anglian artists and artisans.

Proprietor John Dowding is friendly and welcoming. Himself an accomplished musician, he plays saxophone, flute and piano. He has lived in Wymondham since 1986, and plays regularly with the Wymondham Early Music Group. He also founded, in 1995, the annual Wymondham Summer Music Festival which is held at the beginning of July and showcases the talents of musicians from far and wide with a series of events that take place throughout the town.

curious exterior appearance. Step inside, however, and you find a magnificent Norman nave, 112 feet long. (It was originally twice as long, but the eastern end, along with most of the Abbey buildings, was demolished after the Dissolution of the Monasteries in 1539.) The superb hammerbeam roof is supported by 76 beautifully carved angels; there's an interesting 16th century tomb, of the last Abbot, in delicate terracotta work; and a striking modern memorial, a gilded and coloured reredos and tester, commemorating the local men who lost their lives in the First World War.

Wymondham was the home of the Kett brothers, who in 1549 were at the head of a stand made against enclosures of common land by landowners, inflation and a run of bad harvests. The brothers marched at the head of 20,000 supporters to the city of Norwich, which they captured. The Earl of Warwick led his troops against the insurgents and soon quelled the **Norfolk Rebellion** with great loss of life. The Kett brothers were hanged, one from the walls of Norwich Castle, the other from the tower of Wymondham Abbey. On the B1172 between Wymondham and Hethersett stands a somewhat infirm old oak tree on the spot where the brothers roused their supporters before marching on Norwich.

Although many of Wymondham's oldest houses were lost in the fire of 1615 when some 300 dwellings were destroyed, there are still some attractive Elizabethan buildings in the heart of the town. **The Market Place** has a splendid, picturesque octagonal Market Cross, rebuilt two years after the fire. Crowned by a pyramid roof, this appealing timber-framed building is open on all sides on the ground floor, and its upper floor is reached by an outside stairway. Also of interest is

Becket's Chapel, founded in 1174 and restored in 1559. In its long history it has served as a pilgrim's chapel, grammar school, and coal store. Currently, it houses the town library. **The Bridewell**, or House of Correction, in Bridewell Street, was built as a model prison in 1785 along lines recommended by the prison reformer, John Howard, who had condemned the earlier gaol on the site as "one of the vilest in the country". Wymondham's Bridewell is said to have served as a model for the penitentiaries established in the United States. Now owned by the town's Heritage Society, Bridewell is home to several community projects, including the **Wymondham Heritage Museum**.

Railway buffs will also want to visit the historic **Railway Station**, built in 1845 on the Great Eastern's Norwich-Ely line. At its peak, the station and its section employed over 100 people. Still providing a rail link to Norwich, London and the Midlands, the station has been restored, and its buildings house a railway museum, restaurant and tea room, and a piano showroom. Wymondham is at one end of the Mid-Norfolk Railway, a steam or diesel hauled line that runs through 11 miles of rural Norfolk, passing the valleys of the Tud, the Yare and the Tiffey before arriving at Dereham, the line's headquarters.

Diss

20 miles S of Norwich on the A1066

The late Poet Laureate, John Betjeman, voted Diss his favourite Norfolk town, and it's easy to understand his enthusiasm. The River Waveney running alongside forms the boundary between Norfolk and Suffolk, but this attractive old market town keeps itself firmly on the northern bank of the river. The town is a pleasing mixture of Tudor, Georgian and Victorian houses grouped around

The Mere, Diss

The Mere which gives the town its name, derived from the Anglo-Saxon word for standing water. The old town grew up on the hill above The Mere perhaps because, as an 18th century resident observed, *"all the filth of the town centering in the Mere, beside the many conveniences that are placed over it, make the water very bad and altogether useless;...it stinks exceedingly, and sometimes the fish rise in great numbers, so thick that they are easily taken; they are chiefly roach and eels"*. A proper sewerage system was finally installed in 1851.

There's a public park beside the six-acre Mere and from it a narrow street leads to the small Market Place. This former poultry market is dominated by **St Mary's Church**, the oldest parts of which date back some 700 years; the St Nicholas Chapel is particularly enjoyable with its wonderful corbels, angels in the roof, and gargoyles. In the early 1500s, the Rector here was John Skelton, Court poet and tutor to Prince Henry, later Henry VIII. A bitter, quarrelsome man, Skelton was appointed Poet Laureate through the patronage of Cardinal Wolsey despite the fact that most of Skelton's output has been described as 'breathless doggerel'.

Appointed Rector of Diss in 1502, he appears to have been suspended nine years later for having a concubine. Not far from his church is the delightful **Victorian Shambles** with a cast-iron veranda and a small museum inside.

BRESSINGHAM

20 miles S of Norwich off the A1066

A day to remember is guaranteed at Bressingham, where Alan Bloom's **Dell Garden** and Adrian Bloom's **Foggy Bottom Garden** are a paradise for gardeners (see panel below).

The **Steam Experience** will bring a nostalgic tear to railway enthusiasts and lovers of steam power. Bressingham is renowned for its special Steam Days, when the engines can be seen in full steam on the three narrow gauge lines, and footplate rides are given on the diesel standard gauge locomotives. Another helping of nostalgia is on hand in the

Narrow Gauge Steam, Bressingham

form of the **Dad's Army National Collection** with reconstructions of the High Street of Walmington-on-Sea.

The owner, Alan Bloom, is passionate about steam engines and also about plants, and the five acres of landscaped

---

BRESSINGHAM GARDENS

Bressingham, Norfolk IP22 2AB
Tel: 01379 688585 Fax: 01379 688490
website: www.blooms-online.com/about/bressingham.php

A day to remember is guaranteed at Bressingham, where gardeners will be in paradise and children past and present can experience the thrill of the golden age of steam. Alan Bloom, one of the most respected plantsmen of his age, created the Dell Garden and its famous Island Beds between 1955 and 1962, and his garden is now world-renowned for its collection of nearly five thousand species and varieties of hardy perennials. The Garden Centre has a comprehensive collection of hardy perennials including the Blooms Heritage Collection, plus plants for the house and conservatory and all sorts of gardening gifts and accessories, as well as a café and bookshop.

Alan's son-in-law Jaime Blake carries on the family tradition as Curator of Dell Garden, while son Adrian has created a garden for all seasons at nearby Foggy Bottom, where trees, conifers and shrubs provide a backdrop which is enhanced by plantings of perennials and ornamental grasses. The two gardens are open from April to October, the Garden Centre and Steam Experience all year round. There's a full programme of special events, lectures, talks and demonstrations. This really is a place to linger, and Alan Bloom offers B&B accommodation at his Georgian home, Bressingham Hall.

grounds are notable in themselves since they are planted with more than 5,000 perennials and other plants.

SCOLE

20 miles S of Norwich on the A140

Scole's history goes back to Roman times since it grew up alongside the Imperial highway from Ipswich to Norwich at the point where it bridged the River Waveney. Traffic on this road (the A140) became unbearable in the 1980s, but a bypass has now mercifully restored some peace to the village. There are two hostelries of note: a coaching inn of 1655, built in an extravagant style of Dutch gables, giant pilasters and towering chimney stacks, and the Crossways Inn, which must have a good claim to being the prettiest pub in the county.

LANGMERE

15 miles S of Norwich on minor road off the A140 (through Dickleburgh)

Veterans of the Second World War and their families and friends will be interested in the **100th Bomb Group Memorial Museum**, a small museum on the edge of Dickleburgh Airfield (now disused). The Museum is a tribute to the US 8th Air Force which was stationed here during the war, and includes displays of USAAF decorations and uniforms, equipment, combat records and other memorabilia. Facilities include refreshments, a museum shop, visitor centre and a picnic area.

HARLESTON

15 miles S of Norwich off the A143

This pretty market town with some notable half-timbered and Georgian houses, and a splendid 12th century coaching inn, was a favourite of the renowned architectural authority, Nikolaus Pevsner, who particularly

River Waveney, Scole

admired the early Georgian Candlers House at the northern end of the town. Another writer has described the area around the market place as *"the finest street scene in East Anglia"*. The town lies in the heart of the Waveney Valley, a lovely area which inspired many paintings by the locally-born artist, Sir Alfred Munnings.

COLTISHALL

8 miles N of Norwich on the B1150/B1354

This charming village beside the River Bure and the location of a famous World War II RAF station, captivates visitors with its riverside setting, leafy lanes, elegant Dutch-gabled houses, village green and thatched church. Coltishall has a good claim to its title of 'Gateway to Broadland' since for most cruisers this is the beginning of the navigable portion of the Bure (from the north, that is; from the south it marks the limit of navigation). Anyone interested in Norfolk's industrial heritage will want to seek out the **Ancient Lime Kiln**, next door to the Railway Tavern in Station Road. Lime, formerly an important part of Norfolk's rural economy, is obtained by heating chalk to a very high temperature in a kiln. Most of the county sits on a bed of chalk, and in the area around Coltishall and Horstead it is of a particularly high quality. The kiln at Coltishall, one of the few surviving in the country, is a listed building of finely finished brickwork, built in a style unique to Norfolk.

The top of the tapered kiln pot is level with the ground, and down below a vaulted walkway allowed access to the grills through which the lime was raked out. This was uncomfortable and even dangerous work since fresh lime, when it comes into contact with a moist surface, such as a human body, becomes burning hot. The lime had to be slaked with water before it could be used as a fertiliser, for mortar or as whitewash. Access to the kiln is by way of the Railway Tavern, but during the months from October to March the building might well have

BLACKWATER FARM

Great Witchingham, Norfolk NR9 5PH
Tel/Fax: 01362 688227

Blackwater Farm is a leading equestrian venue, home to horse trials, cross-country and schooling courses, set in 160 acres of beautiful undulating countryside. The six courses cater for a range of riders, from pre-novice to experienced. The course hosts several events throughout the year, and its facilities provide the ideal environment for your horses. The course is open for schooling all year round (weather permitting).

THE KNOT GARDEN

Heydon Lane, Wood Dalling, Norwich, Norfolk NR11 6SA
Tel: 01263 587051 (nursery)/01263 587318 (office)
Fax: 01263 587315
e-mail: clarka@btconnect.com website: www.theknotgarden.co.uk

The Knot Garden in Wood Dalling is an extensive and imaginatively designed specialist plant nursery stocking a host of beautiful established trees, specimen plants and shrubs, tree ferns, bamboos, grass trees, topiary and imported exotica. New and exciting additions are arriving all the time. Rhododendrons, azaleas, acers, photinias, pines and numerous other species provide a great variety of choice for any planting scheme. All plants are treated with loving care and attention, to provide customers with the finest quality, backed up by excellent service. This beautifully designed and built setting is the perfect backdrop to the superb hand-picked plants. All stock is in containers and reared in ideal growing conditions, cared for by hand using traditional

methods to ensure an ideal environment suited to every species offered for sale.

This family-owned business is run by keen gardeners Ann and Barry Clark and their son Charles, together with daughter Alex, at present a horticulture student. Their initial interest in creating a spacious water garden, which included sourcing semi-tropical plants for the conservatory, led to the establishment, in October 1998, of this unique 6-acre nursery site. All the staff offer good advice and planning help. Delivery service available.

been taken over by a colony of hibernating bats which, by law, may not be disturbed.

A couple of miles south of Coltishall, on the B1150, is the **Redwings Horse Sanctuary**, founded in 1984 to provide a caring and permanent home for horses, ponies, donkeys and mules rescued from neglect and slaughter. The Sanctuary cares for more than 1000 animals at any one time, and there are no indications that this number is likely to diminish. Even with the help of many volunteers, the work is expensive. To raise funds, the Sanctuary holds regular Open Days, has a gift shop with many horse-related items on sale, and also runs an Adopt-a-Horse scheme.

GREAT WITCHINGHAM
11 miles NW of Norwich off the A1067

Norfolk Wildlife Centre & Country Park is home to an interesting collection of rare, or ancient, breeds of farm livestock such as white-faced woodland and Shetland sheep, pygmy goats and Exmoor ponies. Set in 40 acres of peaceful parkland, the Centre also has reindeer, otters, and badgers, pools teeming with wildfowl and a huge colony of wild herons nesting in the trees. There are also commando and Adventure Play Areas; one of the finest collection of trees and flowering shrubs in the county; a café and gift shop.

A little further southeast, the Dinosaur Adventure Park near Lenwade doesn't have any living creatures, but as you wander through the woods here you will come across some startlingly convincing life-size models of dinosaurs. One of them, the 'Climb-a-Saurus', is a children's activity centre. A woodland maze, a picnic area with gas-fired barbecues, a play area for toddlers, a restaurant, and a Dinostore offering a wide variety of dinosaur models, books and gifts are among the other attractions.

Anyone who has ever read Parson Woodforde's enchanting *Diary of a Country Parson* will want to make a short diversion to the tiny village of **Weston Longville**, a mile or so south of the Dinosaur Park. The Revd James Woodforde was vicar of this remote parish from 1774 until his death in 1803, and throughout that time he conscientiously maintained a daily diary detailing a wonderful mixture of the momentous and the trivial. *"Very great Rebellion in France"* he notes, when ten days after the Fall of the Bastille, the dramatic news eventually arrived at Weston Longville. More often he is recording his copious meals (*"We had for dinner a Calf's head, boiled Fowl and Tongue, a saddle of Mutton roasted on the side table, and a fine Swan roasted with Currant Jelly Sauce for the first Course. The Second Course a couple of Wild Fowl, Larks, Blancmange, Tarts........"*); the weather (during the winter of 1785, for example, the frost was so severe that it froze the chamberpots under the beds); and his frequent dealings with the smuggler Andrews who kept the good parson well supplied with contraband tea, gin and cognac. Inside the simple village church there's a portrait of Parson Woodforde, painted by his nephew, and across the road the inn has been named after this beguiling character.

CAWSTON
12 miles NW of Norwich on the B1145

"Lovers of the Norfolk churches can never agree which is the best", wrote Sir John Betjeman. "I have heard it said that you are either a Salle man or a Cawston man". In this county so rich in exceptionally beautiful churches, Salle and Cawston are indeed in a class of their own. **St Agnes Church** in Cawston, among its many treasures, boasts a magnificent double hammerbeam roof, where angels with protective wings eight feet across float serenely from the roof, and a gorgeous 15th century rood screen embellished with lovely painted panels of saints and Fathers of the Church. The two churches are just a couple of miles apart so you can easily decide for yourself whether you are "a Salle man or a Cawston man".

The attractive little town of Aylsham stands beside the River Bure, the northern terminus of the **Bure Valley Railway** (see panel opposite). It has an unspoilt Market Place, surrounded by late-17th and early-18th century houses, reflecting the prosperity the town enjoyed in those years from the cloth trade. Before that time Aylsham had been

BROADLAND WINERIES LTD

The New Winery, Cawston, Norwich, Norfolk NR10 4BG
Tel: 01603 872474 Fax: 01603 871312
e-mail: broadland-wineries@supanet.com
website: www.broadland-wineries.co.uk

Founded in 1965, **Broadland Wineries** is home to a four-acre site bottling 20 million litres a year. It is best known for its extensive range of Fruit and Country Wines, which are on sale across the UK, and can also be purchased on site. It welcomes potential customers to visit its small shop and taste its range of products.

BLACK SHEEP LTD

9 Penfold Street, Aylsham, Norfolk NR11 6ET
Tel: 01263 733142 Fax: 01263 735074
e-mail: email@blacksheep.ltd.uk
website: www.blacksheep.ltd.uk

With classic countrywear - tweed jackets and coats, heavyweight knitted jerseys and lightweight sweaters, cardigans, scarves, hats, gloves and more - **Black Sheep Ltd** is the place to shop for superb quality woollens. Natural, dyed and undyed wools are used to create an excellent and extensive collection of traditional clothing, all of it from sheep reared in the UK and manufactured here.

THE BUCKINGHAMSHIRE ARMS

nr Aylsham, Norfolk NR11 6NF
Tel: 01263 732133 Fax: 01263 768993

At the superb **Buckinghamshire Arms**, you can enjoy a first-class meal, sup a quiet drink and relax in the luxury of four-poster bedrooms, amid gracious and peaceful surroundings. Here at the gates of Blickling Hall guests can relish the peace and quiet of rural life while partaking of delicious meals in the bars or, in fine weather, in the glorious garden.

famed for its linen, and woollen knitted goods took over as the major industry before the development of the knitting frame killed that activity as a commercial undertaking. The 14th and 15th century church, **St Michael's**, is said to have been built by John O'Gaunt. In the churchyard is the tomb of one of the greatest of the 18th century landscape gardeners, Humphrey Repton, the creator of some 200 parks and gardens around the country. His epitaph requests that his ashes should mingle with the earth to give from and colour to the rose.

One of Repton's many commissions was to landscape the grounds of **Blickling Hall** (National Trust), which stands a mile or so outside Aylsham. Many visitors have marvelled at their first sight of the great Hall built for Sir Henry Hobart in the 1620s. "No-one is prepared on coming downhill past the church into

BURE VALLEY RAILWAY

Aylsham Station, Norwich Road, Aylsham, Norfolk NR11 6BW
Tel: 01263 7338585 Fax: 01263 733814
e-mail: info@bvr.co.uk website: www.bvrw.co.uk

Norfolk's longest narrow gauge heritage railway is a 15" gauge line operating between the old market town of Aylsham and Wroxham, a distance of nine miles. The line was built in 1989-1990 on the track bed of the former East Norfolk Railway, which opened in 1880. The Bure Valley Narrow Gauge Railway was opened in July 1990 with new station buildings and workshops at Aylsham and a new station adjacent to Hoveton and Wroxham station. Unstaffed stations are at Coltishall (the famous RAF Battle of Britain station), Buxton and Brampton. The railway is operated primarily by steam locomotives, of which there are four. Passengers are carried in 22 fully enclosed and luxuriously upholstered coaches. During 1998 two new wheelchair accessible coaches were completed at Aylsham. These can each carry four wheelchairs with their carers. The journey time is 45 minutes.

At Aylsham the workshops are usually open to visitors; on site are a small museum and model railway, a well-stocked gift shop and the Whistlestop Restaurant open for full English breakfasts, lunch and high tea. A shop selling confectionery and drinks is located at Wroxham station. There is ample free car and coach parking at both stations, with fully equipped facilities for disabled visitors.

The Bure Valley Railway specialises in joint operations with other attractions. There is a regular boat train facility from Aylsham connecting with cruises on the Broads from Wroxham. Combined train and boat fares are available, and after arriving at Wroxham passengers take a short stroll to Wroxham Bridge, where the Broad Tours boat will be waiting. After the cruise, normally an hour and a half in duration, passengers are free to return to Aylsham by any train, allowing time to explore the village of Wroxham.

In off-peak periods the Railway operates Steam Locomotive Driving Courses for beginners and the more experienced. The 1-day course offers an ideal introduction to the mysteries of the steam engine and provides ample opportunities to have a go at both shunting and passenger-type train operation. The more detailed 2-day Steam Locomotive Driving Course adds an insight into the operation of a busy railway, the theory being backed up with practical demonstrations and plenty of hands-on experience.

The Bure Valley Railway operates regular services from April to October, Santa Specials towards Christmas and Day out with Thomas the Tank Engine events in May and September. The Railway is paralleled along its whole length by the scenic Bure Valley Walk and cycle path.

the village, to find the main front of this finest of Jacobean mansions, actually looking upon the road, unobstructedly, from behind its velvet lawns," enthused Charles Harper in 1904. "No theatrical manager cunning in all the artful accessories of the stage could devise anything more dramatic."

Blickling Hall

From the outside, Sir Henry's house fully satisfied the current architectural vogue for perfect symmetry. Four towers topped with lead-covered turret-caps rise at each corner, there are lines of matching Dutch gables and mullioned windows, and even the chimneys were placed in corresponding groups of twos, threes or fours.

Inside, the most spectacular feature is the Long Gallery which extends for 135 feet and originally provided space for indoor exercise in bad weather. Its glory is the plaster ceiling, an intricately patterned expanse of heraldic panels bearing the Hobart arms, along with others displaying bizarre and inscrutable emblems such as a naked lady riding a two-legged dragon.

Other treasures at Blickling include a dramatic double-flight carved oak staircase, the Chinese Bedroom lined with 18th century hand-painted wallpaper and the dazzling Peter the Great Room. A descendant of Sir Henry Hobart, the 2nd Earl of Buckinghamshire, was appointed Ambassador to Russia in 1746, and he returned from that posting with a magnificent tapestry, the gift of Empress Catherine the Great. This room was re-designed so as to display the Earl's sumptuous souvenir to its full effect, and portraits of himself and his Countess by Gainsborough were added later.

The Earl was a martyr to gout and his death in 1793 at the age of 50 occurred when, finding the pain unbearable, he thrust his bloated foot into a bucket of icy water, and suffered a heart attack. He was buried beneath the idiosyncratic

Egyptian Pyramid in the grounds, a 45-foot-high structure designed by Ignatius Bonomi, who combined Egyptian and classical elements to create a mausoleum which, if nothing else, is certainly distinctive.

Blickling also offers its visitors miles of footpaths through lovely grounds, a plant centre, picnic area, restaurant and shop.

Mannington Hall

Within a few miles of Blickling Hall are two other stately homes, both the properties of Lord and Lady Walpole. Neither of the houses, **Mannington Hall** and **Wolterton Park**, is normally open to the public but their gardens and grounds are. At Mannington there are country walks and trails, a Heritage Rose Garden featuring thousands of roses set in small gardens reflecting their period of origin, a garden shop, and tea room. Wolterton Park, the stately 18th century Hall built for Horatio Walpole, brother of Sir Robert, England's first Prime Minister, stands in grounds landscaped by Humphrey Repton. Here there are miles of waymarked walks and trails, orienteering, an adventure playground and various special events are held throughout the year.

Just north of Mannington Hall stands the village of **Little Barningham** where

St Mary's Church is a magnet for collectors of ecclesiastical curiosities. Inside, perched on the corner of an ancient box pew, stands a remarkable wood-carved skeletal figure of the Grim Reaper. Its fleshless skull stares hollow-eyed at visitors with a defiant, mirthless grin: a scythe gripped in one clutch of bones, and an hour-glass in the other, symbolise the inescapable fate that awaits us all. This gruesomely powerful memento mori was donated to the church in 1640 by one Stephen Crosbie who, for good measure, added the inscription: "As you are now, even so was I, Remember death for ye must dye." Those words were a conventional enough adjuration at that time, but what is one supposed to make of Stephen's postscript inscribed on the back of the pew: "For

The Saracen's Head

Wolterton, nr Erpingham, Aylsham, Norfolk NR11 7LX
Tel: 01263 768909 Fax: 01263 768993
website: www.broadland.com/saracenshead

The Saracen's Head is truly something special - with its owner-run kitchen, it is well known for its delicious food and unpretentious, welcoming atmosphere. The meals are an imaginative mix of the traditional and the innovative - while the setting is unspoilt. There are 4 en-suite rooms - just the place to get away from it all. It has main entries in most major guides and so booking is advisable!

couples joined in wedlock this seat I did intend"?

THE BROADS

The Broads area covers more than 33 square kilometres that include 200 kilometres of waterways. The broads themselves are shallow lakes formed in

The Broads

medieval times when peat was dug out to provide fuel and over the years the diggings became flooded as the water level rose. These waterways have always been important transport routes, and each village had its own staithe, or quay, many of which are still in use. The traditional Broads boat, originally used

Norfolk Wherries

for commercial purposes, was the wherry, a large, single-sail vessel of shallow draught which plied the broads with cargoes of corn, coal and reed. As rail and road transport gradually took over and the holiday trade began to boom, the wherry's original role was lost and many were converted for leisure use or purpose-built for that purpose, with all mod cons. A few - perhaps no more than half a dozen - still survive, available for regular tours or for private charter, and there really is no finer way to savour the delights of the Broads than from the deck of a wherry.

The Broads, with their wonderful mixture of open water, woodland, fen and marsh, have virtually the status of a National Park; they are protected by the Broads Authority, which is responsible for conservation, recreation and navigation in this unique part of the world. Besides providing peaceful waterborne holidays the area offers great opportunities for walking and cycling, and there are many points from which fishing is permitted. Some of the individual broads are nature reserves, and the waterways are home to an amazing variety of bird, fish and plant life.

There are many picturesque villages and small towns in the area, while on the edges are the city of Norwich and the major towns of Great Yarmouth and Lowestoft.

GREAT YARMOUTH

In Saxon times, Yarmouth was actually an island, a large sandbank dotted with fishermen's cottages. Later, the narrow estuary of the River Bure at the northern end was blocked off, causing it to flow down the western side of the town. It runs parallel to the sea for two miles before joining the larger River Yare, and then their united waters curve around the southern edge of the town for another three miles before finally entering the sea. The seaward side is a 5-mile stretch of sandy beaches and countless amusements, with a breezy promenade from which one can watch the constant traffic of ships in Yarmouth Roads, and two fine old traditional piers, the Britannia (810 feet long) and the Wellington (600 feet). Of the host of entertainments on offer, three are particularly suitable for families. The **Sea Life Centre** includes displays of the kinds of marine life found on the Norfolk coast and an underwater viewing channel passing through shark-infested 'oceans'; Amazonia, which is an indoor tropical paradise among whose reptilian residents are a 13 foot alligator and a python which if fully uncoiled would extend to some 24 feet; and the Merrivale Model Village which offers attractive landscaped gardens, children's rides, and an exceptionally detailed miniature village with more than 200 models.

Also on the sea front are the **Maritime Museum of East Anglia**, housed in what was formerly the Shipwrecked Sailors' Home; the **Elizabethan House** (National Trust), a merchant's house of 1596, now a museum of domestic life with 16th century panelled rooms and a functional Victorian kitchen; and, behind South Beach, the 144 foot high **Nelson's Monument** crowned by a statue, not of Norfolk's most famous son, but of Britannia. A climb up the 217 steps to the viewing platform is rewarded by some striking views.

Most of Yarmouth's older buildings are concentrated in the western, or riverside, part of the town. Here are **The Quay**, which Daniel Defoe considered the most beautiful in England, more than a mile long and in places 150 yards wide; a stately **Town Hall** worth visiting to see its grand staircase, Court Room and Assembly Room; and **The Rows**, a medieval network of tiny courtyards and narrow alleys, a mere two feet wide in places. The Rows were badly damaged during a bombing raid in 1942 but enough remains to show their unique character. There were originally 145 of these rows, about 7 miles in total, all of them built at right angles to the sea and therefore freely ventilated by onshore breezes which, given the urban sanitary conditions of those times, must have been extremely welcome.

The bombing raid of 1942 also completely destroyed the interior of **St Nicholas' Church**, but left its walls standing. Between 1957-60, this huge building - the largest parish church in England - was completely restored and furnished in traditional style, largely by using pieces garnered from redundant churches and other sources. The partly Norman font, for example, came from Highway church in Wiltshire, the organ from St Mary-the-Boltons in Kensington.

Just south of the church, off the Market Place, is the half-timbered house, built in 1641, in which **Anna Sewell** lived. The author of *Black Beauty* was born in the town in 1820 but it was only when she was in her late 50s that she transmuted her concern for the more humane treatment of horses into a classic novel. Anna was paid just £20 for the rights to a book which, in the five months that elapsed between its publication and her death in 1878, had already sold an incredible 100,000 copies.

Sands and Pier, Great Yarmouth

Another famous author associated with the town is Charles Dickens, who stayed at the Royal Hotel on Marine Parade in 1847-48 while writing *David Copperfield*. Dickens had visited the town as a child and had actually seen an upturned boat on the beach being used as a dwelling, complete with a chimney emerging from its keel. In his novel, this becomes Peggotty's house to which young Copperfield is brought following the death of his mother. "One thing I particularly noticed in this delightful house", he writes, "was the smell of fish; which was so searching, that when I took out my pocket-handkerchief to wipe my nose, I found it smelt exactly as if it had wrapped up a lobster".

In fact, the whole town at that time was pervaded with the aroma of smoked herrings, the silvery fish which were the basis of Yarmouth's prosperity. Around the time of Dickens' stay here, the author of the town's directory tried to pre-empt any discouraging effect this might have on visitors by claiming "The wholesome exhalations arising from the fish during the operation of curing are said to have a tendency to dissipate contagious disorders, and to be generally beneficial

Fritton Lake Countryworld

Church Lane, Fritton, Great Yarmouth, Norfolk NR31 9HA
Tel: 01493 488288/488208 Fax: 01493 488355
website: www.frittonlake.co.uk

For an enjoyable day out in the country, **Fritton Lake Countryworld** has few rivals. The beautiful grounds offer a splendid contrast between natural woodland and formal Victorian gardens, and

Fritton Lake, with fishing and boating both available, is one of the loveliest stretches of water in East Anglia. A miniature railway runs by the lake, and among the many new attractions introduced for 2001 are a family cycle trail, an orienteering course and giant outdoor board games. Also on site are a 9 hole par 3 golf course and an18-hole putting green, displays of falconry and basket-making, a growing collection of waterfowl, a children's farm and a heavy horse centre with working Suffolk Punches and Shires.

to the human constitution which is here sometimes preserved to extreme longevity".

Across the town, some 60 curing houses were busy gutting, salting and spicing herrings to produce Yarmouth's great contribution to the English breakfast, the kipper. The process had been invented by a Yarmouth man, John Woodger; a rival of his, a Mr Bishop, developed a different method which left the fish wonderfully moist and flavoursome, and so created the famous Yarmouth bloater.

For centuries, incredible quantities of herring were landed, and at one time the trade had involved so many fishermen that there were more boats (1,123) registered at Yarmouth than at London. But the scale of the over-fishing produced the inevitable result and suddenly, within the space of two decades, the 1950s and 1960s, Yarmouth's herring industry found itself dead in the water. Luckily, the end of that historic trade coincided with the beginning of North Sea oil and gas exploitation, a business which has kept the town in reasonably good economic health up to the present day.

BURGH CASTLE
4 miles W of Great Yarmouth off the A12 or A143

When the Romans established their fortress of Garionnonum, now known as **Burgh Castle**, the surrounding marshes were still under water. The fort then stood on one bank of a vast estuary, commanding a strategic position at the head of an important waterway running into the heart of East Anglia. The ruins are impressive, with walls of alternating flint and brick layers rising 15 feet high in places, and spreading more than 11 feet wide at their base. The Romans abandoned Garionnonum around AD 408 and some two centuries later the Irish missionary St Fursey (or Fursa) founded a

monastery within its walls. Later generations cannibalised both his building, and much of the crumbling Roman castle, as materials for their own churches and houses.

On the northern bank of the Yore, the **Berney Arms Windmill**, the tallest windpump in the country, is one of the best preserved Victorian mills in Norfolk, and the largest, with seven floors to explore. Built to grind cement, it is still fully operational. The mill is accessible by boat, by footpath from Halvergate or Great Yarmouth or from Berney Arms Station (Anglia Railways).

To the south of the village just off the A143 lies **Fritton Lake Countryworld** with its lake, gardens and activities (see panel opposite).

BURGH ST PETER
12 miles S of Great Yarmouth off the A143

Off the A143 Yarmouth-Bungay road, in isolated marshland by the River Waveney, stands the curious **Tower of St Mary**, a pyramid of four stacked brick cubes, each smaller than the one below; it was built in 1793 as a memorial to Samuel Boycott.

CAISTER-ON-SEA
4 miles N of Great Yarmouth on the A149

An important fishing port in Boadicea's time, Caister is now a modern holiday resort with its stretch of fine sands. After the Romans had vanquished her unruly tribe, they settled here some time in the 2nd century and built a castle, or Caister, of which only a few foundations and remains have yet been found. **Caister Castle**, which stands in a picturesque setting about a mile to the west of the town, is a much later construction, built in 1432-5 by the legendary Sir John Fastolf with his spoils from the French wars in which he had served, very profitably, as Governor of Normandy and also distinguished himself leading the

THE VILLAGE EXPERIENCE

Burgh St Margaret, Fleggburgh,
Great Yarmouth, Norfolk NR29 3AF
Tel: 01493 369770
website: www.thevillage-experience.com

Set in over 30 acres of woodland, **The Village Experience** has something for all the family. Working steam and traditional fairground rides such as the Downhill Racer and Victorian Gallopers and unusual attractions like Fun with Science, Myths and Legends and Garden Golf ensure that there's never a dull moment. Live shows include popular concerts given on the magnificent Compton-Christie cinema organ, and Dancing Waters, updating the old tradition of moving water to music. Other entertainment takes in a fairground, train ride, steam-hauled trailer rides, a painting and drawing studio for children, indoor soft play area, junior maze and adventure play area. New attractions for 2001 include the Haunted Conservatory, the Swinging Chairs and the Wareham Bears. Food stops are plentiful, with a restaurant, BBQ, tearooms and traditional pub. The Village Experience is at Fleggburgh on the A1064 between Acle and Caister. It is open daily from the week before Easter to the last Sunday in October.

English bowmen at the Battle of Agincourt. Academics have enjoyed themselves for centuries disputing whether this Sir John was the model for Shakespeare's immortal rogue, Falstaff. Certainly, the historic Sir John was a larger-than-life character, but there's no evidence that he shared Falstaff's other characteristics of cowardliness, boastfulness and general over-indulgence.

Caister Castle was the first in England to be built of brick and is in fact one of the earliest brick buildings in the county. The 90 foot tower remains, together with much of the moated wall and gatehouse, now lapped by still waters and with ivy relentlessly encroaching. The castle is open daily from May to September and, as an additional attraction, there is a motor museum in the grounds. The **Caister Castle Car Collection** is among the finest in the country. Exhibits range from an 1893 Panhard & Levassor to Jim Clark's Formula 1 Lotus, the very first Ford Fiesta and a customised 1990s Harley-Davidson. Also on display are early bicycles, a vintage fire engine, horse-drawn vehicles, baby carriages and pedal cars.

In Caister's **Holy Trinity Church** is a memorial window to nine Caister lifeboatmen who perished in 1901 in the *Beauchamp* while answering a distress call; and in the graveyard is a monument with a broken mast, anchors, sails, oars and a boat tossed by the waves; the names of the nine lifeboatmen are recorded here.

About three miles west of Caister Castle, the pleasantly landscaped grounds surrounding an 1876 Victorian mansion have been transformed into the **Thrigby Hall Wildlife Gardens**, home for a renowned collection of Asian mammals, birds and reptiles. There are snow leopards and rare tigers; gibbons and crocodiles; deer and otters; and other attractions include a tropical house, aviaries, gift shop and café. The Gardens, which in addition to the animals feature Chinese plants, pagodas and bridges across a waterfowl lake, are open every day, all year round.

ORMESBY ST MICHAEL

9 miles NW of Great Yarmouth on the A149

Just to the north of this tiny village, at Decoy Farm, is the **Norfolk Rare Breeds**

Centre, home to a wide variety of domestic and rare breed farm animals enjoying a tranquil Broadland setting. Visitors can inspect the extensive collection of unusual species, see chicks hatching in the incubation room, wander round the museum which houses an interesting collection of old farm-carts, follow the Nature Trail, enjoy home-made cakes in the tearoom and perhaps take home a souvenir from the well-stocked gift shop. Throughout the year, there are special events such as sheep shearing and a Heavy Horse Day.

To the west on the A1064 lies **The Village Experience** set in over 30 acres of woodland and ideal for all the family (see panel opposite).

ACLE

10 miles W of Great Yarmouth off the A47

A thousand years ago, this small market town, now 10 miles inland, was a small fishing port on the coast. Gradually, land has been reclaimed from the estuaries of the Rivers Bure, Waveney and Yare so that today large expanses of flat land stretch away from Acle towards the sea. The town's importance as a boating centre began in the 19th century with boat-building yards springing up beside the bridge, and when Acle's first Regatta was held in 1890, some 150 yachts took part.

Acle was granted permission for a market in 1272 and it's still held every Thursday, attracting visitors from miles around. Others come to see the unusual **Church of St Edmund** with its Saxon round tower, built some time around AD 900, crowned with a 15th century belfry from which eight carved figures look down on the beautifully thatched roof of the nave. The treasures inside include a superbly carved font inscribed with the date 1410, and a fine 15th century screen.

STRUMPSHAW

6 miles E of Norwich off the A47

Strumpshaw Hall Steam Museum houses a collection of steam wagons, steam pumps, engines, tractors and a continental dance organ. Nearby Strumpshaw Fen comprises reed beds, grazing marshes and woodland along the banks of the River Yare. For visitors there are walking trails, hides and an information centre.

WROXHAM

8 miles NE of Norwich on the A1151

This riverside village, linked to its twin, Hoveton, by a hump-backed bridge over the River Bure, is the self-styled 'capital' of the Norfolk Broads and as such, gets extremely busy during the season. The banks of the river are chock-a-block with boatyards full of cruisers of all shapes and sizes, there's a constant traffic of boats making their way to the open spaces of Wroxham Broad, and in July the scene becomes even more hectic when the annual regatta is under way.

Wroxham is also the southern terminus of the **Bure Valley Railway**, a nine-mile long, narrow-gauge (15") steam train service that closely follows the course of the River Bure through lovely countryside to the market town of Aylsham (see panel on page 17).

A couple of miles north of Wroxham is **Wroxham Barns**, a delightful collection of beautifully restored 18th century barns, set in 10 acres of countryside, and housing a community of craftspeople. There are thirteen of them, producing between them a wide range of crafts, from stained glass to woodturning, stitchcraft to handmade children's clothes, pottery to floral artistry, and much more. The complex also includes a cider-pressing centre; a junior farm with lots of hands-on activities; a traditional

(Continued page 28)

WALK 1

Acle and Upton

Start	Acle Recreation Centre
Distance	4½ miles (7.2km)
Approximate time	2 hours
Parking	At start
Refreshments	Pubs at Acle, Upton and Acle Bridge
Ordnance Survey maps	Landranger 134 (Norwich & The Broads), Outdoor Leisure 40 (The Broads)

The village of Acle is situated close between the two river systems of the Broads: the Bure and its tributaries to the north, the rivers Yare and Waveney to the south. The walk begins by using the ancient field path that runs from Acle to the quiet village of Upton, passing the disused round-towered church at Fishley. After walking through Upton, the route follows a footpath skirting the marshes to reach another on the bank of the River Bure that eventually leads back to Acle. Note that Acle holds a busy market on Thursdays. The walk can start from Upton staithe or Acle Bridge if the car park at Acle is full.

Walk out of the car park past the library and Methodist church and turn right. After 100 yds (91m) turn right again down Pyebush Lane and bear left at the cemetery **Ⓐ** on to a short track which soon becomes a field path leading past a pillbox. The churches at Upton and Fishley are prominent in the wide, if rather featureless, landscape. The latter little church is surrounded by trees and has a round tower built of flints. It is rewarding to visit the peaceful churchyard even though the church is locked.

The footpath continues ahead past the churchyard **Ⓑ** over a large field. It is well used and is usually cleared and rolled. It crosses the next, smaller, field in the same direction and comes to an enclosed path leading into Upton. Turn right at the road and then immediately left into the Green. At Boat Dyke Road keep ahead for 100 yds (91m) if you wish to visit the pub, the White Horse, otherwise turn right to continue down Boat Dyke Road.

Bear right at the junction with Back Lane and walk through the car park at the staithe and then up the right-hand side of the dyke. After 50 yds (46m) turn right **Ⓒ** on a footpath running between the ditch and a wood. This leads into carr (scrubland with many elder trees) with a ditch to each side. This, in turn, takes you to open marshland. Birdwatchers will find that the reedbeds here are excellent habitats for reed and sedge warblers while heron will be seen

WALK 1

watching open water for prey. A glance at the map shows that Rattlesnake Carr is not far from the path, and it is puzzling to think why that patch of scrub to the south of Fishley Hall came by that name.

The path crosses a track and then a metal footbridge to enter a wood. The river is close at hand when the path emerges to cross a succession of stiles and then run down the side of a belt of trees. It reaches the river **D** at a sailing club. Turn right to walk along the bank.

The River Bure is the busiest of the Broadland rivers and there is amusement in watching the boats and their crews if the traffic is heavy. Walking on the grassy banktop is pleasant, and it is not long before the boatyards at Acle Bridge come into view. The footpath leaves the riverbank and follows a roadway through the boatyards to the road. Take care in crossing the road to the entrance to the Bridge Inn. Then, if not taking refreshment, continue past the pub with its circular thatched extension (the main part of the pub is old). Note that the footpath runs a few yards inland after the pub garden for a short distance before rejoining the riverbank. The waymarks bear the Weavers Way badge, a long-distance footpath that runs from Great Yarmouth to Cromer

At Acle Dyke the path is forced to turn away from the river and a fence separates it from the boatyard by the dyke. At the head of the dyke the Weavers Way leaves to the left to continue by the river. Instead cross the road and turn left, and then keep ahead to take the road into Acle past the East Norwich Inn (The Cabin) and the fire station. Fork right on the road to return to the starting point. ●

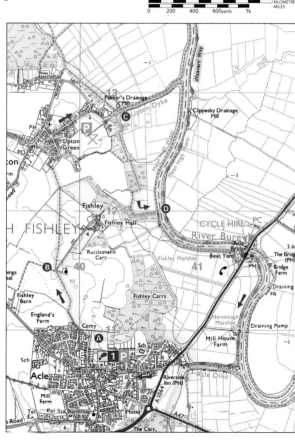

ARTS & CRAFTS

Tunstead Road, Hoveton, Wroxham,
Norfolk NR12 8QG
Tel: 01603 783505

Arts & Crafts supplies an excellent range of painting and artists' materials of all well-known brands. For painting in any media - on glass, silk, porcelain, fabric, parchment, canvas - and craftwork materials for decoupage, stencilling, mosaics and much more - this fine shop has all you need. There is also a good selection of works by local artists, and gifts and cards for all occasions. Open: Monday to Saturday 10.00 am - 4.30 pm.

FAIRHAVEN WOODLAND & WATER GARDEN

South Walsham, Norwich, Norfolk NR13 6EA
Tel/Fax: 01603 270449
website: www.norfolkbroads.com/fairhaven

Nine miles north of Norwich on the B1140, this delightful and unique natural garden is environmentally managed for the benefit of all wildlife. A harmonious mix of wild and cultivated plants grows together, and the natural food chain takes care of any pests. It is a haven of peace and tranquillity, with three miles of paths under trees, over bridges and through sunny glades .

In winter and early spring there are snowdrops, followed by carpets of wild primroses, daffodils, skunk cabbage, butterbur, camellias and early rhododendrons in March and April. May sees the garden's spectacular Candelabra primulas, the largest naturalised collection in England, and the breathtaking blue of the wild bluebells. In June, July and August there are hostas, ligularia, astilbes, hydrangeas, foxgloves and wild flowers such as mullein and meadowsweet providing nectar for a variety of colourful butterflies. In autumn the glow of russet, red and gold leaves and bright berries provide the colour, while in winter the bare trees reveal views of the private Inner Broad that are hidden in other seasons.

Christmas trees and wreaths are on sale in December, and Father Christmas calls in on the three weekends before Christmas. Ninety-two species of garden, woodland and water birds have been recorded here over the seasons, including all three of the native British woodpeckers. The garden is accessible to wheelchairs except in wet weather; the tea room and toilet are also accessible, but visitors need to be able to board on foot the Edwardian-style river boat Beatrice for the Water Trail trip. The garden is open from 10am to 5pm all year and until 9 o'clock on Wednesday and Thursday evenings in May, June, July and August.

Family Fair (with individually priced rides); a gift and craft shop; and a tearoom.

A mile or so north of Wroxham, **Hoveton Hall Gardens** offer visitors a splendid combination of plants, shrubs and trees, with rare rhododendrons, azaleas, water plants and dazzling herbaceous borders within a walled garden. There are woodland and lakeside walks, plant sales, gardening books, and a tea room.

SOUTH WALSHAM
9 miles E of Norwich on the B1140

This small village is notable for having two parish churches built within yards of each other. Just to the north of the village is the **Fairhaven Garden Trust**, an expanse of delightful water gardens lying beside the private South Walsham Inner Broad (see panel).

Norfolk Reed for Thatching, Ranworth

RANWORTH

9 miles E of Norwich off the B1140

This beautiful Broadland village is famous for its church and its position on Ranworth Broad. From the tower of **St Helen's Church** - often known as the Cathedral of the Broads - it is possible to see five Norfolk Broads, Horsey Mill, the sea at Great Yarmouth, and on a clear day, the spire of Norwich Cathedral. Inside, the church houses one of Norfolk's greatest ecclesiastical treasures, a breathtaking early 15th century Gothic choir screen, the most beautiful and the best preserved in the county. In glowing reds, greens and golds, gifted medieval artists painted a gallery of more than thirty saints and martyrs, inserting tiny cameos of such everyday scenes as falcons seizing hares, dogs chasing ducks and, oddly for Norfolk, lions. Cromwell's bigoted vandals, offended by such idolatrous images, smothered them with brown paint - an ideal preservative for these wonderful paintings as became apparent when they were once again revealed during the course of a 19th century restoration of the church. Another treasure is the Antiphoner, a colourfully illuminated 15th century book of services written in Latin. Behind the church is a visitor centre with a photographic display of East Anglian churches.

Norfolk Wildlife Trust's **Ranworth Broad** is one of the few broads totally free of river traffic. The wildlife centre is a floating thatched building on the edge of the broad, reached by a boardwalk that runs through woodland, reed beds and open water. Binoculars and telescopes are positioned at the upper windows for bird-watching. It houses an informative exhibition on the history of the Broads, and there's also an interesting Nature Trail which shows how these wetlands gradually developed over the centuries.

LUDHAM

12 miles NE of Norwich on the A1062

Ludham is a picturesque village well worth a visit in its own right and surrounded by interesting places. South of the village, by the River Bure, is a spot that has long been a favourite with sightseers and painters. This is the gatehouse of **St Benet's Abbey**, which is

"TICKER'S"

c/o Mrs Nicola Arrowsmith-Brown, Forge Cottage, The Street, South Walsham, Norwich, Norfolk NR13 6DQ
Tel: 01603 270457 Fax: 01603 270142
e-mail: arrows270@aol.com website: www.cottageguide.co.uk/tickers

"Ticker's" is a delightful flint and brick self-catering cottage in the lovely village of Cley-next-the-Sea, near the famous windmill and with fine views from upstairs. There are walks from the door to the beach, bird reserve and Blakeney Point. It is decorated and equipped to a high standard of comfort and quality (ETC 4 stars). There are three bedrooms (sleeps 5 plus a baby) and one dog is welcome. Brochure available.

RANWORTH TREES

Woodbastwick Road, Ranworth, Norwich, Norfolk NR13 6HR
Tel: 01603 270755 Fax: 01603 270407
e-mail: neil.m.thomas@112.com
website: www.ranworth-trees.co.uk

In the heart of the Norfolk Broads, **Ranworth Trees** is a specialist tree nursery growing many unusual types of fruit and ornamental trees. With The Norfolk Orchards and Apple project they trace and propagate many of Norfolk's lost varieties. They produce top-quality maiden and container stock and are pleased to supply the trade directly and the public through mail order. Catalogues available on request.

unusual in incorporating an 18th century windmill in its structure. The best way to see the remains of St Benet's Abbey is from a boat along the river (indeed, it's quite difficult to reach it any other way). Rebuilt in 1020 by King Canute, after the Vikings had destroyed an earlier Saxon building, St Benet's became one of the richest abbeys in East Anglia. When Henry VIII closed it down in 1536 he made an unusual deal with its last Abbot. In return for creating the Abbot Bishop of Norwich, the Cathedral estates were to be handed over to the King but St Benet's properties could remain in the Abbot/Bishop's possession. Even today, the Bishop of Norwich retains the additional title of Abbot of St Benet's, and on the first Sunday in August each year, travels the last part of the journey by boat to hold an open-air service near the stately ruins of the Abbey gatehouse.

A healthy stroll or short drive north of Ludham brings visitors to **How Hill**, where the nature reserve on the River Ant is the ideal spot to get close to the unique attractions of the Broads. An alternative to the 1½-mile walking wildlife trail is a trip along the dykes, through the reeds and fens, on the little Edwardian-style boat, the *Electric Eel*, with an experienced guide to point out the great variety of wildlife to be seen. **Toad Hole**, on the banks of the Ant, is a tiny eel-catcher's

cottage that is now a museum giving a fascinating glimpse into Victorian country life.

HORNING
12 miles NE of Norwich off the A1062

The travel writer Arthur Mee described Horning as "Venice in Broadland", where "waterways wandering from the river into the gardens are crossed by tiny bridges". With its pretty reed-thatched cottages lining the bank of the River Bure and its position in the heart of the Broads, there are few more attractive places from which to explore this magical area.

At RAF Neatishead, a couple of miles north of Horning, the **RAF Air Defence Radar Museum** charts the history of radar from 1935 featuring the Battle of Britain, 1942 Operations and the original Cold War operations room.

Horning Broad

THE NORFOLK CHRYSANTHEMUM & HERB CENTRE

Bailey's Norfolk Flowers, Low Road, Martham,
Norfolk NR29 4RE
Tel: 01493 740251 Fax: 01493 748345
e-mail: gareth@norfolk-flowers.co.uk

One of the leading chrysanthemum nurseries within the UK, **Bailey's**
have now expanded into herbs, following the development of the
visitors centre and new herb gardens for 2002 set in 16 acres. The
health foods gift shop provides a range of natural products with the farm shop stocking local produce
and all their own plants and flowers. The tea room serves home made food throughout the day and
there is a nature trail along with a caravan and camping site. Party bookings to the visitor centre is £2
per person. Situated ¼ mile off the A149

POTTER HEIGHAM

14 miles NE of Norwich off the A149

Modern Potter Heigham, generally
regarded as one of the liveliest of the
Broadland boating centres, sprang up
around the medieval bridge over the
River Thurne, a low-arched structure with
a clearance of only 7 foot at its highest, a
notorious test for novice sailors. The
Thurne is a major artery through the
Broads, linking them in a continuous
waterway from Horsey Mere in the east to
Wroxham Broad in the west.

A pleasant excursion from Potter
Heigham is a visit to **Horsey Mere**, about
six miles to the east, and **Horsey
Windpump** (both National Trust). From
this early 20th century four-storey
drainage mill, now restored and fully
working, there are lovely views across the
Mere, which was created by Dutch
engineers in the 17th century. The Mere is

Horsey Windmill

now a wildfowl refuge that attracts
thousands of migratory birds in the
winter.

South of Horsey, at the end of the
navigable stretch of the River Thurne, lies
the hamlet of **West Somerton** and a real
Norfolk curiosity. In the graveyard of **St
Mary's Church** stands a great stone
coffin on four feet, in which is buried
Robert Hales, the tallest man of his time
at a lofty 7'8". For some years he made a
career of his height, meeting Queen
Victoria and causing a sensation in
America. He later ran a pub in Sheffield
and died in retirement at Great Yarmouth
in 1863.

WORSTEAD

12 miles NE of Norwich off the A149 or B1150

It may be hard to imagine now, but
Worstead was a busy little industrial
centre in the Middle Ages. The village
lent its name to the hard-wearing cloth
produced in the region, and many of the
original weavers' cottages can still be seen
in the narrow side-streets. Worsted cloth,
woven from tightly-twisted yarn, was
introduced by Flemish immigrants and
became popular throughout England
from the 13th century onwards. The
Flemish weavers settled happily into the
East Anglian way of life and seem to have
influenced its architecture almost as
strongly as its weaving industry.

(Continued page 34)

WALK 2

How Hill and Ludham

Start	How Hill, near Ludham
Distance	5½ miles (8.9km)
Approximate time	2½ hours
Parking	Car park for Toad Hole Cottage, How Hill
Refreshments	Pubs at Ludham and Ludham Bridge
Ordnance Survey maps	Landranger 134 (Norwich & The Broads), Outdoor Leisure 40 (The Broads)

Looking at the map the River Ant seems to live up to its name – it is a narrow, tortuous waterway connecting Barton Broad with the main network of rivers. The head of navigation is at a tiny village a little way upstream from the Broad though only a few cruisers venture that far. Yet although the Ant may be lacking in stature, its course provides some of the finest scenery of the Broads, at its height in the reaches on each side of How Hill. The walk takes in a delightful village before reaching the riverbank via country lanes and field paths. The How Hill estate now serves as an environmental centre with nature trails and an electric boat providing wildlife water trails (tel. Toad Hole Cottage 01692 678763).

Return to the lane from the Toad Hole Cottage car park and turn left, passing the entrance to How Hill Study Centre. The house was built in 1903 by a Norwich architect as a country retreat though it ended up a grander residence than was originally planned, with elaborate thatched roof inset with dormer windows. Certainly no other house on the Broads can rival its commanding position or landscaped grounds. It stands on one of the rare Broadland hills which just tops 98ft (30m). This is appreciated as the lane drops down after the house through an avenue of fine oak trees. Turn right **A** just before a house as the lane levels on to a pleasant grassy bridleway shaded by more oaks, newly planted ones filling gaps on the left.

The bridleway swings left – follow it for a few paces but look for a path on the right, **B** by an oak tree, which strikes across the field towards a gap in the hedge on the other side, thus cutting off a corner. The path crosses the next field heading directly towards the tower of Ludham church and joins a field-edge track. Turn right on to this to reach a lane and keep ahead on this. Turn left at a T-junction and then keep ahead at a staggered crossroads to walk past modern housing and the village school to reach Ludham village centre. Turn right after the school. The King's Arms stands opposite the church. Keep ahead to pass the east end of the church and pleasing 18th century houses, one of them thatched.

WALK 2

The lane is quiet and pleasant but watch for the next junction, which is well concealed. This is Lovers' Lane, a turn on the right **C** just before a thatched cottage. Walk down this narrow lane, which soon becomes a grassy track running down the edge of a field. At this point it may seem that you are walking back to Ludham, but at the far side of the field the track is joined by another from the southwest. Turn sharply left on to this **D** to head towards buildings on the skyline. To the right of the track is Ludham Hall. The chapel shown on the map is now used as a farm shed, with bricked-up windows and an entrance knocked in its east end, wide enough to accommodate tractors. The rest of the hall retains its ancient beauty. To the left of the farmyard is a fine early-18th century barn, which unfortunately wears a modern roof. Walk through the farmyard and turn right on to the lane, which leads to the main road. Turn left at this junction to reach the Dog Inn within a few yards.

Continue along the main road after the pub – there is a good pavement on the right of the carriageway. Pass the toilets and telephone-box and then turn right **E** to leave the road before the bridge to walk on the riverbank. The reed-fringed path follows the river as it makes a great meander westwards to the foot of Browns Hill. How Hill can now be seen in the distance to the right with a well-preserved drainage mill in the foreground.

The path leaves the riverbank at a dyke **F** and heads toward a wood. When it gets close to this the path divides – take the left fork. Tall reeds screen the vista at first but there are soon views of the How Hill estate with its small lake. Soon afterwards the path is back on the riverbank, which is always busy during holiday months. Walk past the frontage of How Hill and, just before a thatched boathouse, turn right away from the river and cross a footbridge to walk past Toad Hole Cottage, once a marshman's home but now a Broads Authority information centre and free museum with artefacts showing how such people lived in the 19th and early 20th centuries. The garden is planted with herbs that were essential for cooking and medicines at his time. From the cottage, walk to the right of the big house across the greensward to return to the car park at the starting point. ●

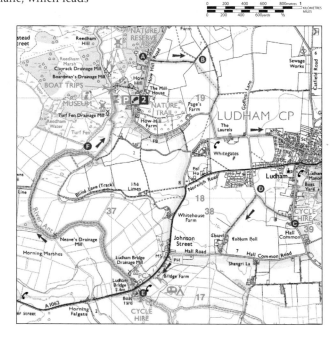

THE OLLANDS

Swanns Loke, Worstead, North Walsham,
Norfolk NR28 9RP
Tel/Fax: 01692 535150
e-mail: ollands@worstead.freeserve.co.uk

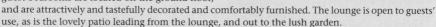

The Ollands Guest House - "Ollands" is a Flemish word meaning "a place of many fields" is set in a picturesque village and amid three-quarters of an acre of garden overlooking farmland. This peaceful retreat offers both bed and breakfast and half-board accommodation. The two double ensuite guest bedrooms are located on the ground floor, and are attractively and tastefully decorated and comfortably furnished. The lounge is open to guests' use, as is the lovely patio leading from the lounge, and out to the lush garden.

Owner Susan Smith provides a full English or Continental breakfast plus, if desired, a two-course evening meal. Packed lunches and flasks are available on request. Any special requests are happily catered for. There's a true home-from-home feeling to this welcoming establishment, and Susan is an attentive and charming host who makes every effort to ensure her guests have a pleasant stay. She has an excellent knowledge of local places of interest - such as the 14th century village church - and places to eat and drink. 4 Diamonds ETC. Pets welcome. Open all year round.

LONG GORES

Hickling, Norfolk NR12 0BE
Tel/Fax: 01692 598185

Long Gores is a special retreat, a holiday cottage with a difference. The setting is truly magical, as the decoration of the cottage has been strongly influenced by the vision and magpie habits of the ecologist and painter Marietta Pallis, who lived at Long Gores for 50 years.

Many of the pictures and objects in the house were created or collected by her. The garden is just as memorable as the house, with winding paths past banks of species roses and the rarities collected by three generations of botanists. The accommodation comprises the original small cottage with two bedrooms under the eaves, reached by a steep winding stair from the charming sitting room, which has an open hearth and which leads, through a windowed door, out into the front garden, and through a back lobby to the light-filled kitchen/dining room; there are also two more bedrooms located in 'The Stables', a series of ground-floor rooms including

the laundry room. Old-fashioned charm permeates every nook and corner.

Repeat bookings by regular visitors and new clients deriving from personal recommendations account for the majority of all visitors here, which always speaks highly of a place's standards and comfort. The 80-acre Long Gores Marsh features a range of acid-marsh, carr-fen and woodland habitats - although the marsh is not open to the public, visitors to Long Gores cottage are offered the opportunity of a guided walk.

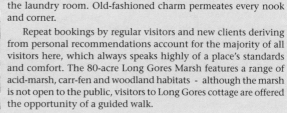

RIVERCRAFT

The Staithe, Stalham, Norfolk NR12 9DA
Tel: 01692 580288 Fax: 01692 582636
e-mail: boats@rivercraft.fsnet.co.uk
website: www.rivercraftnorfolkbroads.co.uk

Rivercraft offer a superb fleet of luxury 2-10 berth cruisers and houseboats for charter on the Norfolk Broads, together with a new four-star riverside lodge with lovely views from the first-floor balcony. Based in a conservation area only five minutes' walk from the village, it's a great base on the River Ant from which to enjoy or begin a broadland holiday.

The lovely 14th century **Church of St Mary** provides ample evidence of Worstead's former prosperity. Its many treasures include a fine hammerbeam roof, a chancel screen with a remarkable painted dado and a magnificent traceried font complete with cover. The village stages an annual weekend of events in July to raise money for the restoration of the church. The festival started up some 35 years ago, and attracts many thousands of visitors each year. The memory of Worstead's days of glory is kept alive by a still-functioning Guild of Weavers. The Guild has placed looms in the north aisle of St Mary's and from time to time there are demonstrations of the ancient skill of weaving.

STALHAM

15 miles NE of Norwich on the A149

Broads history is brought to life at the **Museum of the Broads**, based at Stalham Staithe (Quay) in a collection of old storage buildings and boat sheds. Visitors can experience how Broads people lived and worked as eel-catchers, thatchers, marsh men, reed cutters, boat builders, sailmakers and millwrights. The rich boating heritage of the Broads is illustrated by exhibits that include a vintage holiday cruiser, a river inspector's launch, a traditional steam launch and gun punts complete with guns. The history of the wherries is told with the help of models, drawings and artefacts, and other exhibits not to be missed include the only concrete dinghy ever built, an ice yacht and the story of the destructive coypu.

HICKLING

15 miles NE of Norwich off the A149

Follow the brown tourist signs from Hickling village to reach Norfolk Wildlife Trust's **Hickling Broad National Nature Reserve**. Hickling is the largest and wildest of the Norfolk Broads and a wonderful place to enjoy the scenery and the rich abundance of wildlife. Visitors can explore nature trails, admire the view from a 60 foot tree tower or take a ride in the electric reed lighter boat on the Water Trail. The plant life is very varied, birds like the marsh harrier, barn owl or bittern might be spotted, and eyes should be kept peeled for the Norfolk hawker, one of the rarest of dragonflies, which can be identified by its brown body and vivid green eyes.

A journey along the Norfolk coast rewards the visitor with spectacular sea views, an abundance of sea breezes and miles of sandy beaches that stretch almost without interruption up from Great Yarmouth to Cromer and beyond. The northeast coast includes what could be called the Highlands of Norfolk - the Cromer Ridge, which rises to the not very dizzy heights of 330 feet above sea level.

Substantial stretches of the coast are in the safe hands of the National Trust, including the highest point in the county at West Runton, and the North Norfolk coast is of major importance for its bird life. Morston Marshes and Stiffkey Marshes are sanctuaries to a wide variety of seabirds, and the birds and the seals at

Salthouse Church

Blakeney Point are another favourite tourist attraction. All these are National Trust locations, as are Brancaster, an area of salt marsh and mud flats that includes the site of a Roman fort, and Felbrigg Hall, a superb 17th century house with Grand Tour paintings and marvellous grounds. The house is near Cromer, a charming resort with a 100-year-old pier and a fishing tradition: Cromer crabs are known far and wide. From here a coastal footpath runs all the way west to Holme-next-the-Sea.

The most important town on the northwest coast is the busy seaside resort of Hunstanton, whose cliffs are made up of layers of red, white and brown. Another curious thing about Hunstanton - it is the only east coast resort that actually faces west!

Burnham Overy

LOCATOR MAP

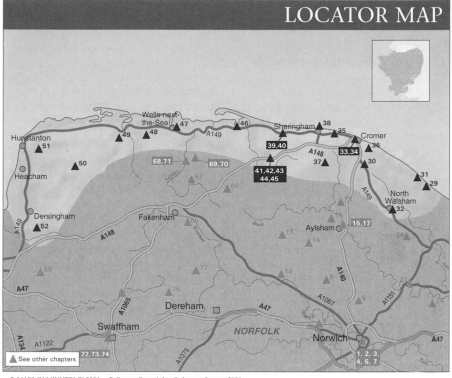

© MAPS IN MINUTES ™ 2001   © Crown Copyright, Ordnance Survey 2001

ADVERTISERS AND PLACES OF INTEREST

HAPPISBURGH TO CROMER

HAPPISBURGH

14 miles SE of Cromer on the B1159

The distinctive **Lighthouse** of this pretty little fishing village, built in 1791 and striped red and white like a barber's pole, has guided many a mariner to the safety of the shore, as has the soaring 110 foot tower of the church of St Mary. But scores of men were lost down the years; the treacherous coastal waters off Happisburgh (pronounced Hazeborough) have seen many a shipwreck over the centuries, and some of the victims lie buried in the graveyard of **St Mary's Church**. The large grassy mound on the north side of the church contains the bodies of the ill-fated crew of *HMS Invincible*, wrecked on the treacherous sandbanks here in 1801. The ship was on its way to join up with Nelson's fleet at

Copenhagen when the tragedy occurred, resulting in the deaths of 119 sailors.

Inside the Church is a splendid 15th century octagonal font carved with the figures of lions, satyrs, and 'wild men'; and embedded in the pillars along the aisle are the marks left by shrapnel from German bombs dropped on the village in 1940.

LESSINGHAM

2 miles S of Happisburgh off the B1159

From this small village a lane winds down through spectacular dunes to the sands at Eccles Beach and, a little further north, to Cart Gap with its gently sloping beach and colourful lines of beach huts. The village of Eccles was overwhelmed by the sea 100 years ago, and the remains of the church are scattered on the beach.

About four miles south of Lessingham stands a windmill that is the tallest not

---

HOLLY TREE COTTAGE

Walcott Green, Walcott-on-Sea, Norwich,
Norfolk NR12 0NS
Tel: 01692 650721
website: www.theaa.com/hotels/102868.html

Holly Tree Cottage is a delightful and traditional Norfolk flint cottage offering superior bed and breakfast accommodation. Set in tranquil countryside just two miles from the sea and four miles from the Norfolk Broads. This lovely establishment was originally a farm barn, refurbished to provide every modern comfort and amenity. There are three attractive and well-appointed double /twin ensuite guest bedrooms. The fresh flowers and home-made biscuits awaiting guests in their room add to the homely ambience. Spotless and tastefully furnished and decorated, the cottage is set in a pleasant garden where guests are welcome to relax. Enjoyable countryside and coastal walks and a wide variety of bird and wildlife in the surrounding farmland help to make this the perfect base. The National Cycle Network Route 30 passes by the front

drive of the cottage. For garden enthusiasts, the fourteen-acre East Ruston Old Vicarage Garden is only one mile away. Four National Trust Properties are within half an hour's drive. Comprehensive details of attractions in the surrounding area are in all the bedrooms.

Owners John and Jennifer Grier are very friendly, helpful hosts. John, prepares and cooks the excellent breakfast from locally sourced products, which is served in a bright, airy and welcoming dining room. The cosy and comfortable guests' lounge has a wood-burning stove. No smoking. No pets. Adults only. Open: Easter - end of September.

Green Farm Hotel and Restaurant

North Walsham Road, Thorpe Market, Norwich,
Norfolk NR11 8TH
Tel: 01263 833602 Fax: 01263 833163
e-mail: grfarmh@aol.com
website: www.greenfarmhotel.co.uk

Green Farm Hotel and Restaurant is a charming flint-faced farmhouse inn offering antique-style double or twin bedrooms (all ensuite) including some four-posters. The converted dairy ground-floor accommodation is particularly well suited for families and guests with disabilities. Established in 1983, owners Philip and Dee Dee Lomax extend a warm welcome to all their guests. The handsome Grade II Listed building was built in 1610, and is thought to have originally been a small monastery.

There's a high standard of quality, comfort and hospitality to be found here in this tranquil location, a convenient and pleasant base from which to explore North Norfolk and its environs. Philip and the hotel's excellent head chef have built up an enviable reputation for quality and presentation of the food served in the a la carte restaurant and bar. Menus change daily, and feature a delicious range of traditional and innovative dishes, all using the freshest local ingredients, home-cooked and home-prepared to provide a truly memorable dining experience.

just in Norfolk, but in the whole of England. Eighty feet high, **Sutton Windmill** was built in the year of the French Revolution, 1789, and its millstones finally ground to a halt only in 1940. Chris Nunn bought the mill in 1976 and since then he has devoted himself to renovating this glorious nine-storey building with the ultimate aim of restoring it to working order. During those years, Chris and his family have also built up a fascinating private collection of artefacts which reflect the social history of Norfolk over the past 150 years or so. These are on display in the family's privately-owned **Broadlands Museum**, a magpie's nest in which you'll find anything from vintage kitchen and veterinary tools to a reconstructed Pharmacy shop of the 1880s, complete with a fine collection of patent medicines, ointments and pills.

North Walsham
9 miles SE of Cromer on the A149

This busy country market town of winding lanes, fine old buildings and an attractive Market Cross of 1600 has some interesting historical associations. Back in 1381, despite its remoteness from London, North Walsham became the focus of an uprising in support of Wat Tyler's Peasants' Revolt. These North Norfolk rebels were led by John Litester, a local dyer, and their object was the abolition of serfdom. Their actions were mainly symbolic: invading manor houses, monasteries and town halls, and burning the documents that recorded their subservient status. In a mass demonstration they gathered on Mousehold Heath outside Norwich, presented a petition to the King, and then retreated to North Walsham to await his answer. It came in the form of the

NORFOLK COASTAL HOLIDAYS

Rainbows End Chalet Park, Mill Lane, Bacton,
Norfolk NR12 0HN
Tel/Fax: 01692 650491 Mobile: 07799 664174
e-mail: info@norfolkcoastalholidays.co.uk
website: www.norfolkcoastalholidays.co.uk

Norfolk Coastal Holidays offers a range of excellent beach chalets which sleep 4 to 6 people (with one double bedroom, one with two single beds and a sofa bed) in a peaceful and relaxing setting. Each holiday chalet is carpeted throughout and handsomely decorated, offering a luxury fitted kitchen with new cooker, fridge and tea/coffee-making facilities, double glazing and colour television for guests' comfort and enjoyment.

Some offer sea views. All are designed for those who prefer those extra touches of comfort and convenience. The lounge is superbly decorated in open-plan style with a new three-piece suite. Each bedroom is beautifully designed with plenty of storage space, and all the beds have interior sprung mattresses.

Each superb chalet is situated in a lovely spot near the splendid sandy beach with private access. Parking is available near each chalet, and there's a safe play area for children. This quiet, undisturbed site covers nearly 13 acres, including 5 acres of traffic-free grassland, while the beach is used almost exclusively by people on the site. This wonderful site also features a putting green. The on-site shop has all the supplies holiday-makers need.

Owners Annette Cini and Margaret Sutton are both Essex-born, and bought this handsome site in 2000, after which they undertook a programme of complete refurbishment to bring all the chalets up to the highest standards of comfort and modernity, and to make each chalet a true home from home. All the

accommodation is clean, well equipped and inexpensive. And improvements continue: plans are underway for a 9-hole golfing facility to be established in 2002, as well as a lounge bar, laundrette and food outlet. The friendly staff are happy to do all they can to ensure that guests enjoy a lovely, relaxing break here on the beautiful and picturesque Norfolk coast.

Centrally located, the site is near Bracton Woods - excellent for walking - and just 6 miles from the Broads, 20 miles from Cromer and Norwich, and 26 miles from Great Yarmouth. Pets and children most welcome. Children under 12 stay free.

Electricity is by £1 coin meter supply. Linen, high chairs, cots and microwave ovens can be hired. Open all year round, there are special out-of-season/Christmas and New Year rates available.

Lord Nelson's School

sanguinary Bishop of Norwich, Henry Despenser, who, as his admiring biographer recorded, led an assault on the rebels, "grinding his teeth like a wild boar, and sparing neither himself nor his enemies,...stabbing some, unhorsing others, hacking and hewing". John Litester was captured, summarily executed and, on the orders of the Bishop, "divided into four parts, and sent throughout the county to Norwich, Yarmouth, Lynn and to the site of his own house".

A more glorious fate awaited the town's most famous resident, Horatio Nelson, who came to **The Paston School** here in 1768 as a boy of ten. Horatio was already dreaming of a naval career and three years later, when he read in the county newspaper that his Uncle Maurice had been appointed commander of a warship, he prevailed on his father to let him join the crew of the *Raisonnable*.

The Paston School had been founded in 1606 by Sir William Paston. His ancestors were the writers of the extraordinary collection of more than a thousand letters, written between 1422 and 1509, which present an astonishingly vivid picture of East Anglian life at the end of the turbulent Middle Ages. Sir William himself is buried in the parish church where he personally supervised (and paid for) the construction of the impressive marble and alabaster monument he desired to be erected in his memory.

About four miles east of North Walsham, near the village of Erpingham on the A140, **Alby Crafts & Gardens** has a Crafts Gallery promoting the excellence of mainly East Anglian and British craftsmanship. The Plantsman's Garden displays a fine collection of unusual shrubs, plants and bulbs in a four-acre site; there are workshops where you can watch craftsmen at work, a Bottle Museum (small charge for admission) and a tearoom.

BACTON
9 miles SE of Cromer on the B1159

Only a few remnants in a field survive of **Broomholm Priory**, founded in the 12th century by William de Glanville and in its day one of the most renowned ecclesiastical establishments in Europe. Pevsner called the village one of the

THE COACH HOUSE

Cromer Road, North Walsham, Norfolk NR28 0HA
Tel/Fax: 01692 403158

The Coach House is comfortable and secluded, an early 17th century converted coach house offering superior bed and breakfast accommodation. The guest bedrooms, lounge and breakfast room are beautifully decorated and furnished. Quiet and peaceful, it is set in a large and lovely garden. This ideal touring base is just 7 miles from the coast and 15 miles from Norwich. The surrounding countryside is perfect for cycling and walking. Cycle hire is available locally and good food can be had at country pubs nearby. The Coach House is only a 5 minute walk from the centre of North Walsham market town.

prettiest in this part of Norfolk, but that was before the arrival of the North Sea Gas Terminal.

PASTON

9 miles SE of Cromer on the B1159

It was in this small village that the Paston family entered the historical record. The vivid collection of letters they wrote to each other during the years that England was being racked by the Wars of the Roses has already been mentioned, and the village boasts another magnificent legacy from this remarkable family. In 1581, Sir William Paston built a cavernous **Tithe-barn** here with flint walls and a thatched roof. It still stands, it's roof still thatched: 160 feet long, almost 60 feet high - the longest, most imposing barn in Norfolk. In the nearby church, the most striking of the family memorials is the one dedicated to Katherine Paston. Sculpted in alabaster by Nicholas Stone in 1628, Katherine lies immaculately dressed in her Jacobean finery of starched ruff, embroidered bodice, puffed sleeves and pearl necklaces. The monument cost £340, a staggering sum of money at that time.

MUNDESLEY

7 miles SE of Cromer on the B1159

"The finest air in the kingdom has been wasted for centuries," said a speaker celebrating the arrival of the railway at Mundesley relatively late, in 1898, "because nobody had the courage to bring the people to the district". The railway has been and gone, but the fresh breezes off the North Sea remain as invigorating as ever.

After the hazards of the coastline immediately to the north where cliffs, fields and houses have all been eroded by the relentless sea, it's a pleasure to arrive at this unassuming holiday resort with its superb sandy beach, considered by many the very best in Norfolk. Mundesley village is quite small (and its **Maritime Museum** is one of the smallest museums in the country) but it provides all the facilities conducive to a relaxing family holiday. Best of all, there is safe swimming in the sea and, when the tide is out, children can spend many a happy hour exploring the many 'lowes', or shallow lagoons, left behind.

CROMER

25 miles N of Norwich on the A149

Cromer had changed from a little-known fishing village to a genteel holiday resort long before the coming of the railway in 1877. In its early days it even received an unsolicited testimonial from Jane Austen. In her novel *Emma* (1816) a character declares "You should have gone to Cromer, my dear, if you went anywhere. Perry was a week at Cromer once, and he holds it to be the best of all the sea-bathing places. A fine open sea, he says, and very pure air". A succession of

Cromer Beach and Pier

CROMER MUSEUM

East Cottages, Tucker Street, Cromer, Norfolk NR27 9HB
Tel: 01263 513543
e-mail: cromer.museum@norfolk.gov.uk
website: www.norfolk.gov.uk/Tourism/Museums/Museums.htm

A row of restored fisherman's cottages houses **Cromer Museum**, where the look and feel of a fisherman's home life 100 years ago is enhanced by the gentle glow of real gas lights. The rooms in

the cottages tell the story of Cromer and the area from the bones of prehistoric animals that once roamed this part of the world to the development of the town, the coming of the railway and the building of the

grand Victorian hotels. Thousands of pictures of old Cromer are stored in the Museum's computer, and visitors can find out about the geology and natural history of the local beaches in the Beachcombers' Shed. The Museum has a small, well-stocked shop.

are launched from the shore (there's no harbour here), sail out to the crab banks about 3 miles offshore, and there the two-man teams on each boat deal with some 200 pots.

The **Lifeboat Museum**, however, is a fairly recent addition. Housed in the former Lifeboat Station, it tells the dramatic story of the courageous men who manned the town's rescue service. Pre-eminent among them was Harry Blogg who was coxswain of the lifeboat for 37 years, from 1910 to 1947. During those years his boat, the *HF Bailey*, was called out 128 times and saved 518 lives. In 1991, the *HF Bailey* was purchased by

celebrities, ranging from Lord Tennyson and Oscar Wilde to Winston Churchill and the Kaiser, all came to see for themselves. The inviting sandy beach remains much as they saw it (horse-drawn bathing machines aside), and so does the **Church of St Peter & St Paul**, which boasts the tallest tower in Norfolk, 160 feet high. And then as now, Cromer Crabs were reckoned to be the most succulent in England. During the season, between April and September, crab-boats

Peter Cadbury of the chocolate manufacturing family and presented to the Museum as its prime exhibit. And what more pleasing sight could there be in a traditional English seaside resort than a traditional seaside pier? **Cromer Pier**, which celebrated its centenary in 2001, is the genuine article, complete with the Pavilion Theatre, which still stages traditional end-of-the-pier shows. The Pier's survival is all the more impressive since it was badly damaged in

DAVIES

7 Garden Street, Cromer, Norfolk NR27 9HN
Tel: 01263 512727 Fax: 01263 514789

Chef Rick Stein included the excellent **Davies** as part of his eight-part television quest for the 'best seafood in Britain'. The shop's fame is well-deserved, as here are sold the most delicious Cromer crabs, lobster, whelks and codling, fresh-caught by owner Richard Davies and his son John. This traditional shop prides itself on its 100 per cent pure shellfish, which are as fresh as can be and contain no additives.

THE NORFOLK SHIRE HORSE CENTRE

West Runton, Cromer, Norfolk NR27 9QH
Tel: 01263 837339 Fax: 01263 837132
e-mail: bakewekk@norfolkshirehorse.fsnet.co.uk
website: www.norfolk-shirehorse-centre.co.uk

Shires, Suffolk Punches and Clydesdales are among the stars of the show at the **Norfolk Shire Horse Centre**, and visitors can meet these wonderful, gentle giants at close quarters in the front yard stables. Two large museum sheds contain a video room and an indoor

demonstration area, and also on show are carts, coaches, gypsy caravans and farm machinery of yesteryear. Next to the museum is a children's play area.

A short walk through a meadow brings visitors to the area where the small animals are kept in their sheds and pens and aviaries. This really is a paradise for animal lovers: native pony mares with their foals, donkeys, Dexter cows, pigs, goats, lambs, guinea pigs, rabbits, chipmunks, chinchillas, cage birds. The ducks and geese have a great time in their own little pond. Twice a day the centre's proprietor, David Blakewell, accompanies demonstrations with a friendly, informative talk about the heavy horses; themes include harnessing and working the horses with the old machinery. Children can have a ride in a cart and join in the feeding of small animals. Numerous specials events are held throughout the summer, including foal days, blacksmiths days, sheepdog days, plough days and harvesting with the heavy horses. Dogs are welcome on leads; the site has a two-acre car park, a café and a gift shop.

Next to the centre, in the same ownership, West Runton Riding Stables offer instruction and accompanied rides for both novice and more experienced riders. The Stables are open throughout the year, the Shire Horse Centre from April to October. Follow the brown tourist signs off the A149 Cromer-Sheringham road or the A148 Cromer-Holt road.

1953 and 1989, and in 1993 sliced in two by a drilling rig which had broken adrift in a storm.

Also well worth visiting is the **Cromer Museum**, housed in a row of restored fishermen's cottages near the church (see panel on page 43).

WEST OF CROMER

WEST RUNTON

3 miles W of Cromer on the A149

The parish of West Runton can boast that within its boundaries lies the highest point in Norfolk - **Beacon Hill**. This eminence is all of 330 feet high, so you won't be needing any oxygen equipment to reach the summit, but there are some excellent views and nearby is the **Roman Camp** (National Trust), a misleading name since there's no evidence that the

---

SHRUBLANDS FARM

Northrepps, Cromer, Norfolk NR27 0AA
Tel/Fax: 01263 579297 e-mail: youngman@farming.co.uk
website: www.broadland.com/shrublands

Shrublands Farm is a charming and welcoming 300-acre family arable farm offering superior accommodation. There are two twin rooms and one double, as well as an attractive and comfortable guests' sitting room and spacious dining room where guests can enjoy fine breakfasts and evening meals made with fresh home-grown and local produce. There are two self-contained properties available: the bungalow adjacent to the farmhouse, which sleeps six, and a cottage in the village itself, which sleeps four.

Romans ever occupied this 70 acres of heathland. Excavations have shown, however, that in Saxon and medieval times this was an iron-working settlement.

West Runton's major tourist attraction is undoubtedly the **Norfolk Shire Horse Centre** where twice a day, during the season, these noble beasts are harnessed up and give a half-hour demonstration of the important role they played in agricultural life right up until the 1930s (see panel opposite).

FELBRIGG

2 miles S of Cromer on minor road off the A148

A couple of miles south of Cromer, on the B1436 signposted from the A140 and A148, is one of Norfolk's grandest houses, **Felbrigg Hall** (National Trust) set in a 1,750-acre estate within North Norfolk's Area of Outstanding Natural Beauty. Thomas Windham began rebuilding the old manor house at Felbrigg in the 1620s, erecting in its place a grand Jacobean mansion with huge mullion windows, pillared porch, and, at roof-level, a dedication in openwork stone: *Gloria Deo in Excelsis*. Later that century, Thomas' grandson William Windham I married a wealthy heiress and added the beautifully proportioned Carolean West Wing where visitors can see portraits of the happily married couple, painted by Sir Peter Lely. Their son, William Windham II, returning from his four-year Grand Tour, filled the house with treasures he had collected - so many of them that he had to extend the Hall yet again. The Windham family's ownership of Felbrigg

Hall came to a tragi-comic end in the 1860s when William Frederick Windham inherited the estate. William was one of the great English eccentrics. He loved uniforms. Attired in the Felbrigg blue and red livery he would insist on serving at the table; in a guard's uniform he caused chaos on the local railway with his arbitrary whistle-blasts; dressed as a policeman, he sternly rounded up the ladies of easy virtue patrolling London's Haymarket. Inevitably, "Mad" Windham fell prey to a pretty fortune-hunter and Felbrigg was only saved from complete bankruptcy by his death at the age of 26.

The Hall was acquired by the National Trust in 1969, complete with its 18th century furnishings, a collection of paintings by artists such as Kneller and van der Velde, and a wonderful Gothic library with a recently restored ceiling. The extensive grounds, perhaps the work of Humphry Repton, include a walled garden containing an elegant octagonal brick dovecote, a vine house, an Orangery from 1707 planted with camellias, a national collection of colchicums (flowering in September), a 500-acre Great Wood, many woodland and lakeside walks, a restaurant, a tea room and a shop. Newly introduced in

Felbrigg Hall

A & J YOUNG POTTERY

Common Farm, Sustead Road, Gresham, Norwich,
Norfolk NR11 8RE
Tel/Fax: 01263 577548

A & J Young Pottery in Gresham is a treat for all fans of unique and decorative stoneware. Owners Andrew and Joanna Young are both gifted potters who met on a ceramics course at art college in Farnham, Surrey and started up the Pottery here in 1981. Specialising in high-fired stoneware which makes for practical and beautiful pots, they produce two types: one in a traditional saltglaze brown, and one made with a white clay glazed in a chrome green. This "white ware" is more decorative, featuring stamps, sprigs (applied raised patterns), roulettes (rolled, indented patterns) and moulded spouts on jugs and teapots, making it quite distinctive.

The green range includes jugs, mugs, various sized bowls (from dessert bowls to large salad bowls), teapots, cups and saucers, plates, butter pots, cooking pots and more. Among the more unusual pieces on sale are the lovely lemon-squeezers and colanders, together with a good selection of plant pots and plant covers made of frost-proof stoneware clay. They also sell a handsome range of plain brown kitchen pottery. All pieces are thrown and fired on site.

The Pottery is set in flintstone barns which were once part of the Felbrigg Estate (now managed by the National Trust), dating back to the mid-19th century. The new showroom, opened in June 2001, displays all the Young's wares in an attractive and welcoming setting.

2001 is a Victory V Walk with an all-weather surface suitable for wheelchairs and pushchairs.

SHERINGHAM

5 miles W of Cromer on the A149

Sheringham has made the transition from fishing village to popular seaside resort with grace and style. There are plenty of activities on offer but Sheringham has managed to avoid the brasher excesses of many English seaside towns. The beach here is among the cleanest in England; consisting mainly of gently sloping sand, it is excellent for bathing and the team of lifeguards makes it ideal for families with children. Rainfall at Sheringham is one of the lowest in the county and the bracing air has also recommended the town to sufferers from rheumatism and respiratory problems.

A small fleet of fishing boats still operates from here, mostly concentrating on crabs and lobsters, but also bringing

Sheringham Beach and Sea Front

in catches of cod, skate, plaice, mackerel and herring. Several original fishermen's' cottages remain, some with lofts where the nets were mended. Sheringham has never had a harbour, so boats are launched from the shore where stacks of creels stand as they have for generations. A golden lobster in the town's coat of arms celebrates this traditional industry.

Like so many other former fishing villages in England, Sheringham owes its transformation into a resort to the arrival of the railway. During the Edwardian peak years of rail travel, some 64 trains a day steamed into the station but the line became

Sheringham Hall and Park

yet another victim of Dr. Beeching, being closed down in stages between 1959 and 1964. Devotees of steam trains joined together and with great effort and enthusiasm managed to re-open the line in 1975 as the **North Norfolk Railway**, better known as **The Poppy Line**.

The name refers to 'Poppyland', a term given to the area by the Victorian journalist Clement Scott, who visited in pre-herbicide days when the summer fields were ablaze with poppies. In 1883, Scott travelled to Cromer on the newly-opened Great Eastern Railway's extension from Norwich. Walking out of the town, he was entranced by the tranquillity of the countryside. In his dispatch to the *Daily Telegraph* he wrote: "It is difficult to convey an idea of the silence of the fields through which I passed, or the beauty of the prospect that surrounded me - a blue sky without a cloud across it, a sea sparkling under a haze of heat, wild flowers in profusion around me, poppies predominating everywhere..." Spurred by Scott's enthusiasm, a succession of

YE OLDE TEA ROOM

7 Lifeboat Plain, Sheringham, Norfolk NR26 8BG
Tel: 01263 821532

As its name tells us, **Ye Olde Tea Room** is a traditional classic: a pretty and comfortable tea room serving delicious cream teas, homemade cakes, light lunches, salads and sandwiches. Featuring a selection of speciality teas and superior coffee, the tempting range of mouth-watering savoury and sweet dishes and snacks will appeal to every palate. Open Tuesday to Sunday 10.30am - 5.00pm April to October; Thursday to Sunday 11.00am - 4.00pm November to March.

notable Victorians made their way here - painters, writers, actors, even a youthful Winston Churchill. Later, during the Second World War, Churchill returned to the area, staying at Pear Tree Cottage in Mundesley.

Although greatly diminished in number, plenty of brilliant poppies can still be seen as you travel the scenic five-mile journey from Sheringham to Holt. The railway, once part of the Midland & Great Northern Railway Company, operates up to eight trains daily in each direction during the season, March to October, and there are special Saturday evening and Sunday lunchtime services when you can dine in style in one of the Pullman coaches from the old Brighton Belle.

Just to the west of the town, at Upper Sheringham, footpaths lead to the lovely grounds of **Sheringham Park** (National Trust). The Park was landscaped by Humphry Repton, who declared it to be his "favourite and darling child in Norfolk"; it is certainly his best known and best preserved work. There are dense growths of oak, beech and fir trees, 15 kinds of magnolia and banks of rhododendrons which are at their most dazzling in late May and June. Waymarked walks are open all year round and there are viewing towers affording spectacular views of coast and countryside; one of the towers is built on the site of a Napoleonic lookout. Humphry Repton (1752-1818) was the most distinguished landscaper in the generation immediately after Capability, of whom he was a great admirer. Repton was known for his selling techniques, producing 'before and after' pictures of his proposals which he bound with explanatory text into what became known as Repton's Red Books (red was the colour of the binding). There's yet

ROSEDALE FARM GUESTHOUSE

Holt Road, Weybourne, Holt, Norfolk NR25 7ST
Tel: 01263 588778 Mobile: 07760 493538
e-mail: rosedale.lacostes@tinyworld.co.uk

Rosedale Farm Guesthouse is a beautiful and distinguished 18th century brick and flint farmhouse offering superb bed and breakfast accommodation. The very comfortable guest bedrooms are traditionally furnished and decorated to a high standard and comprise of one large family en-suite room (with bath and shower),
two large double en-suite rooms, one twin en-suite room and a further double bedroom with a private bathroom. Throughout the house there are many original Georgian features, and a selection of paintings by local artists and by Gerald Lacoste, father of the guesthouse's owner, Charles. Charles and his wife Pauline are warm and welcoming hosts. They started up this superior bed and breakfast establishment in 1996. Pauline is the chef, preparing hearty breakfasts and, by prior arrangement, delicious evening meals and high tea. The freshest local produce is used in the preparation of all meals, with a particular

emphasis on fish meals, a local speciality. There is a large and attractive garden with a croquet lawn and outdoor heated swimming pool.

There is good walking amid the tranquil surroundings of this lovely seaside village, and your hosts can also arrange bicycle hire for those wishing to explore the lovely surrounding landscape. As an added treat, seal trips can be arranged for all guests interested in getting closer to these magnificent sea creatures.

WEYBOURNE FOREST LODGES

Sandy Hill Lane, Weybourne, Holt,
Norfolk NR25 7HW
Tel: 01263 588440 Fax: 01263 588588

Open all year round, **Weybourne Forest Lodges** is a small development of beautiful Scandinavian-style lodges, set in a peaceful glade in a privately owned pine forest. In an Area of Outstanding Natural Beauty on the North Norfolk Coast, two miles above the sea and three miles from Holt and Sheringham. Each lodge has three bedrooms (one en-suite). There are riding stables next door and a leisure centre nearby.

more grand scenery at the aptly-named Pretty Corner, just to the east of the A1082 at its junction with the A148. This is a particularly beautiful area of woodland and also offers superb views over the surrounding countryside.

WEYBOURNE

9 miles W of Cromer on the A149

Here, the shingle beach known as Weybourne Hope (or Hoop) slopes so steeply that an invading fleet could bring its ships right up to the shore. Which is exactly what the Danes did many times during the 9th and 10th centuries. A local adage states that "He who would Old England win, Must at Weybourne Hoop begin", and over the centuries care has been taken to protect this stretch of the coast. A map dated 1588 clearly shows Waborne Fort and Holt's Parish Register for that year of the Armada notes that "in this yeare was the town of Waborne fortified with a continuall garrison of men bothe of horse and foote with sconces (earthworks) ordinaunce and all manner of appoyntment to defend the Spannyards landing theare".

As it turned out, the Spannyards never got close, but during both World Wars the same concern was shown for defending this vulnerable beach. The garrison then became the Anti-Aircraft Permanent Range and Radar Training Wing, providing instruction for National

Servicemen until the camp finally closed in 1959. It was reckoned that by then some 1,500,000 shells had been fired out to sea. The site has since been returned to agricultural use, but the original World War II NAAFI buildings remain and now house the **Muckleburgh Collection**, a fascinating museum of military vehicles, weapons and equipment, most of which has seen action in battlefields all over the world. All the 16 tanks, the armoured cars, the mighty Diamond 'T' tank transporter and the amphibious vehicles on display can be inspected at close quarters, and the tanks - all in working order - take part in daily demonstrations. On weekends (and weekdays during school holidays) visitors can enjoy a ride along the coast in a Gama Goat USA personnel carrier. Besides the real machines, the museum, which is open from mid-February to the end of October, contains 600 models of military vehicles and aircraft, a unique collection of 54 model ships, uniforms, medals and an exhibition of the Suffolk & Norfolk Yeomanry dating back to 1782. Meals and snacks are available, served in a NAAFI-style canteen.

Incidentally, despite Weybourne's exposed position, it has in fact only been attacked once, by the Luftwaffe on 11th July 1940. A stick of bombs landed in the main street and badly damaged two cottages.

WIVETON HALL

Holt, Norfolk NR25 7TE
Tel: 01263 740525 Fax: 01263 741314
e-mail: ddt@wivetonhall.co.uk
website: www.wivetonhall.co.uk

Wiveton Hall is a grand and stately house, one of England's secret architectural gems. It was built in the mid-1600s, and boasts attractive lead-paned windows and tall, patterned chimneys. The wing added during the early 1900s has been converted into self-contained accommodation. For anyone wanting a truly peaceful and pampered holiday, the lovely surroundings feature exposed beams, open log fires, antique furnishings, polished wood floors, fine fabrics, oil paintings and prints alongside every modern amenity. The wing has its own entrances and sunny courtyard garden.

Furnished throughout in traditional country house style, the old ballroom is now a large drawing room with grand piano and open fire, and the former billiard room is now the kitchen/dining room. Surrounded by extensive gardens and set in its own farmland, it is the perfect rural retreat. Fresh fruit, vegetables such as asparagus, strawberries and raspberries straight from the farm are on sale - or guests can pick their own soft fruit. Totally safe for children, this secluded, peaceful and private place is the ideal place to lie back and relax amid gracious and luxurious surroundings. Cooked meals are available, as is a baby-sitting service. This wonderful setting is located on a bird migratory route, making it an ideal place to do a bit of 'twitching'.

YETMANS

37 Norwich Road, Holt, Norfolk NR25 6SA
Tel: 01263 713320
website: www.yetmans.net

When Alison and Peter Yetman (she cooks, he fronts) opened their eponymous restaurant in 1988, they wanted it to be the sort of place that they themselves would like to find in North Norfolk. Thirteen years on and their ethos prevails in this lively, pretty, some would say idiosyncratic place.

The menu, which changes daily and with the seasons, is short - maybe six starters, 5 main courses (one vegetarian) and six or seven puddings. This allows Alison to use farm fresh seasonal produce, most of it sourced locally, and with her trusty team, cook everything to order. She treats the food with respect - first class ingredients cooked simply.

The wine list concentrates mainly on the New World with a strong leaning to New Zealand. To quote from it "we don't stock any wine that we don't enjoy drinking ourselves - basically we sell the sort of food that we like to eat and the wine that we like drinking". There are no half bottles on the list but there are always six or seven wines available by the glass and matched to the day's menu.

Open (winter) Weds - Sat 7.00pm - 9.30pm, Sunday 12.30pm - 2.00pm; (summer) Weds - Sat and Mon 7.00pm - 9.30pm, Sunday 12.30pm - 2.00pm and 7.30pm - 9.30pm.

BODHAM

9 miles W of Cromer off the A148

About midway between Bodham and Weybourne, in the grounds of the Kelling Park Hotel, is the **East Anglian Falconry Centre** which, in addition to having daily flying displays, is also the largest sanctuary in the country for injured owls and birds of prey. The centre keeps and cares for over 200 birds, amongst them kestrels and sparrowhawks, as well as a number of rarer birds such as goshawks, peregrine falcons, harriers and redtail hawks, eagles and snowy owls.

HOLT

10 miles W of Cromer on the A148

Back in 1892, a guide-book to the county described Holt as "a clean and very prettily situated market town, being planted in a well undulating and very woody neighbourhood". More than a century later, one can't quarrel with that characterisation: a perennial finalist in the Anglia in Bloom competition, Holt's town centre always looks a picture with hanging baskets and flowers everywhere. The worst day in the town's history was May 1 1708, when a raging fire consumed most of the town's ancient houses. The consequent rebuilding replaced them with some elegant Georgian houses, gracious buildings which played a large part in earning the town its designation as a Conservation Area.

The town's most famous building, **Gresham's School**, somehow escaped that disastrous conflagration of 1708. Founded in 1555 by Sir John Gresham, the school began as an altruistic educational establishment, its pupils accepted solely on the basis of their academic promise. Since then, the school has abandoned both its town centre location and its founder's

BARON ART

17 Chapel Yard, Holt, Norfolk NR25 6HG
Tel: 01263 713430 Fax: 01263 711670

Anthony Baron and Michael Bellis started **Baron Art** in 1991. A hobby that has grown into a thriving concern, their enterprise, dedication, specialist knowledge and eye for quality have led to the establishment of three distinct shops, all in and around Holt. At 17 Chapel Yard, Holt, the shop specialises in Art Deco ceramics including pieces by Clarice Cliff and other highly sought-after ceramics from the 1920s and

1930s. In addition there are watercolours and artwork by artists such as Eric Gill, Dame Laura Knight, John Nash and many others. New pieces are always being added to their extensive collection of ceramics and paintings. At 9 Chapel Yard, Albert Street, can be found their intimate bookshop featuring modern first editions, antiquarian books, engravings and etchings. A framing service is also available.

Last but definitely not least, at Kelling on the coast road between Weybourne and Salthouse, the Old Reading Room - so named for the original purpose of the building, constructed in 1916 - offers a delightful array of Victorian watercolours and oils, contemporary etchings, woodcuts, thousands of second-hand books, collectibles and postcards. There's also a tasteful and comfortable tea room for light lunches and tempting cream teas.

commitment to free education; among its many distinguished former pupils are Lord Reith, the founder of the BBC, the poets WH Auden and Stephen Spender and the composer Benjamin Britten.

One of Holt's most unusual buildings is **Home Place**. Designed and built in 1903-5 by ES Prior, an architect follower of the Arts & Crafts movement, the exterior of the house is completely covered with an ingeniously contrived cladding of local pebbles.

CLEY-NEXT-THE-SEA
12 miles W of Cromer on the A149

It is no longer 'next-the-sea', in fact it's a mile away from the coast, but in early medieval times, Cley (pronounced Cly, and meaning clay) was a more important port than King's Lynn, with a busy trade exporting wool to the Netherlands. In return, Cley imported a predilection for houses with curved gables, Flemish bricks and pantiles. The windmill overlooking

BIRCHAM CONTEMPORARY ARTS GALLERY

14 Market Place, Holt, Norfolk NR25 6BW
Tel: 01263 713312
e-mail: Birchamgal@aol.com website: bircham-arts.co.uk

Bircham Contemporary Arts Gallery is owned and run by Christopher and Deborah Harrison, who established this excellent gallery in 1988. Since that time they have built up a reputation for the quality of the gallery's featured artists and exhibitions. Christopher studied Fine Art and Art History at Reading University, and brings the benefit of his experience and expertise to bear on sourcing and selling a range of contemporary works of art. Situated in the heart of Holt, this fine gallery occupies a handsome and historic building that was once home to Caxton Press.

Beautiful and contemporary in decor and ambience, its excellent lighting and layout enhance the many fine pieces on display, which include paintings, sculpture, glassware, ceramics and much more. The changing exhibitions can feature watercolour landscapes, abstract prints, works in bronze or wood and modern jewellery. The gallery always offers an exciting and imaginative juxtaposition of a wide range of the best of contemporary pieces, so that visitors invariably find something to admire. Stocking work by many artists, there is a wide range of prices as well as types and subjects, so that there is something to suit every taste and pocket. "Pink Roses, White Daisies" by Judy Scott is an example, illustrated here.

THE LAWNS HOTEL

Station Road, Holt, Norfolk NR25 6BS
Tel: 01263 713390 Fax: 01263 710642
website: www.lawnshotel.co.uk

The Lawns Hotel offers gracious hospitality, courteous service and the highest standards of comfort and quality. The 10 ensuite rooms are spacious and welcoming, all elegantly furnished and decorated. 4 Diamonds ETC. Most rooms have delightful views over Gresham's School playing fields and Holt church, or over the lovely walled gardens in the grounds, where guests are welcome to stroll.

Cley Windmill

finest bird-watching sites in Britain, well known for its rare birds, waders and large flocks of wildfowl. There's something to see at any time of year: avocets among the wading birds arriving in the spring; bitterns in the summer; snow buntings, ducks and Brent geese returning to their favoured feeding grounds as winter approaches. The visitor centre has views across the reserve, with telescopes and binoculars on site, and there are excellent bird-watching hides and a wildlife gift shop. A breezy walk takes in the village, the windmill, the marshes and out along the narrow spit to **Blakeney Point**, the most northerly extremity of East Anglia. This wild and lonely spit of land that stretches three miles out into the sea is another twitcher's paradise and is scarcely less impressive for its flora: almost 200 flowering species have been recorded. Boat trips to see the birds and the seals set out from Blakeney Quay and from Morston.

the harbour adds to the sense that a little piece of Holland has strayed across the North Sea. This is the famous **Cley Mill**, the subject of thousands of paintings. Built in 1713 and in use until 1921, the Mill is now a private residence. Another interesting building is the flint-and-brick **Whalebone House**, whose walls are adorned with panels of flint framed by pieces of whalebone.

The village's prosperity in the past is reflected in the enormous scale of its 14th century parish **Church of St Mary**, whose two-storey south porch is particularly notable for its fine stonework and 16 armorial crests. The gorgeous fan-vaulted roof is decorated with bosses carved with angels, flowers, and a lively scene of an old woman throwing her distaff at a fox making off with her chickens.

Half a mile east of Cley on the A149 coast road, Norfolk Wildlife Trust's **Cley Marshes**, designated Britain's first local nature reserve in 1926, is one of the

BLAKENEY
14 miles W of Cromer on the A149

One of the most enchanting of the North Norfolk coastal villages, Blakeney was a commercial port until the beginning of the 20th century when silting up of the estuary prevented all but pleasure craft from gaining access. The silting has left a fascinating landscape of serpentine creeks and channels twisting their way through mud banks and sand hills. In a side street off the quay is the 14th century **Guildhall** (English Heritage), which was probably a private house and contains little of interest apart from the undercroft, or cellar, which is notable as an early

COUNTRYSIDE COTTAGES

5 Westgate Street, Blakeney, Norfolk NR25 7NQ
Tel : 01263 741777 Fax: 01263 741666
e-mail : ccottages@dialstart.net
website: www.luxury-norfolk-cottages.com

Countryside Cottages is a unique, privately owned company, based in the beautiful village of Blakeney, the jewel of the North Norfolk Coast. Much has been written recently about this select little corner of paradise and it is our pleasure to offer you the perfect base from which to explore the breathtaking coastline. Why are we unique? We have very exacting standards and only add properties of a four and five star standard to our portfolio. We are positively thrilled that many property owners have chosen to trust us with their delightful cottages, most of which have not

been offered to the holiday market previously. We offer our owners and guests alike a professional, friendly, tailor made service and we are 'on call' for advice and help throughout your stay. We have an excellent choice of properties, which we are sure will lure you away for a few days of comfort and relaxation.

From cosy, romantic hideaways with dreamy four-poster beds and roaring log fires to magnificent barn conversions with dramatic galleried rooms or maybe an Aga heated farmhouse with a large garden and tennis court.... We think we can make your holiday really special, so join our increasing number of regular guests and contact us without obligation, after all, you deserve a treat! We also have a "Tailor Made Service" for making a wonderful holiday special - Please call for further information.

example of a brick-built vaulted ceiling. The beautifully restored **Church of St Nicholas**, set on a hill overlooking village and marshland, offers much more

Blakeney Harbour

to the visitor. The chancel, built in 1220, is a lovely example of Early English work, and the magnificent west tower, 100 feet high, is a landmark for miles around. In a small turret on the northeast corner of the chancel a light would once burn as a beacon to guide ships safely into Blakeney Harbour.

GLANDFORD

12 miles W of Cromer off the B1156

Near this delightful village, the **Natural Surroundings Wild Flower Centre** is dedicated to gardening with a strong ecological emphasis. There are wild flower meadows and gardens, organic vegetable and herb gardens, nurseries, a nature trail alongside the unspoilt River Glaven, and the Centre also organises a wide range of events with a conservation theme. A short walk down the valley from the Centre is the **Glandford Shell Museum**, a lovely Dutch-style building which houses the private collection of Sir Alfred Jodrell, a unique accumulation of sea shells gathered from beaches all around the world, together with a fascinating variety of artefacts made from them.

A couple of miles south of Glandford you'll find a building of 1802, which year after year has been awarded the title of Top Tourist Attraction in North Norfolk. **Letheringsett Watermill** stands on the site of an earlier mill recorded in the Domesday Book and was rescued from near-dereliction in the 1980s. This fully functional, water-powered mill produces 100 per cent wholewheat flour from locally grown wheat; there are regular demonstrations of the milling process, with a running commentary from the miller; and the end product can be purchased in the gift shop.

LANGHAM

14 miles W of Cromer off the A149/A148

The minor road leading south from Morston will bring you, after a mile or so, to **Langham Fine Norfolk Rural Crafts** where, in a wonderful collection of restored 18th century barn workshops, you watch a variety of craftspeople exercising their traditional skills. In addition to the now famous Longham Glass works where a master glass-maker will give a running commentary, there's a pyrographer, wood-turner, stained glass maker and glass engraver. The Factory Gift Shop is well stocked with their creations, the Antiques & Collectibles Shop offers a wide variety of items from Victorian china to Lalique, and there's also a walled garden, adventure playground and restaurant.

Letheringsett Mill

MORSTON

13 miles W of Cromer on the A149

Great stretches of salt marshes and mud flats lie between this pleasant village and the sea, which is reached by way of a tidal creek that almost disappears at low tide. Morston is a particularly pleasing village with quiet lanes and clusters of cottages built from local cobbles. If the church tower looks rather patched-up, that's because it was struck by lightning in 1743. It is said that local people took this as a sign that the Second Coming of Christ was imminent and that repairing their church was therefore pointless. It was many years before restoration work was finally undertaken, by which time the fabric of the tower had deteriorated even further. Boat trips to see the birds and seals off Blakeney Point start from Morston and from Blakeney Quay.

STIFFKEY

16 miles W of Cromer on the A149

The Rector of Stiffkey propelled the name of the village into the headlines, but this, one of the prettiest villages in the county, has many more tangible attractions. It takes its name (pronounced Stewkey) from the little river on which it stands; the name means 'island of tree stumps' and is probably derived from the marshy river valley of reed beds and fallen trees which indeed gives the village the appearance of an island. At the east end of the village is the church of St John the Baptist and from the churchyard there are fine views of the river and of **Stiffkey Hall** to the south. All that now remains of this once-impressive building, built by the Bacon family in 1578, are the towers, one wing of the house, and the 17th century gatehouse. The stately ruins of the great hall have been transformed into a rose terrace and sunken garden and are open to the public.

The former **Rectory** is a grand Georgian building, famous as the residence of the Reverend Harold Davidson, Rector of Stiffkey during the 1920s and 1930s. Harold launched a personal crusade to save the fallen women of London's West End, and caused much gossip and scandal by doing so. When arraigned before a Consistory Court at the age of 60 in March 1932 and threatened with defrocking, it was alleged that he spent Sundays in his parish and the rest of the week in a rented bedsit in Shepherd's Bush. Waitresses from ABC and Lyons teashops had complained of being pestered, and other girls testified that he had taken them to Norfolk to work as servants but had been left penniless, forced to live in the fields. In October 1932 the Court found him guilty and he was duly defrocked. There is a rather bizarre ending to his story. After handing over the keys of Stiffkey Rectory, the good vicar, always something of a showman, joined a travelling show and in 1937 in a Skegness amusement park was mauled by a lion whose cage he happened to be sharing; he died two days later.

To the north of the village are the **Stiffkey Salt Marshes**, a National Trust nature reserve which turns a delicate shade of purple in July when the sea lavender is in bloom. Here on the sandflats can be found the famous Stiffkey blues - cockles which have long been highly regarded as a delicacy. They are prepared in the same way as mussels, to which they are preferred by many connoisseurs.

A couple of miles south of Stiffkey stand the picturesque ruins of **Binham Priory** (English Heritage), its magnificent nave still serving as the parish church. This represents only about one-sixth of the original Priory, founded in 1091 by a nephew of William the Conqueror. The church is well worth a visit to see its

Binham Priory

unusually lofty interior with a Monk's Walk at roof level, its Seven Sacraments font, and noble west front.

HUNSTANTON

The busy seaside resort of Hunstanton can boast two unique features: it has the only cliffs in England made up of colourful levels of red, white and brown strata, and it is the only east coast resort that faces west, looking across The Wash to the Lincolnshire coast and the unmistakable tower of the 272 foot high **Boston Stump** (more properly described as the Church of St Botolph).

Hunstanton town is a comparative newcomer, developed in the 1860s by Mr Hamon L'Estrange of nearby Hunstanton Hall to take advantage of the arrival of the railway here, and to exploit the natural appeal of its broad, sandy beaches. The centre is well planned, with mock-Tudor houses grouped around a green that falls away to the shore.

Hunstanton's social standing was assured after the Prince of Wales, later Edward VII, came here to recover from typhoid fever. He stayed at the Sandringham Hotel which, sadly, has since been demolished, along with the grand Victorian pier, and the railway. But *Hunston*, as locals call the town, still has a distinct 19th century charm about it and plenty to entertain visitors.

The huge stretches of sandy beach, framed by those multi-coloured cliffs, are just heaven for children, who will also be fascinated by the **Kingdom of the Sea** on the South Promenade, where an underwater glass tunnel provides a fascinating opportunity to watch the varied and often weird forms of marine life that inhabit Britain's waters. A popular excursion from Hunstanton is the boat trip to **Seal Island**, a sandbank

Hunstanton Cliffs and Beach

in The Wash where seals can indeed often be seen sunbathing at low tide.

AROUND HUNSTANTON

WELLS-NEXT-THE-SEA
17 miles E of Hunstanton on the A149

Wells is a little town of great appeal with its picturesque quayside, narrow streets and ancient houses. Wells has been a working port since at least the 13th century but, as with Cley-next-the-Sea, the town's full name has become increasingly inapt over the years - its harbour now stands more than a mile from the sea. In 1859, to prevent the harbour silting up altogether, Lord Leicester of Holkham Hall built an embankment cutting off some 600 acres of marshland. This now provides a pleasant walk down to the sea.

THE ASHLEY STUDIOS

19 Staithe Street, Wells-next-the-Sea, Norfolk NR23 1AG
Tel/Fax: 01328 710923

The Ashley Studios offers everything you need in the way of art supplies, and more. The shop has two rooms stocking a comprehensive range of artists' materials, including pads, paper, brushes (sable, acrylic, bristle and goat hair), easels, acrylic paints, pastels, every kind of pen, books and a vast selection of Winsor & Newton products. In addition there is a choice variety of hand-painted postcards, framed prints, stationery and much more.

The embankment gave no protection however against the great floods of 1953 and 1978. On the 11th January 1978, the sea rose 16ft 1in above high tide, a few inches less than the 16ft 10in recorded on the 31st January 1953, when the floodwaters lifted a ship on to the quay. A silo on the harbour is marked with these abnormal levels.

Running alongside the embankment is the **Harbour Railway**, which trundles from the small museum on the quay to the lifeboat station by the beach. This narrow-gauge railway is operated by the same company as the **Wells & Walsingham Railway**, which carries passengers on a particularly lovely ride along the route of the former Great Eastern Railway to Little Walsingham. The four mile journey takes about 25 minutes with stops at Warham St Mary and Wighton. Both the WWR and the Harbour Railway services are seasonal. In a curious change of function, the former GER station at Wells is now home to the well-known **Burnham Pottery**, the former signal box is now the station, while the old station at Walsingham is now a church!

In addition to being the largest of North Norfolk's ports, Wells is also a popular resort with one of the best beaches in England bordered by the curiously named **Holkham Meals**, a plantation of pines established here in the 1860s to stabilise the dunes.

HOLKHAM

16 miles E of Hunstanton, on the A149

If the concept of the Grand Tour ever needed any justification, **Holkham Hall** (see panel opposite) amply provides it. For six years, from 1712 to 1718, young Thomas Coke (pronounced Cook) travelled extensively in Italy, France and Germany, studying and absorbing at first hand the glories of European civilisation. And, wherever possible, buying them. When he returned to England, Coke realised that his family's modest Elizabethan manor could not possibly house the collection of treasures he had amassed. The manor, built by his ancestor Sir Edward Coke, Attorney General to Elizabeth and Chief Justice to James I, would have to be demolished and a more fitting building erected in its place.

During his travels in Italy, Coke had been deeply impressed by the cool,

Green State Bedroom, Holkham Hall

Holkham Hall

of pink Derbyshire alabaster transported to nearby Wells by river and sea. Historically, the most important room at Holkham is the Statue Gallery, which contains one of the finest collections of classical sculpture still in private ownership, among them a bust of Thucydides (one of the earliest portrayals of man) and a statue of Diana, both of which have been dated to 4 BC.

classical lines favoured by the Renaissance architect, Andrea Palladio. Working with his friend Lord Burlington - another fervent admirer of Palladio - and the architect William Kent, Coke's monumental project slowly took shape. Building began in 1734 but was not completed until 1762, three years after Coke's death. The completed building, its classical balance and restraint emphasised by the pale honey local brick used throughout, has been described as the ultimate achievement of the English Palladian movement. As you step into the stunning entrance hall, the tone is set for the rest of the house. Modelled on a Roman Temple of Justice, the lofty coved ceiling is supported by 18 huge fluted columns

Each room reveals new treasures: Rubens and Van Dyck in the Saloon (the principal reception room); the Landscape Room with its incomparable collection of

(Continued page 62)

HOLKHAM HALL & BYGONES MUSEUM

Wells-next-the-Sea, Norfolk NR23 1AB
Tel: 01328 710227
Fax: 01328 711707
website: www.holkham.co.uk

In a lakeside deer park on the beautiful North Norfolk coast stands **Holkham Hall**, one of Britain's most majestic stately homes, seat of seven generations of the Earls of Leicester. This classic 18th century mansion in Palladian style is a veritable treasure house of artistic and architectural history, and each part has its separate character and appeal, from the stunning grandeur of the Marble Hall and the magnificence of the State Rooms to the old kitchen with its original pots and pans and the elegant formal gardens. In addition to the superb

house and gardens there are other attractions at Holkham, including a Bygones Museum crammed with over 4,000 domestic and agricultural artefacts, nursery gardens, a pottery shop, restaurant and tearooms.

WALK 3

Warham and Wighton from Wells-Next-The-Sea

Start	Wells harbour
Distance	8½ miles (13.7km)
Approximate time	4 hours
Parking	Harbour car park, Wells-Next-The-Sea
Refreshments	Pubs and cafés at Wells, pub at Warham, pub and seasonal tearoom at Wighton
Ordnance Survey maps	Landranger 132 (North West Norfolk), Explorer 24 (251) (Norfolk Coast Central)

At weekends in summer car parking can be difficult in Wells so it may be easier to begin this route at Wighton, which is a spacious village with room for parking near the church. The walk is a grand mix of country and coast walking, using tracks and byways as well as the coastal path across the salt-marshes. Note that the country pubs are often closed in the afternoon.

In 1845 Wells was described as an 'irregularly built seaport town' and the eccentric charm of its streets survives to attract tourists and numbers of senior citizens who choose to retire here, in spite of the biting winter winds.

Head eastwards along the waterfront (The Quay) at Wells, passing the old granary – now apartments – and the chandlery. The granary is a reminder that until recently Wells was a commercial port, with two or three coasters sometimes lining its quay within the memory of the writer. This activity had gone on for nearly 800 years – Ramsey Abbey was given a charter in 1202 allowing grain from its Norfolk farms to be loaded at Wells. The mid-19th century saw Wells at the height of its prosperity when it had a population of 3,500, and 330 cargoes each year were unloaded at the quays.

Keep ahead when the path divides **A** and pass between boatsheds and workshops

before climbing to the top of the embankment. There are wonderful vistas from here to the pines at East Hills (the eastern sand spit that shelters the entrance to Wells harbour) and inland towards Warham and Wighton. If you look down to the edge of the salt-marsh you will see the skeletal remains of one of the coasters that finished its last voyage here. An English Nature noticeboard stands at the point where a path cut across an inlet over a footbridge. East coast weather saw the end of this bridge some time ago and it has never been replaced.

The walking is excellent on springy turf and there is a sheltered seat overlooking Warham Greens, where the path bends inland for a short way. A second noticeboard stands at the end of Garden Drove. Keep on the coast path to the third noticeboard, **B** where a path runs across the salt-marsh towards the sea. Climb the slight rise and turn inland down Cocklestrand Drove, a good sandy track which soon reaches the main road.

Cross the A149 to the lane opposite, which is a quiet byway that climbs directly into Warham and the crossroads by the Three Horseshoes. Go straight across here on a lane that passes Warham's All Saints' Church and first climbs and then drops to a hump-backed bridge. The tower of the other church of the village, dedicated to St Mary Magdalen, can be seen to the right. Also to the right, reached by a bridleway at the top of the hill, is Warham Camp, an Iron Age fort dating from c.50 BC and covering about 3½ acres (1.4 ha). Twin ditches and earthen ramparts (originally topped by timber palisades) must have made this a conspicuous feature of the windswept landscape.

The lane bends right before dropping into Wighton – there is a good view of the fort before you reach the village. Turn right at the T-junction and pass (or pause at) the Carpenters' Arms before bearing right up the main street to the church. The former school is now an art gallery, and there is a seasonal teashop at the top of the street, open from noon, except Monday and Thursday. Keep ahead on the Wells road, but leave it when it bends right **C** by keeping straight on along a byway going towards a railway bridge. This spans the narrow-gauge steam railway that runs between Wells and Walsingham. Go over the bridge and past the cemetery.

After this the track is stony and must be hard on the tyres of the many bicycles that use it, but at least the scrunching stones give warning of their approach, and it is pleasant walking past a patchwork of fields. On a hot day the shade offered by the trees on Gallow Hill is welcome. Take the second track to the right here **D** to head

northwards down to Wells. The high hedges provide excellent black-berries but screen the view. Wells church can be seen ahead as the track passes cattle-sheds. Keep ahead when the main track leaves to the right after these.

The path leads past a school playing-field, used as a camping-field at summer holiday time, and joins the road to the school by another cemetery. Cross the main road and turn left for 20 yds (18m) before turning right up a footpath that takes you up Plummer Hill and into the Buttlands, which is a delightful green faced by early-19th century houses that were the homes and offices of lawyers, doctors and shipping agents when first built. Cross the grass diagonally to the Globe Inn and then turn right and left to descend Staithe Street, the main thoroughfare, back to the Quay.

paintings by Lorrain, Poussin and other masters; the Brussels tapestries in the State Sitting Room; chimneypiece tablets depicting scenes from *Aesop's Fables* in the North Dining Room and, on a more domestic note, the vast, high-ceilinged kitchen which remained in use until 1939 and still displays the original pots and pans. The 3,000-acre park was laid out originally by William Kent but altered by Coke's great-nephew, Thomas William Coke (1754-1842). Universally known as Coke of Norfolk, Thomas was a pioneer of the Agricultural Revolution, best known for introducing the idea of a four-crop rotation. He was also a generous patron of agricultural innovations and the Sheep Shearings he inaugurated - gatherings to which several hundred people came to exchange ideas on all aspects of agriculture - were the direct forerunners of the modern agricultural show. Lawns sweep down to a vast lake, and other features include a walled kitchen garden in the nursery garden where many plants are for sale. A fountain representing St George and the Dragon is edged by a parterre designed by William Nesfield (1793-1881), who was a distinguished soldier and gifted watercolourist before becoming a landscaper.

The Thomas Coke who built the house had been created Earl of Leicester in 1744, but as his only son died before him, the title lapsed. However, when his grand-nephew, Coke of Norfolk, was elevated to the peerage by Queen Victoria at the very beginning of her reign, he adopted the same title. The present Earl, the 7th of the second creation, lives at Holkham in the private apartments known as the Family Wing but still uses the State Rooms when entertaining guests. The Earl continues in the tradition of Coke of Norfolk by overseeing the vast estate with its 30 tenant farmers and more than 300

houses: the Countess has established a new tradition by setting up the **Holkham Pottery** in the former brickworks. As well as the Pottery and its associated shop, Holkham's other attractions include an 18th century walled garden, a fascinating "bygones" museum, a gift shop and tea room.

BURNHAM THORPE
11 miles E of Hunstanton off the B1355

From the tower of the riverside All Saints' Church the White Ensign flaps in the breeze; the only pub in the village is the Lord Nelson; and the shop next door to it is called the Trafalgar Stores. No prizes for deducing that Burnham Thorpe was the birthplace of **Horatio Nelson**. His father, the Reverend Edmund Nelson was the Rector here for 46 years and Horatio was the sixth of his eleven children. Parsonage House, where he was born seven weeks premature in 1758, was demolished during his lifetime but a plaque marks the site of his birthplace. The pub, where Nelson held a party before setting off aboard *HMS Agamemnon* to fight Napoleon, has become a kind of shrine to his memory, its walls covered with portraits, battle scenes and other marine paintings. There is more Nelson memorabilia in the church, including a crucifix and lectern made with wood from *HMS Victory*, a great chest from the pulpit used by his father, and two flags

Sign at Old Rectory

Nelson's Medicine Chest, Burnham Thorpe

from *HMS Nelson*. Nelson joined the Navy at the tender age of 12 and saw service in many parts of the world before returning to Burnham, where he farmed until resuming naval duties at the outbreak of war with France. Every year on Trafalgar Day, 21 October, members of the Nelson Society gather at the church for a service in commemoration of the man who had specified in his will that he wanted to be buried in its country graveyard, "unless the King decrees otherwise". The King, George III, did indeed decree otherwise and the great hero found his final resting place in St Paul's Cathedral.

A little over a mile to the south of Burnham Thorpe stand the picturesque ruins (notably fragments of the transept and choir) of **Creake Abbey**, an Augustinian monastery founded in 1206. The Abbey's working life came to an abrupt end in 1504 when, within a single week, every one of the monks died of the plague. A stone from the Abbey is incorporated into the altar of North Creake's **Church of St Mary the Virgin**, which contains some excellent brasses and wall paintings.

Burnham Market
9 miles E of Hunstanton, on the B1155

There are seven Burnhams in all, strung along the valley of the little River Burn, and Burnham Market is the largest of them; its past importance reflected in the wealth of Georgian buildings surrounding the green, and the two churches that lie at each end of its broad main street, just 600 yards apart. In the opinion of many, Burnham Market has the best collection of small Georgian houses in Norfolk and it's a delight to wander through the yards and alleys that link the town's three east-west streets.

Burnham Market also boasts two excellent book shops and probably the best hat shop in the county. Auctions are held on the village green every other Monday in Summer.

Treasure Island

North Street, Burnham Market, King's Lynn, Norfolk PE31 8HG
Tel: 01328 738877 e-mail: sally@treasureisland-shop.co.uk

A former Methodist chapel two minutes from the centre of Burnham Market was taken over by Sally Whitworth in 1985, who has filled four rooms with kitchen gadgets and utensils, candles, Italian and Zimbabwean pottery, glassware, Floris toiletries, photo frames, board games, silver jewellery, Alpac salad bowls and trays. There is another room full of soft toys for children and babies, jokes, pocket money toys, fun and smart stationery, a large selection of fun, wacky and naughty stocking fillers. Sally is also well known for her large collection of greetings cards, especially her humorous and adult cards. Sally offers a gift wrapping service using paper from a wide range.

BRANCASTER STAITHE
9 miles NE of Hunstanton, on the A149

In the 18th century, this delightful village was a port of some standing, hence the Staithe, or quay, in its name. The waterborne traffic in the harbour is now almost exclusively pleasure craft, although whelks are still dredged from the sea bed, 15 miles out, and mussels are farmed in the harbour itself.

From the harbour, a short boat trip will take you to **Scolt Head Island** (National Trust), a three and a half mile sand and shingle bar separated from the mainland by a narrow tidal creek. It was originally much smaller but throughout the centuries deposits of silt and sand have steadily increased its size, and continue to do so. Scolt Head is home to England's largest colony of Sandwich terns, who flock here to breed during May, June and July. A **Nature Trail** leads past the ternery (closed during the breeding season), and on to a fascinating area where a rich variety of plantlife and wildlife abounds. During the summer, the sea asters, sea lavender and sea pinks put on a colourful display, attracting many different types of moths and butterflies.

TITCHWELL
7 miles E of Hunstanton, on the A149

Perhaps in keeping with the village's name, the **Church of St Mary** at Titchwell is quite tiny, and very pretty indeed. Its circular, probably Norman, tower is topped by a little whisker of a spire, and inside is some fine late-19th century glass. Just to the west of the village is a path leading to **Titchwell Marsh**, a nationally important RSPB reserve comprising some 420 acres of shingle beach, reed beds, freshwater and salt-marsh. These different habitats encourage a wide variety of birds to visit

the area throughout the year, and many of them breed on or around the reserve. Brent geese, ringed plovers, marsh harriers, terns, waders and shore larks may all be seen, and two of the three hides available are accessible to wheelchairs.

DOCKING

9 miles SE of Hunstanton on the B1454 & B1153

One of the larger inland villages, Docking was at one time called Dry Docking because, perched on a hilltop 300 feet above sea level, it had no water supply of its own. The nearest permanent stream was at Fring, almost three miles away, so in 1760 the villagers began boring for a well. They had to dig some 230 feet down

Great Bircham Windmill

before they finally struck water which was then sold at a farthing (a tenth of today's penny) per bucket. A pump was installed in 1928, but a mains supply didn't reach Docking until the 1930s.

GREAT BIRCHAM

7 miles SE of Hunstanton off the B1153

A couple of miles south of Docking stands the five storey **Great Bircham Windmill**, one of the few in Norfolk to have found a hill to perch on, and it's still working. If you arrive on a day when there's a stiff breeze blowing, the windmill's great arms will be groaning around; on calm days, content yourself with tea and homemade cakes in the tea room, and take home some bread baked at the Mill's own bakery.

RINGSTEAD

3 miles E of Hunstanton off the A149

Another appealing village, with pink and white-washed cottages built in wonderfully decorative Norfolk carrstone. A rare Norman round tower, all that survives of St Peter's Church stands in the grounds of the former Rectory and adds to the visual charm.

In a region well provided with excellent nature reserves, the one on **Ringstead Downs** is particularly attractive, and popular with picnickers. The chalky soil of the valley provides a perfect habitat for the plants that thrive here and for the exquisitely marked butterflies they attract.

HOLME-NEXT-THE-SEA

3 miles NE of Hunstanton off the A149

This village is notable chiefly as the northern end of the **Peddar's Way**, the 50-mile pedestrian trail that starts at the Suffolk border near Thetford and, almost arrow-straight for much of its length, slices across northwest Norfolk to Holme with only an occasional deviation to negotiate a necessary ford or bridge. This determinedly straight route was already long-trodden for centuries before the Romans arrived, but they incorporated long stretches of it into their own network of roads. It was from the Latin word pedester, meaning pedestrian, that the route takes its name. With few gradients of any consequence to negotiate, the Peddar's Way is ideal for the casual walker. At Holme, the Peddar's Way meets with the Norfolk Coastal Footpath, a much more recent creation. Starting at Hunstanton, it closely follows the coastline all the way to Cromer.

Holme-next-the-Sea is the site of **Sea Henge**, a 4,500-year-old Bronze Age tree circle discovered on Holme Beach. This early religious monument was removed by English Heritage for study and preservation to Flag Fen, Peterborough, though after its restoration it is hoped that it will be returned to Holme. For the time being there's a replica - built by Channel 4's *Time Team* - on display in the village.

OLD HUNSTANTON
1 mile N of Hunstanton, off the A149

With its mellow old houses and narrow winding lanes, Old Hunstanton is utterly charming. The sand dunes and creeks provide a perfect habitat for interesting varieties of colourful flora - sea poppies, samphire, marram and sea lavender and more. The glorious sands continue here,

THE RINGSTEAD GALLERY

Ringstead, Hunstanton, Norfolk PE36 5JZ
Tel: 01485 525316 Fax: 01485 525321
e-mail: ringstead.gallery@btinternet.com

The Ringstead Gallery boasts an excellent selection of the work of modern artists in media including oils, watercolours and pastels, bronzes and turned wood. The work of renowned artists such as Lawrie Williamson, Peter Barker and Neil Cox are proudly displayed at this fine gallery, together with sculpture by the likes of Sue Riley and Rosemary Cook, and

wood-turned pieces by Richard Chapman. Owners Don and Margaret Greer are knowledgeable and very helpful to all their visitors. They established the gallery in 1974, in a building that was formerly the old stables. Derelict at the time, it was carefully and tastefully renovated to provide the perfect setting in which to showcase works of art.

The high beamed ceilings and excellent lighting enhance the very pleasant experience of wandering through the gallery to admire the many different pieces on display. A handsome wooden staircase leads to the upper floor gallery, which contains a delightful, eclectic range of paintings and sculpture. The gallery holds between six and eight one-man exhibitions throughout the year, as well as ongoing shows featuring the works of several artists. Please telephone for details of opening times.

and the Norfolk Coastal Footpath leads eastwards all the way to Cromer, some 36 miles distant.

HEACHAM

3 miles S of Hunstanton off the A149

Heacham Park Fishery on Pocahontas Lake is set within the original boundary of Heacham Hall. This three and a half acre freshwater late was re-established in 1996. Spring 1997 saw the introduction to the lake of specimen carp, to be followed in 1998 by rudd, bream, perch and roach. The lake takes its name from the renowned Native American Algonquin princess, who stayed at Heacham Hall in the 1600s, having married, in Virginia, John Rolfe, who originally came from the Hall. She married at 19 and came to England, where she was a great success in society; sadly, she survived only until the age of 22. St Mary's Church contains a memorial to the princess, who is best remembered for saving the life of her beloved Captain Smith when her father ordered him to be clubbed to death.

Just outside this charming village, at Caley Mill, is the famous **Norfolk Lavender**, the largest lavender-growing and distilling operation in the country. Established in 1932, it is also the oldest. The information point at the western entrance is sited in an attractive old watermill which has become something of a Norfolk landmark. On entering the site, visitors instinctively breathe in, savouring the unmistakable aroma that fills the air. Guided tours of the grounds run throughout the day from the spring Bank Holiday until the end of September, and during the lavender harvest, visitors can tour the distillery and see how the wonderful fragrance is produced.

As well as being a working farm, this is also the home of the National Collection of Lavenders, a living botanical dictionary which displays the many different colours, sizes and smells of this lovely plant. Among other attractions at Norfolk Lavender are a four-acre fragrant garden, a fragrant plant centre, a carefully labelled herb garden, a gift shop selling a wide variety of products, and a tea room serving cream teas and even lavender and lemon scones!

SNETTISHAM

5 miles S of Hunstanton off the A149

Snettisham is best known nowadays for its spacious, sandy beaches and the **RSPB Bird Sanctuary**, both about two miles west of the village itself. But for centuries Snettisham was much more famous as a prime quarry for carrstone, an attractive soft-white building-block that provided the 'light relief' for the walls of thousands of Georgian houses around the country, and for nearby Sandringham House, and is still quarried today. But Snettisham's greatest gift to the national heritage is in the British Museum: an opulent collection of gold and silver ornaments from the 1st century AD, the largest hoard of treasure trove ever found in Britain, discovered here in 1991.

DERSINGHAM

7 miles S of Hunstanton off the A149

This large village just north of Sandringham was actually the source of the latter's name: in the Domesday Book, the manor was inscribed as Sant-Dersingham': Norfolk tongues found 'Sandringham' much easier to get around. Dersingham village has expanded greatly in recent years and modern housing has claimed much of Dersingham Common, although there are still many pleasant walks here through Dersingham Wood and the adjoining Sandringham Country Park.

SANDRINGHAM

8 miles S of Hunstanton off the A149/B1140

A couple of miles north of Castle Rising is the entrance to **Sandringham Country Park** and **Sandringham House** (see panel opposite), the royal family's country retreat. Unlike the State Rooms at Windsor Castle and Buckingham Palace, where visitors marvel at the awesome trappings of majesty, at Sandringham they can savour the atmosphere of a family home. The rooms the visitor sees at Sandringham are those used by the royal family when in residence, complete with family portraits and photographs and many treasured personal possessions. In the Saloon, for example, is a weighing-machine with a leather-covered seat, apparently a common amenity in grand houses of the 19th century. In the same room, with its attractively carved Minstrels' Gallery, hangs a fine family portrait by one of Queen Victoria's favourite artists, Heinrich von Angeli. It shows the Prince of Wales (later Edward VII), his wife Alexandra and two of their children, with Sandringham in the background.

The Prince, who at Queen Victoria's instigation had been searching for some time for a country property, first saw Sandringham as a 20-year-old in 1862, and within days the purchase was completed. Most of the house he acquired disappeared a few years later when the Prince rebuilt the main residence, and the grounds have matured into one of the most beautiful landscaped areas in the country. The surrounding countryside, described as 'plain' by a courtier accompanying the Prince on his exploratory visit, has been transformed into a wooded country park, part of the coastal Area of Outstanding Natural Beauty.

One of the additions the Prince made to the house in 1883 was a Ballroom, much to the relief of Princess Alexandra.

Sandringham House

"It is beautiful I think & a great success," and she wrote, "avoids pulling the hall to pieces each time there is a ball or anything". This attractive room is now used for cinema shows and the estate workers

SANDRINGHAM HOUSE

Sandringham, Norfolk PE35 6EN
Tel: 01553 772675 Fax: 01553 541571
e-mail: enquiries@sandringhamestate.co.uk

Sandringham House is the charming country retreat of Her Majesty The Queen hidden in the heart of 60 acres of beautiful wooded gardens. Still maintained in the style of Edward and Alexandra, Prince and Princess of Wales (later King Edward VII and Queen Alexandra), all the main ground-floor rooms used by the Royal Family, full of their treasured ornaments, portraits and furniture, are open to the public. More family possessions are displayed in the Museum housed in the old stable and coach houses; these include vehicles ranging in date from the first car owned by a British monarch, a 1900 Daimler, to a half-scale Aston Martin used by Princes William and Harry. A new display tells the mysterious tale of the Sandringham Company, who fought and died at Gallipoli in 1915, recently the subject of a television film *All the King's Men*. A free Land Train from within the entrance will carry passengers less able to walk through the grounds to the House and back.

Christmas party. Displayed on the walls is a remarkable collection of Indian weapons, presented to the Prince during his state visit in 1875-6, and hidden away in a recess, are the two flags planted at the South Pole by the Shackleton expedition. The house is surrounded by broad lawns and woodland and, among the most notable features, are specimen oaks planted by members of the Royal Family, lakes, rock gardens, a grotto and summerhouse, and a garden designed by Sir Geoffrey Jellicoe for King George VI. Sir Geoffrey's other designs include the Kennedy Memorial at Runnymede and the Cathedral Close in Exeter.

King's Lynn, on the Great Ouse three miles inland from The Wash, was one of England's most important ports in medieval times. Keels were shallower then, of course, but without such modern aids as echo-sounders it must still have taken sailing skills of a high order to navigate one's way into the safety of King's Lynn harbour. To the northeast of King's Lynn is the prosperous market town of Fakenham, around which is a remarkable variety of places of interest. To the north, in the valley of the River Stiffkey, the Shrine of Our Lady of Walsingham was in medieval times second only to that of Thomas à Becket at Canterbury as a pilgrim destination. To the northeast, the Thursford Collection is home to an astonishing gathering of steam-powered engines of every description, including a monumental Wurlitzer organ. On the eastern outskirts of the town you can visit the premier collection of endangered and exotic waterbirds to be found in Europe, and over to the west stands the Marquess of Cholmondely's majestic home, Houghton Hall.

Oxburgh Hall

The area stretching down from Fakenham towards Thetford and into Suffolk is known as Breckland, a region of ancient heathland with breaks (brecks) for cultivation, and of pine forests which were first planted 300 years ago. Traces of 4,000-year-old mines still survive, along with man-made warren banks, a relic of the once important rabbit-breeding industry brought to Breckland by the Normans. Breckland has five market towns - Dereham, Swaffham, Watton, Attleborough and Thetford - each with its own unique character and history, as well as more than 100 villages scattered throughout the quiet countryside. Sandstorms were once frequent in the sandy soil and it is recorded that in 1668 the village of Santon Downham was engulfed. The ancient character of Breckland has changed with the large-scale pine plantations and modern farming methods; much of the remaining Breckland proper is now given over to nature conservation.

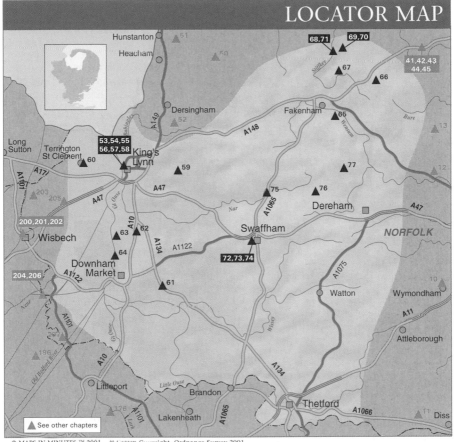

LOCATOR MAP

© MAPS IN MINUTES ™ 2001   © Crown Copyright, Ordnance Survey 2001

ADVERTISERS AND PLACES OF INTEREST

THE TUDOR ROSE HOTEL

St Nicholas Street, off Tuesday Market Place, King's Lynn, Norfolk PE30 1LR
Tel: 01553 762824 Fax: 01553 764894
e-mail: diana@tudorrosehotel.com

The Tudor Rose Hotel provides the ideal base for visitors to historic King's Lynn, combining a central location with a welcoming ambience, abundant comfort, good food and a wealth of history. Frances Bloom and Gordon Hale took over this Grade II listed building - one of the oldest in King's Lynn - in August 2001 and embarked on a top-to-toe refurbishment programme due for completion in the spring of 2002.

The hotel stands on the site of a former winter palace built by the Bishops of Norwich in the 12th century and is located in the oldest part of town opposite the magnificent St Nicholas Chapel. The main part of the current building was the work of a local merchant in about 1500, and behind its timber-framed frontage there was originally a shop below and living quarters above. An extension in brick was added in the 1640s and is now the oldest part of the hotel. Remains of the Dutch gable can be seen from the courtyard.

The guest accommodation comprises 14 bedrooms - singles, doubles, twins and family rooms. Each has its own individual style and character, and all have en suite facilities, telephone, tv, hairdryer and tea/coffee-making equipment. The restaurant, which is open to both residents and non-residents, is an elegant setting for enjoying an excellent meal from interesting menus that include dishes from British, French and Italian cuisines. Bar

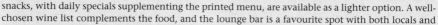

snacks, with daily specials supplementing the printed menu, are available as a lighter option. A well-chosen wine list complements the food, and the lounge bar is a favourite spot with both locals and

hotel guests for relaxing with a drink. The hotel has established a reputation for serving the finest real ales in this part of the county, with four always kept in perfect condition - Timothy Taylor, Batemans XB and two regularly changing guest ales. That's because the man in charge, Roger, treats his ales like a Frenchman treats fine wine.

This friendly hotel, where even the resident ghosts are the benevolent kind, is handily placed for seeing the sights of King's Lynn and is also a perfect start point for exploring further afield into North and West Norfolk. The glorious north coast is a short drive away, and two major attractions nearby are Sandringham, the country retreat of the Monarch, and the superb Holkham Hall, with its fabulous sculptures, Old Master paintings and wonderful gardens.

KING'S LYNN

Tudor, Jacobean and Flemish houses mingle harmoniously with grand medieval churches and stately civic buildings in this marvellous old town, which grew up around two market places. Until the 16th century the town was called Bishop's Lynn as it was, up to the time of the Dissolution of the Monasteries, part of the See of Norwich.

The best place to start an exploration of the town is by the Saturday Market at the beautiful **Church of St Margaret**, founded in 1101 and with a remarkable leaning arch of that original building still intact. The architecture is impressive but the church is especially famous for its two outstanding 14th century brasses, generally reckoned to be the two largest and most monumental in the kingdom. Richly engraved, one shows workers in a vineyard, the other, commemorating

Robert Braunche, represents the great feast which Robert hosted at King's Lynn for Edward III in 1364.

Marks on the tower doorway indicate the church's, and the town's, vulnerability to the waters of The Wash and the River Great Ouse. They show the high-water levels reached during the great floods of 11 March 1883 (the lowest), 31 January 1953 and 11 January 1978.

The organist at St Margaret's in the mid-18th century was the celebrated writer on music, Dr Charles Burney, but his daughter Fanny, born in St Augustine's House in 1752, was perhaps even more interesting. She wrote a best-selling novel, *Evelina*, at the age of 25, became a leading light of London society, a close friend of Dr Johnson and Sir Joshua Reynolds, and at the age of 59 underwent an operation for breast cancer without anaesthetic. It is recorded that

THE GREEN QUAY

Marriott's Warehouse, South Quay,
King's Lynn, Norfolk PE30 5DT
Tel: 01553 818500 Fax: 01553 818501
e-mail: mail@the greenquay.co.uk
website: www.thegreenquay.co.uk

'The closest you can get to the wildlife of The Wash without getting wet!' This is the fully justified claim of the **Green Quay**, a 16th century former warehouse at the heart of King's Lynn's newly restored waterfront. Graphic panels, models, film shows and interactive displays tell visitors all about the origins of this unique part of the British coastline, the forces that created The Wash, and the landscape and wildlife of the area. A saltwater aquarium offers an opportunity to see the fish and shellfish and other denizens of The Wash, while at the Beachcombers Table many strange objects found along the shoreline are on display. A bird-watching gallery looks out to the estuary, with pictures and details of the birds most likely to be seen. iMAC computer work stations provide access to a CD-ROM library for in-depth studies, and supervised school visits include a range of activities in line with the National Curriculum.

Apart from all the many permanent attractions, the Green Quay holds regular special events such as family 'wild walks' and superb photographic exhibitions. The café on the premises sells a range of speciality coffees and delicious sandwiches, cakes and pastries, and the shop is stocked with Green Quay merchandise that reflect the theme of this unique enterprise.

BISHOPS RESTAURANT

19 Chapel Street, King's Lynn, Norfolk PE30 1EB
Tel/Fax: 01553 777662

Built as a public house - the Shoulder of Mutton - these late-18th century premises saw several incarnations before becoming **Bishops Restaurant** on Valentines Day 2001. The owners are Roger Lewis, formerly a regional sales manager with leading international companies, and his wife Roni, whose eye for design has resulted in a very tasteful, comfortable and well-appointed setting for relaxing over a good meal.

The chef is Perry Nadin, whose talent and experience shows throughout his repertoire, which spans an excellent selection of dishes mainly from the classic canon. Typical choices on the three-course evening menu run from creamed Stilton mushrooms or sautéed pigeon breast with berries to main courses such as duck à l'orange, pork loin medallions with coarse mustard, poached salmon mornay and monkfish tail collops with an onion and prawn sauce. There are always main dishes for vegetarians, and desserts like lemon and lime meringue tart or chocolate mousse round off a meal in fine style. Sunday lunch brings a choice of roasts among the main courses, and further variety is provided by special menus like the lobster special (5 courses round a whole lobster and a bottle of Chablis) or the turf special (5 courses round a mixed grill and a bottle of claret). Fine food deserves fine wine, and Bishops has an excellent, well-annotated list that includes a connoisseur's selection. Front of house runs smoothly under manager Lesley.

she only fainted once during the 20-minute operation, and went on to continue her active social life until her death at the ripe old age of 87. Other notable King's Lynn figures include Captain John Smith (of Pocahontas fame) and the surveyor and explorer Captain George Vancouver.

A few steps along from the Saturday Market Place is one of the most striking sights in the town, the **Guildhall of the Holy Trinity**, with its distinctive chequerboard design of black flint and white stone. The Guildhall was built in 1421 and extended in Elizabethan times, and its Great Hall is still used today for wedding ceremonies and various civic events.

Next door to the Guildhall is the Town Hall of 1895, which in a good-neighbourly way is constructed in the same flint and stone pattern. The Town Hall also houses the **Museum of Lynn**

Customs House, King's Lynn

Life where, along with displays telling the story of the town's 900 years, you can also admire the municipal regalia. The greatest treasure in this collection is King John's Cup, a dazzling piece of medieval workmanship with coloured enamel scenes set in gold. The Cup was supposed to be part of King John's treasure which had been lost in 1215 when his overburdened baggage train was crossing the Nene Estuary and sank into the treacherous quicksands. This venerable story won't wash: the Cup was not made until 1340, more than a century after John was dead.

A short distance from the Town Hall, standing proudly by itself on the banks of the River Purfleet, is the handsome **Custom House** of 1683, designed by the celebrated local architect Henry Bell, who was also Mayor at the time. This grand building, perhaps the most distinctive and most photographed in the town, reflects the importance King's Lynn had

attained as a successful commercial port trading with many European countries.

Among other important buildings are the **Hanseatic Warehouse** (1428), the **South Gate** (1440) and the **Greenland Fishery Building** (1605). King's Lynn hosts an annual Arts Festival in July with concerts, theatre and a composer in residence. Some of the concerts are held in the **Guildhall of St George**, the largest surviving medieval guildhall in England and now used as an arts centre, others in **St Nicholas' Chapel**, a medieval building whose acoustics outmatch those of many a modern concert hall. **Red Mount Chapel**, in St James' Park, is a small octagonal building of 1485 used by pilgrims en route to Walsingham. It is said that a long tunnel beneath the chapel runs all the way to Castle Rising, occupied by a ghostly drunken fiddler who entered the tunnel with his dog and never emerged. The greatest period of prosperity for King's Lynn came with the

CONGHAM HALL COUNTRY HOUSE HOTEL

Grimston, King's Lynn, Norfolk PE32 1AH
Tel: 01485 600250 Fax: 01485 601191
e-mail: reception@conghamhallhotel.co.uk
website: www.conghamhallhotel.co.uk

Congham Hall was built in the mid-eighteenth century. This elegant Georgian manor remained a private home until 1982, when it was sympathetically and tastefully transformed into Congham Hall Hotel, one of the finest country house hotels of its size. Retaining the air and appurtenances of a luxurious country home, it nestles in 30 acres of finely manicured lawns and gardens, orchards, a renowned herb garden, parkland and paddocks. Guests here are greeted with warmth and courtesy.

The reception hall boasts an intriguing and delightful 'serpent'-style staircase and welcoming log fire. All rooms are beautifully appointed and have a private bathroom, colour television, radio and direct-dial phone. All are non-smoking. Afternoon tea is served in the gracious lounge. The Orangery Restaurant offers an intimate ambience together with panoramic views of the parkland and gardens. The herb garden is a working kitchen garden providing the hotel's chefs with an array of the freshest salad greens, fruit, vegetables and over 700 different varieties of herbs.

The hotel's Boardroom makes for the perfect setting for private dining, executive meetings or small wedding parties. The outdoor swimming pool and tennis court are available to all guests. In short, this fine country house hotel is the perfect setting for every occasion.

corn-shipping trade in the 18th century, and it is from that century that the **Corn Exchange** and many handsome merchants' houses date. The Millennium North Sea Haven Project is making the waterfront at King's Lynn a vibrant and attractive area for the benefit of both residents and visitors; at its heart is the **Green Quay**, whose discovery centre enables visitors to get as close as possible to the wildlife of The Wash without getting wet (see panel on page 74).

At **Caithness Crystal Visitor Centre**, visitors can watch craftsmen at close quarters as they shape and manipulate the glass into beautiful works of art.

AROUND KING'S LYNN

CASTLE RISING
5 miles NE of King's Lynn off the A148/A149

Overshadowing everything else in this pretty village is the massive Castle Keep (English Heritage), its well-preserved walls rising 50 feet high, and made even more formidable by the huge Norman earthworks on which it stands. The Castle was built in 1150, probably on the site of a chapel, guarding what was then the sea approach to the River Ouse (the sea is depicted in many early representations of the Castle, but the marshy shore is now some three miles distant and still retreating).

Despite its fortress-like appearance, **Castle Rising Castle** was much more of a residential building than a defensive one. In 1331, when Edward III found it necessary to banish his ferocious French-born

mother, Isabella, to some reasonably comfortable place of safety, he chose this far-from-London castle. She was to spend some 27 years here before her death in 1358, never seeing her son again during that time. Her crime, in the view of Edward, was that the 'She-Wolf of France', as all her enemies and many of her friends called Isabella, had joined forces with her lover, Roger Mortimer, against her homosexual husband Edward II (young Edward's father), and later colluded in the king's grisly murder at Berkeley Castle. For three years after the murder, Isabella and Mortimer ruled England as Regents. The moment Edward III achieved his majority, he was swift to act: he had Mortimer tried for treason and hung, drawn and quartered. His mother was spared a similar fate but was banished to Castle Rising, where in her old age she joined the Poor Clares order of nuns. Several rooms have been preserved in fine condition in this mighty castle, which is open for visits throughout the year.

As the bells ring for Sunday morning service in the village, a group of elderly ladies leave the mellow red brick **Bede House**, or **Trinity Hospital**, and walk in procession to the church. They are all

Castle Rising

dressed in long scarlet cloaks, emblazoned on the left breast with a badge of the Howard family arms. Once a year, on Founder's Day, they add to their regular Sunday costume a tall-crowned hat typical of the Jacobean period, just like those worn in stereotypical pictures of broomstick-flying witches. These ladies are the residents of the almshouses founded by Henry Howard, Earl of Northampton, in 1614, and their regular Sunday attendance at church was one of the conditions he imposed on the 11 needy spinsters, who were to enjoy his beneficence. Howard also required that each inmate of his "Hospital of the Holy and Undivided Trinity" must also "be able to read, if such a one may be had, single, 56 at least, no common beggar, harlot, scold, drunkard, haunter of taverns, inns or alehouses". The weekly tableau vivant of the procession of these blameless virgins to the church seems completely in keeping with this picturesque village which rates high on any list of places to visit in Norfolk. The church to which the ladies are making their way, St Lawrence's, although much of it has been reconstructed, is an outstanding example of Norman and Early English work.

Six and a half centuries later, the spacious grounds around the castle provide an appropriate backdrop for an annual display by members of the **White Society**. Caparisoned in colourful medieval garments and armed with more-or-less authentic replicas of swords and halberds, these modern White Knights stage a battle for control of the castle.

TERRINGTON ST CLEMENT

6 miles W of Kings Lynn off the A17

Terrington St Clement is a sizeable village notable for the 'Cathedral of the Marshland', a 14th century Gothic

MOAT ROAD NURSERY

Terrington St Clement, King's Lynn, Norfolk PE34 4PN
Tel: 01553 828723 Fax: 01553 829079

The small but beautifully stocked **Moat Road Nursery** has a vast range of plants including shrubs, bedding plants, alpines, perennials, conifers, climbers, exotic plants, grasses and hostas. There is also a great selection of local and imported cut flowers. This family-run business is set in two acres and is open from the end of March until December.

RAY GRIBBLE

Vine House, Church Road, Wereham, King's Lynn, Norfolk PE33 9AP
Tel: 01366 500387 e-mail: ray@raygribble.co.uk

Ray Gribble hand-makes all the furniture in his workshop, creating a range of sofas, chairs, mirrors, oak refectory tables and more. He can create pieces to customers' exact requirements. Using only the finest woods such as beech and mahogany for the frames and legs, Ray then upholsters with traditional fibre and hair stuffing. He stocks fine fabrics and leathers, though clients are welcome to provide their own choice of fabrics.

masterwork more properly known as **St Clement's Church**, and for the **African Violet Centre** where some quarter of a million violets are grown each year, in a wide range of colour and species.

DOWNHAM MARKET
10 miles S of King's Lynn off the A10/A1122

Once the site for a major horse fair, this compact little market town stands at the very edge of the Fens, with the River Great Ouse and the New Bedford Drain running side by side at its western edge. It was part of an early drainage scheme masterminded by Charles I's Dutch engineer Cornelius Vermuyden (see Denver below), and many of the houses show a Dutch influence.

The parish church has managed to find a small hill on which to perch. It's an unassuming building with a rather incongruously splendid glass chandelier from the 1730s. Another feature of the town, much loved by postcard manufacturers, is the ornate cast-iron **Clock Tower** in the market place. This was erected in 1878 at a cost of £450 and "was worth every penny of it!" The tower's backdrop of attractive cottages provides a charming setting for a holiday photograph. Two great names are associated with this small town: Charles I, disguised as a clergyman, stayed at Downham Market for a night during his flight after the Battle of Naseby, and Horatio (later Lord) Nelson, son of the parson of Burnham Thorpe, was sent to the little school here.

STOW BARDOLPH
8 miles S of King's Lynn off the A10

Holy Trinity Church at Stow Bardolph houses one of the oddest memorials in the country. Before her death in 1744, Sarah Hare, youngest daughter of the Lord of the Manor, Sir Thomas Hare,

arranged for a life-sized and lifelike effigy of herself to be made in wax. Her death was attributed to blood poisoning after she had pricked her finger with a needle, an act of Divine retribution, apparently, for her sin of sewing on a Sunday. Sarah was attired in a dress she had chosen herself, placed in a windowed mahogany cabinet, and the monument set up in the Hare family's chapel, a grandiose structure which is larger than the chancel of the church itself.

DENVER

2 miles S of Downham Market off the A10/A1122

Denver Sluice was originally built in 1651 by the Dutch engineer Vermuyden as part of a scheme to drain 20,000 acres of land owned by the Duke of Bedford. Various modifications were made to the system over the years, but the principle remains the same, and the oldest

surviving sluice, built in 1834, is still in use today. Running parallel with it is the modern Great Denver Sluice, opened in 1964: together these two sluices control the flow of a large complex of rivers and drainage channels, and are able to divert floodwaters into the Flood Relief Channel that runs alongside the Great Ouse. The two great drainage cuts constructed by Vermuyden are known as the Old and New Bedford rivers, and the strip of land between them, never more than 1,000 yards wide, is called the Ouse Washes. This is deliberately allowed to flood during the winter months so that the fields on either side remain dry. The drains run side by side for more than 13 miles, to Earith in Cambridgeshire, and this has become a favourite route for walkers, with a rich variety of bird, animal and insect life to be seen along the way.

SWINTON HOUSE

Stow Bridge, King's Lynn, Norfolk PE34 3PP
Tel/Fax: 01366 383151
e-mail: swinton.house@virgin.uk

Swinton House is a cosy, intimate little non-smoking restaurant overlooking a pretty garden with a pond and a patio for alfresco dining in the summer months. Inside, under a beamed ceiling and warmed by an open fire, there are seats for just 18 diners, so booking is a must at all times.

Owner Graham Kitch, whose entire career has been in catering, established this charming place in 1987 and takes great pride in the quality and freshness of the produce that goes into his kitchen. The cooking is modern English, with 80per cent of the menu sourced by supplies from within a 5-mile radius of the restaurant. Everything, including the bread, is made on the premises. Every dish on the constantly changing menu sounds irresistible, and results on the plate do not disappoint. Typical dishes on a spring menu could include creamy parsnip and pear soup with a hint of cumin; poached whole brill in champagne with hollandaise; breast of thyme-scented chicken with wild mushrooms and madeira; braised diced leg of lamb with coriander, toasted almonds and fine noodles; and for a

finale with a flourish, dark chocolate marquise on a sea of white chocolate or warm lemon flan with vanilla ice cream. Guests can enjoy a drink in the lounge before their meal and take coffee either in the dining room or back in the lounge.

Swinton House is open from 7 o'clock in the evening and for Sunday lunch; it is closed on Monday. The room is ideal for private parties, and Graham offers a personalised outside catering service, specialising in private dinner parties in the customers' own homes.

Denver Windmill, built in 1835 but put out of commission in 1941 when the sails were struck by lightning, re-opened in 2000. This wonderful working mill set on the edge of the Fens has been carefully restored. On-site attractions include a visitor centre, craft workshops, bakery and tea shop. Holiday accommodation is also available.

Oxburgh Hall

HILGAY

3 miles S of Downham Market off the A10

When the Domesday Book was written, Hilgay was recorded as one of only two settlements in the Norfolk fens. It was then an island, its few houses planted on a low hill rising from the surrounding marshland. The village is scarcely any larger today, and there's not a great deal to see, but spotters of unusual gravestones make their way to its churchyard seeking the last resting-place of George William Manby who, during the Napoleonic wars, invented the rocket-powered life line fired to ships in distress. His gravestone is carved with a ship, an anchor, a depiction of his rocket device, and an inscription that ends with the reproachful words "The public should have paid this tribute".

OXBOROUGH

10 miles SE of Downham Market off the A134

Two buildings of great note distinguish this little village. The Church of St John the Evangelist is remarkable for its rare brass eagle lectern of 1498, and for the glorious Bedingfeld Chapel of 1525, sheltering twin monuments to Sir Edmund Bedingfeld and his wife fashioned in the then newly popular material of terracotta.

It was Sir Edmund who in 1482 built **Oxburgh Hall** (National Trust), a hauntingly lovely moated house built of pale-rose brick and white stone. Sir Edmund's descendants still live in what a later architect, Pugin, described as "one of the noblest specimens of domestic architecture of the 15th century". Henry VII and his Queen, Elizabeth of York, visited in 1497 and lodged in the splendid State Apartments which form a bridge between the lofty gatehouse towers, and which ever since have been known as the King's Room and the Queen's Room. On display here is the original Charter of 1482, affixed with Edward IV's Great Seal of England, granting Sir Edmund permission to build with stone, lime and sand, and to fortify the building with battlements. These rooms also house some magnificent period furniture, a collection of royal letters to the Bedingfelds, and the huge Sheldon Tapestry Map of 1647 showing Oxfordshire and Berkshire. Another, more poignant, tapestry, known as the Marian Needlework, was the joint handiwork of Mary, Queen of Scots and Elizabeth, Countess of Shrewsbury (Bess of Hardwick) during the former's captivity here in 1570. The Bedingfelds seemed always to draw the short straw when the Tudors needed someone to discharge an unpleasant or difficult task. It was an earlier Sir Edmund who was charged with the care of Henry VIII's discarded wife, Catherine of Aragon, and his son, Sir Henry, was given the even more onerous task of looking after the King's official bastard, the Princess Elizabeth. After Elizabeth's accession as Queen, Sir Henry presented himself at Court, no doubt with some misgivings. Elizabeth received him civilly but, as he was leaving, tartly observed that "if we have any prisoner whom we would have hardlie and strictly kept, we will send him to you".

As staunch Catholics, the Bedingfelds were, for the next two and a half centuries, consigned to the margins of English political life. Their estates dwindled as portions were sold to meet the punitive taxes imposed on adherents of the Old Faith. By the middle of the 20th century, the Bedingfelds' long tenure of Oxburgh was drawing to a close. In 1951, the 9th Baronet, another Sir Edmund, was constrained to put Oxburgh Hall on the market, and the only prospective purchaser was a builder who promptly announced his intention of demolishing the house. Sir Edmund's mother, the Dowager Lady Sybil, was shocked by the prospect of such vandalism and used her considerable powers of persuasion to raise sufficient funds to buy back the house. She then conveyed it into the safe keeping of the National Trust.

The grounds at Oxburgh provide the perfect foil for the mellow old building, reflected in its broad moat. There's a colourful Victorian parterre, a Victorian wilderness garden, a walled kitchen garden, an orchard, woodland walks and an interesting Catholic chapel.

FAKENHAM

Fakenham is a busy market town best known for its National Hunt Racecourse and antique and bric-a-brac markets, and as a major agricultural centre for the region. Straddling the River Wensum, this attractive country town has a number of fine late-18th and early-19th century brick buildings in and around the Market Place. And it must surely be one of the few towns in England where the former gasworks (still intact) have been turned into a **Museum of Gas & Local History**, housing an impressive historical display of domestic gas appliances of every kind. **Fakenham Church** also has an unusual feature, a powder room above the porch, built in 1497 and used for storing gunpowder. Even older than the church is the 700-year-old hunting lodge, built for the Duchy of Lancaster, which is now part of the Crown Hotel. As an antidote to the idea that Norfolk is unremittingly flat, take the B1105 north out of Fakenham and after about half a mile take the first minor road to the left. This quiet road loops over and around the rolling hills, a 10-mile drive of wonderfully soothing countryside that only ends at Wells-next-the-Sea.

AROUND FAKENHAM

Southeast of Fakenham, off the A1067, **Pensthorpe Waterfowl Park** (see panel opposite) is home to Europe's best collection of endangered and exotic waterbirds. Over 120 species of waterfowl can be seen here in their natural surroundings on the park's five lakes, a wonderful avian refuge where you may come across anything from a scarlet ibis to the more familiar oystercatcher, along with avocets and ruffs. The spacious walk-through enclosures offer close

PENSTHORPE WATERFOWL PARK & NATURE RESERVE

Pensthorpe, Fakenham, Norfolk NR21 0LN
Tel: 01328 851465 Fax: 01328 855905

Southeast of Fakenham, off the A1067, the **Pensthorpe Waterfowl Park & Nature Reserve** is a 200-acre site with a world-renowned collection of waterfowl. As well as familiar native breeds, birds from all over the world are represented, including king eiders and harlequins from the Arctic; diminutive pygmy geese from tropical Africa; the Javan tree duck; and the sacred, glossy and scarlet ibises. The flock of endangered red-breasted geese, native to northern Siberia, is a special attraction, as is the unusual oldsquaw (long-tailed duck) that is the symbol of the Pensthorpe Waterfowl Trust. Walk-through aviaries, bird hides and strategically sited feeding stations around the lakes allow close contact with the birds, and access to all areas is easy thanks to specially built colour-coded paths. Animal life as well as bird life abounds here, including otters, voles, red squirrels and the secretive, humble slow worm, and there is also a wide range of insect and plant life to be discovered. Among other attractions within the site are a children's adventure playground, exhibition centre, wildlife gift shop and licensed restaurant.

Pensthorpe Waterfowl Trust is a charitable trust whose aims are to protect waterfowl and wetland habitats; to encourage public appreciation of the importance of wetlands for wildlife; to work with young people and schools to develop a sense of enjoyment of the natural world and an appreciation of the need for wildlife conservation; and to provide facilities to promote the enjoyment of waterfowl and other wildlife on the Pensthorpe Reserve.

contact with shy wading birds, and in the Dulverton Aviary elegant spoonbills and bearded tits vie for your attention. There are good facilities for disabled visitors and children, a Wildlife Brass Rubbing Centre, nature trails through 200 acres of the Wensum Valley countryside, a restaurant and a shop.

THURSFORD GREEN
4 miles NE of Fakenham off the A148

About two minutes' walk from Thursford Green stands what is perhaps the most unusual museum in Norfolk, **The Thursford Collection**. George Cushing began this extraordinary collection of steam-powered traction engines, fairground organs and carousels back in

1946 when "one ton of tractor cost £1". Perhaps the most astonishing exhibit is a 1931 Wurlitzer organ whose 1,339 pipes can produce an amazing repertoire of sounds - horses' hooves, fire engine sirens, claps of thunder, waves crashing on sand, and the toot-toot of an old railway engine are just some of the Wurlitzer's marvellous effects. There are regular live music shows when the Wurlitzer displays its virtuosity and other attractions include a steam-powered Venetian Gondola switchback ride, a 98-key French organ, shops selling a wide variety of goods, many of them locally made, and a tearoom. A mile or so north of the Thursford museum, in the village of Hindringham, **Mill Farm Rare Breeds** is home to dozens of cattle, sheep, pigs, goats, ponies, poultry and waterfowl, which were once commonplace but are now very rare. These creatures have some 30 acres of lovely countryside to roam around. Children are encouraged to feed the animals and there's also an Adventure Playground, crazy golf course, craft and gift shop, picnic area and tearoom.

GREAT SNORING
5 miles NE of Fakenham off the A148

The names of the twin villages, Great and Little Snoring, are such a perennial source of amusement to visitors it seems almost churlish to explain that they are derived from a Saxon family called Snear. At Great Snoring, the main street rises from a bridge over the River Stiffkey and climbs up to St Mary's Church. On a hill above Little Snoring stands the Church of St Andrew with its ancient detached round tower.

LITTLE WALSINGHAM
5 miles N of Fakenham on the B1105

A world-renowned place of pilgrimage since the 11th century, this small village attracts some half a million visitors annually to worship at the **Shrine of Our Lady of Walsingham**. In 1061 the Lady of the Manor of Walsingham, Lady Richeld, had a vision of the Holy Virgin in which she was instructed to build a replica of the Holy House in Nazareth, the house in which the Archangel Gabriel had told Mary that she would be the mother of Christ. Archaeologists have located the original house erected by Lady Richeld; it measured just 13 feet by 23 feet and was made of wood, later to be enclosed in stone. These were the years of the Crusades, and the Holy House at Walsingham soon became a major centre of pilgrimage, because it was regarded by the pious as an authentic piece of the Holy Land. Around 1153, an Augustinian

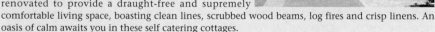

WHITE HORSE FARM

Gunthorpe, Norfolk NR24 2PB
Tel: 01263 860693 Fax: 01263 861178
e-mail: dianne.c.@virgin.net

White Horse Farm in the tiny village of Gunthorpe combines the best of both worlds: a rural retreat with style, sophistication and charm. No chintz here! Each of the three exquisite original farm buildings has been sensitively renovated to provide a draught-free and supremely comfortable living space, boasting clean lines, scrubbed wood beams, log fires and crisp linens. An oasis of calm awaits you in these self catering cottages.

renowned for hosting guests since 1978.

THE MANOR HOUSE

Barsham Road, Great Snoring, Norfolk NR21 0HP
Tel: 01328 820597 Fax: 01328 820048
e-mail: gtsnoringmanorhouse.com
website: www.norfolkmanorhouse.com

An idyllic venue where elegance is still a way of life, **The Manor House** with supremely comfortable and handsomely appointed rooms, can accommodate a party of up to 12 guests for one night or longer. The staff are friendly and attentive. This prestigious house, built in the late 1400's, is

Shrine of Our Lady of Walsingham

in 1511 and was critical of the rampant commercialisation of the Shrine with its plethora of bogus relics and religious souvenirs for sale. He was shown a gigantic bone, "the finger-joint of St Peter" no less, and in return for a small piece of translation was presented with a fragment of wood - a sliver of a bench on which the Virgin had once seated herself.

In the same year that Erasmus visited, Henry VIII also made the pilgrimage that all his royal predecessors since Richard I had undertaken. He stayed overnight at the enchanting early-Tudor mansion, **East Barsham Hall**, a glorious medley of mullion windows, towers, turrets, and a group of ten chimneys, each one individually carved with an amazing variety of styles. Since the King's visit, the Hall has had a succession of owners over the years, among them a Hapsburg Duke who entertained his neighbours in truly Imperial style before disappearing, leaving behind some truly imperial debts, and the pop group the Bee Gees. The Hall is today owned by a London businessman and is not open to the public, but it stands for all to see at the entrance to the village.

Priory was established to protect the shrine, now encrusted with jewels, gold and silver, and to provide accommodation for the pilgrims. The Priory is in ruins but the largest surviving part, a stately 15th century gatehouse on the east side of the High Street, is very impressive.

For almost 500 years, Walsingham prospered. Erasmus of Rotterdam visited

After his overnight stay at East Barsham Hall, Henry VIII, like most other pilgrims, went first to the **Slipper Chapel**, a beautiful 14th century building about a mile away in **Houghton St Giles**. Here he removed his shoes and

NORTH NORFOLK RIDING CENTRE

138 Edgar Road, Little Walsingham, Norfolk NR22 6BA
Tel: 01328 820796

The North Norfolk Riding Centre enjoys an enviable reputation for quality and value, and offers instruction for anyone of any age, from beginners to experienced riders. Novices can explore the quiet, pretty lanes, more advanced riders can make use of the bridle paths, fields or the beach. This excellent family-run centre also features stabling in five stalls for up to eight horses.

completed the last stretch on foot. Despite this show of piety, some 25 years later Henry had no hesitation in closing the Priory along with all the other monastic institutions in his realm, seizing its treasures and endowments, and having its image of the Virgin publicly burnt at Chelsea. Walsingham resumed its role as a place of pilgrimage towards the end of the 19th century, and the new shrine was completed in 1937.

The 15th century **Church of St Mary**, restored after a fire in the 1960s, has a number of treasures, including a Seven Sacraments font and an Epstein sculpture, the Risen Christ.

Little Walsingham itself is an exceptionally attractive village, set in the midst of parks and woodlands, and with fine medieval and Georgian houses lining its streets. Also of interest is the 16th century octagonal **Clink in Common**

MURRAY CARPETS

Hindringham Road, Great Walsingham Barns,
Norfolk NR22 6DR Tel: 01328 820961
website: www.murraycarpets.co.uk

Murray Carpets are specialists dealing in fine Afghan, Chinese, Indian, Persian and contemporary rugs and runners in a variety of sizes and patterns. All are guaranteed original handmade and authentic. They also stock a select range of needlepoint (including Aubusson). The helpful, knowledgeable staff are happy to seek out any special or unusual size or design required. A repair and cleaning service is also available. Open: Wednesday - Sunday; 10.00am - 5.00pm.

GREAT WALSINGHAM GALLERY

Hindringham Road, Great Walsingham,
Norfolk NR22 6DR
Tel/Fax: 01328 820900
e-mail: gwframing@msn.com
website: www.walsinghamgallery.co.uk

Run by husband and wife team Joanna and Timothy Lant and their daughter Victoria, **Great Walsingham Gallery** is housed in a converted traditional Norfolk barn in a lovely courtyard setting, and offers two services and attractions in one. The Gallery and shop feature an excellent selection of English-made jewellery, paintings and other artwork, including Heather Green's woodcarvings and sculpture. Exhibitions are held regularly and include a special Christmas exhibition in late November. The Gallery has fine displays of contemporary crafts, including pottery and textiles, with many pieces originating in East Anglia.

The Gallery also stocks a comprehensive range of fine art greeting cards and the largest selection of prints in East Anglia, being the sole UK distributor of the extensive range of The Medici Society's fine art prints, with a large showroom for retail and trade sales. Picture-framing is the second strand of what's on offer. Tim and Jo specialise in all types of framing, and are Fine Art Trade Guild-commended framers. Open Monday - Friday; 9.30am - 5.00pm, weekends and Bank Holidays; 10.00am - 5.00pm.

Place, used in medieval times as a lock-up for petty offenders; the scanty ruins of **Walsingham's Franciscan Friary** of 1347; and the former **Shire Hall**, which is now a museum (see below).

GREAT WALSINGHAM

5 miles N of Fakenham on the B1388

English place names observe a logic of their own, so Great Walsingham is of course smaller than Little Walsingham. The two villages are very different in atmosphere and appearance, Great Walsingham displaying the typical layout of a rural Norfolk settlement, with attractive cottages set around a green watered by the River Stiffkey, and dominated by a fine 14th century church, **St Peter's**, noted for its superb window tracery, elaborately carved Norman font and perfectly preserved 15th century carved bench ends.

WIGHTON

7 miles N of Fakenham, on the B1105

Wighton Post Office must be one of very few in the country where you can buy a postal order and a pint at the same time.

This happy state of affairs has come about because the post office desk is located in the bar of the village pub, **The Carpenters Arms**. The desk is open two days a week and provides all the normal post office services apart from passports and Road Tax licences. This unusual arrangement has been featured on the TV programme *Country File*.

Just outside the village, the Wells & Walsingham Railway trundles its way between Little Walsingham and Wells-next-the-Sea.

TATTERFORD

5 miles SW of Fakenham off the A148 or A1065

This tiny village is well known to botanists for **Tatterford Common**, an unspoilt tract of rough heathland with tiny ponds, some wild apple trees, and the River Tat running through it to join the River Wensum about a mile away.

About four miles west of Tatterford, approached by a long avenue, stands **Houghton Hall**, home of the Marquess of Cholmondely and one of Norfolk's most magnificent buildings. This glorious demi-palace was built in the Palladian

WALSINGHAM SHIREHALL MUSEUM & ABBEY GROUNDS

Common Place, Little Walsingham, Norfolk NR22 6BP
Tel: 01328 820510/820259 Fax: 01328 820098
e-mail: walsingham.museum@farmline.com

Set in the picturesque village of Little Walsingham, the early 16th century building that now houses the **Walsingham Shirehall Museum** was used as a hostel for important visitors as it was only 80 feet away from the Priory Church. In the 1770s it was converted into the shirehall for the quarter sessions, which were held here until 1861; the petty sessions continued until 1971.

The courtroom has survived unaltered since it was last used and is now part of the 'hands-on' museum, which includes a comprehensive display on Walsingham as a place of pilgrimage since 1061, as well as local artefacts and photographs. The building also houses local tourist information and a well-stocked gift shop, and is the entrance to the historic Abbey grounds, which contain the remains of the Augustinian Priory and the site of the original shrine and holy house.

style during the 1720s by Sir Robert Walpole, England's first Prime Minister. The Walpoles had been gentlemen of substance here since the 14th century. With his family revenues augmented by the considerable profits Sir Robert extracted from his political office, he was in a position to spend lavishly and ostentatiously on his new house. The first step was to destroy the village of Houghton (it spoilt the view), and re-house the villagers a mile away at New Houghton. All that remains of the original village is a double row of little whitewashed houses. Although Sir Robert deliberately cultivated the manner of a bluff, down-to-earth Norfolk squire, the personal decisions he made regarding the design and furnishings of the house reveal a man of deep culture and refined taste. It was he who insisted that the Hall could not be built in homely Norfolk brick, but in the whole of the county there is virtually no stone suitable for construction on this scale. The expensive decision was taken to use the exceptionally durable stone quarried at Aislaby in North Yorkshire, transporting it by sea from Whitby to King's Lynn. Nearly three centuries later, the Aislaby stone is still flawless, the only sign of its age a slight weathering that has softened its colour to a creamy gold.

To decorate the interior and design the furniture, Sir Robert commissioned the versatile William Kent, equally renowned for his romantic landscaping. Kent was at the peak of his powers - witness the decoration in the Stone Hall, the exquisite canopied bed in the Green Velvet Bedchamber, and the finely-carved woodwork throughout which made impressive use of the newly-discovered hardwood called mahogany. And the paintings were an incomparable collection of Old Masters personally selected by Sir Robert. Sadly, many of

them are now in the Hermitage Museum in St Petersburg, sold by his wastrel grandson to the Empress Catherine of Russia.

This grandson, George, 3rd Earl of Orford, succeeded to the title at the age of 21 and spent the next 40 years dissipating his enormous inheritance. When his uncle Horace (the 4th Earl, but better known as Horace Walpole, novelist, MP and inveterate gossip) succeeded to the title he found: "Houghton half a ruin ... the two great staircases exposed to all weathers; every room in the wings rotting with wet; the park half-covered with nettles and weeds; mortgages swallowing the estate, and a debt of above £40,000."

Houghton's decline was arrested when the Hall passed by marriage to the Marquess of Cholmondely, Lord Great Chamberlain, in 1797. But it wasn't until 1913, when George, later the 5th Marquess, moved into the house with his new wife, Sybil Sassoon, that Houghton was fully restored to its former state of grace. The depleted collection of paintings was augmented with fine works by Sir Joshua Reynolds and others from Cholmondely Castle in Cheshire, and the Marchioness introduced new collections of exquisite French furniture and porcelain.

One of the 6th Marquess' interests was military history, and in 1928 he began the astonishing Model Soldiers Collection now on display at Houghton. More than 20,000 perfectly preserved models are deployed in meticulous reconstructions of battles such as Culloden and Waterloo, and in one exhibit, recreating the Grand Review of the British Army in 1895, no fewer than 3,000 figures are on parade.

The grounds, still being developed by the present Marquess, include a superb rose garden with a sunken pool, a water garden with a fountain, and a marvellous fruit and vegetable garden.

East Raynham

3 miles SW of Fakenham, on the A1065

Raynham Hall is another superb Palladian mansion, designed by Inigo Jones and with magnificent rooms created a century later by William Kent. The house is only open to the public by appointment since it is the private residence of the 7th Marquess of Townshend. It was his 18th century ancestor, the 2nd Viscount (better known as 'Turnip' Townshend), who revolutionised English agriculture by promoting the humble turnip as an effective means of reclaiming untended land, for feeding cattle in winter, and along with wheat, barley and clover, as part of the four year rotation of crops that provided a cycle of essential nutrients for the soil. The Townshend family have owned extensive estates in this area for centuries and in St Mary's Church there are some fine monuments to their ancestors, the oldest and most sumptuous of which commemorates Sir Roger, who died in 1493.

SWAFFHAM

Swaffham's one-time claim to be the 'Montpellier of England' was justified by the abundance of handsome Georgian houses that used to surround the large, wedge-shaped market place. A good number still survive, along with the **Assembly Room** of 1817 where the gentry would foregather for concerts, balls and soirees. The central focus of the market square is the elegant **Butter Cross** presented to the town by the Earl of Orford in 1783. This is actually not a cross at all but a classical lead-covered

The Swaffham Florist

23 Market Place, Swaffham, Norfolk PE37 7LA
Tel: 01760 721726

Flowers for every occasion are the main stock-in-trade at the **Swaffham Florist**, which Diane Tighe took over as a going concern in April 2000. Born and raised in Norwich, Diane completed a course there that led to a national certificate in floristry, and her friendly, helpful assistants Anne, Hazel and Sue also hold diplomas in floristry.

The Swaffham Florist enjoys a central location in 1200-year-old building that was once part of the King's Arms stable block; it then saw service as a cobblers, gunsmith, wool shop and toy shop before adopting its present role in 1988. As well as the colourful variety of fresh flowers, the shop sells indoor

and outdoor plants, dried and silk flowers available singly or in lovely artistic arrangements, vases, pots and glassware, helium-filled balloons and collectable soft toys. Wonderful bouquets can be made up for special occasions, and the shop will undertake orders and deliveries not only locally but nationally and internationally, including beautifully presented chocolates and fruit by special arrangement.

Presentation is always a strong point at the Swaffham Florist, which won a Best Window Display Award at the Swaffham Carnival in August 2000.

STRATTONS HOTEL

4 Ash Close, Swaffham, Norfolk PE37 7NH
Tel: 01760 723845 Fax: 01760 720458
e-mail: strattonshotel@btinternet.com
website: www.strattons-hotel.co.uk

Strattons Hotel is proof positive that living well and living in an environmentally friendly way are not mutually exclusive. The inspiration behind this luxury establishment came in the 1980s, when owners Vanessa and Les Scott found a way to combine their love of food and entertaining with a business based at home. Their dream to create a business that could stand with the cream of the industry without sacrificing their principles for the environment, and making the most of the local produce, artisans and work force, has stood the test of time, and they have gone from strength to strength.

Their beautiful Grade II listed Palladian villa set in its own walled gardens has won several awards, a high point coming in 2000 when it was named Green Globe's global Best Small Hotel, a BCE (Business Commitment to the Environment) premier award winner, a Beazer Homes' Business Environment Award winner, and BA's UK winner for sustainable tourism. The Hotel was the first in the UK to win the DTI's Queen's Award for outstanding environmental performance. From the lounge's open fire, which uses fuel bricks made from compressed newspapers, to the flock of free-range hens which produce all the eggs used in the restaurant's dishes, this wonderful hotel excels in all its aims.

Strattons Hotel has six individual letting rooms and suites; each of them - and the interior throughout - is spectacular, with imaginative use of colour and paint effects, beautiful, comfortable furnishings, and a classic sense of style that informs every square inch, as for example in the exotic Red Room, a Moroccan extravagance with plush sofas, four-poster bed and tented bathroom, or in the delightful modern room called, simply, The Sea, with a glass block wall and tiny green wavy tiles.

The menu in the 20-seat restaurant offers a superb, daily-changing choice of delicious dishes such as warm goat's cheese and leek cheesecake with pesto sauce, grilled fillet of sea bass with wild mushroom risotto, or Norfolk beef with spicy parsnip mash and Savoy cabbage. Using local and organic produce whenever possible, the restaurant has won many accolades for its food and for its award-winning wine list. The accommodation, the service, the food and drink and the always-welcoming atmosphere contribute to ensuring a break that is both cosseting and relaxing.

Swaffham is a Georgian market town of historical importance but very much in the 21st century with its environmental centre Eco Tech and the tallest wind turbine in England designed by Sir Norman Foster. Swaffham lies within the stunning Brecks countryside, one of English Natures areas of International Conservation.

dome standing on eight columns and surmounted by a life-size statue of Ceres, the Roman goddess of agriculture, an appropriate symbol for this busy market town from which ten roads radiate out across the county. From the market place an avenue of limes leads to the quite outstanding **Church of St Peter & St Paul**, a 15th century masterpiece with one of the very best double hammerbeam roofs in the county, strikingly embellished with a host of angels, their wings widespread. The unknown mason who devised the church's harmonious proportions made it 51 feet wide, 51 feet high and 102 feet long. Carved on a bench-end here is a man in medieval dress accompanied by a dog on a chain. The same two figures are incorporated in the town's attractive coat of arms, and also appear in the elegantly designed town sign just beyond the market place. The man is the **'Pedlar of Swaffham'**, a certain John Chapman who, according to legend, dreamed that if he made his way to London Bridge he would meet a stranger who would make him rich. The pedlar and his dog set off for London, and on the bridge he was eventually accosted by a stranger who asked him what he was doing there. John recounted his dream. Scoffingly, the stranger said "If I were a dreamer, I should go to Swaffham. Recently I dreamt that in Swaffham lived a man named Chapman, and in his garden, buried under a tree, lay a treasure." John hastily returned home, uprooted the only tree in his garden, and unearthed two jugs full of gold coins.

How much truth there in this story will never be known, but there was indeed a John Chapman who contributed generously to the building of the church in the late 1400s. Cynics claim that he was a wealthy merchant, and that similar tales occur in the folklore of most

European countries. Whatever the truth, there's no doubt that the people of Swaffham took the story to their hearts.

John Chapman may be Swaffham's best known character locally, but internationally the name of **Howard Carter**, the discoverer of Tutankhamen's tomb, is much better known. Carter was born at Swaffham in 1874 and his death in 1939 was attributed by the popular press to the 'Curse of Tutankhamen'. The curse took a long time to come into effect, as 17 years had elapsed since Carter had knelt by a dark, underground opening, swivelled his torch and found himself the first human being in centuries to gaze on the astonishing treasures buried in the tomb of the teenage Pharaoh.

Swaffham Museum in the Town Hall is the setting for the story of the town's past. Visitors can follow Howard Carter's road to the Valley of the Kings, see the Symonds Collection of handmade figurines, follow the pedlar on his journeys and admire the Sporle collection of locally-found artefacts (see panel on page 92).

Move on some 1,400 years from the death of Tutankhamen to Norfolk in the 1st century AD. Before a battle, members of the Iceni tribe, led by Boadicea, would squeeze the blue sap of the woad plant on to their faces in the hope of frightening the Roman invaders (or any other of their many enemies). At **Cockley Cley Iceni Village and Museums**, three miles southwest of Swaffham, archaeologists have reconstructed a village of Boadicea's time, complete with wooden huts, moat, drawbridge and palisades. Reconstruction though it is, the village is remarkably effective in evoking a sense of what daily life for our ancestors entailed more than 1,900 years ago.

SWAFFHAM MUSEUM

Town Hall, 4 London Street, Swaffham,
Norfolk PE37 7DQ
Tel: 01760 721230 Fax: 01760 720469
e-mail: swaffhammuseum@ic24.net
website: www.aboutswaffham.co.uk

Swaffham's Town Hall, a handsome redbrick building in the heart of the market place, is the setting for the excellent **Swaffham Museum**. The building itself has an interesting history: originally the home of 18th century brewer John Morse, it became the home of Swaffham Urban District Council in 1955; the Museum has been here since it opened in 1986. The Museum focuses on the social history of the town and the surrounding villages, and the collections cover many aspects of life including trade, industry and domestic life from prehistoric times to the present. This 'house of mystery and discovery' has many individual attractions. One of the highlights is the DM Symonds Collection of handmade figurines, donated by Mrs Ann Peal in memory of her father Derrick Maurice Symonds (1922-1993), author, teacher, artist and craftsman. The collection consists of 66 hand-crafted figures or groups based on characters taken from the works of Tolkien, Dickens, Shakespeare and the Commedia dell'Arte. All the costumes were designed and made by Mr Symonds over a period of years.

One of the town's best-known stories, illustrated in the Museum, concerns John Chapman, 'ye pedlar of Swaffham who did by a dream find a great treasure'. John had a recurring dream that he would find his fortune in London and, with his dog, his staff and his pedlar's pack, set out on his search for gold. On London Bridge he met a man who heard his story and declared that he, too, had a dream - but his was

about a pot of gold buried under a tree in the garden of a John Chapman, a pedlar of Swaffham. Back went John to Swaffham, where he did indeed find pots of gold, which meant wealth and comfort for him and his family. They moved to a grand house and became respected citizens; John was appointed a churchwarden and was a generous benefactor of the parish church. John Chapman is perhaps a figure of legend, but two who were very much real-life sons of Swaffham were Captain William Earl Johns, author of the Biggles stories, and Howard Carter, the Egyptologist who discovered the tomb of Tutankhamun in the Valley of the Kings at Luxor in 1922. His mummy was a Swaffham girl, the daughter of a builder, while his father was a fairly successful artist. The fascinating stories of Captain Johns and Howard Carter are told in the Museum, and one of the other major attractions is the splendid Sporle Collection of locally-found artefacts.

Swaffham Museum offers excellent research and education facilities through a library of pictures, photographs, press cuttings and other documents, and staff are on hand to help with family trees or identifying objects found by visitors. The Museum and its souvenir shop are open Tuesday to Sunday from April to October.

A more recent addition to Swaffham's attractions is the **EcoTech Discovery Centre** and Ecotricity Wind Turbine, opened in 1998. Through intriguing interactive displays and hands-on demonstrations, visitors can discover what startling innovations technology may have in store for us during the millennium we have just entered.

Castle Acre

AROUND SWAFFHAM

Castle Acre

4 miles N of Swaffham off the A1065

Set on a hill surrounded by water meadows, Castle Acre is the only village of any size on the Peddars Way (see Holme-next-the-Sea in Chapter 2). William de Warenne, William the Conqueror's son-in-law, came here very soon after the Conquest and built a huge mound and a castle that was one of the first, and largest, in the country to be built by the Normans. Of that vast fortress, little remains apart from the gargantuan earthworks and a squat 13th century stone bailey gateway leading on to the village green.

Much more has survived of **Castle Acre Priory**, also the work of William de Warenne, founded in 1090 and set in fields beside the River Nar. Its glorious West Front gives a powerful indication of how majestic a triumph of late Norman architecture the complete Priory must have been. With five apses and twin towers, the ground plan was modelled on

the Cluniac mother church in Burgundy where William de Warenne had stayed while making a pilgrimage to Rome. Despite the Priory's great size, it appears that perhaps as few as 25 monks lived here during the Middle Ages. And in some comfort, to judge from the well-preserved Prior's House (still with its roof) which has its own bath and built-in wash-basin. The Priory lay on the main route to the famous Shrine at Walsingham with which it tried to compete by offering pilgrims a rival attraction to the finger of St Peter in the form of an arm of St Philip. Today the noble ruins of the Priory are powerfully atmospheric, a brooding scene skilfully exploited by Roger Corman when he filmed here for his screen version of Edgar Allan Poe's ghostly story, *The Tomb of Ligeia*.

Castle Acre village is extremely picturesque and in 1971 became the first place in Norfolk to be designated a Conservation Area. Most of the village, including the 15th century parish church, is built in traditional flint, in many cases recycled from the ruins of the castle and priory; the later houses of brick blend in remarkably happily in this most picturesque of villages.

(Continued page 96)

WALK 4

Marham Fen and the Nar Valley Way

Start	Narborough
Distance	5½ miles (8.9km)
Approximate time	2½ hours
Parking	At start in the cul-de-sac behind the bus shelter at the end of Narford Road
Refreshments	Pub at Narborough
Ordnance Survey maps	Landranger 143 (Ely & Wisbech), Explorer 236 (King's Lynn, Downham Market & Swaffham)

Only short lengths of road are used on this route, at the beginning and end at Narborough. For the rest of the time the walker is on footpaths, woodland tracks, and on the riverbank of the lovely River Nar. This is one of the best sections of the Nar Valley Way, and having sampled it here many will be encouraged to try other lengths, either downstream to King's Lynn or towards the source at Gressenhall.

Cross the main road and keep ahead into Denny's Walk (also known as Meadow Close at this end). Keep ahead into Meadow Road when the major road swings right, and keep ahead too when a lane leaves to the left and a footpath joins on the right. About 50 yds (46m) before the track ends at a gate go left **Ⓐ** across a field following a bridleway waymark to a belt of conifers. Pass through this on to a path to follow a hedgerow, which at the end of the field becomes a farm track.

Cross a field from an electricity pole to come to a concrete track and turn left on to this. After 100 yds (91m) turn right off the track to take a track that twists and turns as it skirts the edge of the wood (Marham Fen).

Marham Fen was originally cut by the people of the village for wood and fodder. It is now managed by Anglian Water with the involvement of the Norfolk Wildlife Trust and the British Trust for Conservation Volunteers. The fen has a range of habitats. The woodland is noted for its butterfly species, and the open grassland supports a variety of flora and insect life.

After crossing another concrete track, keep ahead through a metal gate – the bridleway leaves to the left here. **Ⓑ**

A delightful woodland walk follows on a good track. Unfortunately, the pub at the east end of Marham village has closed and the surviving one is at the other end, more than a mile (1.6km) away. Thus it is best to turn right at a T-junction **C** away from Marham and a large pumping station to continue walking through the wood.

The track runs in a north-easterly direction now, but is no less beautiful as it passes through the heart of the fen. There are occasional patches of reed, which show that this is wetland, and the shrubby and somewhat unkept nature of the trees reflect this too.

At the end of the wood, cross over a farm track to a broader one ahead and walk down towards a pumping station that stands by the River Nar. Turn right here **D** to walk with the river to the left. The walking is somewhat more difficult now, grass hiding ruts made by tractors. The sound of rushing water heralds a weir where a large waterwheel stands in a state of decay.

Almost too soon Narborough church appears to the right and the roofs of the bungalows that house most of the inhabitants of the village. Near to the road the way ahead is blocked by a garden, and there is a detour via a narrow path leading into a cul-de-sac. Turn right to the main road. The Ship Inn is to the left, just a few steps away on the other side of the Nar.

Narborough had two working watermills until comparatively recently but now both have been put to other purposes.

Turn right to return to the starting point, passing the church (which has a Norman nave) on the right. •

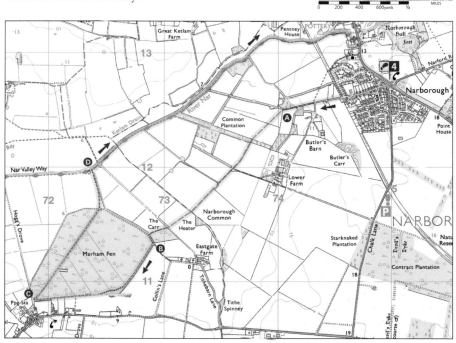

THE GEORGE & DRAGON

Newton-by-Castle Acre, King's Lynn, Norfolk PE32 2BX
Tel: 01760 755046

On the A1064 four miles north of Swaffham, the **George & Dragon** is a Grade II listed building dating from the mid-18th century. It was taken over in June 2001 by the family team of Lee Gordon and his parents Brian and Pat, who celebrated their arrival with an evening of canapés and jazz. The two bars have a warm, traditional appeal, and in the 70-seat restaurant, Lee produces a wide range of superb dishes, from honey ham and chicken liver brochettes to salmon with a Thai red curry sauce or sirloin steak grilled to perfection and served with a pepper sauce. Cask ales and good wines complement the fine food.

LITCHAM

11 miles NE of Swaffham on the B1145

Small though it is, this village strung alongside the infant River Nar can boast an intriguing **Village Museum**, with displays of local artefacts from Roman times to the present, an extensive collection of photographs, some of which date back to 1865, and an underground lime kiln.

EAST DEREHAM

16 miles W of Norwich on the A47

One of the most ancient towns in the county, Dereham has a recorded history stretching back to 654 AD when St Withburga founded a Nunnery here. Her name lives on at **St Withburga's Well**, just to the west of the church. This is where she was laid to rest but, some 300 years later, the Abbot and monks of Ely robbed her grave and ensconced the precious, fund-raising relic in their own Cathedral. In the saint's desecrated grave a spring suddenly bubbled forth, its waters possessed of miraculous healing properties, and St Withburga's shrine attracted even more pilgrims than before. Some still come.

In the **Church of St Nicholas**, the second largest in Norfolk, there are features from every century from the 12th to the 16th: a magnificent lantern tower, a lofty Bell Tower, painted roofs, and a Seven Sacrament Font. This is the largest

of these notable fonts of which only 30 have survived, 28 of them in Norfolk and Suffolk.

In the northeast transept is buried a poet some of whose lines have become embedded in the language:

*Variety's the very spice of life, the
monarch of all I survey*
*God made the country and man made the
town.*

They came from the pen of **William Cowper** who, despite being the author of such cheery poems as *John Gilpin*, suffered from serious depression, a condition not improved by his association with John Newton, a former slave trader who had repented and become "a man of gloomy piety". The two men collaborated on a book of hymns which included such perennial favourites as *Oh! for a closer walk with God, Hark, my soul, it is the Lord*, and *God moves in a mysterious way*. Cowper spent the last four years of his life at East Dereham, veering in and out of madness. In a late-flowering romance, he had married the widow Mary Unwin, but the strain of caring for the deranged poet drove her to insanity and death. She too is buried in the church.

William died four years after Mary, in 1800. Three years later another celebrated writer was born at the quaintly named hamlet of Dumpling Green on the edge of the town. **George Borrow** was to

Dereham Centre

Protestant 'heretics' during the unhappy reign of Mary Tudor. He was rector of the town before being appointed Bishop of London and he lived in the exquisite thatched terrace now called **Bishop Bonner's Cottages**. The exterior is ornamented with delightful pargetting, a frieze of flower and fruit designs below the eaves, a form of decoration which is common in Suffolk but very unusual in Norfolk. The cottages now house a charming little local history museum.

A few miles northeast of Dereham, at Elsing, Elsing Hall is a fine moated, half-timbered house whose lush garden features wild orchids, masses of old roses and a wide variety of trees.

become one of the great English travel writers, producing books full of character and colour such as *Wild Wales* and *The Bible in Spain*. In his autobiographical novel *Lavengro* he begins with a warm recollection of the town where he was born: "I love to think on thee, pretty, quiet D[ereham], thou pattern of an English market town, with thy clean but narrow streets branching out from thy modest market place, with thine old-fashioned houses, with here and there a roof of venerable thatch." The house in which George Borrow was born, Borrow's Hall, still stands in Dumpling Green.

A much less attractive character connected with East Dereham is Bishop Bonner, the enthusiastic burner of

BRADENHAM

5 miles W of East Dereham off the A47

The grounds of **Bradenham Hall** cover 27 acres that include a paved garden, old-fashioned rose garden, herbaceous borders, a walled kitchen garden, two glasshouses and an arboretum with about 1,000 varieties, all labelled. The gardens, which offer fine views from one of the

HOLMDENE FARM

Beeston, King's Lynn, Norfolk PE32 2NJ
Tel: 01328 701284 e-mail: holmdenefarm@farmersweekly.net
website: www.northnorfolk.co.uk/holmdenefarm

A home-from-home can be found at **Holmdene Farm**, set in peaceful rural surroundings and offering superior bed and breakfast accommodation, and self-catering accommodation in two lovely cottages converted from traditional farm buildings. All accommodation is comfortable and spacious, handsomely decorated and furnished. Owner Gaye Davidson offers a warm welcome to all her guests, as well as an excellent English breakfast - home-made bread, jams and pickles, fresh farm produce and more - to start them on their day!

county's loftier spots, is also noted for its daffodils and fritillaries.

GRESSENHALL

3 miles NW of East Dereham off the B1146

The **Norfolk Rural Life Museum** is housed in a former workhouse which, like so many of those institutions, is an extremely imposing late 18th century building, this one built in rose-red brick. Gressenhall Workhouse was designed to accommodate some 700 unfortunates, so it was built on a very grand scale indeed. There's ample room for the many exhibits illuminating the working and domestic life of Norfolk people over the last 150 years. The surrounding 50 acres of countryside, Union Farm, is run as a typical 1920s farm, with rare breeds of sheep, pigs, cattle and poultry, and demonstrations of the real nature of bygone agricultural labour. The museum

hosts numerous special events during the season, ranging from Steam Days to an international folk dance festival with more than 200 dancers taking part.

BRISLEY

7 miles N of East Dereham on the B1145

Brisley village is well known to local historians and naturalists for its huge expanse of heathland, some 170 acres of it. It is considered to be the best example of unspoilt common in Norfolk and at its centre are scores of pits which were dug out in medieval times to provide clay for the wattle and daub houses of the period. Another feature of interest in the village is Gately Manor (private), an Elizabethan manor house standing within the remains of a medieval moat. there is yet another moated house at Old Hall Farm in the southwest corner of the village green.

THE BRISLEY BELL INN AND RESTAURANT

The Green, Brisley, East Dereham, Norfolk NR20 5DW
Tel: 01362 668686

The Brisley Bell Inn and Restaurant is a family-run concern offering excellent food and first-class hospitality. Husband and wife Roger and Jean Greer are ably assisted by their son James, daughter Sarah and son-in-law Gary.

Jean and chef Janet are responsible for the superb home-cooked and home-prepared meals. Guests can enjoy freshly prepared bar meals in the cosy and comfortable bar. The beamed restaurant features an extensive menu of chef's specialities, steaks from the grill, stir-fry dishes, a comprehensive vegetarian selection and a special fish menu. To accompany your meal there is a good selection of beers, cask ales from local Norfolk breweries and an extensive range of wines and spirits (including a wide choice of single malt whiskies).

This traditional Norfolk inn overlooks Brisley Common - the largest privately owned common in Europe - and enjoys a tranquil and picturesque setting in this lovely village. Ideally situated for exploring the Broads, the coast and Norwich, the inn has spacious ensuite double, twin and family rooms decorated and furnished to a high standard of comfort and quality. Facilities for people with disabilities are available.

NORTH ELMHAM

6 miles N of East Dereham off the B1110

Near the village of North Elmham stand the sparse remains of a **Saxon Cathedral**. North Elmham was the seat of the Bishops of East Anglia until 1071 when they removed to Thetford, and 20 years later to Norwich. Although there had been a cathedral here since the late 7th century, what has survived is mostly from the 11th century. Despite its grand title, the T-shaped ground plan reveals that the cathedral was no larger than a small parish church.

FOXLEY

6 miles NE of East Dereham on the A1067

Norfolk Wildlife Trust's **Foxley Wood** is the county's largest ancient woodland, thought to be 6,000 years old. Features include majestic oaks and a wide variety of birdlife and wildlife.

WATTON

14 miles NE of Thetford on the A1075

The striking town sign of Watton, smallest of the five Breckland market towns, depicts the **Babes in the Wood** of the famous nursery story. The story, which was already current hereabouts in the 1500s, relates that as Arthur Truelove lay dying, he decided that the only hope for his two children was to leave them in the care of their uncle. Unfortunately, the uncle decided to help himself to their inheritance and paid two men to take the children into nearby Wayland Wood and kill them. In a moment of unexpected compassion, one of the men decided that he could not commit the dastardly act. He disposed of his accomplice instead and abandoned the children in the wood to suffer whatever fate might befall them. Sadly, unlike the nursery tale in which the children find their way back home and live happily ever after, this

unfortunate brother and sister perished. Their ghosts are said to wander hand in hand through the woods to this day.

Wayland Wood, now owned by the Norfolk Naturalist Trust, is believed to be one of the oldest in England; Griston Hall (private), half a mile south of the wood, is a Grade II listed building, reputedly the home of the Wicked Uncle in the Babes in the Wood story.

Watton itself boasts an unusual **Clock Tower**, dated 1679, standing at the centre of its long main street. It was built after a great fire so that the townspeople could be warned if a similar disaster should ever arise again.

THOMPSON

10 miles NE of Thetford on a minor road off the A1075

This is a quiet village with a marshy man-made lake, **Thompson Water**, and a wild common. The Peddars Way long-distance footpath passes about a mile to the west and, about the same distance to the north-east, the church is a splendid early 14th century building notable for its fine carved screen and choice 17th century fittings. On **Thompson Common** can be seen pingo ponds, little water-filled depressions in the ground created by nature during the great Ice Age.

ATTLEBOROUGH

16 miles NE of Thetford off the A11

The greatest glory of this pleasant market town is to be found in its **Church of St Mary**. Here, a remarkable 15th century chancel screen stretches the width of the church and is beautifully embellished with the arms of the 24 bishoprics into which England was divided at that time. The screen is generally reckoned to be one of the most outstanding in the country, a remarkable survivor of the Reformation purging of such beautiful creations from churches across the land.

Collectors of curiosities will be interested in a strange memorial in the churchyard. It takes the form of a pyramid, about six feet high, and was erected in 1929 to mark the grave of a local solicitor with the rather splendid name of Melancthon William Henry Brooke, or 'Lawyer' Brooke as he was more familiarly known. Melancthon was an amateur Egyptologist who became convinced by his studies of the Pharaohs' tombs that the only way to ensure an agreeable after-life was to be buried beneath a pyramid, precisely placed, and of the correct physical dimensions. Several years before his death, he gave the most punctilious instructions as to how this assurance of his immortal existence should be constructed and located.

Attleborough's town sign depicts two industries that were once important here - turkey farming and cider-making: the turkeys on the sign have tarred feet, the better to stand the journey to London's markets, and Gaymers were based in the town until recently.

A couple of miles west of Attleborough, the **Tropical Butterfly Gardens and Bird Park** is set in 2,400 square feet of landscaped tropical gardens and provides a congenial home for hundreds of exotic tropical butterflies. There's also a Falconry Centre with flying displays twice daily; one and a half miles of paths and a waterside walk, a two-acre garden centre with more than 2,000 plant varieties on offer, a gift shop, coffee shop and tea gardens.

Euston Hall, Thetford

THETFORD

The ancient capital of East Anglia, Thetford has a very long history and 2,000 years ago may well have been the site of Boadicea's Palace. In the 1980s excavations for building development at Gallows Hill, north of the town, revealed an Iron Age enclosure. It is so extensive that it may well have been the capital of the Iceni tribe which gave the Romans so much trouble. Certainly, the town's strategic location at the meeting of the Rivers Thet and Little Ouse made it an important settlement for centuries. At the time of the Domesday Book, 1086, Thetford was the sixth largest town in the country and the seat of the Bishop of East Anglia, with its own castle, mint and pottery.

Of **Thetford Castle**, only the 80 foot motte remains, but it's worth climbing to the top of this mighty mound for the views across the town. An early Victorian traveller described Thetford as "An ancient and princely little town....one of the most charming country towns in England". Despite major development all around, the heart of the town still fits that description, with a fair number of medieval and Georgian houses presenting an attractive medley of flint and half-timbered buildings. Perhaps the most striking is the **Ancient House Museum** in White Hart Street, a magnificent 15th century timber-framed house with superb carved oak ceilings. It houses the Tourist Information Centre and a museum where some of the most interesting exhibits are replicas of the Thetford Treasure, a 4th century hoard of gold and silver jewellery discovered as recently as 1979 by an amateur archaeologist with a metal detector. The originals of these sumptuous artefacts are housed in the British Museum.

Even older than the Ancient House is the 12th century **Cluniac Priory** (English Heritage), now mostly in ruins but with an impressive 14th century gatehouse still standing. During the Middle Ages, Thetford could boast 24 churches; today, only three remain.

Thetford's industrial heritage is vividly displayed in the **Burrell Steam Museum**, in Minstergate, which has full-size steam engines regularly in steam, re-created workshops and many examples of vintage agricultural machinery. The Museum tells the story of the Burrell Steam Company, which formed the backbone of the town's industry from the late 18th to the early 20th centuries, their sturdy machines famous around the world.

In King Street, the **Thomas Paine Statue** commemorates the town's most famous son, born here in 1737. The revolutionary philosopher, and author of *The Rights of Man*, emigrated to America in 1774 where he helped formulate the American Bill of Rights. Paine's democratic views were so detested in England that even ten years after his

death in New York State, the authorities refused permission for his admirer, William Cobbett, to have Paine's remains buried in his home country. And it wasn't until the 1950s that Thetford finally got around to erecting a statue in his honour. Ironically for such a robust democrat, his statue stands in King Street opposite The King's House, named after James I who was a frequent visitor here between 1608 and 1618. At the Thomas Paine Hotel in White Hart Street, the room in which it is believed that Paine was born is now the Honeymoon Suite, complete with four-poster bed.

To the west of the town stretch the 90 square miles of **Thetford Forest**, the most extensive lowland forest in Britain. The Forestry Commission began planting in 1922, and although the woodland is

Statue of Thomas Paine

largely given over to conifers, with Scots and Corsican Pine and Douglas Fir predominating, oak, sycamore and beech can also be seen throughout. There is a particularly varied trail leading from the Forestry Commission Information Centre, which has detailed information about this and other walks through the area.

On the edge of the forest, about two miles west of Thetford, are the ruins of **Thetford Warren Lodge**, built around 1400. At that time a huge area here was preserved for farming rabbits, a major element of the medieval diet. The vast warren was owned by the Abbot of Thetford Priory and it was he who built the Lodge for his gamekeeper. Still in the forest, reached by a footpath from the village of Santon Downham, is the 34-acre site of **Grimes Graves** (English Heritage), the earliest major industrial site to be discovered in Europe. At this extensive network of unique Neolithic flint mines, Stone Age labourers extracted the flint for their sharp-edged axes and knives, arrows and spears from the chalk either in opencast mines or from deep pits. It's a strange experience entering these 4,000-year-old shafts which descend some 30 feet to an underground chamber. (The experience is even better if you bring your own high-powered torch.)

AROUND THETFORD

MUNDFORD
8 miles NW of Thetford on the A1065/A134

Mundford is a large Breckland village of flint cottages, set on the northern edge of Thetford Forest and with the River Wissey running by. If you ever watch television, you've almost certainly seen **Lynford Hall**, a mile or so northwest of Mundford. It has provided an impressive

location for scenes in *Dad's Army*, *Allo, Allo*, *You Rang My Lord?* and *Love on a Branch Line*, as well as featuring in numerous television commercials. The Hall is a superb Grade II-listed mansion, built for the Lyne-Stevens family in 1885 (as a hunting-lodge, incredibly), and designed in the Jacobean Renaissance style by William Burn.

BANHAM
12 miles E of Thetford on the B1114

Banham Zoo, about five miles to the east of East Harling, provides the opportunity of coming face to face with some of the world's rarest wildlife - many of the animals who find a home here otherwise face extinction. The Zoo is particularly concerned with monkeys and apes, but in the 25 acres of landscaped gardens, you'll also come across Siberian tigers, snow leopards, cheetahs, zebras, lemurs, penguins, and many other species. There are educational talks and displays, a children's play area, Shire Horse dray rides, a safari road train and a restaurant.

WEETING
5 miles NW of Thetford off the A1065

This village close to Grimes Graves boasts the longest row of thatched cottages in Britain and the remains of a fortified manor house dating from the 11th century. Two miles west of the village, signposted from the Weeting-Hockwold road, **Weeting Heath National Nature Reserve** is considered to be the place in Britain to see the rare and elusive stone curlew. Rabbits contribute greatly to the success of the curlew, for where they nibble and dig they provide a perfect nesting and feeding place for the bird. Weeting Heath was given to Norfolk Wildlife Trust in 1942 by JC Cadbury of the famous chocolate-making family.

The area of central Suffolk between the heathland and the coast is a delightful place for getting away from the urban rush to the real countryside, with unchanged ancient villages, gently flowing rivers, rich farming land, markets and fairs, churches and museums, and some of the best-preserved windmills and watermills in the whole country.

While inland Suffolk has few equals in terms of picturesque countryside and villages, Suffolk is also very much a maritime county, with more than 50 miles of coastline. The whole stretch is a conservation area, with miles of waymarked walks and cycle trails and an abundance of birdlife and wildlife, and the coast has been a constant source of inspiration for distinguished writers, artists

St Mary the Virgin Flint Tower, Wortham

and musicians. The sea brings natural dangers and the coast has for centuries been under constant threat from the forces of nature. It also brings danger in human form, and it was against the threat of a Napoleonic invasion that Martello Towers were built, in the tradition of Saxon and Tudor forts and anticipating concrete pillboxes. Starting just before the end of the 18th century, at least 80 of these forts were built, the most northerly being at Slaughden (Aldeburgh), the most southerly at Shoreham in Sussex.

Somerleyton Hall and Maze

LOCATOR MAP

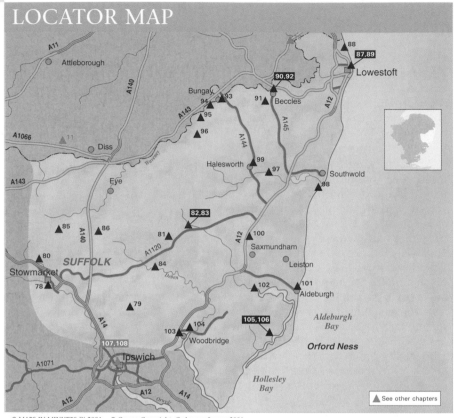

© MAPS IN MINUTES ™ 2001   © Crown Copyright, Ordnance Survey 2001

ADVERTISERS AND PLACES OF INTEREST

STOWMARKET

The largest town in the heart of Suffolk, Stowmarket enjoyed a period of rapid growth when the River Gipping was still navigable to Ipswich and when the railway arrived.

Much of the town's history and legacy are brought vividly to life in the splendid **Museum of East Anglian Life**, which is situated in the centre of town to the west of the market place, in a 70-acre meadowland site on the old Abbot's Hall Estate (the aisled original barn dates from the 13th century). Part of the open-air section features several historic buildings which have been moved from elsewhere in the region and carefully re-erected on site (see panel below). Besides the buildings there's also a collection of working steam engines, farm animals and year-round demonstrations of all manner of local arts and crafts, from coopering to candle-making, from sheep shearing to saddlery.

The town certainly merits a major stroll, while for a peaceful picnic the riverbank beckons. Serious scenic walkers should make for the **Gipping Valley River Park walk**, which runs all the way to Ipswich.

AROUND STOWMARKET

ELMSWELL
7 miles W of Stowmarket off the A14

Clearly visible from the A14, the impressive **Church of St John the Baptist** with its massive flint tower stands at the entrance to the village facing Woolpit across the valley. A short drive north of Elmswell lies **Great Ashfield**, an unspoilt village whose now disused airfield played key roles in both World Wars. In the churchyard of the 13th century All Saints is a memorial to the Americans who died during the Second World War and inside is a commemorative altar. Some accounts say that Edmund was buried here in 903 after dying at the hands of the Danes; a cross was put up in his memory. The cross was replaced in the 19th century and now stands in the garden of Ashfield House.

HAUGHLEY
4 miles W of Stowmarket off the A14

On the run into Stowmarket, Haughley once had the largest motte and bailey castle in Suffolk. All that now remains is a mound behind the church. **Haughley Park** is a handsome redbrick mansion set

---

MUSEUM OF EAST ANGLIAN LIFE

Stowmarket, Suffolk IP14 1DL
Tel: 01449 612229 Fax: 01449 672307
website: www.suffolkcc.gov.uk/central/meal

The Museum of East Anglian Life occupies a 70-acre site in the heart of Stowmarket. Its rich collections of social, rural and industrial history include a number of historic buildings such as a working watermill, a smithy, a chapel and a 13th century farmhouse. There is something for the whole family to enjoy with a variety of farm animals, adventure playground, picnic sites, café and gift shop.

Throughout the year the Museum holds special events as well as demonstrations of crafts and engines in steam. The Museum is open from April to October.

THE CROCKERY BARN

Ashbocking, Ipswich, Suffolk IP6 9JS
Tel/Fax: 01473 890123
e-mail: info@thecrockerybarn.co.uk
website: www.thecrockerybarn.co.uk

The Crockery Barn in Ashbocking is a cornucopia of everything you need to grace your kitchen, table, or any room you please, or to find the perfect gift. Tableware, cookware - all manner of beautiful and practical treasures can be found here. Flamboyant, lavish, homely and eye-catching pots, plates, tea cups, mugs, tea pots, soup tureens, bowls, serving dishes, jugs, candelabra and more, fashioned in clay, earthenware, china, brass and stainless steel, to name but a few of the variety of wares sold here - are displayed in tidy rows throughout this wonderful barn.

Set in a tastefully and handsomely converted former farm building, in the midst of unspoilt open scenery, there is plenty of room to browse at your leisure among the many fine pieces on display.

Owner Trish Sargent has been running this thriving concern since 1993. Ceramics from Portugal, France, Italy and the Far East - together with work from named potters throughout the UK, such as Portmeirion, Spode, Poole Pottery, Queens, Cloverleaf, Emma Bridgewater and Nicholas Mosse - grace the many shelves brimming with expertly crafted and designed pieces. All these well-known names and many other superior makes are here in great quantity and a wealth of colours, shapes, sizes and styles, across the range of the best tableware and cookware available.

Trish and her husband Michael travel regularly to mainland Europe in search of the most exciting and beautiful examples of the potter's and metalsmith's art. The white china imported from Sri Lanka is in particularly great demand by many hotels and restaurants throughout the region and nationwide, as it is justly prized for its durability and classic style. Wholesale enquiries are just as welcome as retail ones. Much of the stock is imported direct from manufacturers, so that the extra choice and value are passed on to the customer. Newly opened is the Basket Barn, which is filled with wickerware, basketware and all kinds of unique hand-woven goods.

The Barnyard Cafe has recently opened and specialises in bistro-style snacks and speciality teas and coffees - just the place to relax over a quiet cuppa and a cake or hot or cold snack after a few hours' happy browsing and shopping through The Crockery Barn's elegant and practical wares. The Crockery Barn is open seven days a week from 10 am to 5 pm (11 am to 4 pm on Sunday), and is located just six miles north of Ipswich on the B1077.

RED HOUSE FARM

Haughley, Stowmarket, Suffolk IP14 3QP
Tel: 01449 673323 Fax: 01449 675413

Set amid beautiful surroundings over 17 acres, **Red House Farm** offers comfortable bed and breakfast accommodation and a warm welcome to all guests. There are four ensuite guest bedrooms in this charming establishment. Breakfast features the farm's own free-range eggs, home-made fruit preserves and home-baked bread. Tranquil and relaxed yet just half a mile from Haughley, there's also a self-catering cottage and small caravan site within the grounds.

in eight acres of gardens and surrounding woodland featuring ancient oaks and splendid magnolias. Woodland paths take you past a half-mile stretch of rhododendrons, and in springtime the bluebells and lilies of the valley are a magical sight. The gardens are open on Tuesdays between May and September, the house by appointment only.

HARLESTON

4 miles W of Stowmarket off the A14

The churches of Shelland and Harleston lie in close proximity on a minor road between Woolpit and Haughley picnic site. At Shelland, the tiny **Church of King Charles the Martyr** is one of only four in England to be dedicated to King Charles I. The brick floor is laid in a herringbone pattern, there are high box pews and a three-decker pulpit, but the most unusual accessory is a working barrel organ dating from the early 19th century.

The **Church of St Augustine** at Harleston stands all alone among pine trees and is reached by a track across a field. It has a thatched roof, early English windows and a tower with a single bell.

BUXHALL

3 miles W of Stowmarket just off the B1115

The village church is notable for its six heavy bells, but the best-known landmark in this quiet village is

undoubtedly the majestic **Tower Mill**, without sails since a gale removed them in 1929 but still standing as a silent, sturdy reminder of its working days. This is good walking country, with an ancient wood and many signposted footpaths.

NEEDHAM MARKET

4 miles SE of Stowmarket off the A14

A thriving village whose greatest glory is the wonderful carvings on the ceiling of the **Church of St John the Baptist**. The church, both outside and within, is otherwise not remarkable, so the ornate double hammerbeam roof seems all the more magnificent, especially when bathed in light from the strategically placed skylight. The roof is massive, as high as the walls of the church itself; the renowned authority on Suffolk churches, H Munro Cautley, described the work at Needham as "the culminating achievement of the English carpenter".

The River Gipping flows to the east of the High Street and its banks provide miles of walks: the towpath is a public right of way walkable all the way from Stowmarket to Ipswich and the on riverbank at Needham is a 25-acre picnic site and a nature reserve.

BAYLHAM

7 miles SE of Stowmarket off the B11130

The Roman site of Combretrovium is home to **Baylham House Rare Breeds**

Farm, and visitors (April-early October) will find displays and information relating to both Rome and rare animals. The farm's chief concern is the survival of rare breeds and there are breeding groups of cattle, sheep, pigs, goats and poultry.

EARL STONHAM

6 miles E of Stowmarket on the A1120

A scattered village set around three greens in farming land. The **Church of St Mary the Virgin** boasts one of Suffolk's finest single hammerbeam roofs, and is also notable for its Bible scene murals, the doom (Last Judgement scene) placed, as was usual, over the chancel arch and a triple hour-glass, presumably to record just how protracted some of the sermons were.

STONHAM ASPAL

7 miles E of Stowmarket on the A1120

The Suffolk Owl Sanctuary at the **British Birds of Prey and Nature Centre** is home to every British owl and raptors from Britain and around the world. The Sanctuary is open all year round, with flying displays from Easter to September, and there are conservation talks and demonstrations, plus some red squirrels and bird hides. Also on site are a café, garden centre and craft shops.

In 1962 the remains of a Roman bath house were unearthed at Stonham. The parish church has an unusual wooden top to its tower, a necessary addition to house the ten bells that a keen campanologist insisted on installing.

SAXTEAD GREEN

14 miles E of Stowmarket off the A1120

One of the prettiest sights in Suffolk is the white 18th century mill that graces the marshy green on a site where a post mill has stood since 1287. This is a wonderful example of a post mill, perhaps the best in the world, dating back to 1796 and renovated first in the 19th century. The **Saxtead Green Mill** worked until 1947 and has since been kept in working order, with the mechanism turning on its post to face the wind and the sails turning, though the mill no longer grinds. You can climb into the buck (body) of the elegant weatherboarded construction and explore the machinery. It is open for visits in the summer.

FRAMLINGHAM

18 miles E of Stowmarket on the B1119

The marvellous **Castle**, brooding on a hilltop, dominates this agreeable market town, as it has since Roger Bigod, 2nd Earl of Norfolk, built it in the 12th century (his grandfather built the first a century earlier but this wooden construction was soon demolished). The Earls and Dukes of

SAXTEAD BOTTOM EQUESTRIAN CENTRE

Saxtead Bottom Farm, Saxtead, Framlingham, Suffolk IP13 9QS
Tel: 01728 621016

Louise Howie B.H.S.A.I. (British Horse Society Assistant Instructor) set up the **Saxtead Bottom Equestrian Centre**, set in the beautiful Suffolk countryside, in 1995.

She has worked professionally with horses for 13 years, including two years at Goodwood, and brings a wealth of experience to giving riding lessons (from beginners to advanced), and re-schooling and breaking horses. She also offers a livery and transport service.

Framlingham Castle

apostles in shell niches. Also of note is the Carolean organ of 1674, a gift of Sir Robert Hitcham, to whom the Howards sold the estate. Cromwell and the Puritans were anti-organ so this instrument was lucky to escape the mass destruction of organs at the time of the Commonwealth. On a humbler level, the people of Framlingham are very proud of their two Victorian post boxes, which were installed in 1856.

DENNINGTON
2 miles N of Framlingham on the B1116

The pretty little village of Dennington boasts one of the oldest post offices in the country, this one having occupied the same site since 1830. The village church has some very unusual features, none more so than the hanging pyx canopy above the altar. A pyx served as a receptacle for the Reserved Sacrament, which would be kept under a canopy attached to weights and pulleys so that the whole thing could be lowered when the sacrament was required for the sick and the dying.

The church also has many interesting carvings, the most remarkable being that of a sciapod, the only known representation in this county of a mythical creature of the African desert, humanoid but with a huge boat-shaped foot with which he could cover himself against the sun. This curious beast was referred to by Herodotus and to Pliny, who remarked that it had 'great pertinacity in leaping'. In the chapel at the top of the south aisle stands the tomb of Lord Bardolph, who fought at

Norfolk, the Howards, were here for many generations before moving to Arundel in 1635. The castle is in remarkably good condition, partly because it was rarely attacked - though King John put it under siege in 1215. Its most famous occupant was Mary Tudor, who was in residence when proclaimed Queen in 1553. In the reign of Elizabeth I it was used as a prison for defiant priests and in the 17th century, after being bequeathed to Pembroke College, Cambridge, it saw service as a home and school for local paupers. Nine of the castle's 13 towers are accessible and the climb up the spiral staircase and walk round the battlements are well worth the effort. On one side the view is of the Meres, which is a bird sanctuary. In the north wing is the **Lanman Museum**, devoted to farm and craft tools and domestic bygones.

The castle brought considerable prestige and prosperity to Framlingham, evidence of which can be found in the splendid **Church of St Michael**, which has two wonderful works of art. One is the tomb of Henry Fitzroy, bastard son of Henry VIII, beautifully adorned with scenes from Genesis and Exodus and in a superb state of repair. The other is the tomb of the 3rd Duke with carvings of the

(Continued page 112)

WALK 5

Framlingham from Dennington

Start	Dennington church
Distance	6 miles (9.7km). Shorter version 5 miles (8km)
Approximate time	3 hours
Parking	At start
Refreshments	Pub at Dennington, pubs and tearooms at Framlingham
Ordnance Survey maps	Landranger 156 (Saxmundham, Aldeburgh & Southwold), Explorer 212 (Woodbridge & Saxmundham)

Large fields surround Framlingham and too many footpaths here have been lost to agriculture. This walk takes you on field paths and byways from the lovely village of Dennington to Framlingham, with its great castle and a church that contains some of the finest 16th century monuments in England.

St Mary's Church at Dennington is famous for the wonderful medieval craftsmanship to be seen in its chapels – work done both in stone and wood – and in the decoration of its benches. There are also box pews and an unusual and intricate pyx canopy as well as medieval stained glass.

From the church, cross the Framlingham road and take the one to Saxtead, passing a telephone-box. At a Z-bend, where the road begins to swing right, turn left **A** on to a footpath that passes the front of a pink house and goes behind the gardens of new properties. Keep ahead to reach a path along the edge of a field and turn sharp right on to a concrete drive before reaching the road at Glebe Cottage. When the track ends, go left to find a field-edge path heading for a wood. The path turns left and then right and then goes left again at the end of a field just before it reaches the wood. This is a broader path but one that is often muddy (the mud in this part of Suffolk clings to boots in a particularly annoying way). When the path comes to a junction, **B** take the permissive path ahead that follows a ditch to go behind Dairy Farm. Unfortunately, all the paths

marked on the map as crossing the vast field southwards have been lost. The Gothic outline of Framlingham College appears at the right-hand end of the wood ahead. After the wood the path crosses a footbridge. Turn left after this **C** along the edge of the field and follow the stream to Durrant's Bridge and an opening on to the road a few yards further on.

Cross the road here and continue along the right bank of the River Ore. After a stile the path crosses a meadow (usually containing goats or sheep), and head towards a house just beyond farm buildings. The path crosses a stream and stiles near the corner of the pasture **D** before climbing a rise at the top of which Framlingham Castle comes into view. Follow the fence on the left, heading towards the church to come to a lane. **E**

If you prefer not to visit Framlingham you can turn left here and follow the lane to rejoin the main route at Ash Grove. **G**

Otherwise turn right along the lane that leads past the Mere. You may care to take the footpath to the left of the lane but this is often virtually unwalkable because of mud.

Pass the Hitcham Almshouses of 1654 and turn left into Bridge Street. When you reach Market Hill, turn left up Church Lane to see the church (notable for its hammerbeam roof and magnificent monuments to several significant noblemen of the 16th and 17th centuries. Continue past the east end of the church to turn left into a lane.

This takes you to the castle entrance. The remains are chiefly of the stronghold put up by the 2nd Earl of Norfolk between 1190 and 1210 that replaced an earlier castle. Its size and shape show the influence of the fortresses that the Crusaders had seen on their expeditions in the Holy Land; unlike other East Anglian castles there is no keep to dominate outer defence works, just a curtain wall with thirteen towers. The gatehouse was added in the 16th century, and in the 17th century a bequest made by Sir Robert Hitcham turned the castle's great hall into a Poor House.

Go up to the castle entrance but before crossing the bridge go through a turnstile on the left (it is not the sort of turnstile where you have to pay). The route descends to cross a moat and then a green in front of the castle walls. It then goes down steps and crosses a footbridge. Walk past a Suffolk Wildlife Trust noticeboard after a stile and go through a gate. A choice of three paths are presented here. **F** Take the middle one that climbs to a field and then bear right to pass a mound and walk along the left-hand side of a hedgerow. Pause to look back at the fine view of the castle. When the path divides, take the left fork heading across a field to Ash Grove. Turn right at the edge of the wood and follow it to a footbridge leading on to a lane. **G**

Turn right and keep ahead past black gates on to the drive to Great Lodge Farm when the lane bends right. The surfaced drive provides excellent walking through attractively wooded countryside. Turn left at a crossways before Great Lodge, a large modern house. An unsurfaced drive takes you past cottages on a brief stretch of Roman road to meet a road. Turn right

along the road for nearly ½ mile (800m) before turning left at Clay Hill Farm. **H**

The path begins by following the ditch by the side of the property and when this ends it strikes across the field to head for the tower of Dennington church. It veers slightly to the left of the church across a second field. At a third field it heads for a barn on the far side and then goes through a meadow and follows the edge of a playing-field to come to the churchyard and the possibility of refreshment at the 15th century Queen's Head back near the starting point. ●

GRANGE FARM

Dennington, Woodbridge, Suffolk IP13 8BT
Tel: 01986 798388   Mobile: 07774 182835
website: www.framlingham.com/grangefarm

Situated in the handsome village of Dennington off the main A1120, **Grange Farm** is an enchanting moated farmhouse dating back to the 13th century. Every room in this characterful home is beamed, and in winter cosy log fires burn in the sitting rooms, where guests can enjoy rest and relaxation, a game of billiards, quiet reading or some television. There are three supremely comfortable guest bedrooms , all looking out over the very pretty and extensive (two and a half acre) gardens, which are full of bird life and where guests are welcome to wander. The grounds include an all-weather tennis court. Owner Libby Hickson has lived at the farm since 1971. Farming ceased in 1992; now the house and grounds make for a charming rural hideaway. The choice of breakfasts

includes local produce and home-made bread and marmalade, while the honey is locally produced. Dinner and supper are available by arrangement; these delicious repasts boast home-grown vegetables when available. In warm weather tea may be served beside the moat, for a truly peaceful experience. The surrounding countryside is perfect for walking and cycling, while Snape, Minsmere, the seaside and a wealth of historic and picturesque attractions are within easy reach. For a true taste of rural bliss, look no further.

FIELDWAY BED & BREAKFAST

Saxtead Road, Dennington,
nr Framlingham, Woodbridge,
Suffolk IP13 8AP
Tel/Fax: 01728 638456
e-mail: fieldway@framlingham.com
website: www.framlingham.com/fieldway

Enjoying their fourth year of business, owners Omer and Diana Turan create a relaxed, informal and welcoming ambience at **Fieldway** for all their guests. The house is comfortable and attractive, with antique furniture and exquisite Oriental rugs.

Each of the three lovely guest bedrooms is spacious and comfortable, and command beautiful views. The double bedroom is located on the ground floor - and boasts its own conservatory! The twin and single rooms occupy the first floor Guests also have their own sitting room and are free to explore the large, secluded gardens. Horse riding, golf and cycling can be arranged for guests. The delightful dining room overlooks the gardens. The traditional English breakfast is expertly prepared, and cooked on Diana's much-loved Aga. The alternative 'Continental' breakfast comprises fresh fruit salad and croissants. Dinner is available by request, and there is also a very good pub/restaurant within walking distance.

The setting of this charming establishment is serene, overlooking the village green and church. The surroundings are the epitome of rural tranquillity, while still being within easy distance of the many attractions in the area. ETB 4 Diamonds.

Agincourt, and his wife, their effigies carved in alabaster. Lord Bardolph was the head of the Phelip family of Dennington Court and after his elevation was honoured with the task of managing the funeral of King Henry V.

CHARSFIELD

5 miles S of Framlington off the B1078

A minor road runs from Framlingham through picturesque Kettleburgh and Hoo to Charsfield, best known as the inspiration for Ronald Blyth's book *Akenfield*, later memorably filmed by Sir Peter Hall. A cottage garden in the village displays the Akenfield village sign and is open to visitors in the summer.

OTLEY

7 miles SW of Framlingham on the B1079

Standing in ten acres of gardens that include a canal, a nuttery and a knot garden, the exquisite moated **Otley Hall** was built by and long associated with the Gosnold family, whose coat of arms is also that of the village. The best-known member of that family is Bartholomew Gosnold, who sailed to the New World, named Martha's Vineyard, discovered Cape Cod and founded the settlement of Jamestown, Virginia. The 13th century **Church of St Mary** has a remarkable baptistry font measuring six feet in length and two feet eight inches in

Otley Hall

depth. Though filled with water, the font is not used and was only discovered in 1950 when the vestry floor was raised. It is thought that it may have been used for adult baptisms; it would also have been an efficient way of baptising twins.

HELMINGHAM

7 miles SW of Framlingham on the B1077

Another moated hall, this one a Tudor construction. **Helmingham Hall** itself is only open to the public by appointment but on Tuesdays in summer and on certain other days the extensive grounds can be visited; attractions include herbaceous and spring borders, a knot and herb garden designed by Lady Salisbury in 1982, many varieties of rose, a giant ancient oak and a walled kitchen garden. In the woodland are not only newly planted trees but ornamental shrubs, and masses of bluebells and lilies of the valley. The Tollemache family were here for many years, and one of their number founded a brewery which, after a merger, became the Tolly Cobbold brewery based in Ipswich.

FRAMSDEN

7 miles SW of Framlingham on the B1077

The scenery in these parts is real picture postcard stuff, and in the village of Framsden the picture is completed by a fine **Post Mill**, this one built high on a hill in 1760, refitted and raised in 1836 and in commercial use until 1934. The milling machinery is still in place and the mill is open by appointment for visits at the weekend.

CRETINGHAM

4 miles SW of Framlingham off the A1120

The village sign is the unusual item here, in that it has two different panels: one shows an everyday Anglo-Saxon farming scene, the other a group (perhaps of Danes) sailing up the River Deben, with the locals fleeing. The signs are made from mosaic tiles.

Brandeston

3 miles SW of Framlingham off the A1120

Brandeston is a delightful spot with a row of beautiful thatched cottages and the parish **Church of All Saints** with a 13th century font. The best-known vicar of Brandeston was John Lowes (1572-1646), who was accused of witchcraft by the villagers, interrogated by Witchfinder General Matthew Hopkins and hanged at Bury St Edmunds. His sad end was made even sadder by the fact that before being strung up he had himself to read out the burial service of a condemned witch, as no priest was allowed to conduct the service. Hopkins was an obscure lawyer practising in Essex who came into prominence during a craze for hunting out witches during the Civil War. He made a handsome living out of this bizarre business, preying on the superstitions of the times and using the foulest means to obtain confessions. One account of his 'career' claims that his victims numbered well over 200. The best-known method of determining guilt was to hurl the bound accused into water, because a witch, having denied her/his baptism, would be repelled by the water and float; that would be proof of guilt (but if the accused did not resurface, there was surely a good chance of drowning). Eventually Hopkins was himself accused of being a witch, 'failed' the water test and was hanged. The less satisfactory alternative is that he died of tuberculosis. Who knows 'witch' is true!

Debenham

10 miles E of Stowmarket on the B1077

A sizeable village of architectural distinction, with a profusion of attractive timber-framed buildings dating from the

---

Shrubbery Farmhouse

Chapel Hill, Cretingham, Suffolk IP13 7DN
Tel: 01473 737494 Fax: 01473 737312
e-mail: sm@marmar.co.uk
www.shrubberyfarmhouse.co.uk

Owners St John and Christine Marston have created a wonderful rural retreat at **Shrubbery Farmhouse**. They offer all their guests a warm and sincere welcome, and make every effort to ensure that guests enjoy a comfortable and relaxing stay. Christine's artistic flair is evident in every room, particularly in the lovely floral arrangements.

Located just 15 miles from the Suffolk Heritage Coast, the farm house is within easy reach of The Suffolk Way - the long-distance walk through rural Suffolk beginning at Flatford - as well as of many of the interesting and attractive sights of the region. This delightful listed part-16th century home retains many original features, including the exposed oak beams and inglenook fireplaces. The excellent facilities include a fully-equipped gym, football lawn, croquet lawn and tennis court. The grounds are also perfect just for relaxing or having a quiet stroll. Indoors, there is a library, welcoming lounge, and piano, all for guests to enjoy. Each of the three guest bedrooms is beautifully decorated and comfortably furnished. Breakfast times are flexible; the meal can be taken indoors or out and features fresh duck, goose or chicken eggs, locally cured Suffolk bacon and traditional sausages from the local village butcher, fresh fruit, yoghurt and tasty breads.

To get to this superb establishment, from Cretingham village take the Otley Road towards Otley, then left towards Monewden, 400 yards up Chapel Hill and then right, along a bumpy farm track, to Shrubbery Farmhouse.

14th to the 17th century. The River Deben flows beside and beneath the main street and, by one of the little bridges, weavers still practise their craft. There is also a pottery centre. **St Mary's Church** is unusual in having an original Saxon tower, and the roof alternates hammerbeams and crested tie beams.

MENDLESHAM

6 miles NE of Stowmarket off the A140

On the green in Old Market Street lies an enormous stone which is said to have been used as a preaching stone, mounted by itinerant Wesleyan preachers. In the **Church of St Mary** there is a collection of parish armour assembled 400 years ago, and also some fine carvings. The least hidden local landmark is a 1,000ft TV mast put up by the IBA in 1959; it stands on the site (now an industrial area) of Mendlesham Airfield, wartime home of the 34th Bomb Group. This Group did not lose a single aircraft over enemy territory but lost four over their own airfield; a memorial stands on the A140.

COTTON

16 miles E of Bury St Edmunds off the B1113

The village of Cotton should be visited for several reasons, one of which is to see the splendid 14th century flint **Church of St Andrew**, impressive in its dimensions and notable for its double hammerbeam roof with carved angels. In Blacksmith,

MECHANICAL MUSIC MUSEUM & BYGONES

Blacksmith Road, Cotton, Nr. Stowmarket, Suffolk IP14 4QN
Tel: 01449 613876

There are musical treasures aplenty at the **Mechanical Music Museum & Bygones**, which houses a unique collection of music boxes, polyphons, street pianos, pianolas and organs. Stars of the show include a Limonaire fairground organ dating from around 1850 and a mighty Wurlitzer theatre organ originally installed in the Stilwell Theatre, Brooklyn, in 1926. It was later shipped to England and for many years graced London's Luxury Theatre (later the Leicester Square Theatre), which was built by the great star Jack Buchanan. The Mechanical Museum acquired

the Wurlitzer in the early 1980s. The Museum, which also boasts a large collection of teapots and musical memorabilia, is open on Sunday afternoons from June to September, and for an annual fair organ enthusiasts day on the first Sunday in October.

the **Mechanical Music Museum & Bygones** is a unique attraction with a fascinating collection of mechanical musical instruments of all kinds. (see panel above)

WETHERINGSETT

7 miles NE of Stowmarket off the A140

On the other side of the A140, Wetheringsett is where you'll find the **Mid-Suffolk Light Railway Museum**, open on summer Sundays and during summer school holidays. The museum recreates the 'Middy' as it was 90 years ago, with station buildings, a steam locomotive and Great Eastern Railway coaches including a refreshment car. Visitors will also find a trackbed walk, a nature pond and a woodland picnic area. During the Second World War the railway transported goods and ammunition to Mendlesham and Horham Airfields.

Wetheringsett has had two well-known rectors, famous for very different reasons. Richard Hakluyt, incumbent from 1590 till his death in 1616, is remembered for his major work *Voyages* (full title *Principal Navigation, Voiages, Traffiques and Discoveries of the English Nation*). Hakluyt was a fervent promoter of overseas expansion by Britain, particularly in North America, and knew all the famous sea captains and sailors of his day. He married Duglesse Cavendish, the daughter of the circumnavigator Thomas Cavendish, and maintained his great interest in travel after his appointment to the parish of Wetheringsett. The rector between 1858 and 1883 was a certain George Wilfrid Ellis, sometime tailor and butler, and finally a bogus clergyman. After he was unmasked as a sham it needed a special Act of Parliament to validate the marriage ceremonies he had illegally conducted and to legitimise the issue of those marriages.

THORNHAM MAGNA & PARVA

10 miles N of Stowmarket off the A140

The **Thornham Walks and Field Centre**, with 12 miles of walks and a herb garden and nursery, cater admirably for hikers, horticulturists and students of the countryside. The tiny thatched **Church of St Mary** at Thornham Parva houses a considerable treasure in the shape of an exquisite medieval altar painting, known

as a retable, with a central panel depicting the Crucifixion and four saints on each side panel. Its origins are uncertain but it was possibly the work of the Royal Workshops at Westminster Abbey, and made for Thetford Priory, or a nearby Dominican monastery. Also to be admired is the 14th century octagonal font and a series of fascinating wall paintings. In the churchyard is a monument to Sir Basil Spence (1907-76), architect of Coventry Cathedral.

YAXLEY

12 miles N of Stowmarket on the A140

Another **Church of St Mary** and more treasures. One is an extremely rare sexton's wheel, which hangs above the south door and was used in medieval times to select fast days in honour of the Virgin. When a pair of iron wheels were spun on their axle, strings attached to the outer wheel would catch on the inner, stopping both and indicating the chosen day. The 17th century pulpit is one of the finest in the country, with the most glorious, sumptuous carvings. Yaxley's most famous son is Sir Frederick Ashton, who is buried in the churchyard.

EYE

13 miles NE of Stowmarket on the B1117

The name is derived from the Saxon for an island, as this super little town was once surrounded by water and marshes.

The Church of St Peter and St Paul
stands in the shadow of a mound on
which a castle once stood (the remains
are worth a look and the mound offers a
panoramic view of the town - almost a
bird's eye view, in fact). The church's 100
foot tower is described by Pevsner as "one
of the wonders of Suffolk" and the
interior is a masterpiece of restoration,
with all the essential medieval features in
place. The rood screen, with painted
panels depicting St Edmund, St Ursula,
Edward the Confessor and Henry VI, is
particularly fine.

Other interesting Eye sights are the
ornate redbrick town hall; the timbered
Guildhall, with the archangel Gabriel
carved on a corner post; a crinkle-crankle
(serpentine) wall fronting Chandos
Lodge, where Sir Frederick Ashton once
lived; and a thriving theatre, one of the
smallest professional theatres in the
country. Eye Airfield, the first to be built
in this part of the world by the US army,
is now part of an industrial area, but
there is a memorial to the 490th Bomb
Group by the village hall at Brome, a
short drive north of Eye.

Hoxne
4 miles NE of Eye on the B1118

Palaeolithic remains indicate the
exceptionally long history of Hoxne (call
it Hoxon), which stands along the banks
of the River Waveney near the Norfolk
border. It is best known for its links with
King Edmund, who was reputedly killed
here, though Bradfield St Clare and
Shottisham have rival claims. The Hoxne
legend is that Edmund was betrayed to
the Danes by a newlywed couple who
were crossing **Goldbrook Bridge** and
spotted his golden spurs reflected from
his hiding place below the bridge.
Edmund put a curse on all newlyweds
crossing the bridge, and to this day some
brides take care to avoid it. The present

bridge, built in 1878, bears an inscription
recalling the King's capture. The story
continues that Edmund was tied to an
oak tree and killed with arrows. That
same oak mysteriously fell down in 1848
while apparently in good health, and a
monument at the site is a popular tourist
attraction. In the Church of St Peter and
St Paul an oak screen (perhaps that very
same oak?) depicts scenes from the
martyr's life. A more cheerful event is the
Harvest Breakfast on the village green
that follows the annual service.

Horham
6 miles E of Eye on the B1117

There are no fewer than three distinct
musical connections in this dapper little
village. The Norman church has had its
tower strengthened for the rehanging of
the peal of eight bells, which is believed
to be the oldest in the world. Benjamin
Britten, later associated with the
Aldeburgh Festival, lived and composed
in Horham for a time, and on a famous
day during World War II, Glenn Miller
brought his band here to celebrate the
200th flying mission from the American
airfield. Horham and Stradbrooke
churches have memorials to the airfield
personnel, and also nearby is the 95th
Bomb Group Hospital Museum.

Worlingworth
8 miles SE of Eye off the B1118

It's well worth taking the country road to
Worlingworth, a long, straggling village
whose **Church of St Mary** has a
remarkable font cover reaching up about
30 feet. It is brilliantly coloured and
intricately carved, and near the top is an
inscription in Greek which translates as
'wash my sin and not my body only'.
Note, too, the Carolean box pews, the
carved pulpit and an oil painting of
Worlingworth's Great Feast of 1810 to
celebrate George III's jubilee.

WINGFIELD

6 miles E of Eye off the B1118

Wingfield College is one of the country's most historic seats of learning, founded in 1362 as a college for priests with a bequest from Sir John de Wingfield, Chief Staff Officer to the Black Prince. Sir John's wealth came from ransoming a French nobleman at the Battle of Poitiers in 1356. Surrendered to Henry VIII at the time of the Dissolution, the college became a farmhouse and is now in private hands. The facade is now Georgian, but the original medieval Great Hall still stands, and the college and its three acres of gardens are open to the public at weekends during the summer. Attractions include regular artistic events, a play garden, a photographic display on the college's history and restoration, paintings, sculptures and handprinted items produced on a 19th century Columbian printing press.

The **Church of St Andrew** was built as the collegiate church and has an extra-large chancel to accommodate the college choir. The church contains three really fine monuments: to Sir John (in stone); to Michael de la Pole, 2nd Earl of Suffolk (in wood); and to John de la Pole, Duke of Suffolk (in alabaster). In the churchyard is a hudd - a shelter for the priest for use at the graveside in bad weather.

On a hill outside the village are the imposing remains of a castle built by the 1st Earl.

FRESSINGFIELD

10 miles E of Eye on the B1116

The Fox and Goose restaurant is one of the best in Suffolk, but the spiritual centre is the **Church of St Peter and St Paul**. It has a superb hammerbeam roof and a lovely stone bell tower that was built in the 14th century. On one of the pews the initials AP are carved. These are believed to be the work of Alice de la Pole, Duchess of Norfolk and grand-daughter of Geoffrey Chaucer. Was this a work of art or a bout of vandalism brought on by a dull sermon?

At nearby Ufford Hall lived the Sancroft family, one of whom became Archbishop of Canterbury. He led the revolt of the bishops against James II and was imprisoned in the Tower of London. Released by William IV and sacked for refusing to swear the oath of allegiance, he returned home and is entombed by the south porch of the church.

The village sign is a pilgrim and a donkey, recording that Fressingfield was a stopping place on the pilgrim route from Dunwich to Bury St Edmunds.

LAXFIELD

12 miles E of Eye on the B1117

Laxfield & District Museum, in the 16th century Guildhall, gives a fine insight into bygone ages with geology and natural history exhibits, farm and domestic tools, a Victorian kitchen, a village shop and a costume room. The museum is open Saturday and Sunday afternoons in summer.

Heveningham Hall

Drawing Room, Heveningham Hall

All Saints Church is distinguished by some wonderful flint flashwork on its tower, roof and nave. In the 1808 Baptist church is a plaque remembering John Noyes, burnt at the stake in 1557 for refusing to take Catholic vows. History relates that the villagers, with a single exception, dowsed their fires in protest, and the one remaining fire was used to light the stake.

A couple of miles east of Laxfield, **Heveningham Hall** is a fine Georgian mansion, a model of classical elegance designed by James Wyatt with lovely grounds by Capability Brown. As it runs through the grounds, the River Blyth widens into a lake.

LOWESTOFT AND THE COAST

The most easterly town in Britain had its heyday as a major fishing port during the late 19th and early 20th centuries, when it was a mighty rival to Great Yarmouth in the herring fishing industry. That industry has been in major decline since World War I but Lowestoft is still a fishing port, and the trawlers still chug into the harbour in the early morning with the catches of the night. Guided tours of the fish market and the harbour are available.

Lowestoft is also a popular holiday resort, the star attraction being the lovely **South Beach** with its golden sands, safe swimming, two piers and all the expected seaside amusement and entertainment. **Claremont Pier**, over 600 feet in length, was built in 1902, ready to receive day trippers on the famous Belle steamers. The buildings in this part of town were developed in mid-Victorian times by the company of Sir Samuel Morton Peto, also responsible for Nelson's Column, the statues in the Houses of Parliament and the Reform Club, and also for Somerleyton Hall, about which more anon.

At the heart of the town is the old harbour, home to the Royal Norfolk & Suffolk Yacht Club and the lifeboat station. Further upriver is the commercial part of the port, used chiefly by ships carrying grain and timber. The history of Lowestoft is naturally tied up with the sea, and much of that history is recorded

Fishing Boats, Lowestoft

in fascinating detail in the **Lowestoft & East Suffolk Maritime Museum** with model boats, fishing gear, a lifeboat cockpit, paintings and shipwrights' tools. The setting is a flint-built fisherman's cottage in Sparrow's Nest Gardens (see panel below). **The Royal Naval Patrol Museum** nearby remembers the minesweeping service in models, photographs, documents and uniforms.

Lowestoft had England's first lighthouse, installed in 1609. The present one dates from 1874. Also in Sparrow's Nest Gardens is the **War Memorial Museum**, dedicated to those who served during the Second World War. There's a photographic collection of the bombing of the town, aircraft models and a chapel of remembrance.

Lowestoft has some interesting literary and musical connections. The Elizabethan playwright, poet and pamphleteer, Thomas Nash(e), was born here in 1567. His last work, *Lenten Stuffe*, was a eulogy to the herring trade and specifically Great Yarmouth. Joseph Conrad (Jozef Teodor Konrad Korzeniowski), working as a deckhand on a British freighter bound for Constantinople, jumped ship here in 1878, speaking only a few words of the language in which he was to become one of the modern masters. Benjamin Britten, the greatest English composer of the 20th century, is associated with several places in Suffolk, but Lowestoft has the earliest claim, for it is here that he was born in 1913.

LOWESTOFT MARITIME MUSEUM

Sparrows Nest Park, Whapload Road, Lowestoft, Suffolk NR32 1XG
Tel: 01502 561963

Anyone with an interest in the sea and ships should steer a steady course for Britain's most easterly museum under the lighthouse on Whapload Road. Open daily from May to September, **Lowestoft Maritime Museum** specialises in the history of the Lowestoft fishing fleet, from early sail to steam and through to the modern diesel-powered vessels. Methods of fishing are recorded, including trawling and the no longer practised driftnet fishing for herring, and other displays depict the evolution of lifeboats and the town's association with the Royal Navy. A replica of the aft cabin of a steam drifter and a fine picture gallery are other attractions of this fascinating museum, where the attendants are ex-seamen and others interested in the port of Lowestoft. They are all delighted to answer any questions visitors have about the Museum and its exhibits. School

parties are particularly welcome, with takeaway educational packs available, and out-of-season parties can be catered for with notice. The Museum, which is maintained by members of the Lowestoft and East Suffolk Maritime Society, was established in 1968 and extended in 1978, when the Duke of Edinburgh was guest of honour. The objects of the Society are to educate the public in shipping, old and modern, in Lowestoft and the County of Suffolk, and in trades and crafts associated with shipping lore in general and in particular to maintain the Museum.

Just north of town with access from the B1385, **Pleasurewood Hill** is the largest theme park in East Anglia.

Oulton Broad, on the western edge of Lowestoft, is a major centre of amusement afloat, with boats for hire and cruises on the Waveney. It also attracts visitors to Nicholas Everitt Park to look around **Lowestoft Museum**, housed in historic Broad House. Opened by the Queen and Prince Philip in 1985, the museum displays archaeological finds from local sites, some now lost to the sea, costumes, toys, domestic bygones, and a fine collection of Lowestoft porcelain. (The porcelain industry lasted from about 1760 to 1800, using clay from the nearby Gunton Hall Estate. The soft-paste ware, resembling Bow porcelain, was usually decorated in white and blue.)

Another museum, the **ISCA Maritime Museum**, has a unique collection of ethnic working boats, including coracles, gondolas, junks, dhows, sampans and proas.

BLUNDESTON

4 miles N of Lowestoft off the A12

Known chiefly as the village used by Charles Dickens as the birthplace of that writer's 'favourite child', David Copperfield. The morning light shining on the sundial of the church - which has the tallest, narrowest Saxon round tower of any in East Anglia - greeted young David as he looked out of his bedroom window in the nearby Rookery. He said of the churchyard: "There is nothing half so green that I know anywhere, as the grass of that churchyard, nothing half so shady as its trees; nothing half so quiet as its tombstones."

Blundeston has another notable literary connection: Blundeston Lodge was once the home of Norton Nichols, whose friend the poet Gray is reputed to

MIDWAY NURSERIES

Yarmouth Road, Corton, Lowestoft, Suffolk NR32 5NG
Tel: 01502 730419 Fax: 01502 732761
e-mail: midwaynurseries@ic24.net
website: midwaynurseries.ic24.net

Midway Nurseries in Corton is a delightful one-stop plant centre specialising in helping clients find "the right place for the right plants". Among the many popular plants on sale here are fuchsias, bedding plants, petunias, begonias and more, together with shrubs, climbers and soft woods.

Owner Penny is happy to discuss location, soil type and position with all her customers, and her advice is never biased - she would rather not sell to a customer unless she is sure that the planting will be a success in their garden. With over 60 varieties of fuchsias, as these have become more popular Penny has extended the range of plants on offer to include a wider choice of flowering plants and shrubs. Wooden structures such as pergolas, all made to order on site, are another speciality of this excellent nursery.

Penny also offers a straightforward and very helpful garden design service, assisted by a specially prepared questionnaire on existing soil type, who will use the garden, type of property, aspect and more - she really listens to what the client requires, and this makes her computer-aided design service both efficient and truly appropriate for the needs of each gardener.

have taken his inspiration for *An Elegy Written in a Country Church Yard* while staying there.

LOUND

5 miles N of Lowestoft off the A12

Lound's parish **Church of St John the Baptist**, in the very north of the county, is sometimes known as the 'golden church'. This epithet is the result of the handiwork of designer/architect Sir Ninian Comper, seen most memorably in the gilded organ-case with two trumpeting angels, the font cover and the rood screen. The last is a very elaborate affair, with several heraldic arms displayed. The surprise package here is the modern St Christopher mural on the north wall. It includes Sir Ninian at the wheel of his Rolls Royce, and, in 1976, an aeroplane was added!

SOMERLEYTON

5 miles NW of Lowestoft on the B1074

Somerleyton Hall, one of the grandest and most distinctive of stately homes, is a splendid Victorian mansion built in Anglo-Italian style by Samuel Morton

SOMERLEYTON HALL & GARDENS

Lowestoft, Suffolk NR32 5QQ
Tel: 01502 730224 Fax: 01502 732143
website: www.somerleyton.co.uk

The stately home of Lord and Lady Somerleyton is a splendid early Victorian mansion virtually rebuilt from the Tudor and Jacobean house that stood on the site. The Victorian building was designed by Sir Morton Peto and his architect John Thomas in elaborate Anglo-Italian style, and the facade has many lavish features and magnificent carved stonework. The house was bought from Sir Morton in 1863 by the carpet manufacturer Sir Francis Crossley, whose descendants have occupied it ever since; the present Lord Somerleyton is the great-grandson of Sir Francis.

The Oak Room, with 17th century panelling from the original Jacobean house, some outstanding wood carvings and an exquisite silver and gilt mirror made for the Doge's Palace in Venice, is one of

several superb rooms in this grandest of houses; others include the elegant Library, its walls lined with over 3,500 books; the Dining Room, adorned by some of the Hall's best paintings and some unusual pieces of silver; and the sumptuous ballroom. The splendour of the house is matched by the magnificent gardens, which contain a wide variety of beautiful trees, plants and borders, along with attractive displays of flowers provided by the Victorian glasshouses, which were designed by Sir Joseph Paxton, creator of the Crystal Palace. One of the highlights of the garden is the yew hedge maze, the work of the celebrated landscape gardener William Nesfield. It was planted in 1846, and has had visitors going round in circles ever since. Other features include some interesting statuary, the walled and sunken gardens and a 70' pergola with an unusual iron framework. A more recent attraction that appeals to all ages is a miniature railway offering fine views of the Hall and surrounding parkland.

Peto. Its lavish architectural features are complemented by fine state rooms, magnificent wood carvings (some by Grinling Gibbons) and notable paintings. The grounds include a renowned yew-hedge maze, where people have been going round in circles since 1846, walled and sunken gardens and a 300-foot pergola. There's also a sweet little miniature railway, and Fritton Lake Countryworld, part of the Somerleyton Estate, is a 10-minute drive away. The Hall is open to the public on most days in summer (see panel opposite).

Samuel Morton Peto learned his skills as a civil engineer and businessman from his uncle and was still a young man when he put the Reform Club and Nelson's Column into his CV. The Somerleyton Hall he bought in 1843 was a Tudor and Jacobean mansion. He and his architect virtually rebuilt the place, and also built Somerleyton village, a cluster of thatched redbrick cottages. Nor was this the limit of Peto's achievements, for he ran a company which laid railways all over the world and was a Liberal MP, first for Norwich, then for Finsbury and finally for Bristol. His company foundered in 1863 and Somerleyton Hall was sold to Sir Francis Crossley, one of three brothers who made a fortune in mass-producing carpets. Crossley's son became Baron Somerleyton in 1916, and the Baron's grandson is the present Lord Somerleyton.

HERRINGFLEET

5 miles NW of Lowestoft on the B1074

Standing above the River Waveney, the parish Church of St Margaret is a charming sight with its Saxon round tower, thatched roof and lovely glass. **Herringfleet Windmill** is a beautiful black-tarred smock mill in working order, the last survivor of the Broadland wind pump, whose job was to assist in draining the marshes. This example was built in 1820 and worked regularly until the 1950s. It contains a fireplace and a wooden bench, providing a modicum of comfort for a millman on a cold night shift.

BECCLES

9 miles W of Lowestoft on the A146

Beccles is the largest town in the Waveney district at the southernmost point of the Broads. The Saxons were here, the Vikings were here, and at one time the market was a major supplier of herring (up to 60,000 a year) to the Abbey at Bury St Edmunds. At the height of its trading importance Beccles must have painted a splendidly animated picture, with wherries constantly on the move transporting goods from seaports to inland towns. The same stretch of river is still alive, but now with the yachts and pleasure boats of the holidaymakers and weekenders who fill the town in summer.

HUNGATE HEALTH STORE

4 Hungate, Beccles, Suffolk NR34 9TL
Tel: 01502 715009

Hungate Health Store in Beccles is a welcoming and attractive shop offering all manner of delicious and healthy foods, drinks, vitamins and more. Set in a Grade II listed mid-18th century building, the many wares in this fine shop are well displayed and offer an excellent selection of superior products. The shop specialises in organic foods and foods for special diets, such as a range of gluten-free items. Owner Theresa Hale and her friendly staff provide helpful advice to all their customers.

RINGSFIELD HALL

Ringsfield, Beccles, Suffolk NR34 8JR
Tel/Fax: 01502 713020
e-mail: info@ringsfield-hall.freeserve.co.uk
website: www.ringsfield-hall.freeserve.co.uk

Ringsfield Hall Residential Country Centre is a charitable trust that offers educational and retreat facilities, as well as holiday accommodation when available, in peaceful surroundings deep in the Suffolk countryside. This marvellous venue is set in 14 acres of varied woodland, parkland, meadows and gardens. The Victorian house was opened in 1972 by the Ringsfield Hall Charitable Trust as a residential centre for schools, church groups, youth groups and families.

The Trust has continued in its role by working with school groups from deprived areas, special schools, disadvantaged groups and those with a specific programme, to develop either curriculum-based study or social and relationship skills as well as church related groups to provide retreats, seminars or conferences, or holidays for those in need.

The Centre creates a safe place of welcome for all, with hospitality that includes attention to group and individual needs. The house's decor and ambience are directed to inspire guests; meals encourage an awareness of the connection between the land and the food we eat (using the Centre's own garden

and local produce where possible) and foster a sense of community. The large grounds provide the ideal space and security for children of all ages. The idyllic setting also encourages awareness of the human spirit and its values of honesty, love, caring, imagination, creativity and contemplation.

Sample programmes and workshops at this superb Centre include 'Earthkeepers' - a three-day course where children can learn about ecological concepts and discover the environment around them - 'Childkeepers' - a course for teachers dealing with issues of child protection using materials from the Department of Health training pack entitled Protecting the Children and the NSPCC's publication, Bullying - 'Spills and Skills' - a one-day programme introducing children to the concepts and practice of self-esteem social skills and emotional awareness.

Children's courses are appropriate for either Key Stage 1 (infants/years 1-2) or Key Stage 2 (juniors/ years 3-6). 'Earthkeepers' is part of the Centre's special Outdoor Earth Education series, a residential programme with aims and objectives that include helping children understand how energy and materials tie all of life together, and encouraging them to experience good feelings for the natural world. Shorter sessions use orienteering, games, storytelling, drama and arts and crafts to help children learn about the environment and to enhance their social and emotional skills. These shorter sessions must be booked well in advance. For more details about any of the Centre's programmes, please telephone.

The regatta in July and August is a particularly busy time.

The fires that are sadly such a common part of small-town history ravaged Beccles at various times in the 16th and 17th centuries, destroying much of the old town. For that reason the dwellings are largely Georgian in origin, with handsome redbrick facades. One that is not is **Roos Hall**, a gabled building dating from 1583. Just outside the town, far enough away to escape the great fire of 1586, it was built to a Dutch design, underlining the links between East Anglia and the Low Countries forged by the wool and weaving trades. Elizabeth I stayed at the hall just after it was completed, when she visited Beccles to present the town's charter; the occasion is depicted in the town sign. One of the hall's owners was Sir John Suckling (later to become Controller of the Household to James I), one of whose descendants was Lord Nelson. Any old hall worth its salt has a ghost, and the Roos representative is a headless coachman who appears on Christmas Eve.

The parish **Church of St Michael** was built in the second half of the 14th century by the Abbot of Bury. Its tower stands separate, built in the 16th century, rising almost 100 feet and containing a peal of bells. An unusual feature at the north facade is an outside pulpit taking the form of a small balcony. The priest could enter the pulpit from inside the church and preach to lepers, who were not allowed inside. Nelson's parents, the Reverend Edmund Nelson and Catherine Suckling, were married in St Michael's, so too the Suffolk poet George Crabbe.

Another building with Dutch-style gables houses **Beccles & District Museum**, whose contents include 19th century toys and costume, farm implements, items from the old town jail and memorabilia from the sailing wherries. Beccles, like Bungay, is a printing town, and has its own **Printing Museum** at the Newgate works of printer William Clowes. Here the visitor will learn about the history of printing since the 1800s, with woodcuts, books and machinery, and it is also possible to tour the factory.

At **North Cove**, east of Beccles just off the A146, **North Cove Hall** is a Georgian house set in lawns and parkland. Open by appointment for visits, the ground includes a walled garden, an attractive pond, a little stream with waterfalls, borders, pergolas and woodland walks.

BUNGAY

9 miles N of Halesworth on the A144

The River Waveney played an important part in the fortunes of this ancient fortress town until well into the 18th century, with barges laden with coal, corn, malt and timber plying the route to

the coast. The river is no longer navigable above Geldeston but is a great attraction for anglers and yachtsmen.

Bungay is best known for its **Castle**, built in its original form by Hugh Bigod, 1st Earl of Norfolk, as a rival to Henry II's castle at Orford. In 1173 Hugh took the side of the rebellious sons of Henry, but this insurrection ended with the surrender of the castle to the king. Hugh was killed not long after this episode while on the Third Crusade; his son Roger inherited the title and the castle, but it was another Roger Bigod who came to Bungay in 1294 and built the round tower and mighty outer walls which stand today.

To the north of the castle are Bungay's two surviving churches of note (the Domesday Book recorded five). The Saxon round tower of **Holy Trinity Church** is the oldest complete structure in the town, and a brass plate on the

door commemorates the church's narrow escape from the fire of 1688 that destroyed much of the town (similar disasters overtook many other towns with close-set timber-and-thatch buildings). The **Church of St Mary** - now redundant - was not so lucky, being more or less completely gutted. The tower survives to dominate the townscape, and points of interest in the church itself include a woodcarving of the Resurrection presented by Rider Haggard, and a monument to General Robert Kelso, who fought in the American War of Independence.

A century before the fire the church received a visit, during a storm, from the devilish Black Shuck, a retriever-like hound who, hot from causing severe damage at Blythburgh, raced down the nave and killed two worshippers. A weather vane in the market place puts the legend into verse:

THE BROAD STREET GUILD

Broad Street, Bungay, Suffolk NR35 1FE
Tel: 01986 896196 Mobile: 0794 772 6521

The Broad Street Guild is a workshop occupying a handsome brick former coach house. Here visitors can see sculptor Mark Goldsworthy at work. Mark produces fine figurative pieces that range in size from one inch high to 20 feet. Commissions are designed and carved in the workshop, larger works on site. He has created works for the Sandringham Estate and various District Councils. Please telephone before visiting.

EARSHAM PARK FARM

Harleston Road, Earsham, Bungay, Suffolk NR35 2AQ
Tel/Fax: 01986 892180

Earsham Park Farm offers good quality farmhouse accommodation in tranquil and beautiful surroundings. This Victorian farmhouse is set in 600 acres, originally one of the Duke of Norfolk's deer parks. Beautifully restored to offer every modern amenity but with a wealth of handsome original features, there are three tastefully furnished and attractively decorated ensuite guest bedrooms. The home-cooked breakfasts are served in the lovely, dining room; there is also a cosy guests' lounge. No smoking.

All down the church in midst of fire
The Hellish Monster Flew
And Passing onwards to the Quire
He many people slew.

Nearby is the famous octagonal **Butter Cross**, rebuilt after the Great Fire and topped by Justice with her scales and sword. This building was once used as a prison, with a dungeon below.

EARSHAM

1 mile SW of Bungay off the A143

All Saints Church and Earsham Hall are well worth a visit, but what brings most people here is the **Otter Trust**, on the banks of the Waveney, where the largest collection of otters in natural enclosures is bred for re-introduction into the wild. Waterfowl, herons, carp, deer and wallabies are also kept in the 30 attractive acres, which include an island garden, an illustrated nature trail, a visitor centre and a gift/refreshment shop.

FLIXTON

2 miles SW of Bungay on the B1062

Javelin, Meteor, Sea Vixen, Westland Whirlwind: names that evoke earlier days of flying, and just four of the 20 aircraft on show at The **Norfolk and Suffolk Aviation Museum**, on the site of a USAAF Liberator base during the Second World War (see below). Flixton is named after St Flik, the first Bishop of East Anglia, and he is depicted in the village sign.

MENDHAM

6 miles SW of Bungay off the A143

This pretty little village on the Waveney is the birthplace of Sir Alfred Munnings RA, who was born at Mendham Mill,

NORFOLK & SUFFOLK AVIATION MUSEUM

The Street, Flixton, Nr. Bungay, Suffolk NR35 1NZ
Tel: 01986 896644
e-mail: nsam.flixton@virgin.net website: www.aviationmuseum.net
Founded in 1972, the **Norfolk & Suffolk Aviation Museum** was officially opened to the public in 1976. Set in the picturesque Waveney Valley, the complex covers 7½ acres, with unique undercover exhibitions, military and civil, from the pioneer days through World War, the inter-war years, World War II right up to the present day.

The Museum incorporates the Museums of the 446th Bomber Group, Royal Observer Corps, RAF Bomber Command, Air-Sea Rescue and Coastal Command. More than 25 historic aircraft are on display, along with engines, missiles, guns, bombs and ejector seats. Throughout the Museum there are examples of aviation art, together with themed

displays, including WWII decoy sites, Civil Defence, telephones, compasses, models and (perhaps the most fascinating of all) wreckology - the digging for the remains of aircraft in areas where they are known to have crashed.

Among the aircraft on display are an Avro Anson C19, the first aircraft acquired by the Museum; a Dassault Mystère IVA, a Vampire, a Meteor, a Javelin and two Westland helicopters. The Museum, officially recognised as East Anglia's Aviation Heritage Centre, is located on the B1062 off the A143 a mile west of Bungay. Admission is free, the Museum relying on money put in the donation boxes or spent in the shop or NAAFI.

SOUTH ELMHAM HALL

St Cross South Elmham, Harleston,
Norfolk IP20 0PZ
Tel: 01986 782526 Fax: 01986 782203
e-mail: enquiries@southelmham.co.uk
website: www.southelmham.co.uk

The ancient landscape and buildings of
South Elmham Hall Farm at St Cross South
Elmham are evidence of a fascinating and
complex past that is still being researched
by archaeologists and historians. This
impressive historic home and farm comprises
182 hectares (455 acres) and is situated in
Suffolk's 'Saints' country, south of the
Waveney Valley. This exceptionally picturesque spot is welcoming and peaceful. The farm itself is
mainly arable, growing wheat, sugar beet and vining peas.

Owners Jo and John Sanderson have lived and farmed here since 1983, with a mixed farm that
includes pedigree beef cows and calves. Rare British White cattle, with their black noses and ears,
graze alongside the large Simmental cows. Both Jo and John are locals born and bred, John is the third

generation of Sandersons to live on the
farm. In 1906, when the Sandersons first
arrived, the farm was worked by 12 men
with as many horses. While the farm is not
organic, sprays and fertilisers are kept to a
carefully monitored minimum, and on
most of the grassland none is used. The
historic landscape has changed little, as the
ancient trees and meadows - relics of a
medieval deer park where the Bishops of
Norwich and their royal guests would hunt
- have been preserved.

The history of South Elmham Hall is
best appreciated by walking the farm on
the specially marked paths. Five different
routes of varying length can be easily followed with the help of the Wildlife Walks map available. A
walk along the water meadows lead to the 11th century Minster ruin in its atmospheric enclosure, and
beyond that to Park Barn. All along the way there's a rich variety of flora and fauna. Hedgerows and
woodland have been replanted - including the community wood, accessible to all. These and other
conservation projects have won several awards.

In the Spring of 2001 a new Visitor Centre and
Tearoom opened at Bateman's Barn, offering full
facilities for walkers, educational groups, business
conferences, corporate hospitality and weddings
(website www.batemansbarn.co.uk; open Thu, Fri
Sat & Bank Hols 10 am - 5 pm).

At Hall Farm Cottage, self-catering accommodation is available for up to six, with three
bedrooms, bathroom, kitchen, sitting and dining
rooms, available all year round. The Hall itself is
open for guided tours Thursdays, some Sundays
and Bank Holiday Mondays at 2 pm from 1st May
to 28th October.

where his father was the miller. Sir Alfred's *Charlotte and her Pony* was the inspiration for the village sign, which was unveiled by his niece Kathleen Hadingham.

CARLTON COLVILLE

3 miles SW of Lowestoft on the B1384

'History in motion at East Anglia's premier working transport museum'. Many an old bus-spotter has shed a nostalgic tear at the **East Anglia Transport Museum**, where children and ex-children climb aboard to enjoy rides on buses, trams and trolleybuses (one of the resident trolleybuses was built at the Garrett works in Leiston). A special London Trolleybus weekend is scheduled for September 2002 to celebrate the 40th anniversary of the last trolleybus running in the capital and the 50th anniversary of the last London tram in service. The East Suffolk narrow-gauge railway winds its way around the site, and there's a 1930s' street with all the authentic accessories, plus lorries, vans and steamrollers. If you think it's far too long since you saw a tram or trolleybus, this is the place for you.

Also in Carlton Colville is the 15th century Church of St Peter, which incorporated parts of other buildings when restored in the 19th century.

Suffolk Broads Centre & **Carlton Marshes Nature Reserve** is a wetland nature reserve in the Waveney Valley at the southern tip of the Broads. Run by the Suffolk Wildlife Trust, the 120-acre miniature version of the Broads consists of reed beds, marshes, fens, swampy woodlands and mini-broads. The one-kilometre nature trail is one of several paths on the reserve, where the dykes in particular support a colourful collection of wetland plants such as water soldier, arowhead, frogbit and bladderwort;

dragonflies including the Norfolk Hawker; water shrews; water voles; marsh harriers, Cetti's warblers, sedge warblers, reed warblers, snipe, dabchicks, hobbies and short-eared owls.

KESSINGLAND

3 miles S of Lowestoft off the A12

A small resort with a big history. Palaeolithic and Neolithic remains have come to light, and traces of an ancient forest have been unearthed on the sea bed. At the time of William the Conqueror, Kessingland prospered with its herring industry and was a major fishing port rivalled only by Dunwich. The estuary gradually silted up, sealing off the river with a shingle bank and cutting off the major source of wealth. The tower of the Church of St Edmund reaches up almost 100 feet - not unusual on the coast, where it provides a conspicuous landmark for sailors and fishermen. Most of the maritime trappings have disappeared: the lighthouse on the cliffs was scrapped 100 years ago, the lifeboat lasted until 1936 (having saved 144 lives), and there were several coastguard stations, one of them bought as a holiday home by the writer Rider Haggard.

The major tourist attraction is the **Suffolk Wildlife Park**, 100 acres of coastal parkland that are home to a wide range of wild animals, from aardvarks to zebras by way of bats, flamingos, giraffes, meerkats and sitatunga. The flamingos have their own enclosure. The park has been home to several film stars, including two chimps who appeared in *Gorillas in the Mist* and *Joey*, leading player in the PG Tips TV commercials. Burmese pythons are used for snake-handling sessions - an attraction that's definitely not for everyone!

COVEHITHE
7 miles S of Lowestoft off the A12

Leave the A12 at Wrentham and head for the tiny coastal village of Covehithe which is remarkable for its 'church within a church'. The massive **Church of St Andrew**, partly funded by the Benedictine monks at Cluniac, was left to decline after being laid waste by Dowsing's men. The villagers could not afford a replacement on the same grand scale so in 1672 it was decided to remove the roof and sell off some of the material. From what was left a small new church was built within the old walls. The original tower still stands, spared by Cromwell for use as a landmark for sailors.

SOUTHWOLD

A town full of character, and full of interest for the holidaymaker and for the historian. Though one of the most popular resorts on the east coast, Southwold has very little of the kiss-me-quick commercialism that spoils so many seaside towns. It's practically an island, bounded by creeks and marshes, the River Blyth and the North Sea, and has managed to retain the atmosphere of the last century. There are some attractive buildings, from pink-washed cottages to elegant Georgian town houses, many of them ranged around a series of greens which were left undeveloped to act as firebreaks after much of the town was lost in the great fire of 1659.

In a seaside town whose buildings present a wide variety of styles, shapes and sizes, William Denny's **Buckenham House** is among the most elegant and interesting. On the face of it a classic Georgian town house, it's actually much older, dating probably from the middle of the 16th century. Richard Buckenham, a wealthy Tudor merchant, was the man who had it built and it was truly impressive in size, as can be deduced from the dimensions of the cellar (now the Coffee House). Many fine features survive, including moulded cornices, carefully restored sash windows, Tudor brickwork and heavy timbers in the ceilings.

The town, which was granted its charter by Henry VII in 1489, once prospered, like many of its neighbours, through herring fishing, and the few remaining fishermen share the harbour on the River Blyth with pleasure craft. Also adding to the period atmosphere is Southwold's new pier, the first to be built in Britain since the 1950s. There are also colourful bathing huts and a brilliant white lighthouse that stands 100 feet tall, its light visible 17 miles out to sea. Beneath the lighthouse stands a little

Sole Bay Inn and Lighthouse, Southwold

Victorian pub, the **Sole Bay Inn**, whose name recalls a battle fought off Southwold in 1672 between the British and French fleets and the Dutch. This was an episode in the Third Anglo-Dutch War, but why Sole Bay? Because the Duke of York, Lord High Admiral of England and later to be crowned James II, had taken Sutherland House in Southwold as his headquarters and it was from there that his fleet (along with the French) set sail. There were many casualties on both sides, and when the Dutch withdrew both sides claimed victory. A distinguished victim of the battle was Edward Montagu, 1st Earl of Sandwich, great-grandfather of the man whose gambling mania did not allow him time for a formal meal. By inserting slices of meat between slices of bread, the 4th Earl ensured that his name would live on.

The Sole Bay Inn is one of several owned by the local brewery Adnams. One of the best known is the **Lord Nelson**, where traces can be seen of a smugglers' passageway leading to the cliffs. Where there were smugglers there are usually ghosts, and here it's a man in a frock coat who disappears into the cliff face. Adnams still use horse-drawn drays for local beer deliveries.

Southwold's maritime past is recorded in the **Museum** set in a Dutch-style cottage in Victoria Street. Open daily in the summer, it records the famous battle and also local archaeology, geology and natural history, and the history of the Southwold railway. The Southwold Sailors' Reading Room contains pictures, ship models and other items, and at **Gun Hill** the **Lifeboat Museum** has a small collection of RNLI-related material with particular reference to Southwold. The main attraction at Gun Hill is a set of six 18-pounder guns, captured in 1746 at the Battle of Culloden and presented to the town (hitherto more or less undefended)

by the Duke of Cumberland. They have never been pressed into use. Another Southwold museum, and one unique in its scope, is the **Amber Museum** in the market place, dedicated to the story and history of amber, with examples from all over the world showing the variety of colours and the creatures trapped within.

No visitor to Southwold should leave without spending some time in the splendid **Church of St Edmund, King and Martyr**, which emerged relatively unscathed from the ravages of the Commonwealth. The imposing flint tower, the screens, the 15th century pulpit, the vast font cover and the richly wrought choir stalls are just some of the glories of this outstanding church; it's a very light, bright place, because almost all the glass is clear, replacing Victorian stained glass blown out in wartime raids. The exception is Sir Ninian Comper's superb window showing the martyrdom of St Edmund. Outside the church, a splendid Jack o'the Clock - a little wooden man in War of the Roses armour - strikes his bell on the hour.

AROUND SOUTHWOLD

WANGFORD

2 miles NW of Southwold off the A12

There's some great walking in the country around Southwold, both along the coast and inland. At Wangford, a mile or so inland, **Henham Walks** are waymarked paths through Repton Park, lake and woods. A splendid place for a ramble or a picnic, or to see the wildlife, rare-breed sheep and Highland cattle. Also at Wangford is the Perpendicular Church of St Peter and St Paul, built on the site of a Benedictine priory. Even closer to Southwold is **Reydon Wood Nature Reserve**.

BLYTHBURGH

2 miles SW of Southwold, A1095 then A12

Blythburgh's **Church of Holy Trinity** is one of the wonders of Suffolk, a stirring sight as it rises from the reed beds, visible for miles around and floodlit at night to spectacular effect. This 'Cathedral of the Marshes' reflects the days when Blythburgh was a prosperous port with a bustling quayside wool trade. With the silting up of the river trade rapidly fell off and the church fell into decay. In 1577 the steeple of the 14th century tower was struck by lightning in a severe storm; it fell into the nave, shattering the font and taking two lives. The scorch marks visible to this day on the north door are said to be the claw marks of the Devil in the guise of hellhound Black Shuck, left as he sped towards Bungay to terrify the congregation of St Mary's.

Disaster struck again in 1644, when Dowsing and his men smashed windows, ornaments and statues, blasted the wooden angels in the roof with hundreds of bullets and used the nave as a stable, with tethering rings screwed into the pillars of the nave. Luckily, the bench-end carvings escaped the desecration, not being labelled idolatrous. These depict the Labours of the Months, and the Seven Deadly Sins. Blythburgh also has a Jack o'the Clock, a brother of the figure at Southwold, and the priest's chamber over the south porch has been lovingly restored complete with an altar made with wood from HMS Victory. The angels may have survived, but the font was defaced to remove the signs of the sacraments.

A mile south, at the junction of the A12 and the Walberswick road, **Toby's Walks** is an ideal place for a picnic and, like so many places in Suffolk, has its own ghost story. This concerns Tobias Gill, a dragoon drummer who murdered a

WOOTTENS OF WENHASTON

Blackheath, Wenhaston, Halesworth, Suffolk IP19 9HD
Tel: 01502 478258 e-mail: woottensplants@hotmail.com
Fax: 01502 478888 website: woottensplants.co.uk

Woottens of Wenhaston is a fine nursery specialising in traditional pelargoniums, ornamental grasses, penstemons and hemerocallis, together with a huge range of hardy herbaceous plants. Featured on the BBC's Gardener's World in 2000 and 2001, Anna Pavord in The Independent writes, 'The plants are thumping with good health and the range is extraordinary: a beautiful nursery.' Open seven days a week from 9.30 am to 5.00 pm.

THE PARISH LANTERN LTD

The Village Green, Walberswick, Southwold, Suffolk IP18 6TT
Tel: 01502 723173 Fax: 01502 725474

The Parish Lantern is set on two floors of a handsome Georgian building right on the village green in Walberswick. Here visitors will find a wealth of innovative crafts, gifts, pottery, toys, and paintings by local artists. This charming shop is well known for its tea room, where a range of freshly made cakes and light lunches can be enjoyed.

local girl and was hanged here after a trial at Ipswich. His ghost is said to haunt the heath, but he is very unlikely to interrupt a picnic.

The **Norman Gwatkin Nature Reserve** is an area of marsh and fen with two hides, walkways and a willow coppice.

WENHASTON

5 miles W of Southwold off the A12

The **Church of St Peter** cannot compete as a spectacle with Blythburgh's Holy Trinity, but is well worth a detour. Saxon stones are embedded in its walls but the most remarkable feature is the Doom (portrayal of the Last Judgement), said to have been painted around 1500 by a monk from Blythburgh.

WALBERSWICK

1 miles SW of Southwold on the B1387

The story is familiar: flourishing fishing port; grand church; changing of the coastline due to erosion and silting; decline of fishing and trading; no money to maintain the church; church falls into disrepair. Towards the end of the 16th

The River Blithe, Walberswick

century, a smaller church was built within the original St Andrew's, by then in ruins through neglect. The situation in Walberswick had been exacerbated by the seizing of church lands and revenues by the king, and by a severe fire.

Fishing hardly exists today, and boating in Walberswick is almost entirely a weekend and holiday activity. The tiny 'church within a church' is still in use, its churchyard a nature reserve. South of the village is the bird sanctuary of Walberswick & Westleton Heaths. Walberswick has, for two centuries, been a magnet for painters, the religious ruins, the beach and the sea being favourite subject for visiting artists. The tradition continues unabated, and many academics have made their homes here.

HALESWORTH

16 miles SW of Lowestoft on the A144

Granted a market in 1222, Halesworth reached the peak of its trading importance when the River Blyth was made navigable as far as the town in 1756. A stroll around the streets reveals several buildings of architectural interest. The Market Place has a handsome Elizabethan timber-framed house, but the chief attraction for the visitor is the **Halesworth and District Museum** at Steeple End, a conversion of a row of 17th century almshouses. Local geology and archaeology are the main interests, with various fossils and flints on display, and there's a fascinating account of the Halesworth witchcraft trials of 1645. An art gallery is in the same building. During the Second World War the 56th Fighter Group was based at Halesworth (Holton) Airfield, along with the 489th Bomb Group and the 5th Emergency Rescue Squadron. The Halesworth Airfield Memorial Museum tells their story, and there is a memorial in nearby Holton church.

FOCUS ORGANIC

14 Thoroughfare, Halesworth, Suffolk IP19 8AH
Tel: 01986 872899 Fax: 01986 872995

The word 'organic' brings to mind of images of healthy living and the freshest natural produce. All of these designs for living can be found at **Focus Organic** in Halesworth and Southwold.

The Halesworth shop is deceptively small from the outside, but the interior is actually two shops in one, in an extensive, well-laid out open-plan space with beamed ceiling and exposed brick uprights. Along the walls and on the many attractively laid out shelves occupying the central area, visitors will find a wealth of wholefoods and health products, including organically grown food and drink, including breads, cakes, pastries, wines, beers, confectionery, nuts, seeds, pulses, fresh herbs and plants, coffees, and, of course, the freshest fruits and vegetables. The shop also stocks a selection of gluten-free products including pastas, locally baked breads and pastries.

Together with all this there is a variety of chilled and frozen foods including organic meats, and a range of healthy snack foods such as rice cakes, flapjacks and organic chocolate. Every aspect of home

life is catered for with the range of household cleaning products for sale. Among the toiletries for sale are an impressive selection of homoeopathic and herbal remedies, aromatherapy oils, soaps and vitamin creams and cosmetics.

On the premises are also an aromatherapist, who can offer a relaxing aromatherapy massage, a nutritionist, for expert dietary advice, and an allergy-tester. The second shop within a shop features an exciting range of extraordinary and unique gifts and home decorating items, from lampshades, curtains, mirrors, mobiles, pottery, individually made china pieces and photo frames to stationery, a good selection

of cards and wrapping paper, incense, calendars, rugs, wall hangings, and didgeridoos! There's also a lovely array of distinctive jewellery crafted in silver and precious and semi-precious stones. The range of clothing for sale includes scarves, dresses, jeans and hats, together with a wonderful selection of toys, games, and also books covering diet, healing and health issues.

For those travelling out that way, there is also another branch of this fine shop situated in Southwold, offering a similar range of products together with a good selection of vitamins and a variety of delicious organic cakes, bread and pastries, set in cosy premises - for details and directions, please telephone the Halesworth shop.

BRAMFIELD

3 miles S of Halesworth on the A144

The massive Norman round tower of **St Andrew's Church** is separate from the main building and was built as a defensive structure, with walls over 3 feet thick. Dowsing ran riot here in 1643, destroyed 24 superstitious pictures, one crucifix, a picture of Christ and 12 angels on the roof. The most important monument is one to Sir Arthur Coke, sometime Lord Chief Justice, who died in 1629, and his wife Elizabeth. Arthur is kneeling, resplendent in full armour, while Elizabeth is lying on her bed with a baby in her arms. This monument is the work of Nicholas Stone, the most important English mason and sculptor of his day. The Cokes at one time occupied Bramfield Hall, and another family, in residence for 300 years, were the Rabetts, whose coat of arms in the church punningly depicts rabbits on its shield.

DUNWICH

4 miles SW of Southwold off the B1105

Dunwich is renowned as the town that disappeared. Founded in Roman times, it was later taken over by the invading Sigebert, who made it the capital of the Kingdom and appointed Felix as his Bishop in 636. For several centuries it was a major trading port (wool and grain out; wine, timber and cloth in) and a centre of fishing and shipbuilding, with many fine buildings. The records show that in 1241 no fewer than 80 ships were built for the king. By the middle of the next century the best days were over as the sea attacked from the east and a vast bank of sand and shingle silted up the harbour. The course of the river was diverted, the town was cut off from the sea and the town's trade was effectively dead. For the next 700 years, the relentless forces of nature continued to take their toll, and all that remains now of ancient Dunwich are the ruins of a Norman leper hospital, the archways of a medieval friary and a buttress of one of the nine churches that once served the community.

Today's village comprises a 19th century church and a row of Victorian cottages, one of which houses the **Dunwich Museum**. Local residents set up the museum in 1972 to tell the Dunwich story; the historical section has displays and exhibits from Roman, Saxon and medieval times, the centrepiece being a large model of the town at its 12th century peak. There are also sections for natural history, social history and the arts. Experts have calculated that the main part of old Dunwich extended up to seven miles beyond its present boundaries, and the vengeance of the sea has thrown up inevitable stories of drama and mystery. The locals say that when a storm is threatening, the sound of

(Continued page 138)

WALK 6

Dingle Marshes from Dunwich

Start	Dunwich beach
Distance	4½ miles (7.2km)
Approximate time	2½ hours
Parking	Car park at beach
Refreshments	Pub, café and tearoom at Dunwich
Ordnance Survey maps	Landranger 156 (Saxmundham, Aldeburgh & Southwold), Explorer 231 (Southwold & Bungay)

Dunwich is the Avalon of Suffolk. Stand on the beach on a still, moonlit night and you may well think that you can hear the bells of its six churches that lie beneath the waves. Certainly Dunwich has a romance all its own, with marshes, forest and lonely shore all to be seen on this short walk.

Dunwich, a city in Anglo-Saxon times and until the 14th century a thriving seaport, suffered its demise long before global warming became a fact of life. Its decline took place in a matter of a 100 years, when a series of violent storms not only blocked off the harbour but also wrought havoc in eroding the shoreline to such an extent that the large town virtually vanished. The last of its six medieval churches slipped down the cliff in 1904, and now only the remains of the Franciscan priory remain to reflect the splendour that once was Dunwich (and even the priory was rebuilt in its present position in 1289 after the initial foundation had become threatened by the waves).

Turn northwards along the shore. Initially there is a good grassy path behind the shingle bank that makes good walking. However, once this reaches the reedy lagoons it becomes damp so it is best to walk on the top of the bank. Anyone with an interest in ornithology will have his binoculars at the ready as the lagoons attract a wide range of native and migrating birds. The landmarks of Southwold – lighthouse, church and brewery – become more distinct as you progress northwards.

After about an hour of walking by the sea, after passing Great Dingle Farm nestled in its clump of trees, look for a ramp A leading down to an English Nature noticeboard. From here there is a path on top of the flood bank that snakes across the marshes. Follow this until it turns towards a drainage mill and the tower of Walberswick church. There are more reedy lagoons to the right as you come to a yellow-topped post where the Suffolk Coast and Heaths Path goes to the left. B Take this path through the reedbeds which skirts a small nameless promontory and crosses a bank before swinging left round the flank of Dingle Great Hill. It then climbs past Great Dingle Farm to join a track leading into woodland. C

The track may be muddy at first but improves steadily and gives wide views across the marshes. After passing the imposing Dingle Stone House the walking is excellent on a sandy track with the forest to the right and the marshes and shoreline to the left. Pass

old farm buildings to come to the road at Bridge Farm D which has a tearoom.

Turn left on to the road and fork left at the church. This was built in Victorian times to replace the church that went over the cliff. Passing the pub on the way, return to the car park at the starting point. ●

Westwood Marshes

FB

Point Marsh B

Dingle Great Hill

73

Great Dingle Farm A

C

Sandymount Covert

Foxburrow Wood

Dingle Stone House

8

Dingle Marshes

72

Reedland Marshes

rest

47

48

Little Dingle

Hog's Grove

G

Bridge Farm

20

15

D

P PC

6

Maison Dieu Hill

71

Chapel (rems of)

Dunwich

Sandy Lane Farm

Remains of Friary (Franciscan)

submerged church bells can still be heard tolling under the waves as they shift in the current. Other tales tell of strange lights in the ruined priory and the eerie chanting of long-gone monks.

Dunwich Forest, immediately inland from the village, is one of three - the others are further south at Tunstall and Rendlesham - named by the Forestry Commission as Aldewood Forest. Work started on these in 1920 with the planting of Scots pine, Corsican pine and some Douglas fir; oak and poplar were tried but did not thrive in the sandy soil. The three forests, which between them cover nearly 9,000 acres, were almost completely devastated in the hurricane of October 1987, Rendlesham alone losing more than a million trees, and the replanting will take many years to restore them.

South of the village lies **Dunwich Heath**, one of Suffolk's most important conservation areas, comprising Minsmere Beach, splendid heather and gorse, a field study centre, a public hide, and an information centre and restaurant in converted coastguard cottages. The whole area from just below Lowestoft to the mouth of the River Deben is the Suffolk Coast & Heaths Area of Outstanding Natural Beauty and Project Area. Walkers' and Cyclists' trails run through coastal countryside that includes the Sandling Heaths, once used primarily as sheepwalks. The heathland, formerly tracts of sandy soil, has gradually been eroded down the centuries and now exists in isolated pockets amid arable farming, forests and the encroachment of the built environment. The Sandlings Group, part of the Suffolk Coast & Heaths Partnership, is engaged on a programme of heathland management, supported by the Heritage Lottery Fund, to create and improve the heathland to provide protected habitats for a variety of

wildlife. Sheep have been re-introduced and the land made habitable by many species. Heather blankets the heath, along with three species of gorse, and bird-watchers should look out in particular for the stonechat and the winchat, the woodlark (especially in April), the nightjar (June) and the hobby (August). Everyone should look out for the adder, Britain's only venomous snake; shy and nervous, the adder can occasionally be seen sunning itself on open ground, but it will invariably slither into cover once it detects human presence. Lizards, grass snakes, glow worms, heather beetles and heather gossamer spiders are other creatures that inhabit the heathland, along with butterflies, including the lovely silver-studded blue.

1998 marked the 30th anniversary of Dunwich Heath being in the care of the National Trust, who organise many special events each year: 2001 saw, among others, an Easter Egg hunt; Dunwich Heath 1939-1945; Moths, Bats and BBQ; Wildflowers of the Heath; Children's Activity Days; and the Warden's Ramble with Brunch.

Around Dunwich Heath are the attractive villages of **Westleton**, **Middleton**, **Theberton** and **Eastbridge**.

In Westleton, the 14th century thatched **Church of St Peter**, built by the monks of Sibton Abbey, has twice seen the collapse of its tower. The first fell down in a hurricane in 1776 and its smaller wooden replacement collapsed when a bomb fell in World War II. The village is the main route of access to the RSPB-managed **Minsmere Bird Sanctuary**, the most important sanctuary for wading birds in eastern England. The marshland was flooded during World War II, and nature and this wartime emergency measure created the perfect habitat for innumerable birds. More than 100 species nest here, and a similar number visit. It's a birdwatcher's paradise, with many hides, and the Suffolk Coastal Path runs along the foreshore.

YOXFORD

10 miles SW of Southwold on the A12

Once an important stop on the London-Yarmouth coaching route, Yoxford now attracts visitors with its pink-washed cottages and its arts and crafts, antique and food shops. Look for the cast-iron signpost outside the church, with hands pointing to London, Yarmouth and Framlingham set high enough to be seen by the driver sitting high up on his stagecoach.

SIBTON

12 miles SW of Southwold on the A1120

Two miles west of Yoxford, on the A1120, Sibton is known chiefly for its abbey (now in ruins), the only Cistercian house in Suffolk. The Church of St Peter is certainly not a ruin and should be seen for its fine hammerbeam and collar roof.

PEASENHALL

6 miles NW of Saxmundham on the A1120

A little stream runs along the side of the main street, whose buildings present several styles and ages. Most distinguished is the old timbered Woolhall, splendidly restored to its 15th century grandeur. The oddest is certainly a hall in the style of a Swiss chalet, built for his workers by James Josiah Smyth, grandson of the founder of James Smyth & Sons. This company, renowned for its agricultural drills, was for more than two centuries the dominant industrial presence in Peasenhall. On the south side of St Michael's churchyard stands the 1805 drill mill where James Smyth manufactured his Nonpareil seed drills, one of which is on display in Stowmarket's museum.

SAXMUNDHAM

12 miles SW of Southwold off the A12

A pretty name for a little town that was granted its market charter in 1272. On the font of the church is the carving of a woodwose, a tree spirit or green man - he, and others like him, have given their name to a large number of pubs, in Suffolk and elsewhere. The only thing in ruins in Sax is the bus garage!

LEISTON

4 miles E of Saxmundham off the B1119

The first **Leiston Abbey** was built on Nunsmere marshes in 1182 but in 1363 the Earl of Suffolk rebuilt it on its present site. It became one of the largest and most prestigious monasteries in the country, and its wealth probably spelt its ruin, as it fell within Henry VIII's plan for the dissolution of the monasteries. A new abbey was built by the ruins of the

old, and the restored old hall is used as a base for PROCORDA, a group promoting musical excellence.

For 200 years the biggest name in Leiston was that of Richard Garrett, who founded an engineering works here in 1778 after starting business in Woodbridge. In the early years ploughs, threshers, seed drills and other agricultural machinery were the main products, but the company later started one of the country's first production lines for steam machines. The Garrett works are now the **Long Shop Museum**, the factory buildings having been lovingly restored, and many of the Garrett machines are now on display, including traction engines, a steam-driven tractor and a road roller. There's also a section where the history and workings of steam engines are explained. A small area of the museum recalls the USAAF's 357th fighter group, who flew from an airfield outside Leiston during World War II. One of their number, a Captain Chuck Yeager, was the first man to fly at more than the speed of sound.

The Garrett works closed in 1980 and what could have been a disastrous unemployment situation was to some extent alleviated by the nuclear power station at **Sizewell**. The coast road in the centre of Leiston leads to this establishment, where visitors can take tours, on foot with access to buildings at Sizewell A or by minibus, with guide and videos, round the newer PWR Sizewell B.

ALDRINGHAM

4 miles E of Saxmundham on the B1122

The village church is notable for its superb 15th century font, and the village inn was once a haunt of smugglers. It now helps to refresh the visitors who flock to the **Aldringham Craft Market**, founded in 1958 and extending over three galleries, with a serious selection of arts and crafts, clothes and gifts, pottery, basketry, books and cards.

FRISTON

3 miles SE of Saxmundham off the A1094

The tallest **Post Mill** in England is a prominent sight on the Aldeburgh-Snape road, moved from Woodbridge in 1812, just after its construction. It worked by wind until 1956, then by engine until 1972.

THORPENESS

6 miles E of Saxmundham on the B1353

Thorpeness, which started life as a remote farming and fishing hamlet, was transformed into a unique holiday village with mock-Tudor houses and the general look of a series of eccentric film sets. Buying a considerable pocket of land

House in the Clouds, Thorpeness

called the Sizewell estate in 1910, the architect, barrister and playwright Glencairn Stuart Ogilvie created what he hoped would be a fashionable resort with cottages, some larger houses and a large, shallow boating and pleasure lake called **The Meare**. That came in 1910, followed by the Country Club in 1912 and a collection of highly distinctive and individualistic buildings mainly in neo-Tudor or modernist style. The 85' water tower, built to aid in the lake's construction, looked out of place, so Ogilvie disguised it as a house, known ever since as the **House in the Clouds**, and now available for rent as a holiday home. The neighbouring **Mill**, moved lock, stock and millstones from Aldringham, stopped pumping in 1940 but has been restored and now houses a visitor centre. Every August, in the week following the Aldeburgh Carnival, a regatta is held on the Meare, culminating in a splendid fireworks show. Thorpeness is very much a one-off, not at all a typical Suffolk community, but with a droll charm that is all its own.

Aldeburgh

6 miles SE of Saxmundham on the A1094

And so down the coast road to Aldeburgh, another of those coastal towns that once prospered as a port with major fishing and shipbuilding industries. Drake's *Greyhound* and *Pelican* were built just south of present-day Aldeburgh at Slaughden, now taken by the sea, and during the 16th century some 1,500 people were engaged in fishing. Both industries declined as shipbuilding moved elsewhere and the fishing boats became too large to be hauled up the shingle. Suffolk's best-known poet, **George Crabbe**, grandson of the local customs collector, was born at Slaughden in 1754 and lived in the poor times. He

Aldeburgh

clearly reflected the melancholy of those days when he wrote of his fellow townsmen in terms of stark realism:

> *Here joyless roam a wild amphibious race,*
> *With sullen woe displayed in every face;*
> *Who far from civil arts and social fly,*
> *And scowl at strangers with suspicious eye.*

But even in Crabbe's time Aldeburgh has begun to attract a more civilised band to the joys of the fresh sea air, so that he could write:

> *Soon as the season comes, and crowds arrive,*
> *To their superior rooms the wealthy drive...*
> *Observe how various parties take their way,*
> *By seaside walks, or make the sand-hills gay...*

He was equally evocative concerning the sea and the river, and the following lines written about the River Alde could apply to several others in the county.

> *With ceaseless motion comes and goes the tide*
> *Flowing, it fills the channel vast and wide;*
> *Then back to sea, with strong majestic sweep*
> *It rolls, in ebb yet terrible and deep;*
> *Here samphire-banks and salt-wort bound the flood*
> *There stakes and seaweed withering on the mud;*
> *And higher up, a ridge of all things base,*
> *Which some strong tide has rolled upon the place*

STRAND GALLERY

164 High Street, Aldeburgh,
Suffolk IP 15 5AQ
Tel: 01728 454695
Fax: 01728 453662
e-mail: strandg@strandg.screaming.net
website: www.strandgallery.co.uk

Strand Gallery was established permanently in Aldeburgh in 1997, after several years of occasional exhibitions in the town.

It shows a changing selection of pictures and artists'prints by noted artists and sculptors, sometimes with a local connection. It also aims to give the opportunity to discover the work of lesser known 20th century artists such as Bryan Ingham, Henry Cliffe and Allin Braund.

There is usually a selection of work by artists such as Henry Moore, Sir Terry Frost RA, Geoffrey Clarke RA, Margaret Thomas, Guy Taplin alongside the current show. Those with increasing reputations - younger sculptors such as Jonathan Clarke and artists such as Tessa Newcomb and Emma McClure - are also regularly shown.

The gallery aims to ignore the distinction between 'fine art' and 'craft' and shows ceramics, jewellery and other craftsman made objects. European work is regularly featured. Italian glass is a particular interest, showing contemporary work as well as that by Sottsass, other members of 'Memphis' and other 20th century makers and designers.

Some work is specially commissioned by the gallery and always there is a deliberate policy of showing the best work across a wide price range. Some books are available, including artists' books and signed copies.

The gallery is listed by the National List of Craftshops and Galleries and shows many makers on the Crafts Council's list.

Crabbe it was who created the character of the solitary fisherman Peter Grimes, later the subject of an opera composed by another Aldeburgh resident, Benjamin Britten.

The Marquess of Salisbury, visiting early in the 19th century, was one of the first to be attracted by the idea of sea-bathing without the crowds and subsequently spent much of the year here. By the

Beach, Aldeburgh

middle of the century the grand houses that had sprung up were joined by smaller residences, the railway arrived, a handsome water tower was put up (1860) and Aldeburgh prospered once more. There were even plans for a pier, and construction started in 1878, but the project proved too difficult or too expensive and was halted, the rusting girders being removed some time later.

One of the town's major benefactors was Newson Garrett, a wealthy businessman who was the first mayor under the charter of the Local Government Act of 1875. This colourful character designed and built much of modern Aldeburgh and also developed the Maltings at Snape, but is perhaps best remembered through his remarkable daughter Elizabeth, who was the first woman doctor in England (having qualified in Paris at a time when women could not qualify here) and the first woman mayor (of Aldeburgh, in 1908). This lady married the shipowner James Skelton Anderson, who established the golf club at Aldeburgh in 1884.

If the poet were alive today he would have a rather less crabbed opinion of his fellows, especially at carnival time on a Monday in August, when the town

celebrates with a colourful procession of floats and pedestrians, a fireworks display and numerous other social events.

As for the arts, there is, of course, the **Aldeburgh Festival**, started in 1948 by Britten and others; the festival's main venue is Snape Maltings, but many performances take place in Aldeburgh itself.

The maritime connection remains very strong. There has been a lifeboat here since 1851 and down the years many acts of great heroism are recorded. The very modern **Lifeboat Station** is one of the town's chief attractions for visitors, and there are regular practice launches from the shingle beach. A handful of fishermen still put out to sea from the beach, selling their catch from their little wooden huts, while down at Slaughden a thriving yacht club is the base for sailing on the Orde and sometimes on the sea. At the very southern tip of the town the **Martello Tower** serves as a reminder of the power of the sea: old pictures show it standing well back from the waves, but now the seaward side of the moat has disappeared and the shingle is constantly being shored up to protect it. This tower, which had four guns but saw no action, is the most northerly of the 75 or more built against the threat of a Napoleonic invasion at the beginning of the 19th century. Stretching along the coast from Suffolk to Sussex, the towers took their name from the Torre della Mortella on Corsica. Beyond Aldeburgh's Tower is a long strip of marsh and shingle stretching right down to the mouth of the River Alde at Shingle Street.

Back in town, there are several interesting buildings, notably the **Moot Hall** and the parish **Church of St Peter and St Paul**. Moot Hall is a 16th century half-timbered flint and brick building that once stood in the centre of town. It hasn't moved, but the sea long ago took away several houses and streets, so it now stands a few paces from the sea. Inside the hall, which was restored in mid-Victorian times and given tall Jacobean-style chimneys, is a museum of town history and finds from the nearby Snape burial ship. Britten set the first scene of *Peter Grimes* in the Moot Hall. A sundial on the south face of the hall proclaims, in Latin, that it only tells the time when the sun shines.

The church, which stands above the town as a very visible landmark for mariners, contains a memorial bust of George Crabbe and a beautiful stained-glass window, designed by John Piper and executed by Patrick Reyntiens, depicting the three Britten parables for church performance. *Curlew River* is a non-biblical story from a Japanese Noh play; the design of *The Burning Fiery Furnace* was inspired by Romanesque sculpture at Autun; and the composition of *The Prodigal Son* was taken from a picture by

Rembrandt in the Hermitage at St Petersburg. Britten is buried in the churchyard, as are his lifelong friend the singer Peter Pears,   and their close associate Imogen Holst. Elizabeth Garrett Anderson is also buried here. Aldeburgh has a number of good hotels and fine restaurants specialising in locally-caught fish and shellfish - the best of the restaurants is the Lighthouse.

SNAPE

3 miles S of Saxmundham on the A1094

The "boggy place" has a long and interesting history, and in 1862 an Anglo-Saxon ship was discovered. Since that time regular finds have been made, with some remarkable cases of almost perfect preservation. Snape, like Aldeburgh, benefited from the philanthropy of the Garrett family, one of whose members built the primary school and set up the Maltings, centre of the **Aldeburgh Music Festival**.

The last 30-odd years have seen the development of the **Snape Maltings Riverside Centre**, which incorporates shops and galleries. The site is a complex of restored Victorian granaries and malthouses that is also the setting for the renowned Aldeburgh festival.

The Maltings, Snape

VALLEY FARM BARNS

Aldeburgh Road, Snape, Saxmundham, Suffolk IP17 1QH
Tel: 01728 689071 e-mail: chrisvalleyfarm@aol.com

Valley Farm Barns offer three delightful accommodations: Harvest Cottage, Granary Cottage, and Hayloft Cottage. The 'youngest' of these thatched and timber-framed cottages dates back to 1650! All three retain original features such as the exposed beams, and include a fitted kitchen, living/dining area and double bedroom. Each occupies two floors, with a extensive open-plan ground floor and solid wooden stairs leading up to the galleried bedroom. There are private patio areas and a communal garden. Dog friendly!

The Maltings began their designated task in the 1840s and continued thus until 1965, when the pressure of modern techniques brought them to a halt. There was a real risk of the buildings being demolished but George Gooderham, a local farmer, bought the site to expand his animal feeds business and soon saw the potential of the redundant buildings (his family still own the site).

The concert hall came first, in 1967, and in 1971 the Craft Shop was established as the first conversion of the old buildings for retailing. Conversion and expansion continue to this day, and in the numerous stylish outlets visitors can buy anything from fudge to country-style clothing, from herbs to household furniture, from silver buttons to top hats. Plants and garden accessories are also sold, and art galleries feature the work of local painters, potters and sculptors. The centre hosts regular painting, craft and decorative art courses; there's a pub, tea shop and restaurant, and the latest expansion has seen the creation of an impressive country-style department store. Hour-long trips on the River Alde start from the quay, and cottages are available all year round for self-catering holidays.

A short distance west of Snape, off the B1069, lies Blaxhall, best known for its 'growing' stone. The **Blaxhall Stone**, which lies in the yard of Stone Farm, is reputed to have grown to its present size (5 tons) from a comparative pebble, the size of a football, when it first came to local attention 100 years ago. Blaxhall getting mixed up with 'Blarney'?

WOODBRIDGE

Udebyge, Wiebryge, Wodebryge, Wudebrige ... just some of the ways of spelling this splendid old market town since first recorded in 970. As to what it means, it could simply be 'wooden bridge' or 'bridge by the wood', but the most likely and most interesting explanation is that it is derived from Anglo-Saxon words meaning 'Woden's (or Odin's) town'. Standing at the head of the Deben estuary, it is a place of considerable charm, with a wealth of handsome, often historic buildings and a considerable sense of history, as both a market town and a port.

The shipbuilding and allied industries flourished here as at most towns on the Suffolk coast, and it is recorded that both Edward III, in the 14th century, and Drake in the 16th sailed in Woodbridge ships. There's still plenty of activity on and by the river, though nowadays it is all leisure-oriented. The town's greatest benefactor was Thomas Seckford, who rebuilt the abbey, paid for the chapel in the north aisle of St Mary's Church and founded the original almshouses in Seckford Street. In 1575 he gave the town the splendid Shire Hall on Market Hill. Originally used as a corn exchange, it now houses the **Suffolk Horse Museum**, which is an exhibition devoted to the Suffolk Punch breed of heavy working horse, the oldest such breed in the world. The history of the breed and its rescue from near-extinction in the 1960s is covered in fascinating detail, and there's a section dealing with the other famous Suffolk breeds - the Red Poll cattle, the Suffolk

River Deben, Woodbridge

sheep and the Large Black pigs. Opposite the Shire Hall is **Woodbridge Museum**, a treasure trove of information on the history of the town and its more notable residents, and from here it is a short stroll down the cobbled alleyway to the magnificent parish Church of St Mary, where Seckford was buried in 1587.

Seckford naturally features prominently in the museum, along with the painter Thomas Churchyard, the map-maker Isaac Johnson and the poet Edward Fitzgerald. 'Old Fitz' was

something of an eccentric and, for the most part, fairly reclusive. He loved Woodbridge and particularly the River Deben, where he often sailed in his little boat *Scandal*.

Woodbridge is lucky enough to have two marvellous mills, both in working order, and both great attractions for the visitor. The weather-boarded **Tide Mill**, standing bright and white on the quayside close to the town centre, dates from the late 18th century (though the site was mentioned 600 years previously)

Melton Road, Melton, Woodbridge, Suffolk IP12 1NZ
Tel: 01394 386232

Melton Antiques holds an eclectic mix of small decorative items, silver and collectibles including Victoriana such as a fine bird cage from 1880 and Victorian sewing accessories, glass and jewellery amidst a constantly changing selection of wonderful pieces, any of which would make an attractive addition to any home. Owner Anna Harvey-Jones established this thriving concern in 1981, turning her hobby into a successful business.

and worked by the power of the tide until 1957. It has been meticulously restored and the waterwheel still turns, fed by a recently created pond which replaced the original huge mill pond when it was turned into a marina. **Buttrum's Mill**, named after the last miller, is a tower mill standing just off the A12 by-pass a mile west of the town centre. She is a marvellous sight, and her six storeys make her the tallest surviving tower mill in Suffolk. There is a ground-floor display of the history and workings of the mill.

Many of the town's streets are traffic-free, so shopping is a real pleasure, and the town has a good variety of pubs and restaurants.

AROUND WOODBRIDGE

WICKHAM MARKET

5 miles N of Woodbridge off the A12

Places to see in this straggling village are a picturesque **Watermill** by the River Deben and **All Saints Church**, whose 137' octagonal tower has a little roof to shelter the bell. At Boulge, a couple of miles southwest of Wickham Market, is the grave of Edward Fitzgerald, whose free translation of *The Rubaiyat of Omar Khayyam* from the Persian is an English masterpiece. Many lines from the Rubaiyat have become almost universally known - "a jug of wine, a loaf of bread, and thou beside me in the wilderness...."; "The moving finger writes, and having writ moves on". Fitzgerald was educated at Trinity College, Cambridge, where he struck up a lifelong friendship with Thackeray. He retired to the quiet country life at Woodbridge, where he led a mainly solitary life, though he had many friends, including Alfred, Lord Tennyson and Thomas Carlyle. The Rubaiyat was published in 1859, but attracted very little attention until it was 'discovered' by Dante Gabriel Rossetti, and later by Algernon Swinburne. Tradition has it that on his grave is a rose bush grown from one on Omar Khayyam's grave in Iran.

EASTON

5 miles N of Woodbridge off the B1078

A scenic drive leads to the lovely village of Easton, one of the most colourful, flower-bedecked places in the county. A remarkable sight to the west of the village is the 2-mile-long crinkle-crankle wall that surrounds **Easton Park**. This extraordinary type of wall, also known as a ribbon wall, wavers snake-like in and out and is much stronger than if it were straight. This particular wall, said to be the world's longest, was built by Lord of the Manor the Earl of Rochford in the 1820s.

Tucked away three miles off the A12 in the beautiful Deben valley, **Easton Park Farm** is one of Suffolk's greatest attractions. 2001 sees its 28th year, and in that time more than a million visitors have passed through the gates to have a great day out and to leave knowing a lot more about the ways of the countryside than when they arrived. It's a marvellous place to bring the family, as the children can have endless fun feeding and making friends with the little animals in Pets Paddock, riding ponies or simply running around in the adventure playground. The showpiece of the park is the Victorian dairy, an ornate octagonal building, while the Dairy Centre is contrastingly modern, with walkways over the top of the stalls and a viewing gallery over the milking parlour.

PARHAM

8 miles N of Woodbridge on the B1116

Parham Airfield (also known as Framlingham) is now agricultural land, but in the control tower and a hut is a museum of the 390th Bomb Group of the USAAF. Volunteers worked on the restoration since 1976 and their efforts were rewarded when in 1991 the museum was chosen as the Suffolk Museum of the Year. The airfield was built for the RAF in 1942 but in the following year was taken over by the USAAF, who flew missions in Flying Fortresses. One of these aircraft crashed nearby shortly after take-off and the museum includes photographs of the event, along with uniforms, weapons and parts of a Liberator bomber that came to grief over Blythburgh.

UFFORD

4 miles N of Woodbridge off the A12

Pride of place in a village that takes its name from Uffa (or Wuffa), the founder of the leading Anglo-Saxon dynasty, goes to the 13th century church. The font cover, which telescopes from five feet to eighteen feet in height, is a masterpiece of craftsmanship, its elaborate carving crowned by a pelican. Many 15th century benches have survived but Dowsing smashed the organ and most of the stained glass - what's there now is mainly Victorian, some of it a copy of 15th century work at All Souls College, Oxford. Ufford is where the Suffolk Punch originated, Crisp's 404 being, in 1768, the progenitor of the breed.

BREDFIELD

3 miles N of Woodbridge off the A12

The funny thing about Bredfield is that sometimes nothing happens, and a plaque on the wall of the village pub actually records nothing at all happening on a day in 1742. On a day in 1809, however, something did happen: Edward Fitzgerald was born (see under Wickham Market). Something else happened in 1953: a wrought-iron canopy with a golden crown, made at the village forge, was put on the crossroads pump to celebrate Queen Elizabeth II's coronation.

SUTTON HOO

1 mile E of Woodbridge off the B1083

A mile or so east of Woodbridge on the opposite bank of the Deben is the **Sutton Hoo Burial Site**, a group of a dozen grassy barrows which hit the headlines in 1939. Excavations brought to light the outline of an 80-foot long Anglo-Saxon ship, filled with one of the greatest hoards of treasure ever discovered in Britain. The priceless find includes gold coins and ornaments, silverware, weapons and armoury, drinking horns and leather cups; the bulk of the find is in the British Museum, but there are exhibitions, replicas and plenty of other interest at the site. Research continues, and it is now believed that the ship was the burial place of the pagan kings of East Anglia, notably Raedwald, of the Wuffinga dynasty, who was King of East Anglia from about 610 to 625. The National Trust has undertaken a multi-million pound project to allow visitors close access to the site while balancing the needs of conservation. A circular route, including a viewing platform above the ship burial mound, caters for the many thousands of visitors annually attracted to the site, and new buildings house an exhibition whose centrepiece is a re-creation of the burial chamber.

RENDLESHAM

5 miles NE of Woodbridge on the A1152

Rendlesham Forest, part of the Forest of Aldewood, was ravaged by the great hurricane of October 1987 but seven years before that, on Christmas night 1980, another visitation had occurred. Security guards at RAF Woodbridge, at that time a front line NATO base, spotted strange lights in the forest and went to investigate. They came upon a 9-foot high triangular object with a series of lights around it. As they approached, it did what all good UFOs do and flew off before it could be photographed. The next day the guards returned to the spot where it had landed and found three depressions in the ground. The UFO was apparently sighted again two days later and security in the area was tightened. No explanation has ever been forthcoming about the incident, but interest in it continues and from time to time guided walks to the landing site are arranged.

Victorian Rendlesham Hall no longer exists, but one of its lodges is described by Pevsner as one of the most remarkable follies in the county. **Woodbridge Lodge**, otherwise fairly modest, has a tall

chimney supported by vast flying buttresses that are totally out of proportion, creating a site that is both imposing and slightly comical.

BUTLEY

5 miles NE of Woodbridge on the B1084

At the northern edge of Rendlesham Forest, the village has a splendid 14th century gatehouse, all that remains of **Butley Priory**, an Augustinian priory founded by Ranulf de Glanville in 1171. The gatehouse is, by itself, a fairly imposing building, with some interesting flintwork on the north facade (1320) and baronial carvings. Butley still has a **Working Mill**, remarkable for its fine Regency porch, and the parish church is Norman, with a 14th century tower.

There are some splendid country walks here, notably by **Staverton Thicks**, which has a deer park and woods of oak and holly. The oldest trees date back more than 400 years. Butley Clumps is an avenue of beech trees planted in clumps of four, with a pine tree at the centre of each clump - the technical term for such an arrangement is a quincunx. Butley was long renowned for its oysters, and the beds have recently been revived.

ORFORD

12 miles E of Woodbridge at the end of the B1084

Without doubt one of the most charming and interesting of all the places in Suffolk, with something to please everyone, from delightful old fishermen's cottages and ancient, atmospheric pubs to one of the oldest castles in the country. The ruins of **Orford Castle**, one of the most important castles in medieval England, are a most impressive sight, even though the keep is all that remains of the original building commissioned by Henry II in 1165. The walls of the keep are 10-feet deep, and behind them are many rooms and passages in a remarkable state of preservation. Visitors can hear the story of the Orford Merman, a legendary man of the sea who was for a while held in captivity at the castle. A climb up the spiral staircase to the top provides splendid views out over Orford Ness.

Orford

St Bartholomew's Church was built at the same time, though the present church dates from the 14th century. A wonderful sight at night when floodlit, the church is regularly used for the performance of concerts and recitals, and many of Benjamin Britten's works were first heard here, including *Noye's Fludde*, based on the Chester miracle play, and the three one-act church parables. At the east end lie the still-splendid Norman remains, all that is left of the original chancel.

These two grand buildings indicate that Orford was a very important town at one time. Indeed it was once a thriving port, but the steadily growing shingle bank of Orford Ness gradually cut it off from the sea, and down the years its appeal has changed. The sea may have gone, but the river is still there, and in summer the quayside is alive with yachts and pleasure craft. On the other side of the river is **Orford Ness**, the largest vegetated shingle spit in England which is home to a variety of rare flora and fauna. The lighthouse marks the most easterly point in Britain (jointly with Lowestoft).

Access to the spit, which is in the hands of the National Trust, is by ferry from Orford quay only. For many years the ness was out of bounds to the public, being used for various military purposes, including pre-war radar research under Sir Robert Watson-Watt. Boat trips also leave Orford quay for the RSPB reserve of **Havergate Island**, haunt of avocet and tern (the former returned in 1947 after being long absent).

RICHARDSON'S SMOKEHOUSE

Baker's Lane, Orford, Suffolk IP12 2LH
Tel/Fax: 01394 450103

Richardson's Smokehouse is the place to find traditionally cured, meats, game, poultry and fish. Among the gastronomic delights for sale from this charming shop are molasses-coated hams, chicken, duck, guinea fowl, pheasant, pigeon, kippers, salmon, trout, mackerel, mature English cheddar, Stilton and exquisite pates. The art of long, slow smoking using only oak wood is the secret of their

delicious, moist succulence. No preservatives, dyes or additives are used; only pure salt is added to the wholesome goodness of the food here.

Other specialities include ham roasted in cider and a range of mouth-watering sausages such as pork and garlic, pork and venison and pork and apple. This thriving business has been going strong since 1986, and is set in a side lane off the Main Square in Orford, with a small serving area, kitchens to the rear, and the adjoining brickbuilt smoke rooms, one hot - for the game and some fish - and one cold - for the haddock, prawns, cheese and other delicacies. For a taste of high quality food at very reasonable prices, prepared in a simple and natural way, look no further.

Open: Seven days a week, Easter to end September 9.30-5; October to Easter 10-4. Wednesdays 9.30-2.45. Telephone orders are welcome, and there's a mail order service on request.

Back in the market square are a handsome town hall, two pubs with a fair quota of smuggling tales, a well-loved restaurant serving Butley oysters and a smokehouse where kippers, salmon, trout, ham, sausages, chicken and even garlic are smoked over Suffolk oak.

BAWDSEY

7 miles SE of Woodbridge on the B1083

The B1083 runs from Woodbridge through farming country and several villages (Sutton, Shottisham, Alderton) to Bawdsey, beyond which lie the mouth of the River Deben, the end of the Suffolk Coastal Path, and the ferry to Felixstowe. The late-Victorian **Bawdsey Manor** was taken over by the Government and became the centre for radar development

when Orford Ness was deemed unsuitable. By the beginning of World War II there were two dozen secret radar stations in Britain and radar HQ moved to Dundee from Bawdsey. The manor is now a leisure centre.

HOLLESLEY

5 miles SE of Woodbridge off the B1083

The Deben and the Ore turn this part of Suffolk almost into a peninsula and on the seaward side lie **Hollesley** and **Shingle Street**. The latter stands up on a shingle bank at the entrance to the Ore and comprises a row of little houses, a coastguard cottage and a Martello Tower. Its very isolation is an attraction, and the sight of the sea rushing into and out of the river is worth the journey.

Much of Suffolk's character comes from its rivers, and in the part of the county surrounding Ipswich, the Orwell and the Stour mark the boundaries of the Shotley Peninsula. Much of the countryside is largely unspoilt, with wide-open spaces between scattered villages. The relative flatness of Suffolk gives every encouragement for motorists to leave their machines, and the

Timbered House, Bildeston

peninsula, still relatively peaceful, is ideal for a spot of walking or cycling or boating. Southeast of Ipswich, the peninsula created by the River Deben and the River Orwell is one of the prettiest areas in Suffolk, its winding lanes leading through a delightful series of quiet rural villages and colourful riverside communities.

John Constable, England's greatest landscape painter, was born at East Bergholt in 1776 and remained at heart a Suffolk man throughout his life. He painted the occasional portrait and even attempted a couple of religious works, but he concentrated almost entirely on the scenes that he knew and loved as a boy. The Suffolk tradition of painting continues to this day, with many artists drawn particularly to the coast and to the beautiful Constable country.

Cambridgeshire, Norfolk, the A134 and the A14 frame the northern part of West Suffolk, which includes Bury St Edmunds, a gem of a town that is rich in archaeological treasures and places of religious and historical interest, and Newmarket, one of the major centres of the horseracing world. Between and above them are

Willy Lotts Cottage, Flatford Mill

picturesque villages, bustling market towns, rich farming countryside, the fens, and the expanse of sandy heath and pine forest that is Breckland.

The area south and west of Bury towards the Essex border contains some of Suffolk's most attractive and peaceful countryside. The beauty is largely unspoilt and the motorist will come upon a succession of picturesque villages, historic churches, stately homes, heritage centres and nature reserves. In the south, along the River Stour, stand the historic wool towns of Long Melford, Cavendish and Clare.

LOCATOR MAP

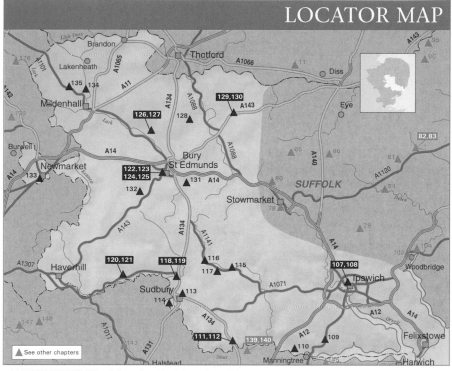

© MAPS IN MINUTES ™ 2001   © Crown Copyright, Ordnance Survey 2001

ADVERTISERS AND PLACES OF INTEREST

IPSWICH

Ipswich is renowned as the birthplace of Cardinal Wolsey, but the story of Suffolk's county town starts very much earlier. It has been a port since the time of the Roman occupation and by the 7th century the Anglo-Saxons had expanded it into the largest port in the country. King John granted a civic charter in 1200, confirming the townspeople's right to their own laws and administration, and for several centuries the town prospered as a port exporting wool, textiles and agricultural products.

Thomas Wolsey arrived on the scene in 1475, the son of a wealthy butcher and grazier. Educated at Magdalen College, Oxford, he was ordained a priest in 1498 and rose quickly in influence, becoming chaplain to Henry VII and then Archbishop of York, a cardinal and Lord Chancellor under Henry VIII. He was quite indispensable to the king and had charge of foreign policy as well as powerful sway over judicial institutions. He also managed to amass enormous wealth, enabling him to found a grammar school in Ipswich and Cardinal's College (later Christ Church) in Oxford. Wolsey had long been hated by certain nobles for his low birth and arrogance, and they were easily able to turn Henry against him when his attempts to secure an annulment from the Pope of the king's marriage to Catherine of Aragon met with failure. Stripped of most of his offices following a charge of overstepping his authority as a legate, he was later charged with treason but died while travelling from York to London to face the king. His death put an end to his plans for the grammar school, and all that remains now is a red-brick gateway.

FRIARS TO FLYERS

St Edmund House, County Hall, Ipswich, Suffolk IP4 1LZ
Tel: 01473 583179 Fax: 01473 230078
e-mail: susan.brookes@et.suffolkcc.gov.uk
website: www.heartofsuffolk.com

Friars to Flyers is a unique initiative that promotes several outstanding attractions, including historic friaries and priories, abbeys and colleges, medieval moats and Second World War airfields. A good way to start is with Laxfield and District Museum, for the background on Suffolk's religious power bases of the past, continuing on to the impressive South Elmham Hall, a former Bishop's Palace, with the nearby atmospheric ruins of the Minster. St Mary's Church in Bungay was founded as a nunnery in 1183. Wingfield Old College was a community of priests in the 14th century, while the small monastery of Rumburgh Priory was established just before the Norman Conquest. The "museum of moats" at The Lanman Museum inside Framlingham Castle is the starting point for an exploration of the many fine moats in the region, which include those at Dennington Place, St Peter's Hall and Tannington Hall. Over 30 airfields were built in the county during the Second World War, including those at Debach, Eye, Halesworth, Horham, Parham and Thorpe Abbotts. A good way to begin a tour of these is from the Norfolk and Suffolk Aviation Museum near Bungay.

Events throughout the year at these wonderful attractions include aviation enthusiasts' days, military vehicle rallies, tours, walks and other fun and educational ways to explore the past, for visitors of all ages. There's free admission to most museums, though donations are always most welcome. Friars to Flyers is funded by the European Union structural fund, East of England Development Agency and Suffolk County Council.

St Peter's Dock, Ipswich

beers. In Grimwade Street stands **Peter's Ice Cream Factory**, built 100 years ago. Guided tours take place several times a day, and there's a museum, restaurant and shop. Victorian enterprise depleted the older buildings, but a number survive, notably the Tudor houses where Wolsey was born, the **Ancient House** with its wonderful pargeting, and a dozen medieval churches. **St Margaret's** is the finest of these, boasting some very splendid flintwork and a double hammerbeam roof.

When the cloth market fell into decline in the 17th century a respite followed in the next century, when the town was a food distribution port during the Napoleonic Wars. At the beginning of the 19th century the risk from silting was becoming acute at a time when trade was improving and industries were springing up. The **Wet Dock**, constructed in 1842, solved the silting problem and, with the railway arriving shortly after, Ipswich could once more look forward to a safe future. The Victorians were responsible for considerable development and symbols of their civic pride include the handsome Old Custom House by the Wet Dock, the Town Hall and the splendid **Tolly Cobbold Brewery**, rebuilt at the end of the 19th century, 150 years after brewing started on the site. Guided tours take visitors through the whole brewing process and start in the Bottlers Room, which boasts the country's largest collection of commemorative bottled

The Ancient House, Ipswich

Christchurch Mansion is a beautiful Tudor home standing in a 65-acre park. Furnished as an English country house, it contains a major collection of works by Constable and Gainsborough and many other paintings, prints and sculptures by Suffolk artists from the 17th century on.

The town's main **Museum** is in a Victorian building in the High Street. Displays include a natural history gallery, a wildlife gallery complete with a model of a mammoth, a reconstruction of a Roman villa and replicas of Sutton Hoo treasures. A recent addition is a display of elaborately carved timbers from the homes of wealthy 17th century merchants.

In a former trolleybus depot on Cobham Road is the **Ipswich Transport Museum**, a fascinating collection of vehicles, from prams to fire engines, all made or used around Ipswich (see below).

On the outskirts of town, signposted from Nacton Road, is **Orwell Country Park**, a 150-acre site of wood, heath and reedbeds by the Orwell estuary. At this point the river is crossed by the imposing Orwell Bridge, a graceful construction in pre-stressed concrete that was completed in 1982 and is almost a mile in length. There are three lowland heath areas within Ipswich's boundaries: Bixley Heath, Rushmore Common and Pipers Vale by the bridge.

Notables from the world of the arts with Ipswich connections include Thomas Gainsborough, who got his first major commissions here to paint portraits of local people; David Garrick, the renowned actor-manager, who made his debut here in 1741 as Aboan in Thomas Southerne's *Oroonoko*; and the peripatetic Charles Dickens, who stayed at the Great White Horse while still a young reporter

IPSWICH TRANSPORT MUSEUM

Old Trolleybus Depot, Cobham Road,
Ipswich, Suffolk IP3 9JD
Tel: 01473 715666
website: www.ipswichtransportmuseum.co.uk

The **Ipswich Transport Museum** is dedicated to preserving the transport and engineering heritage of the Ipswich area. The collection is believed to be the largest in the country devoted to just one area and is an entirely volunteer run and funded museum, housed in a former trolleybus depot. The building has been altered to include a gift shop, tearoom and outdoor picnic area.

Among the more unusual exhibits are a monorail for transporting spoil, a road sweeper conversion from a Morris car, a petrol roller for rolling grass runways, a horse drawn tower wagon for maintaining overhead wires, the oldest trolleybus in the world (Ipswich no. 2, built by Railless in 1923), and a collection of wheelchairs. There are additional exhibition rooms covering air, water and rail transport of the Ipswich area, with exhibits and photographs. The Ipswich area was the hub of experimentation in the 1930's with research bases for fixed wing aircraft, seaplanes and bombing ranges. Radar was developed nearby at Bawdsey Manor.

Ipswich was an engineering town throughout the 19th and 20th centuries. The museum commemorates this heritage through its collection of Ipswich-made exhibits, which include lawnmowers, mobile cranes, fork lift trucks and factory trucks. Photographs depict the huge Walking Draglines built in Ipswich, weighing up to 2,000 tons.

with the Morning Chronicle. Soon afterwards, he featured the tavern in *The Pickwick Papers* as the place where Mr Pickwick wanders inadvertently into a lady's bedroom. Sir V S Pritchett was born in Ipswich, while Enid Blyton trained as a kindergarten teacher at Ipswich High School. Ipswich caters well for the young, with plenty of sports facilities. They also, of course, have a football team of note, Ipswich Town, nicknamed the "Super Blues". The **Ipswich Town Experience** includes a stadium tour and relates the history of the team from 1878 to the day in May at Wembley 2000 when the whole county celebrated the team winning the Divison 1 Play-off Final.

AROUND IPSWICH

NACTON
4 miles SE of Ipswich off the A14

South of Nacton's medieval church lies **Orwell Park House**, which was built in the 18th century by Admiral Edward Vernon, sometime Member of Parliament for Ipswich. The admiral, who had won an important victory over the Spanish in the War of Jenkins' Ear, was known to his men as Old Grog, because of his habit of wearing a cloak of coarse grogram cloth. His nickname passed into the language when he ordered that the rum ration dished out daily to sailors should be diluted with water to combat the drunkenness that was rife in the service. That was in 1740, and a ration of 'grog' was officially issued to sailors until 1970.

George Tomline bought the splendid house in 1857 and made it even more splendid, adding a conservatory, a ballroom and towers. He also changed the façade to handsome Georgian. The house became the setting for some of the grandest shooting parties ever seen in

this part of the world, and such was the power of the Tomlines that they were able to move the village away from the house to its present site.

Nacton picnic site in Shore Lane (signposted from the village) commands wonderful views of the Orwell and is a prime spot in winter for birdwatchers. The birds feed very well off the mud flats.

LEVINGTON
5 miles SE of Ipswich off the A14

A pretty village on the banks of the Orwell. Fisons established a factory here in 1956 and developed the now famous "Levington Compost". On the foreshore below the village is an extensive marina which has brought an extra bustle to the area. The coastal footpath along the bank of the Orwell leads across the nature reserve of Trimley Marshes and on to Felixstowe.

TRIMLEY ST MARY & TRIMLEY ST MARTIN
6 miles SE of Ipswich off the A14

Twin villages with two churches in the same churchyard. The Cavendish family were famous Trimley residents, their best known member being the adventurer Thomas Cavendish. In 1590 he became the second man to sail round the world and two years later he died on another voyage. He is depicted on the village sign.

Trimley Marshes were created from farmland and comprise grazing marsh, reed beds and wetland home to an abundance of interesting plant life and many species of wildfowl, waders and migrant birds. Access is on foot from Trimley St Mary.

NEWBOURNE
7 miles E of Ipswich off the A12

A small miracle occurred here on the night of the hurricane of October 1987. One wall of the ancient **St Mary's**

Church was blown out and with it the stained glass, which shattered into fragments. One piece, showing the face of Christ, was found undamaged and was later incorporated into the rebuilt wall. Two remarkable inhabitants of Newbourne were the Page brothers, who both stood over 7 feet tall; they enjoyed a career touring the fairs and are buried in Newbourne churchyard.

WALDRINGFIELD

7 miles E of Ipswich off the A12

Waldringfield lies on a particularly beautiful stretch of the Deben estuary, and the waterfront is largely given over to leisure boating and cruising. The quay was once busy with barges, many of them laden with coprolite. This fossilised dung, the forerunner of fertiliser, was found in great abundance in and around Waldringfield, and a number of exhausted pits can still be seen.

FELIXSTOWE

12 miles SE of Ipswich off the A14

Until the early 17th century Felixstowe was a little known village of no great importance, but it was the good Colonel Tomline of Orwell Park who put it on the map by creating a port to rival its near neighbour Harwich. He also started work on the Ipswich-Felixstowe railway (with a stop at Nacton for the grand parties), and 1887 saw the completion of both projects. Tomline also developed the resort aspects of Felixstowe, rivalling the amenities of Dovercourt, and when he died in 1887 most of his dreams had become reality. (He was, incidentally, cremated, one of the first in the county to be so disposed of in the modern era.) What he didn't live to see was the pier, opened in 1904 and still in use. The town received a further boost when the Empress of Germany paid a visit in 1891.

The town has suffered a number of ups and during the 20th century, but still thrives as one of England's busiest ports, having been much extended in the 1960s. It is the largest container port in the UK and the fourth largest in Europe; over 2,500 are directly employed in the port, and perhaps 10,000 in port-related industries. The resort is strung out round a wide, gently curving bay, where the long seafront road is prettified by trim lawns and gardens.

The **Martello Tower** is a noted landmark, as is the **Pier**, which was once long enough to merit an electric tramway. It was shortened as a security measure during the Second World War, a precaution applied to many east coast piers. All the usual attractions are provided for the holidaymaker, and a very unusual one. This is the **Felixstowe**

Sailing at Felixstowe

Water Clock, a curious piece assembled from dozens of industrial bits and pieces.

The original fishing hamlet from which the Victorian resort was developed lies beyond a golf course north of the town. This is **Felixstowe Ferry**, a cluster of holiday homes, an inn, a boatyard, fishing sheds, a Martello Tower and a new Millennium site still being developed. The sailing club is involved mainly with dinghy racing and the whole place becomes a hive of activity during the class meetings. A ferry takes foot passengers (plus bicycles) across to Bawdsey.

At the southernmost tip of the peninsula is Landguard Point, where a nature reserve supports rare plants and migrating birds.

Just north on this shingle bank is **Landguard Fort**, built in 1718 (replacing an earlier construction) to protect

Harwich harbour and now home to **Felixstowe Museum**. The museum is actually housed in the Ravelin Block (1878), which was used as a mine storage depot by the army when a mine barrier was laid across the Orwell in World War I. A fascinating variety of exhibits includes local history, model aircraft and model paddle steamers, Roman coins and the history of the fort itself, which was the scene of the last invasion of English soil, by the Dutch in 1667. Beyond the fort is an excellent viewing point for watching the comings and goings of the ships.

FRESTON

3 miles S of Ipswich off the B1080

A 4,000-year-old archaeological site was revealed by aerial photography in this ancient village on the south bank of the Orwell. It is well worth visiting for some fine old buildings and some curiosities. The most curious and best known of

ROOKERY FARM SHOP

Tattingstone, Ipswich, Suffolk IP9 2LU
Tel: 01473 327220
website: www.rookeryfarm.co.uk

Located just a few miles southeast of Tattingstone on the A137, **Rookery Farm Shop** is a wonderful place well worth seeking out, offering as it does an impressive variety of the freshest, most delicious home-grown and local produce according to season. Fresh, seasonal, local fruits, vegetables and other goods offer great quality and value to discerning customers.

Set in an attractive 18th century oak farm building, this charming and friendly shop is a delight just to visit; laid out with chequered-clothed tables laden with all manner of tempting seasonal fruit and vegetables, fruit cream ices, farmhouse cakes and biscuits, free-range eggs, preserves, chutneys,

pickles and honey, farm-pressed fruit juices, meats from local farms, local dairy produce, and fresh flowers. Owner Sarah Caldwell opened the shop in June 1998, and it has gone from strength to strength. Some of her 70-plus suppliers are award winners in competitions run by the National Farmers' Union, and Sarah is a member of the Farm Retail Association and Tastes of Anglia, an assurance of quality and service. Open: Tuesday to Saturday 10 a.m. - 5.30 p.m.; Sundays 10 a.m. - 1 p.m.

The adjoining field is also available for up to five touring caravans.

these buildings is the six-storey **Tudor Tower** by the river in Freston Park (it's actually best viewed from across the river). The red-brick house, built around 1570, has just six rooms, one per storey. It might be a folly, but it was probably put up as a lookout tower to warn of enemies sailing up the river. The nicest theory is that it was built for Ellen, daughter of Lord Freston, to study a different subject each day, progressing floor by floor up the tower (and with Sundays off, presumably).

House by the Waterside, Pin Mill

TATTINGSTONE

4 miles S of Ipswich off the A137

Tattingstone Wonder, on the road between Tattingstone and Stutton, looks like a church from the front, but it isn't. It was built by a local landowner to provide accommodation for estate workers. He presumably preferred to look at a church from his mansion than some plain little cottages. Tattingstone lies at the western edge of **Alton Water**, a vast man-made lake created as a reservoir in the late 1970s. A footpath runs round the perimeter, and there's a wildlife sanctuary. On the water itself all sorts of leisure activities are on offer, including angling, sailing and windsurfing.

CHELMONDISTON

5 miles S of Ipswich on the B1456

The church here is modern, but incorporates some parts of the original building, which was destroyed by a flying bomb in 1944. In the same parish is the tiny riverside community of **Pin Mill**, a well-known beauty spot and sailing centre. The river views are particularly lovely at this point, and it's also a favourite place for woodland and heathland walks. Pin Mill was once a major manufacturer of barges and those imposing craft can still be seen sharing the river with sailing boats and pleasure craft. Each year veteran barges gather for a race that starts here at Buttermans Bay and ends at Harwich. Arthur Ransome, author of *Swallows and Amazons*, stayed in Pin Mill. In fact he had boats built here and one of his books *We Didn't Mean to Go to Sea* starts aboard a yacht moored at the local quay.

ERWARTON

6 miles S of Ipswich off the B1456

An impressive red-brick Jacobean gatehouse with a rounded arch, buttresses and pinnacles is part of **Erwarton Hall**, the family home of the Calthorpes. Anne Boleyn was the niece of Philip Calthorpe and visited as a child and as queen. Just before her execution Anne apparently requested that her heart be buried in the family vault at St Mary's Church. A casket in the shape of a heart was found there in 1836 and when it was opened was found to contain dust. It was resealed and laid in the Lady Chapel.

SHOTLEY

8 miles S of Ipswich on the B1456

Right at the end of the peninsula, with the Orwell on one side and the Stour on the other, Shotley is best known as the home of **HMS Ganges**, where generations of sailors received their training. The main feature is the 142 ft mast up which trainees would shin at the passing-out ceremony. A small museum records the history of the establishment from 1905 to 1976, when it became a policy academy. At the very tip is a large marina where a classic boat festival is an annual occasion.

HINTLESHAM

7 miles W of Ipswich on the A1071

Hintlesham's glory is the magnificent **Hintlesham Hall** dating from the 1570s, when it was the home of the Timperley family. It was considerably altered during the 18th century, when it acquired its splendid Georgian façade. For some years the hall was owned by the celebrated chef Robert Carrier, who developed it into the county's leading restaurant.

CONSTABLE COUNTRY

England's greatest landscape painter was born at East Bergholt in 1776 and remained at heart a Suffolk man throughout his life. His father, Golding Constable, was a wealthy man who owned both Flatford Mill and Dedham Mill, the latter on the Essex side of the Stour. The river was a major source of inspiration to the young John Constable, and his constant involvement in country matters gave him an expert knowledge of the elements and a keen eye for the details of nature. He was later to declare "I associate my careless boyhood with all that lies on the banks of the Stour. Those scenes made me a painter and I am

grateful." That interest in painting developed early and was fostered by his friendship with John Dunthorne, a local plumber and amateur artist. He became a probationer at the Royal Academy Schools in 1799 and over the following years developed the technical skills to match his powers of observation. He painted the occasional portrait and even attempted a couple of religious works, but he concentrated almost entirely on the scenes that he knew and loved as a boy.

The most significant works of the earlier years were the numerous sketches in oil which were forerunners of the major paintings of Constable's mature years. He had exhibited at the Royal Academy every year since 1802, but it was not until 1817 that the first of his important canvases, *Flatford Mill on the River Stour*, was hung. This was succeeded by the six large paintings which became

Artist, Flatford Mill

his best known works. These were all set on a short stretch of the Stour, and all except *The Hay Wain* show barges at work. These broad, flat-bottomed craft were displayed in scenes remarkable for the realism of the colours, the effects of light and water and, above all, the beautiful depiction of clouds. His fellow-artist Fuseli declared that whenever he saw a Constable painting

Georgian House, East Bergholt

he felt the need to reach for his coat and umbrella. Though more realistic than anything that preceded them, Constable's paintings were never lacking soul, and his work was much admired by the painters of the French Romantic School. One of the best-known quotations from the man himself reveal much about his aims and philosophy:

"I never saw any ugly thing in my life; in fact, whatever may be the shape of an object, light, shade or perspective can always make it beautiful."

At the time of his death in 1837, Constable's reputation at home was relatively modest, though he had many followers and admirers in France. Awareness and understanding of his unique talent grew in the ensuing years, and his place as England's foremost landscape painter is rarely disputed.

The Suffolk tradition of painting continues to this day, with many artists drawn particularly to Walberswick and the beautiful Constable country. That beauty is not always easy to appreciate when crowds throng through the Stour valley at summer weekends, but at other times the peace and beauty are much as they were in Constable's day.

BRANTHAM
8 miles SW of Ipswich on the A137

Brantham is also known as 'Burnt Village' - possibly because it was sacked during a Danish invasion 1,000 years ago. The Church of St Michael owns one of the only two known religious paintings by Constable, *Christ Blessing the Children*, which he executed in the style of the American painter Benjamin West. It is kept in safety in Ipswich Museum. Just off the junction of the A137 and the B1070 is Cattawade picnic site, a small area on the edge of the Stour estuary. It's a good spot for birdwatching, and redshanks, lapwings and oystercatchers all breed on the well-known **Cattawade Marshes**. Fishing and canoeing are available, and there are public footpaths to Flatford Mill.

EAST BERGHOLT
8 miles SW of Ipswich on the B1070

Narrow lanes lead to this picturesque and much visited little village. The **Constable Country Trail** starts here, where the painter was born, and passes through Flatford Mill and on to Dedham in Essex. The actual house where he was born no longer stands, but the site is marked by a plaque on the fence of its successor, a private house called Constables. A little further along Church Street is **Moss Cottage**, which Constable once used as his studio. **St Mary's Church** is one of the many grand churches built with the wealth brought by the wool trade. This one should have been even grander, with a tower to rival that of Dedham across the river. The story goes that Cardinal Wolsey pledged the money to build the tower but fell from grace before the funds were forthcoming. The tower got no further than did his college in Ipswich, but a bellcage constructed in the churchyard as a temporary house for the bells became their permanent home, which it remains to this day. In this unique timber-framed structure the massive bells hang upside down and are rung by hand by pulling on the wooden shoulder stocks; an arduous task, as the five bells are among the heaviest in England.

The church is naturally something of a shrine to Constable, his family and his friends. There are memorial windows to the artist and to his beloved wife Maria Bicknell, who bore him seven children and whose early death was an enormous blow to him. His parents, to whom he was clearly devoted, and his old friend Willy Lott, whose cottage is featured famously in *The Hay Wain*, are buried in the churchyard.

East Bergholt has an interesting mix of houses, some dating back as far as the 14th century. One of the grandest is **Stour House**, once the home of Randolph Churchill. Its gardens are open to the public, as is **East Bergholt Place Garden** on the B1070.

A leafy lane leads south from the village to the Stour, where two of Constable's favourite subjects, **Flatford Mill** and **Willy Lott's Cottage**, both looking much as they did when he

(Continued page 167)

Flatford Mill Field Centre

Field Studies Council, Flatford Mill, East Bergholt, Suffolk, CO7 6UL
Tel: 01206 298283 Fax: 01206 298892
e-mail: fsc.flatford@ukonline.co.uk

Flatford Mill Field Centre lies at the heart of 'Constable Country', on the banks of the River Stour near the Suffolk-Essex border. The Field Centre buildings (which include the Mill and Willy Lott's House) are leased by the Field Studies Council from the National Trust and are instantly recognisable since they feature in many paintings by John Constable. The rich mosaic of lowland landscapes, wildlife habitats and places of historic interest in this beautiful part of East Anglia are all reflected in the Centre's extensive programme of environmental, art and craft 'leisure learning' courses.

Over 180 short courses, lasting from two to seven days, are offered each year from January through to December. 'Flowers of Woodlands and Hedgerows', 'Watercolour for Absolute Beginners', 'Suffolk's Medieval Houses', 'Gardening for Wildlife' and 'Family Birdwatching' are typical of the variety of courses on offer over just a single weekend. You can browse the full programme by visiting the FSC website at www.field-studies-council.org or by contacting Flatford Mill directly to ask for the current Course Guide. The Field Centre is at the end of a lane with no through traffic and offers resident and non resident visitors on courses a much sought-after sense of tranquillity to complement a wonderful learning environment. Accommodation in twin, family and sole occupancy rooms makes full use of the historic buildings, where Edward Jackson and his Centre Staff create a relaxed and informal atmosphere to make your stay a special experience.

WALK 7

Constable Country – Flatford and East Bergholt

Start	East Bergholt
Distance	5½ miles (8.9km)
Approximate time	2½ hours
Parking	Car park at village centre
Refreshments	Pubs and tearooms at East Bergholt and Flatford
Ordnance Survey maps	Landrangers 168 (Colchester, Halstead & Maldon) and 169 (Ipswich & The Naze, Clacton-on-Sea), Explorer 196 (Sudbury, Hadleigh & Dedham Vale)

John Constable, the most famous painter of the English landscape, grew up in the lovely surroundings of the Stour valley, which forms the boundary between Suffolk and Essex. Although Constable died more than 150 years ago, much of the landscape he painted survives almost unaltered and is instantly recognisable.

Turn right out of the car park in East Bergholt and walk past the Red Lion and the post office. Turn right into the lane by the post office – Constable's early studio is the building on the other side of the road and belongs to the East Bergholt Society, having been purchased in 1802, thirty-five years before the painter's death. Pass the Congregational church and a cemetery and after a gate into Vale Farm follow the fence to the left, on a path descending to a footbridge. Cross the stream and a driveway to take the path climbing through a pasture on the other side. A classic view of Dedham Vale is revealed at the top, one that featured in several of Constable's works. To the left is Dedham, with the great tower of the church the dominating feature. Ahead is Stratford St Mary and its smaller church with the A12 beyond, a modern feature that mars the scene but does not spoil it.

Turn left at the footpath junction **A** to take a sunken footpath signposted to

Dedham Road. In winter the path serves as the bed of a stream. Turn left again at the bottom of this path **B** on to a field-edge path that is soon enclosed by fences on each side and rapidly growing young trees. Turn right and then left to cross the stream again, which flows down from Vale Farm. Climb a stile and walk a few yards along the end of Fishpond Wood. After another stile the path follows the lower edge of a field before switching to the other side of the hedge and then crossing back again.

When the path comes to another belt of trees, bear left to a footpath junction **C** and turn right on to a track. Follow the track, taking the right fork when it divides to cross a tributary stream. When the footpath divides again, keep ahead on the main track to follow a sign to Flatford. Cross the River Stour and turn left along the riverbank. **D** This part of the route is magnificent – one of the finest riverside walks in England, though the meadows are grazed by cattle who may

be inquisitive if you have a dog (which should be kept on its lead). All sorts of wildlife may be seen, including herons and even kingfishers. At length, just beyond a picturesque footbridge, a cottage can be seen ahead. Cross the river and turn right to walk along the lane to pass Flatford Mill Field Centre and then Willy Lott's House.

Bear left to pass the private car park but then go right **E** to take a National Trust permissive path that takes you round the bank of a lovely pond, the habitat of a wide variety of water birds and geese. Turn right at the end of the pond if you wish to use the bird hide, otherwise go left to pass beneath power lines, which are a hazard to geese and herons using the Stour wetlands. Go left again and then turn right to rejoin the Stour Valley Way and go beneath the power lines again.

Turn left **F** to follow a hedgerow through a succession of meadows that are extremely damp in winter. Pass an opening on the left which is the end of Hog's Lane – not a right of way. The going becomes even more damp, especially at gateways. Eventually you will see the timber of a small cattle enclosure and a gateway on the left. **G** This is the start of Dazeley's Lane, a track which climbs steadily to a road. Turn left, and after 50 yds (46m) go left again at the end of Clarence Villas **H** down an extremely narrow enclosed path. Cross a field to another length of enclosed path.

Cross Hog's Lane to a footpath on the other side and keep ahead past

Clapper Farm and then follow its drive to a lane, though note that about 20 yds (18m) from the lane a stile on the right takes the right of way across the end of a paddock. Cross the lane and continue on the footpath that goes through a small wood passing a water treatment plant on the way. Cross a track at the top of the wood and then a meadow to a stile above a sunken lane **J** You can turn right here on the footpath that runs by the edge of the road. This is rather narrow but avoids the traffic coming from Flatford. It ends at a seat by a footpath junction. Continue on the lane, being aware of the traffic approaching from the rear. Turn left on to the main road by East Bergholt church. This is worth visiting for the unique Bell House in the churchyard and for other features to be seen within. The Bell House was built when the construction of the enormous west tower was abandoned in 1525.

Walk past the sadly incomplete west end of the church to pass the site of East Bergholt House, Constable's childhood home, and return to the car park at the village centre. ●

GLADWINS FARM

Harper's Hill, Nayland, Suffolk CO6 4NU
Tel: 01206 262261 Fax: 01206 263001
e-mail: gladwinsfarm@compuserve.com
website: www.gladwinsfarm.co.uk

Set in 22 acres of rolling Suffolk countryside, within the Dedham Vale Area of Outstanding Natural Beauty, made famous by John Constable and Thomas Gainsborough, **Gladwins Farm** overlooks the beautiful Stour Valley. This is the perfect location for a peaceful, relaxing holiday, or just an overnight stay in the lovely farmhouse bed and breakfast. Although no longer a working farm, its wooded meadows are a haven for wildlife including badgers, pheasants, owls and bats. Here guests will find 500 years of history tastefully converted to modern standards of convenience and comfort. All the original cottages have been awarded "4 Star" ratings by the English Tourism Council.

Six of these welcoming self-catering cottages have been converted from original Tudor buildings to up-to-date standards, while *Hadleigh* forms part of the farmhouse. Attractive open-plan beamed living/dining rooms are furnished to a high standard of quality and comfort; the kitchens are modern

and fully fitted. The newest cottage, *Chelsworth*, has been purpose-built to achieve the highest accolade of "5 Stars", and includes everything guests might need. All the bedrooms in this cottage are ensuite; one has a delightful four-poster bed, and there is a television in every bedroom. The ground-floor bedroom is designed to suit less able guests. All the cottages have remote-controlled TV and video players. *Chelsworth*, *Constable*, *Gainsborough* and *Hadleigh* have log-burning stoves for cooler evenings. *Gainsborough* and *Hadleigh* are both ground-floor cottages suitable for visitors with disabilities. Every cottage also has outdoor furniture and sun loungers, as well as barbecues for cooking al fresco in the summer. Owners Robert and Pauline are also happy to provide frozen gourmet meals, although you will be spoilt for choice from a wide range of superb restaurants in the area, ranging from Michel Roux cuisine to seafood bistros. For those who prefer bed and

breakfast accommodation, the "4 Diamonds" graded bedrooms within the farmhouse are comfortably furnished and handsomely decorated. The residents' lounge area has its own colour TV, books, papers and magazines. Breakfast - which makes use of only the freshest local produce from local farms and the village butcher, as well as home-made preserves - can be served on the terrace on fine mornings.

The new indoor heated pool adds another luxurious feature to this wonderful retreat. It has a sauna and an aromatherapy steam capsule, while the pool building is fully air-conditioned. In

the grounds, the lake is stocked with trout and coarse fish for guests wishing to spend a quiet time casting a fly. Other amenities include an all-weather tennis court, playground and picnic area. Not far from the sea and with lovely views across the Dedham Vale, this wonderful retreat is an excellent base for any holiday and you should not miss the opportunity to explore the romantic Constable Country villages such as Dedham, Flatford, Kersey and Lavenham which make South Suffolk so special.

Willy Lott's Cottage

painted them, are to be found. Neither is open to the public, and the brick watermill is run as a residential field study centre. Nearby **Bridge Cottage** at Flatford is a restored 16th century building housing a Constable display, a tea room and a shop. There's also a restored dry dock, and the whole area is a delight for walkers; it is easy to see how Constable drew constant inspiration from the wonderful riverside setting.

NAYLAND

14 miles SW of Ipswich on the B1087

On a particularly beautiful stretch of the Stour in Dedham Vale, Nayland has charming colour-washed cottages in narrow, winding streets, as well as two very fine 15th century buildings in Alston Court and the Guildhall. **Abels Bridge**, originally built of wood in the 15th century by wealthy merchant John Abel, divides Suffolk from Essex. In the 16th century a hump bridge replaced it, allowing barges to pass beneath, and the current bridge carries the original keystone bearing the initial A. In the **Church of St James** stands an altarpiece by Constable entitled *Christ Blessing the Bread and Wine*.

THE OLD POST OFFICE

19 High Street, Nayland, nr Colchester, Essex CO6 4JG
Tel/Fax: 01206 262210

Colin and Patricia Ford have owned the exceptional **Old Post Office** since 1981. As its name tells us, part of the property is still the village post office, with Patricia as post-mistress, as she has been since she moved here. Formerly the Rose Inn and, in the 19th century, a chemist's shop, Literary Institute and later a coffee tavern, this handsome establishment has been carefully refurbished and decorated to a high standard, with period furniture and fittings, to provide excellent self-catering accommodation which sleeps up to 12. There are five bedrooms and large communal spaces. Each of the bedrooms is comfortable and welcoming. Original features include the vaulted ceilings, Victorian fireplaces and ceramic-tiled floors. The kitchen/dining room boasts the original beamed ceiling and wooden Tudor staircase. The spacious and handsomely appointed guests' lounge has an open fire.

Outside there are extensive grounds which include gardens, a wonderful heated swimming pool and a full-sized trampoline. This superb establishment is ideally placed for exploring Nayland, Colchester and further afield. Colin and Patricia also own and run three other self-catering cottages beside the castle in central Colchester, available for both short-and long-term lets. Two of these sleep three to five people, while the third is a romantic two-person cottage.

STRATFORD ST MARY

10 miles SW of Ipswich off the A12

Another of Constable's favourite locations, Stratford St Mary, is the most southerly village in Suffolk and is right on the Essex border. *The Young Waltonians* and *A House in Water Lane* (the house still stands today) are the best known of his works set in this picturesque spot. The village church is typically large and imposing, with parts dating back to 1200. At the top of the village are two splendid half-timbered cottages called the Ancient House and the Priest's House. Stratford was once on the main coaching route to London, and the largest of the four pubs had stabling for 200 horses. It is claimed that Henry Williamson, author of *Tarka the Otter*, saw his first otter here.

STOKE BY NAYLAND

12 miles SW of Ipswich on the B1087

The drive from Nayland reveals quite stunning views, and the village itself has a large number of listed buildings. The magnificent **Church of St Mary**, with its 120 foot tower, dominates the scene from its hilltop position; it dominated more than one Constable painting, the most famous showing the church lit up by a rainbow. William Dowsing destroyed 100 'superstitious pictures' here in his Puritan purges, but plenty of fine work is still to be seen, including several monumental brasses.

The Guildhall is another very fine building, now private residences but in the 16th century a busy centre of trade and commerce. When the wool trade declined, so did the importance of the Guildhall, and for a time the noble building saw service as a workhouse.

The decline of the cloth trade in East Anglia had several causes. Fierce competition came from the northern and western weaving industries, which generally had easier access to water supplies for fulling; the wars on the continent of Europe led to the closure of some trading routes and markets; and East Anglia had no supplies of the coal that was used to drive the new steam-powered machinery. In some cases, as at Sudbury, weaving or silk took over as smaller industries.

POLSTEAD

11 miles SW of Ipswich off the B1068

Polstead is a very pretty village in wooded, hilly countryside, with thatched, colour-washed cottages around the green and a wide duck pond at the bottom of the hill. Standing on a rise above the pond are **Polstead Hall**, a handsome Georgian mansion, and the 12th century **Church of St Mary**. The church has two features not found elsewhere in Suffolk - a stone spire and the very early bricks used in its construction. The builders used not only these bricks, but also tiles and tufa, a soft, porous stone much used in Italy. In the grounds of the hall stand the remains of a 'Gospel Oak' said to have been 1,300 years old when it collapsed in 1953. Legend has it that Saxon missionaries preached beneath it in the 7th century; an open-air service is still held here annually.

Polstead has two other claims to fame. One is for **Polstead Blacks**, a particularly tasty variety of cherry which was cultivated in orchards around the village and which used to be honoured with an annual fair. The other is much less agreeable, for it was here that the notorious **Red Barn Murder** hit the headlines in 1827 (see under Moyse's Hall in Bury St Edmunds). The incident aroused a great deal of interest and today's visitors to the village will still find reminders of the ghastly deed: the thatched cottage where Maria lived stands, in what is now called Marten's Lane, and the farm where the murderer lived is now called Corder's Farm.

BURES

17 miles W of Ipswich on the B1508

At this point the River Stour turns sharply to the east, creating a natural boundary between Suffolk and Essex. The little village of Bures straddles the river, lying partly in each county. Bures St Mary in Suffolk is where the church is located, overlooked by brick and half-timbered houses. Bures wrote itself very early into the history books when on Christmas Day 855 it is thought that Edmund the Martyr, the Saxon king, was crowned at the age of 15 in the Chapel of St Stephen. For some time after that momentous occasion Bures was the capital seat of the East Anglian kings. Bures has a long connection with the Waldegrave family, possibly from as far back as Chaucer's day. One of the Waldegrave memorials shows graphically the results of a visitation by William Dowsing and the Puritan iconoclasts: all the figures of the kneeling children have had their hands cut off.

Gainsborough's House, Sudbury

SUDBURY

Another wonderful town, the largest of the 'wool towns' and still home to a number of weaving concerns. Unlike Lavenham, it kept its industry because it was a port, and the result is a much more varied architectural picture. The surrounding countryside is some of the loveliest in Suffolk, and the River Stour is a further plus, with launch trips, rowing boats and fishing all available. Most visitors make a beeline for **Gainsborough's House** on Market Hill. The painter Thomas Gainsborough was

GAINSBOROUGH'S HOUSE

46 Gainsborough Street, Sudbury, Suffolk CO10 2EU
Tel: 01787 372958 Fax: 01787 376991
e-mail: mail@gainsborough.org
website: www.gainsborough.org

Gainsborough's House is the birthplace museum of Thomas Gainsborough (1727-1788), one of England's most celebrated artists. An exceptional collection of his paintings, drawings and prints is on display in this charming town house with a Georgian façade built by the artist's father. Around 25 oil paintings are on show, including a magnificent landscape of 1782 and a touching miniature of his wife, and among the Gainsborough memorabilia to be seen in the house are the artist's studio cabinet, his swordstick and his pocket watch. Two galleries and the garden showcase contemporary art and craft, and the print workshop hosts evening classes and summer courses in the techniques of etching, screenprinting, stone lithography and relief printing.

BULMER BRICK & TILE COMPANY LTD

Brickfields, Bulmer, Sudbury, Suffolk CO10 7EF
Tel: 01787 269232 Fax: 01787 269040

A brickworks has stood on the site of **Bulmer Brick & Tile** since the 15th century. The skilled staff produce hand-moulded facings and specials to nearly 5,000 patterns, together with a range of terracotta pieces.

They specialise in purpose-made bricks for restoration, using London Bed clay to produce the mellow reds seen in the nation's finest buildings, as in their restoration work at Hampton Court and Windsor Castle.

born here in 1727 in the house built by his father John. More of the artist's work is displayed in this Georgian-fronted house than in any other gallery, and there are also assorted 18th century memorabilia and furnishings (see panel below). A bronze statue of Gainsborough stands in the square.

Sudbury boasts three medieval churches; **All Saints** dates from the 15th century and has a glorious carved tracery pulpit and screens; 14th century **St Gregory's** is notable for a wonderful medieval font; and **St Peter's** has some marvellous painted screen panels and a piece of 15th century embroidered velvet.

Other buildings of interest are the Victorian Corn Exchange, now a library;

Salter's Hall, a 15th century timbered house; and the Quay Theatre, a thriving centre for the arts.

AROUND SUDBURY

HADLEIGH

12 miles E of Sudbury on the A1071

Old and not-so-old blend harmoniously in a variety of architectural styles. Timber-framed buildings, often with elaborate plasterwork, stand in the long main street as a reminder of the prosperity generated by the wool trade in the 14th to 16th centuries, and there are also some fine houses from the Regency and Victorian periods. The 15th century **Guildhall** with two overhanging storeys, the **Deanery Tower** and the church are a magnificent trio of huge appeal and contrasting construction - timber for the Guildhall, brick for the tower and flint for the church.

Guthrun, the Danish leader who was captured by Alfred and pardoned on condition that he became a

Hadleigh Guild Hall

Christian, made Hadleigh his HQ and lived here for 12 years. He was buried in the church, then a wooden construction but later twice rebuilt. In the south chapel of the present church is a 14th century bench-end carving depicting the scene of the wolf guarding the head of St Edmund. The wolf is wearing a monk's habit, indicating a satirical sense of humour in the carpenter. Also of interest is the clock bell, which stands outside the tower. A famous resident of Hadleigh was the rector Dr Rowland Taylor, who was burnt at the stake on **Aldham Common** for refusing to hold a mass. A large stone, inscribed and dated 1555, marks the spot.

Kersey Ford

There are two good walks from Hadleigh, the first being along the Brett with access over medieval Toppesfield Bridge. The other is a walk along the disused railway line between Hadleigh and Raydon through peaceful, picturesque countryside. At **Raydon** a few buildings survive from the wartime base of the 353rd, 357th and 358th Fighter Groups of the USAAF.

Two miles east of Hadleigh is **Wolves Wood**, an RSPB reserve with woodland nature trails and no wolves.

KERSEY
11 miles E of Sudbury off the A1141

The ultimate Suffolk picture-postcard village, a wonderful collection of timbered merchants' houses and weavers' cottages with paint and thatch. The main street has a **Water Splash**, which, along with the 700-year-old Bell Inn, has featured in many films and travelogues. The **Church of St Mary**, which overlooks the village from its hilltop position, is of massive proportions, testimony to the wealth that came with the wool and cloth industry. Kersey's speciality was a coarse twill broadcloth much favoured for greatcoats and army uniforms. Headless angels and mutilated carvings are reminders of the Puritans' visit to the church, though some treasures survive, including the ornate flintwork of the 15th century south porch. Traditional craftsmanship can still be seen in practice at the **Kersey Pottery**, which sells many items of stoneware plus paintings by Suffolk artists.

CHELSWORTH
10 miles NE of Sudbury off the A1141

Chelsworth is an unspoilt delight in the lovely valley of the River Brett, which is crossed by a little double hump-backed bridge. The timbered houses and

Chelsworth Village Street

CORNCRAFT

Monks Eleigh, Ipswich, Suffolk IP7 7AY
Tel: 01449 740456 e-mail: info@corncraft.co.uk
Fax: 01449 741665 website: www.corncraft.co.uk

Corncraft brings together some of East Anglia's most creative artists and craftspeople in converted farm buildings where a variety of traditional corn dollies, pottery, ceramics, tea pots and more can be found. The centre's showroom also features dried and silk flowers and loose bunches of dried flowers in basket arrangements. In the charming tea room guests can enjoy a range of delicious cakes, biscuits and light snacks all day.

HEDGEROWS FARM SHOP & NURSERY

Brent Eleigh, Sudbury, Suffolk CO10 9NU
Tel: 01787 247772

Set in beautiful countryside, **Hedgerows Farm Shop & Nursery** offers a wide range of unusual and well-priced plants, including hardy perennials and herbaceous plants, notably geraniums and grasses, as well as home-grown vegetables in season, free-range eggs, pick-your-own fruit (raspberries, black- and redcurrants, strawberries) and more. Open Monday to Saturday 8.30-5; Sundays 9-12 and 2-4, there's expert advice on hand.

thatched cottages look much the same as when they were built, and every year the village opens its gardens to the public. Nearby **Monks Eleigh**, with its thatched cottages, a 14th century church and a pump on the village green is so traditional that it was regularly used on railway posters as a lure to this wonderful part of the country.

BRENT ELEIGH

8 miles NE of Sudbury off the A1141

The church at Brent Eleigh, on a side road off the A1141, is remarkable for a number of quite beautiful ancient wall paintings, discovered during maintenance work as recently as 1960. The most striking and moving of the paintings is one of the Crucifixion.

LAVENHAM

6 miles N of Sudbury on the A1141

Lavenham is an absolute gem of a town,

the most complete and original of the medieval 'wool towns', with crooked timbered and whitewashed buildings lining the narrow streets. From the 14th to the 16th centuries, Lavenham flourished as one of the leading wool and cloth-making centres in the land, but with the decline of that industry the prosperous times soon came to an end. It is largely due to the fact that Lavenham found no

Restored Medieval Houses, Lavenham

THE GUILDHALL, LAVENHAM

Market Place, Lavenham, Suffolk CO10 9QZ
Tel: 01787 247646
e-mail: almjtg@smtp.ntrust.org.uk

The Guildhall, built around 1530 by the prosperous Corpus Christi religious guild, has been at the heart of village life ever since. It is a fine example of close-studded timber framing, with exuberant carvings that show off the impressive skills of the carpenters of the time. In 1547, when religious guilds were abolished as part of the Reformation, the Guildhall became parish property and in the ensuing centuries was put to various uses, including a house of correction, parish workhouse, home for WWII evacuees, Red Cross restaurant and nursery school. In 1951 it was vested in the National Trust and now houses a local history museum that includes exhibitions on the cloth industry, farming and the railway. The peaceful walled garden contains examples of the that were plants used to dye cloth in medieval times.

replacement industry that so much of the medieval character remains: there was simply not enough money for the rebuilding and development programmes that changed many towns, often for the worse. The medieval street pattern still exists, complete with market place and market cross.

More than 300 buildings are officially listed as being of architectural and historical interest, and none of them is finer than the **Guildhall**. This superb 16th century timbered building was originally the meeting place of the Guild of Corpus Christi, an organisation that regulated the production of wool. It now houses exhibitions of local history and the wool trade, and its walled garden has a special area devoted to dye plants (see panel).

Little Hall is hardly less remarkable, a 15th century hall house with a superb crown post roof. It was restored by the Gayer Anderson brothers, and has a fine collection of their furniture. The **Church of St Peter and St Paul** dominates the town from its elevated position. It's a building of great distinction, perhaps the greatest of all the 'wool churches' and declared by the 19th century architect August Pugin to be the finest example of Late Perpendicular style in the world. It was built, with generous help from wealthy local families (notably the Spryngs and the de Veres) in the late 15th and early 16th centuries to celebrate the end of the Wars of the Roses. Its flint tower is a mighty 140 feet in height and it's possible to climb to the top to take in the glorious views over Lavenham and the surrounding countryside. Richly carved screens and fine (Victorian) stained glass are eye-catching features within.

The **Priory** originated in the 13th century as a home for Benedictine monks and the beautiful timber-framed house on the site dates from about 1600. In the original hall, at the centre of the building, is an important collection of paintings and stained glass. The extensive grounds include a kitchen garden, a herb garden and a pond.

John Constable went to school in Lavenham, where one of his friends was Jane Taylor, who wrote the words to *Twinkle Twinkle Little Star*.

LONG MELFORD

2 miles N of Sudbury off the A134

The heart of this atmospheric wool town is a very long and, in stretches, fairly broad main street, set on an ancient Roman site in a particularly beautiful part of South Suffolk. In Roman times the Stour was a navigable river and trade flourished. Various Roman finds have been unearthed, notably a blue glass vase which is now on display in the British Museum. The street is filled with antique shops, book shops and art galleries and is a favourite place for collectors and browsers. Some of the houses are washed in the characteristic Suffolk pink, which might originally have been achieved by mixing ox blood or sloe juice into the plaster.

Holy Trinity Church, on a 14-acre green at the north end of Hall Street, is a typical exuberant manifestation of the

Long Melford

THE PERSIAN CARPET STUDIO

The Old White Hart, Long Melford, Sudbury, Suffolk CO10 9HX
Tel: 01787 882214 Fax: 01787 882213
e-mail: sarabarber@persian-carpet-studio.net
website: www.persian-carpet-studio.net

As its name tells us, **The Persian Carpet Studio** is a showroom of a glorious spectrum of antique and contemporary rugs and carpets. A kaleidoscope of colour and pattern awaits visitors to this 18th century former coaching inn. Masterpieces of the Oriental weavers' craft are on display in a spacious, relaxed setting flooded with natural light, where visitors can enjoy and examine the range of sensuous textiles, superb colours and exquisite patterns of the carefully selected stock. Leading UK retailers and restorers of Oriental and contemporary rugs and carpets, the Studio was established in 1990 and has since that time moved from strength to strength. Customer care is second to none, with a sourcing service for unusual and higher value items, an at-home service for those who find themselves unable to decide from among the tremendous range of quality rugs in the showroom, a cleaning and restoration service.

From inexpensive small furnishing pieces to Oriental carpets in excess of 20 by 15 feet, and rare antiques, the extensive stock offers something for every taste and pocket. With a wide variety of Persian, Caucasian, Anatolian and Central Asian tribal and village rugs and kilims, the shop also offers lectures, exhibitions and training days for those who wish to learn more about the craftsmanship and care of Oriental carpets. Member of the Rug Restorers Association. For information on training days and exhibitions, please ask to be put on the mailing list.

wealth of the wool and textile trade. It's big enough to be a cathedral, but served (and still serves) comparatively few parishioners. John Clopton, who became a very wealthy man through the woollen business, was largely responsible for this magnificent Perpendicular-style edifice, which has a 180-foot nave, chancel, half timbers, flint flashwork of the highest quality and 100 large windows to give a marvellous sense of light and space. Medieval glass in the north aisle depicts religious scenes and the womenfolk of the Clopton family. There are many interesting monuments and brasses, and in the chantry entrance is a bas relief of the Three Wise Men, the Virgin and Child, and St Joseph. In the Lady Chapel, reached by way of the churchyard, a children's multiplication table written on a wall is a reminder that the chapel served as the village school for a long period after the Reformation.

John Clopton's largesse is recorded rather modestly in inscriptions on the roof parapets. His tower was struck by lightning in the early 18th century and the present brick construction dates from around 1900. The detail of this great church is of endless fascination, but it's

KENTWELL HALL

Long Melford, Suffolk CO10 9BA
Tel: 01787 310207 Fax: 01787 379318
e-mail: info@kentwell.co.uk
website: www.kentwell.co.uk

Kentwell Hall, a romantic, mellow, moated redbrick Tudor mansion in a tranquil parkland setting, has a great deal to offer the visitor. The house was built by the Clopton family in the first half of the 16th century with wealth accrued from the wool trade, and the exterior has changed little down the centuries. After the Cloptons, the house saw a succession of owners and tenants before being requisitioned by the Army in the Second World War. It was in a poor state of repair when acquired by the present owner Patrick Phillips in 1971, since when he and his wife Judith have been lovingly restoring the house and its gardens.

Visitors can enjoy the Tudor service rooms such as the Great Kitchen and the Wardrobe Privy in the main house and the Bakehouse, Brewhouse and Dairy in the separate 15th century service building. Hopper's Gothic Great Hall and Dining Room and a series of classical 18th century rooms should also be seen, along with the newly redecorated State Bedroom, the Chinese Room, the brick-paved Tudor Rose Maze Courtyard and some very fine early heraldic stained glass. The owners have created a rare breeds farm in the superb grounds, where other features include a newly restored working ice house, a new rose garden, a fern stumpery, a coppice walk, a living sundial and the largest carved tree in England, representing the Tower of Babel.

Kentwell is famous for its recreations of Tudor domestic life and of wartime Britain, when it saw of wartime Britain, when it saw service as a transit camp. These events take place on Bank Holidays and selected weekends throughout the year, and in the summer a series of open-air entertainment, from jazz to Shakespeare, is invariably well attended. The Hall was the setting for the film version of *Toad of Toad Hall*.

the overall impression that stays in the memory, and the sight of the building floodlit at night is truly spectacular. The distinguished 20th century poet Edmund Blunden spent his last years in Long Melford and is buried in the churchyard. The inscription on his gravestone reads "I live still to love still things quiet and unconcerned".

Melford Hall, east of town beyond an imposing 16th gateway, was built around 1570 by Sir William Cordell on the site of an earlier hall that served as a country retreat, before the Dissolution of the Monasteries, for the monks of St Edmundsbury Abbey. There exists an account of Cordell entertaining Queen Elizabeth I at the Hall in 1578, when she was welcomed by "200 young gentlemen in white velvet, 300 in black and 1,500 serving men". Much of the fine work of Sir William (whose body lies in Holy Trinity Church) has been altered in restoration, but the pepperpot chimneys are original, as is the panelled banqueting hall. The rooms are in various styles, some with ornate walnut furniture, and there's a notable collection of Chinese porcelain on show. Most delightful of all is the Beatrix Potter room, with some of her water colours, first editions of books and, among the toys, the original of Jemima Puddleduck. She was a frequent visitor here (her cousins the Hyde Parkers were the owners), bringing small animals to draw. The Jeremy Fisher illustrations were mostly drawn at Melford Hall's fishponds, and the book is dedicated to Stephanie Hyde Parker. The Hall, which is a National Trust property, stands in a lovely garden with some distinguished clipped box hedges. William Cordell was also responsible for the red-brick almshouses, built in 1593 for '12 poor men', which stand near Holy Trinity.

Kentwell Hall is a red-brick Tudor moated mansion approached by a long avenue of limes. It sets out to illustrate and recreate Tudor times, with a walled garden, a bakery, a dairy and several varieties of rare-breed farm animals (see panel on page 175).

Long Melford is a great place for leisurely strolls, and for the slightly more energetic there's a scenic 3-mile walk along a disused railway track and farm tracks that lead straight into Lavenham.

GLEMSFORD
5 miles NW of Cavendish on the B1065

Textiles and weaving have long played a prominent part in Glemsford's history, and thread from the silk factory, which opened in 1824 and is still growing strongly, has been woven into dresses and robes for various members of the present royal family, including the late Princess Diana's wedding dress. During the last century several factories produced matting from coconut fibres and in 1906 Glemsford was responsible for the largest carpet in the world to cover the floor at London's Olympia. To this day one factory processes horse hair for use in judges' wigs, sporrans and busbies. The old Church of St Mary makes an impressive sight on what, for Suffolk, is a quite considerable hill at the north end of town.

CAVENDISH
5 miles W of Sudbury on the A1092

A most attractive village, where the Romans stayed awhile (the odd remains have been unearthed) and the Saxons settled. The look is splendidly traditional, with the church, thatched cottages, almshouses, **Nether Hall** and the **Sue Ryder Foundation Museum** spread around the green. The last, in a 16th century rectory by the pond, illustrates the work of the Sue Ryder Foundation, and was formally opened by Queen Elizabeth in 1979. Once a refuge for concentration camp victims, it houses abundant war photographs and memorabilia. Nether Hall is a well-restored 16th century building and the headquarters of Cavendish Vineyards.

In the **Church of St Mary**, whose tower has a pointed bellcote and a room inside complete with fireplace and shuttered windows look for the two handsome lecterns, one with a brass eagle (15th century), the other with two chained books; and for the Flemish and Italian statues. In 1381 Wat Tyler, leader of the Peasants revolt, was killed at Smithfield in London, by John Cavendish, son of Sir John Cavendish, Lord of the Manor and Chief Justice of England. Sir John was hounded by the peasants, who caught him and killed him near Bury St Edmunds. He managed en route to hide

some valuables in the belfry of St Mary's, Cavendish, and bequeathed to the church £40, sufficient to restore the chancel. A later Cavendish - Thomas - sailed round the world in the 1580s and perished on a second voyage. In the shadow of the church, on the edge of the village green, is a cluster of immaculate thatched cottages at a spot known as **Hyde Park Corner**. Pink-washed and pretty as a picture, they look almost too good to be true - and they almost are, having been rebuilt twice since the Second World War due to a combination of fire and dilapidation.

CLARE

7 miles W of Sudbury on the A1092

A medieval wool town of great importance, Clare repays a visit today with its fine old buildings and some old ruins. Perhaps the most renowned tourist attraction is **Ancient House**, a timber-

---

THE CLARE HALL COMPANY

The Barns, Clare Hall, Clare, Sudbury, Suffolk CO10 8PJ
Tel: 01787 278445 Fax: 01787 278803
Answerphone: 01787 277510

The Clare Hall Company at The Barns in Clare Hall is a distinctive workshop producing fine quality globes of the world, furniture making and restoration work for all types of antiques, all under one roof. The

setting alone is impressive: a converted barn where owner Michael Moore and his team of five cabinet-makers and restorers, most of whom have been in the business for 20 years or more, work to create and restore pieces of lasting beauty and value.

Mr Moore himself has been in the antiques trade for over 35 years. Much of the company's work now entails bespoke period furniture, particularly for the film industry. These are master craftsmen whose work has adorned the sets of motion pictures from *Shakespeare in Love* and *Braveheart* to James Bond films. They also supply many of the finest interior design shops in London, exquisite boardroom tables for some of the nation's biggest companies, and, of course, their speciality: globes for top emporia such as Aspreys, and the export market. Their restoration work is also second to none.

F D SALTER ANTIQUES

1-2 Church Street, Clare, Suffolk CO10 8PD
Tel: 01787 277693

F D Salter Antiques is a treasure trove: two floors of mainly 18th and 19th century furniture, porcelain and glass. Most pieces are English; the furnishings mostly hardwoods (mahogany, rosewood, oak). There is also a fine range of decorative items. Owners David and Pauline Salter established the shop in 1981; David has been in the trade for over 40 years, bringing the benefit of his expertise to all his customers.

framed building dated 1473 and remarkable for its pargeting (the word comes from the French 'pour jeter' - to throw). This is the decorative treatment of external plasterwork, usually by dividing the surface into rectangles and decorating each panel. It was very much a Suffolk speciality, particularly in the 16th and 17th centuries, with some examples also being found in Cambridgeshire and Essex. The decoration could be representations of plants, animals or people, with simple brushes of a comb, scrolls or squiggles, or more elaborate, with religious motifs, guild signs, family crests or abstract geometric patterns. Some pargeting is incised, but the best is in relief - pressing moulds into wet plaster or shaping by hand. Ancient House sports some splendid twining flowers and branches, and a representation of two figures holding a shield. The best-known workers in this unique skill had their own distinctive styles, and the expert eye could spot the particular 'trademarks' of each man (the same is the case with the master thatchers). Ancient House is now a museum, open during the summer months with an exhibition of local history.

Another place of historical significance is **Nethergate House**, once the work place of dyers, weavers and spinners. The **Swan Inn**, in the High Street, has a sign which lays claim to being the oldest in the land. Ten feet in length and carved from a solid piece of wood, it portrays the arms of England and France. Clare Castle was a motte and bailey fortress that sheltered a household of 250. **Clare Castle Country Park**, with a visitor centre in the goods shed of a disused railway line, contains the remains of the castle and the moat, the latter now a series of ponds and home to varied wild life. At the Prior's House, the original cellar and infirmary are still in use. Established in 1248 by Augustine friars and used by them until the Dissolution of 1538, the priory was handed back to that order in 1953 and remains their property.

A mile or so west of Clare on the A1092 lies **Stoke-by-Clare**, a pretty village on one of the region's most picturesque routes. It once housed a Benedictine priory, whose remains are now in the grounds of a school. There's a fine 15th century church and a vineyard: Boyton Vineyards at Hill Farm, Boyton End, is open early April-end October for a tour, a talk and a taste.

KEDINGTON

12 miles W of Sudbury on the B1061

Haverhill intrudes somewhat, but the heart of the old village gains in appeal from the presence of the River Stour.

Known to many as the 'Cathedral of West Suffolk', the **Church of St Peter and St Paul** is the chief attraction of Kedington. Almost 150ft in length, it stands on a ridge overlooking the Stour Valley. It has several interesting features, including a 15th century font, a Saxon cross in the chancel window, a three-decker pulpit (with a clerk's desk and a reading desk) and a sermon-timer, looking rather like a grand egg-timer. The foundations of a Roman building have been found beneath the floorboards.

Following the Stour along the B1061, the visitor will find a number of interesting little villages. In **Little Wratting**, Holy Trinity Church has a shingled oak-framed steeple (a feature more usually associated with Essex churches). John Sainsbury was a local resident, while in **Great Wratting** another magnate, WH Smith, financed the restoration of St Mary's Church in 1887. This church boasts some diverting topiary in the shape of a church, a cross and an armchair.

HAVERHILL
14 miles W of Sudbury on the A604

Haverhill is notable for its fine Victorian architecture. Fire destroyed many of the town's buildings in 1665, but **Anne of Cleves House** was restored and is well worth a visit. Anne was the fourth wife of Henry VIII and after a brief political marriage she was given an allowance and spent the remainder of her days at Haverhill and Richmond. East Town Park is a new country park on the east side of Haverhill.

GREAT & LITTLE THURLOW
15 miles W of Sudbury on the B1061

Great and Little Thurlow form a continuous village on the west bank of the Stour four miles north of Haverhill. Largely undamaged thanks to being in a conservation area, they have many 17th century cottages and a Georgian manor house.

A short distance further up the B1061 stands the village of **Great Bradley**, divided in two by the River Stour, which rises just outside the village boundary. Chief points of note in the tranquil parish church are a fine Norman doorway sheltering a Tudor brick porch and some beautiful stained glass poignantly depicting a soldier in the trenches during the First World War. The three bells in the tower include one cast in the 14th century, one of the oldest in Suffolk.

BURY ST EDMUNDS

The town takes its name from St Edmund, who was born in Nuremberg in 841 and came here as a teenager where he became the last king of East Anglia. He was a

---

ASH COTTAGE
59 Whiting Street, Bury St Edmunds, Suffolk IP33 1NP
Tel/Fax: 01284 755098
e-mail: ashcottage@freebie.net
website: www.members.tripod.com/ashcottage

Charm doesn't come more readily than at **Ash Cottage**, a superb 16th century townhouse set in the heart of town, within walking distance of the Theatre Royal, restaurants, the lovely Abbey Gardens and countless places of historic interest. Offering bed and breakfast accommodation in two supremely comfortable rooms (a double and a twin),both with their own shower room, a warm welcome awaits all guests.

staunch Christian, and his refusal to deny his faith caused him to be tortured and killed by the Danes in 869. Legend has it that although his body was recovered, his head (cut off by the Danes) could not be found. His men searched for it for 40 days, then heard his voice directing them to it from the depths of a wood, where they discovered it lying protected between the paws of a wolf. The head and the body were reunited and, to commemorate the wolf's deed, the crest of the town's armorial bearings depicts a wolf with a man's head.

Abbey, Bury St Edmunds

THE ANGEL HOTEL

Angel Hill, Bury St Edmunds, Suffolk IP33 1LT
Tel: 01284 714000 Fax: 01284 714001
e-mail: sales@theangel.co.uk website: www.theangel.co.uk

The Angel Hotel is a charming and historic coaching inn that dates back to 1452. It has been in the Gough family for 28 years. Originally three inns serving the pilgrims visiting the great Abbey of St Edmundsbury, it has a long and impressive history as host to scores of artists, renowned writers including Charles Dickens (who wrote part of *The Pickwick Papers* whilst in residence), and members of the royal family. Noted for its beautiful location on Angel Hill, it is set in one of the prettiest squares in the country. It enjoys a well-earned reputation for quality and service. The warm, relaxed atmosphere is enhanced by the friendly staff and beautiful surroundings.

Each room contains interesting collections of antiques, art and photographs reflecting the hotel's rich heritage. There is a choice of two restaurants, a superb guests' lounge and the convivial Pickwick Bar. Meals range from brasserie-style informal dishes to local specialities and a range of imaginative and delicious English and Continental delights. The wine list happily provides a variety of Old and New World vintages. The guest bedrooms are exquisitely appointed and include ground-floor rooms and rooms decorated and furnished in different styles, including some with four-poster beds and some suitable for families. This elegant hotel makes the perfect base from which to explore this lovely and historic part of East Anglia.

Edmund was possibly buried first at Hoxne, the site of his murder, but when he was canonised in about 910 his remains were moved to the monastery at Beodricsworth, which changed its name to St Edmundsbury. A shrine was built in his honour, later incorporated into the Norman Abbey Church after the monastery was granted abbey status by King Canute in 1032. The town soon became a place of pilgrimage and for many years St Edmund was the patron saint of England, until replaced by St George. Growing rapidly around the great abbey, which became one of the largest and most influential in the land, Bury prospered as a centre of trade and commerce, thanks notably to the cloth industry.

The next historical landmark was reached in 1214, when on St Edmund's Feast Day the Archbishop of Canterbury, Simon Langton, met the Barons of England at the high altar of the Abbey and swore that they would force King John to honour the proposals of the Magna Carta. The twin elements of Edmund's canonisation and the resolution of the Barons explain the motto on the town's crest: 'sacrarium regis, cunabula legis' - 'shrine of a king, cradle of the law'.

Rebuilt in the 15th century, the **Abbey** was largely dismantled after its dissolution by Henry VIII, but

imposing ruins remain in the colourful **Abbey Gardens** beyond the splendid Abbey Gate and Norman Tower. **St Edmundsbury Cathedral** was originally the Church of St James, built in the 15th/16th century and accorded cathedral status (alone in Suffolk) in 1914. The original building has been much extended down the years (notably when being adapted for its role as a cathedral) and outstanding features include a magnificent hammerbeam roof, whose 38 beams are decorated with angels bearing the emblems of St James, St Edmund and St George. The monumental Bishop's throne depicts wolves guarding the crowned head of St Edmund, and there's a fascinating collection of 1,000 embroidered kneelers. Millennium funds granted in 1997 should guarantee that the tower which the cathedral lacks is finally built (see panel below). Services are held at the Cathedral daily at 7.30am,

St Edmundsbury Cathedral

Angel Hill, Bury St Edmunds, Suffolk IP33 1LS
Tel: 01284 754933 Fax: 01284 768655
website: www.stedscathedral.co.uk

The site of Suffolk's Cathedral has been one of pilgrimage and worship for almost 1,000 years. One church within the precinct of a Norman Abbey was built by Abbot Anselm in the 12th century and was dedicated to St James. The nave of today's church, started in 1503, is the successor to that church, and though little remains of the abbey following the dissolution in 1539, St James' Church has continued to grow over the years and in 1914 it became the Cathedral Church of the Diocese of Saint Edmundsbury and Ipswich.

The last 40 years have seen several additions to the church as well as the building of the Cathedral Centre, which houses the Song School, the refectory and meeting rooms. Outstanding features of the Cathedral include a magnificent hammerbeam roof and a monumental bishop's throne.

1pm and 5.30pm, and on Sundays at 8am, 10am, 11.30am and 3.30pm. There are also frequent organ recitals and a full programme of concerts and other musical events.

St Mary's Church, in the same complex, is also well worth a visit: an equally impressive hammerbeam roof, the detached tower standing much as Abbot Anselm built it in the 12th century, and several interesting monuments, the most important to Mary Tudor, sister of Henry VIII, Queen of France and Duchess of Suffolk. Her remains were moved here when the Abbey was suppressed; a window in the Lady Chapel which records this fact was the gift of Queen Victoria.

The **Abbey Visitor Centre**, open daily from Easter to the end of October, is situated in Samson's Tower, part of the west front of the Abbey. The centre has displays and hands-on activities concerning the Abbey's history.

Bury is full of fine non-ecclesiastical buildings, many with Georgian frontages concealing medieval interiors. Among the most interesting are the handsome **Manor House Museum** with its amazing collection of clocks and watches, along with paintings, furniture, costumes and objets d'art; the Victorian Corn Exchange with its imposing colonnade; the Athenaeum, hub of social life since

Regency times and scene of Charles Dickens's public readings; Cupola House, where Daniel Defoe once stayed; the Angel Hotel, where Dickens and his marvellous creation Mr Pickwick stayed; and the **Nutshell**, owned by Greene King Brewery and a contender for the title of the smallest pub in the country. Its single bar measures 16ft by 7ft. The **Theatre Royal** in Westgate Street, now in the care of the National Trust, was built in 1819 by William Wilkins, who was also responsible for the National Gallery. It once staged the premiere of *Charley's Aunt* and still operates as a working theatre, with a year-round programme of professional and amateur drama, comedy, dance, mime and pantomime.

The **Bury St Edmunds Art Gallery** is housed in one of Bury's noblest buildings, built to a Robert Adam design in 1774. It filled many roles down the years, and was rescued from decline in the 1960s to be restored to Adam's original plans. It is now one of the county's premier art galleries, with eight exhibitions each year and a thriving craft shop.

Perhaps the most fascinating building of all is **Moyse's Hall** at one end of the Buttermarket. Built of flint and limestone about 1180, it has claims to being the oldest stone domestic building in England. Originally a rich man's residence, it later saw service as a prison,

OUNCE HOUSE

Northgate Street, Bury St Edmunds, Suffolk IP33 1HP
Tel: 01284 761779 Fax: 01284 768315
e-mail: pott@globalnet.co.uk
website: www.ouncehouse.co.uk

Ounce House is a charming and gracious Victorian house hotel set in the centre of Bury, on one of the finest residential street in the town. Elegant and quiet, each of the ensuite rooms is individually decorated and equipped with every amenity guests have come to expect. This welcoming hotel makes the perfect base from which to explore the delights of the region.

a workhouse, a police station and a railway office, and for the past 100 years it has been a museum. It houses some 10,000 items, from a Bronze Age hoard, Roman pottery and Anglo-Saxon jewellery to a 19th century doll's house and some grisly relics of the notorious **Red Barn Murder**. A local girl, Maria Martin, was murdered in 1827 by William Corder, a farmer with whom she had been having an affair, at the Red Barn in Polstead, near Sudbury. The girl's body was found only a year later after her stepmother had a dream that it lay in the Red Barn. Corder was hunted down in London, arrested, tried and found guilty. Public interest in the murder was enormous, and a crowd of 20,000 watched his hanging. His body was put on show for a time, after which his skeleton was used for teaching purposes at a local hospital. Relics in Moyse's Hall include his scalp, an ear and a book bound with his skin, as well as the murder weapon and a death mask.

Steeped though it is in history, Bury also moves with the times, and its sporting and leisure facilities are impressive. A mile and a half outside town on the A14 (just off the East Exit) is **Nowton Park**, almost 200 acres of countryside landscaped in Victorian style and supporting a wealth of flora and fauna. The mature woods and specimen trees, the wildflower meadows and the avenue of limes, carpeted with daffodils in the spring, are particular delights. There are also timber sculptures, circular walks, picnic sites, a play area, a ranger centre and an all-weather sports pitch.

Bury is a wonderful place to visit, with almost 1,000 preserved buildings and a disciplined network of streets (the layout was devised in the 11th century) that provide long, alluring views. William Cobbett (1763-1835), a visitor when chronicling his *Rural Rides*, did not disagree with the view that Bury St Edmunds was "the nicest town in the world" - a view which would be endorsed by many of its inhabitants and by many of the millions of visitors who have been charmed by this jewel in Suffolk's crown.

ICKLINGHAM
8 miles NW of Bury St Edmunds on the A1101

There are two churches in this village - the parish church of St James (mentioned in the Domesday Book) and the redundant thatched-roofed All Saints, with medieval tiles on the chancels and beautiful east windows in the south aisle. Standing at the point where the Icknield Way crosses the River Lark, Icklingham has a long history, brought to light in frequent archaeological finds, from pagan bronzes to Roman coins. The place abounds in tales of the supernatural, notably of the white rabbit who is seen at dusk in the company of a witch, causing horses to bolt and men to die!

Just south of Icklingham, at the A1101, is **Rampart Field** picnic site, where pleasant walks through gorse-filled gravel workings reveal the varied plant life of a typical Breckland heath.

WEST STOW
4 miles NW of Bury St Edmunds off the A1101

The villages of West Stow, Culford, Ingham, Timworth and Wordwell were for several centuries part of a single estate covering almost 10,000 acres. Half the estate was sold to the Forestry Commission in 1935 and was renamed the King's Forest in honour of King George V's Jubilee in that year. An Anglo-Saxon cemetery was discovered in the village in 1849 and the years since have revealed traces of Roman settlements and the actual layout of the original Anglo-Saxon village (see panel on page 186). A trust was established to investigate

(Continued page 186)

WALK 8

Forest and Riverside from West Stow

Start	Forest Lodge, West Stow
Distance	5 miles (8km)
Approximate time	2½ hours
Parking	Car park at Forest Lodge picnic site, the King's Forest
Refreshments	None on route
Ordnance Survey maps	Landranger 144 (Thetford & Diss, Breckland & Wymondham), Explorer 229 (Thetford Forest in The Brecks)

This short walk in the Breckland of north Suffolk displays a wide variety of scenery: forest at first, then farmland, the parkland surrounding Culford School, and then a short length along the new footpath on the north bank of the River Lark. Note that on this section the path may be encroached by nettles.

Leave the car park at its entrance and turn left to walk past black sheds on a sandy track. Turn right at the first crossways Ⓐ on to a path which follows the edge of the forest with open fields to the right. It becomes even more narrow as it progresses, threading its way through trees and bushes. Keep ahead when the path swings left and duck under or climb over a wooden barrier and then bear left on a farm track which passes through a meadow, heading towards tiny Wordwell church. A little further on, the track veers away from the church to pass in front of the pink-washed Wordwell Hall and reach a road.

Cross straight over Ⓑ to the track on the other side and continue across a field to Blake's Spinney to join a track

that takes you to a another belt of trees and the Icknield Way Path, a prehistoric trackway that pre-dates the Peddars Way and runs down the chalky spine of southern England from the north Norfolk coast to Avebury on the Wiltshire downs.

Turn right Ⓒ and walk down the dead-straight track to the village of Brockley. Turn right along the road (the verge is broad on the right) and after about 1Ú3 mile (536m) turn left Ⓓ to take a farm track heading towards a water-tower and then a wood. The path goes through the latter and comes out on to the Culford School playing-fields, where the right of way is not marked. Cross the field from an ancient beech tree, heading to the right of the main building, and turn right on the main drive to pass the cricket field and graceful iron bridge to the left.

Keep to the drive, which passes close to the lower end of the lovely lake, but leave it just before the end of the lake to fork right **E** on to a path going towards West Stow church. Turn left at the road and then take the first right on to the lane going to Flempton. Keep on the main road and, just before the bridge, take the riverbank footpath on the right to follow the riverbank. **F**

This is part of the Lark Valley Path – a 13-mile (20.9km) route that follows the course of the River Lark from Mildenhall to Bury St Edmunds. This section may be overgrown with nettles

in early summer. There is a fishing lake close to the right which, with the reedbeds, helps to make this part of the route a birdwatcher's delight, with a good chance of seeing kingfishers or herons.

Soon you will be walking on a raised bank between two branches of the river. When they join, fork right off the riverside path on to a track that bends right away from the sewage treatment works and passes behind houses before reaching the road. Turn right and then in 50 yds (46m) turn left to take the road back to the starting point at the King's Forest picnic site. ●

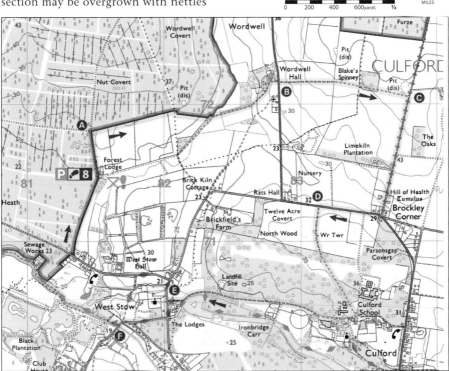

further the Anglo-Saxon way of life and their building and farming techniques. Several buildings were constructed using, as accurately as could be achieved, the tools and methods of the 5th century. The undertaking has become a major tourist attraction, with assistance from both human (in Anglo-Saxon costume) and cassette guides. There are pigs and hens and growing crops, craft courses, a Saxon market at Easter, a festival in August and special events all year round. This fascinating village, which is entered through the Visitor Centre, is part of **West Stow Country Park**, a large part of which is designated a Site of Special Scientific Interest (SSSI). Over 120 species of bird and 25 species of animal have been sighted in this Breckland setting, and a well-marked five-mile nature trail

CHIMNEY MILL GALLERIES

West Stow, Bury St Edmunds, Suffolk IP28 6ER
Tel: 01284 728234

Specialising in antique stripped pine furniture and paintings, **Chimney Mill Galleries** is set in the grounds of a former water mill on the River Lark. Opened in 1976 to show the work of local artists and sculptors, the Galleries now exhibit work from all over East Anglia in a wide range of media. Owned and run by Hilary and Adrian Murfitt, the Galleries are open 11am to 5pm Tuesday to Saturday and at any other time by prior arrangement.

WEST STOW ANGLO-SAXON VILLAGE

The Visitor Centre, Icklingham Road, West Stow, Bury St Edmunds, Suffolk IP28 6HG
Tel: 01284 728718 Fax: 01284 728277
website: www.stedmundsbury.gov.uk/weststow.htm

Between 1965 and 1972 the low hill by the River Lark in Suffolk was excavated to reveal several periods of occupation, but in particular, over 70 buildings from an early Anglo Saxon village. There was also information from about 100 graves in the nearby cemetery. It was decided that such extensive evidence about these people should be used to carry out a practical experiment to test ideas about the buildings that formed the elements of the original village.

Part of the Anglo Saxon Village has been reconstructed on the site where the original (inhabited from around 420 650 AD) was excavated. The reconstructions have been built over a period of more than 20 years. Each of the eight buildings is different, to test different ideas, and each has been built using the tools and techniques available to the early Anglo Saxons. Exploring the houses is an excellent way of finding out about the Anglo Saxons who lived at West Stow. Costumed "Anglo Saxons" bring the village to life at certain times, especially at Easter and during August. The new Anglo Saxon Centre is an exciting addition to the site, housing the original objects found there and at other local sites. Many of the objects have never been seen by the public before. The displays show aspects of village life and the focal point is a series of life size reconstructions of costume, based upon the grave finds.

West Stow Anglo Saxon Village lies in the middle of a beautiful 125 acre Country Park, part of which is a Site of Special Scientific Interest. The park has a number of different habitats, including woodland, heathland, a lake and a river. There is a play area, a bird feeding area and bird hides. The Park is open daily all year, from 9am-5pm in winter, 9am-8pm in summer. Entry to the park is free.

links this nature reserve with the woods, a large lake and the River Lark. Very near the park and village is **Cow Wise**, a working dairy farm with lots of animals for young visitors to feed.

HENGRAVE

3 miles NW of Bury St Edmunds on the A1101

A captivating old-world village of flint and thatch. Excavations and aerial photography indicate that a settlement has been here since Neolithic times, and the parts of the village of archaeological interest are now protected. The chief attraction is **Hengrave Hall**, a rambling Tudor mansion built partly of Northamptonshire limestone and partly of yellow brick between 1525 and 1538 by Sir Thomas Kytson, a wool merchant. A notable visitor in the early days was Elizabeth I, who brought her court here in 1578. Several generations of the Gage family were later the owners and one of them, with a particular interest in horticulture, imported various kinds of plum tree from France. Most of the bundles were properly labelled with their names but one had lost its label. When it produced its first crop of luscious green fruit someone had the bright idea of calling it the green Gage. The name stuck, and the descendants of the trees, planted in 1724, are still at the Hall, which may be visited by appointment. The fruit trees had come from Italy to France and the Loire Valley town of Blois, where the King of France had his seat. The King's wife Claude was much taken with the new fruit and had many trees planted; hence the French for greengage is 'reine-claude'. In the grounds of the Hall stands a lovely little church with a round Saxon tower and a wealth of interesting monuments. The church was for some time a family mausoleum; restored by Sir John Wood, it became a private chapel and it now hosts services of various denominations.

EUSTON

9 miles N of Bury St Edmunds on the A1088

Euston Hall has been the seat of the Dukes of Grafton for 300 years. It's open to the public on Thursday afternoons and is well worth a visit, not least for its portraits of Charles II and its paintings by Van Dyck, Lely and Stubbs. In the colourful landscaped grounds is an ice house disguised as an Italianate temple, the distinguished work of John Evelyn and William Kent.

Euston's church, in the grounds of the Hall, is the only one in the county dedicated to **St Genevieve**. It's also one of only two Classical designs in the county, being rebuilt in 1676 on part of the original structure. The interior is richly decorated, with beautiful carving on the hexagonal pulpit, panelling around the walls and a carved panel of

THE KITCHEN GARDEN

Church Cottage, Troston, Bury St Edmunds, Suffolk IP31 1EX
Tel/Fax: 01359 268322 website: www.kitchen-garden-hens.co.uk

The Kitchen Garden is a beautiful and charming place where two-thirds of an acre are divided into 'rooms' featuring different plantings, including a wild garden with pond and ducks. Owner Francine Raymond is a renowned expert on hens; on sale are her own books as well as plants, seeds, tools and more.

Tea, coffee and home-made cakes are served in the garden or farmhouse kitchen. Please telephone for opening times.

the *Last Supper*. Parts of this lovely wood carving have been attributed to Grinling Gibbons. Behind the family pew is a marble memorial to Lord Arlington, who built the church.

PAKENHAM

4 mile NE of Bury St Edmunds off the A143

On a side road just off the A143 (turn right just north of Great Barton), lies the village of Pakenham, whose long history has been unearthed in the shape of a Bronze Age barrow and kiln, and another kiln from Roman times.

Elsewhere in Pakenham are the 17th century Nether Hall, from whose lake in the park the village stream flows through the fen into the millpond, and from the same period Newe House, a handsome Jacobean building with Dutch gables and a two-storey porch. The **Church of St Mary** has an impressive carved Perpendicular font and in its adjacent vicarage is the famous Whistler Window - a painting by Rex Whistler of an 18th century parish priest. The fens were an important source of reeds, and many of Pakenham's buildings show off the thatcher's art.

Pakenham's current unique claim to fame is in being the only parish in England with a windmill and a watermill, both in working order. The **Pakenham Watermill** was built around 1814 on a site mentioned in the Domesday Book (the Roman excavations suggest that there could have been a mill here as far back as the 1st century AD). The mill, which is fed from Pakenham fen, has many interesting features, including the Blackstone oil engine, dating from around 1900, and the Tattersall Midget rollermill from 1913, a brave but not successful attempt to compete with the larger roller mills in the production of flour. The mill and the neighbouring recreation park are well

worth a visit. No less remarkable is the **Pakenham Windmill**, one of the most famous in Suffolk. The black-tarred tower was built in 1831 and was in regular use until the 1950s. One of the best preserved mills in the county, it survived a lightning strike in 1971.

IXWORTH

5 miles NE of Bury St Edmunds on the A143

One of the Iceni tribe's major settlements, with important Roman connections and, in the 12th century, the site of an Augustinian priory. The remains of the priory were incorporated into a Georgian house known as **Ixworth Abbey**, which stands among trees by the River Blackbourne. The village has many 14th century timber-framed dwellings, and the Church of St Mary dates from the same period, though with many later additions.

BARDWELL

7 miles NE of Bury St Edmunds just off the A1088

Here's another **Tower Windmill**. This one dates from the 1820s and was worked by wind for 100 years, then by an oil engine until 1941. It was restored in the 1980s, only to suffer severe damage in the great storm of October 1987, when its sails were torn off. Stoneground flour is still produced by an auxiliary engine, and there's an on-site bakery. Also in this delightful village are a 16th century inn and the Church of St Peter and St Paul, known particularly for its medieval stained glass.

HONINGTON

7 miles NE of Bury St Edmunds on the A1088

The little village of Honington is the birthplace of the shoemaker and pastoral poet Robert Bloomfield (1766-1823), whose best known work is *The Farmer's Boy*. The house where he was born is now divided, one part called Bloomfield Cottage, the other Bloomfield Farmhouse. A brass plaque to his memory can be seen in All Saints Church, in whose graveyard his parents are buried.

BARNINGHAM

8 miles NE of Bury St Edmunds on the B1111

Near the Norfolk border, Barningham was the first home of the firm of Fisons, which started in the late 18th century. Starting with a couple of windmills, they later installed one of the earliest steam mills in existence. The engine saw service for nearly 100 years and is now in an American museum; the mill building exists to this day, supplying animal feed.

This is marvellous walking country, and **Knettishall Heath Country Park**, on 400 acres of prime Breckland terrain, is the official starting place of the Peddars Way National Trail and of a path that stretches 77 miles to Great Yarmouth and

beyond by way of the Little Ouse and Waveney valleys. Waymarked trails provide shorter excursions.

STANTON

7 miles NE of Bury St Edmunds on the A143

Stanton was mentioned in the Domesday Book and the Romans were here before that. A double ration of medieval churches - All Saints and St John the Baptist - will satisfy the ecclesiastical scholar, while for more worldly indulgences Wyken Vineyards will have a strong appeal. On the same site, the four acres of **Wyken Hall Garden** feature herb and knot gardens designed by Arabella Lennox-Boyd, rose, kitchen and woodland gardens, a fritillary meadow, a nuttery, an orchard, a splendid woodland walk, an eccentric dog kennel in Gothic style and a Deep South-style veranda complete with rocking chair. New for 2001 is a 'Giant's Stride', a type of Maypole that swings

HILLCREST NURSERIES

Barningham Road, Stanton, Bury St Edmunds, Suffolk IP31 2DU
Tel: 01359 250327 Fax: 01359 250940

Owner Kathy Fulcher operates **Hillcrest Nurseries**, a family-run business, with flair and style. First opened in 1990, it enjoys a fine reputation for quality and service. There's a vast selection of superb quality bedding and herbaceous plants, shrubs, fruit and vegetable plants, bare-rooted trees, hedging and the ever-popular zonal geraniums.

There's also a very good range of pots, statues and other garden ornaments. This extensive nursery is easy to roam through, enjoying the many plants on display in the green

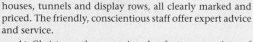

houses, tunnels and display rows, all clearly marked and priced. The friendly, conscientious staff offer expert advice and service.

At Christmas the nurseries also feature a variety of handsome trees and wreaths. The attractive garden shop offers a selection of fruits and vegetables, sweets, bird and pet food, garden produce and garden accessories. Everything the beginner or expert gardener needs can be found here. The nurseries are easy to find on the Barningham Road, and are open seven days a week: Monday to Friday 8 am - 5.30 pm; Saturdays and Sundays 8.30 am - 5.30 pm.

WYKEN VINEYARDS

Stanton, Bury St Edmunds,
Suffolk IP31 2DW
Tel: 01359 250287
Fax: 01359 252372

At the heart of a quintessential Suffolk estate that was first settled 6,000 years ago stands Wyken Hall, a romantic Elizabethan manor house owned by Englishman Sir Kenneth Carlisle and his American wife Carla. Their collaboration has produced a garden which has something to delight every visitor: blue rocking chairs on a Southern-style veranda, a dog chapel and a US mail box typify the American humour, while a herb garden, knot garden, nuttery and rose garden planted with old-fashioned roses, hardy geraniums and delphiniums assert the Englishness of the setting. And everywhere Carla's eye for design and instinct for colour are evident.

A stroll through ancient woodland brings visitors to **Wyken Vineyards**, set in seven acres on a south-facing slope where the Romans perhaps planted the first vines. The present enterprise was started in 1988, since when it has been producing grapes for some of the very best wines in England. Wyken Bacchus, a dry white, is a winner of the English Vineyard Association's Wine of the Year Award, and the full, dark red is also establishing an excellent and well-deserved reputation.

Inspired by the cultural and viticultural traditions of life in California's Napa Valley, Carla has converted an imposing 400-year-old flint barn on the estate into the Leaping Hare Vineyard Restaurant, where Wyken wines accompany food that is in tune with the seasons, the land and the customers' appetites. Only the best and freshest of local ingredients find their way into the kitchen, including vegetables, fruit and herbs from the Wyken's kitchen garden. The style is mainly English (salmon fishcakes are among the favourites), but with influences from France and from California, where Carla spent some time as an apprentice pastry chef at the world-renowned Chez Panisse restaurant. The restaurant is open every lunchtime and Friday and Saturday evenings, while the adjacent café is open every day for teas, coffees, cakes and light lunches.

Alongside the restaurant and café, the Leaping Hare Country Store is committed to selling the very best of everything that is both special and useful: the eclectic range runs from Suffolk and Norfolk crafts to clothes for women, American quilts, French grape-picking baskets and English bicycles.

visitors up in the air. The complex also includes an Elizabethan manor house, a 16th century barn, a country shop and a restaurant (see panel on page 190)

WALSHAM-LE-WILLOWS
9 miles NE of Bury St Edmunds off the A143

A pretty name for a pretty village, with weatherboarded and timber-framed cottages along the willow-banked river which flows throughout its length. **St Mary's Church** is no less pleasing to the eye, with its sturdy western tower and handsome windows in the Perpendicular style. Of particular interest inside is the superb tie and hammerbeam roof of the nave, and (unique in Suffolk and very rare elsewhere) a tiny circular medallion which hangs suspended from the nave wall, known as a 'Maiden's Garland' or 'Virgin's Crant'. These marked the pew seats of unmarried girls who had passed away, and the old custom was for the young men of the village to hang garlands of flowers from them on the anniversary of the girl's death. This particular example celebrates the virginity of one Mary Boyce, who died (so the inscription says) of a broken heart in 1685, just 20 years old. There is also a carving on the rood screen which looks rather like the face of a wolf: this may well be a reference to the benevolent creature that plays such an important role in the legend of St Edmund. A museum by the church has changing exhibitions of local history.

REDGRAVE
13 miles NE of Bury St Edmunds on the B1113

Arachnophobes beware! Redgrave and Lopham Fens form a 360-acre reserve of reed and sedge beds where one of the most interesting inhabitants is the Great Raft Spider. The village is the source of

Half Moon Street, Redgrave

the Little Ouse and Waveney rivers, which rise on either side of the B1113 and set off on their seaward journeys in opposite directions.

THELNETHAM
12 miles NE of Bury St Edmunds off the B111

West of Redgrave, between the B1113 and the B1111, lies Thelnetham - another village, another windmill. This one, a tower mill, was built in 1819 to replace a post mill on the same site, and worked for 100 years. It has been lovingly restored. Stoneground flour is produced and sold at the mill. If you wish to visit you should set sail on a summer Sunday.

HESSETT
4 miles E of Bury St Edmunds off the A14

Dedicated to St Ethelbert, King of East Anglia, Hessett's church has many remarkable features, particularly some beautiful 16th century glass and wall paintings, both of which somehow escaped the Puritan wave of destruction. Ethelbert was unlucky enough to get on the wrong side of the mighty Offa, King of the Mercians, and was killed by him at Hereford, in 794.

THE LUCY REDMAN SCHOOL OF GARDEN DESIGN

6 The Village, Rushbrooke, Bury St Edmunds, Suffolk IP30 0ER
Tel: 01284 386250
e-mail: lucyredman@redmangardendesigns.fsnet.co.uk

Design your own garden with the help of distinguished Garden Designer,
Lucy Redman. Short courses range from the one-day "Plantaholic Days"
or 5-day Intensive Garden Design Course, to the 10 week part-time courses,
where a design consultation visit is made to each students garden, based
on which they can then transform their gardens. Small group sizes ensure
individual tuition.

WOOLPIT

6 miles E of Bury St Edmunds on the A14

The **Church of St Mary the Virgin** is
Woolpit's crowning glory, with a
marvellous porch and one of the most
magnificent double hammerbeam roofs,
with two rows of angels. The village was
long famous for its brick industry, and
the majority of the old buildings are
faced with 'Woolpit Whites'. The
yellowish-white brick looked very much
like more expensive stone and for several
centuries was widely exported. Some was
used in the building of the Senate wing of
the Capitol in Washington DC. Red bricks
were also produced, and the **Bygones
Museum** has a brick-making display and
also tells the story of the evolution of the
village.

Nearby is a moated site known as
Lady's Well, a place of pilgrimage in the
Middle Ages. The water from the spring
was reputed to have healing properties,
most efficacious in curing eye troubles.

A favourite Woolpit legend concerns
the **Green Children**, a brother and sister
with green complexions who appeared
one day in a field, apparently attracted by
church bells. Though hungry, they would
eat nothing until some green beans were
produced. Given shelter by the lord of the
manor, they learned to speak English and
said that they came from a place called St
Martin. The boy survived for only a short
time, but the girl thrived, lost her green

colour, was baptised and married a man
from King's Lynn - no doubt leaving
many a Suffolk man green with envy!

THE BRADFIELDS

7 miles SE of Bury St Edmunds off the A134

The Bradfields - St George, St Clare and
Combust - thread their way through a
delightful part of the countryside and are
well worth a little exploration, not only to
see the picturesque villages themselves
but for a stroll in the historic **Bradfield
Woods**. These woods stand on the eastern
edge of the parish of **Bradfield St George**
and have been turned into an outstanding
nature reserve, tended and coppiced in
the same way for more than 700 years and
home to a wide variety of flora and fauna.
They once belonged to the Abbey of St
Edmundsbury and part of them is still
today called Monk's Park Wood.

Coppicing involves cutting a tree back
down to the ground every ten years or so.
Woodlands were managed in this way to
provide an annual crop of timber for
local use, and the regrowth after
coppicing is very fast as the root is
already strongly established. Willow and
hazel are the trees most commonly
coppiced. Willow is often pollarded, a
less drastic form of coppicing where the
trees are cut far enough from the ground
to stop grazing animals having a free
lunch.

Bradfield St Clare, the central of the three Bradfields, has a rival claim to that of Hoxne as the site of the martyrdom of St Edmund. The St Clare family arrived with the Normans and added their name to the village, and the church, originally All Saints, was rededicated to St Clare; it is the only church in England dedicated to her. **Bradfield Combust**, where the pretty River Lark rises, probably takes it curious name from the fact that the local hall was burnt to the ground during the 14th century riots against the Abbot of St Edmundsbury's crippling tax demands. Arthur Young (1741-1820), noted writer on social, economic and agricultural subjects, is buried in the village churchyard.

COCKFIELD

8 miles SE of Bury St Edmunds off the A1141

Cockfield is perhaps the most widely spread village in all Suffolk, its little thatched cottages scattered around and between no fewer than nine greens. Great Green is the largest, with two football pitches and other recreation areas, and Parsonage Green has a literary connection: the Old Rectory was once home to a Dr Babbington, whose nephew Robert Louis Stevenson was a frequent visitor and who is said to have written *Treasure Island* while staying there. Cockfield also shelters one of the last windmills to have been built in Suffolk (1891). Its working life was very short but the tower still stands, now in use as a private residence.

THORPE MORIEUX

9 miles SE of Bury St Edmunds off the B1071

St Mary's Church in Thorpe Morieux is situated in as pleasant a setting as anyone could wish to find. With water meadows, ponds, a stream and a fine Tudor farmhouse to set it off, this 14th century church presents a memorable picture of old England. Look at the church, then take the time to wander around the peaceful churchyard with its profusion of springtime aconites, followed by the colourful flowering of limes and chestnuts in summer.

GREAT WELNETHAM

2 miles S of Bury St Edmunds off the A134

One of the many surviving Suffolk windmills is to be found here, just south of the village. The sails were lost in a gale 80 years ago but the tower and a neighbouring old barn make an attractive sight.

HAWKEDON

9 miles S of Bury St Edmunds off the A143

Hawkedon is designated a place of outstanding beauty and the **Church of St Mary** is located untypically in the middle of the village green. The pews and intricately carved bench-ends take the eye here, along with a canopied stoup (a recess for holding holy water) and a Norman font. There is a wide variety of carved animals, many on the bench-ends but some on the roof cornice. One of the stalls is decorated with the carving of a crane holding a stone in its claw; legend says that if the crane was on watch and fell asleep, the stone would drop and the noise would wake it.

ALPHETON

10 miles S of Bury St Edmunds on the A134

Several points of interest at this little village straddling the main road. It was first settled in 991 and its name means the *farm of Aefflaed*. That lady was the wife of Ealdorman Beorhtnoth of Essex, who was killed resisting the Danes at the Battle of Maldon and is buried in Ely Minster.

The hall, the farm and the church stand in a quiet location away from the main road and about a mile from the village. This remoteness is not unusual: some attribute it to the villagers moving during times of plague but the more likely explanation is simply that the scattered cottages, originally in several tiny hamlets, centred, for whatever reason, in a more convenient site than that of the church. Equally possible is that it was built to suit the local landed family (that is to say, next door). The main features at the **Church of St Peter and St Paul** are the flintwork around the parapet (the exterior is otherwise fairly undistinguished), the carefully restored 15th century porch and some traces of an ancient wall painting of St Christopher with the Christ Child. All in all, a typical country church of unpretentious dignity and well worth a short detour from the busy main roads.

Back in the village, two oak trees were planted and a pump installed in 1887, to commemorate Queen Victoria's 50 years on the throne. Another of the village's claims to fame is that its American airfield was used as the setting for the classic film *Twelve o'Clock High*, in which Gregory Peck memorably plays a Second World War flight commander cracking up under the strain of countless missions.

SHIMPLING

9 miles S of Bury St Edmunds off the B1066

Shimpling is a peaceful farming community whose church, **St George's**, is approached by a lime avenue. It is notable for Victorian stained glass and a Norman font, and in the churchyard is the Faint House, a small stone building where ladies overcome by the tightness of their stays could decently retreat from the service. The banker Thomas Halifax built many of Shimpling's cottages and also the village school and Chadacre Hall, which Lord Iveagh later turned into an agricultural college. That role

ceased in 1989 and the Hall is again in private hands.

LAWSHALL

8 miles S of Bury St Edmunds off the A134

A spread-out village first documented in 972 but regularly giving up evidence of earlier occupation. A Bronze Age sword dated at around 600BC was found here and is now in Bury Museum. The Church of All Saints, Perpendicular with some Early English bits, stands on one of the highest points in Suffolk, and next to it is Lawshall Hall whose owners once entertained Queen Elizabeth I. Another interesting site in Lawshall is the Wishing Well, a well-cover on the green put up in memory of Charles Tyrwhitt Drake, who worked for the Royal Geographic Society and was killed in Jerusalem.

HARTEST

9 miles S of Bury St Edmunds on the B1066

Hartest, which has a history as long as Alpheton's, celebrated its millennium in 1990 with the erection of a village sign (the hart, or stag). It's an agreeable spot in a valley, with colour-washed houses and chestnut trees on the green. Also on the green are All Saints Church (mentioned in the Domesday Book) and a large glacial stone, the **Hartest Stone**, which was dragged by a team of 45 horses from where it was found in a field in neighbouring Somerton. From 1789 until the 1930s Hartest staged a St George's Day Fair, an annual jolly celebrating King George III's recovery from one of his spells of madness. Just outside the village is **Gifford's Hall**, a smallholding which includes 12 acres of vines and a winery producing white and rosé wines and fruit liqueurs. There are also organic vegetable gardens, wild flower meadows, black St Kilda sheep, black Berkshire pigs, goats and free-range fowl. The Hall is particularly famous for its sweet peas and roses, and an annual festival is held on the last weekend in June. Open from Easter to the end of October.

HORRINGER

3 miles SW of Bury St Edmunds on the A143

Rejoining the A143 by Chedburgh, the motorist will soon arrive at Horringer, whose village green is dominated by the flintstone Church of St Leonard. Beside

Approach to Ickworth House

the church are the gates of one of the country's most extraordinary and fascinating houses, now run by the National Trust. **Ickworth House** was the brainchild of the eccentric 4th Earl of Bristol and Bishop of Derry, whose inspiration for the house was Belle Isle, a house built on an island in Lake Windermere, and the massive structure is a central rotunda linking two semi-circular wings. As well as some wonderful Old Master paintings, the house has a notable collection of Georgian silver, friezes and sculptures by John Flaxman and frescoes copied from wall paintings discovered at the Villa Negroni in Rome in 1777 (see panel).

Arable land surrounds Horringer, with a large annual crop of sugar beet grown for processing at the factory in Bury, the largest of its kind in Europe.

CHEDBURGH

6 miles SW of Bury St Edmunds on the A1430

Farm parks are an excellent way of discovering the county's rural and agricultural legacy and **Rede Hall Farm Park**, near Chedburgh, is modelled on a working farm of the 1930-1950 period. The Suffolk Punch can be seen at work here, and there are rare breeds of farm animals, a nature trail, cart rides and working displays. There are picnic and play areas, a tea room and a gift shop. Open April-September.

ICKWORTH PARK & GARDENS

Ickworth, Horringer, Bury St Edmunds,
Suffolk IP29 5QE
Tel: 01284 735270 Fax: 01284 735175
e-mail: aihusr@smtp.ntrust.org.uk
website: www.nationaltrust.org.uk

Ickworth is one of the most unusual and surprising of National Trust properties, an elegant Italianate House and Gardens set within spectacular English parkland. The present house was begun in 1795, the creation of the famously eccentric Frederick, 4th Earl of Bristol and Bishop of Derry. The extraordinary central rotunda houses magnificent state rooms displaying Old Master paintings including works by Titian, Velasquez and Gainsborough. Ickworth is also noted for its Georgian silver and Regency furniture. Surrounding the house are the superb Italianate grounds featuring gold and silver gardens, a Victorian stumpery and the temple rose garden. The extensive wooded parkland created in part by Capability Brown is a living landscape rich in plant, animal and bird life. Ickworth has something for everyone with miles of waymarked walks, a vineyard which produces award-winning Ickworth wine, plant centre, challenging children's play area, deer hide, trim trail and family cycle route. There's also a shop and a restaurant.

NATIONAL HORSERACING MUSEUM

99 High Street, Newmarket, Suffolk CB8 8JL
Tel: 01638 667333 Fax: 01638 665600
website: www.nationalstud.co.uk

"The Newmarket Experience" comprises two separate attractions: **The National Horseracing Museum** and **The National Stud**. The story of racing throughout the ages is told through the Museum's permanent collections, featuring the horses, people, events and scandals that make the sport so colourful.

Highlights include the head of Persimmon, a great Royal Derby winner in 1896; a special display about Fred Archer, the Victorian jockey who committed suicide after losing the struggle to keep his weight down; the skeleton of Eclipse, ancestor of 90 per cent of modern thoroughbreds; items associated with Red Rum, Lester Piggott, Frankie Dettori and other heroes of the Turf. In the Practical Gallery, visitors can learn everything there is to know about the horse and jockey, and experience the thrill of riding on the horse simulator. The Gallery is staffed by retired jockeys and trainers, who make the world of racing come alive. Special exhibitions have included "*Why did you get that hat?*", a display of Gertrude Shilling's outrageous Ascot outfits. Mrs Shilling (1910-1999) was one of the most colourful and eccentric personalities ever to grace the sport.

The Museum also boasts a range of exciting temporary exhibitions, including paintings and other works of art with a racing theme. The daily minibus tours of working establishments in Newmarket are another treat, offering visitors a chance to see horses at close quarters and meet stable staff in a two-hour tour, as well as horses training on the gallops, the horses' swimming pool and a training yard, together with the historic town itself.

The National Stud extends a warm welcome to all its visitors. Breeding top-class thoroughbreds, the 500-acre site has 12 yards, 9 miles of roads and tracks, 60 miles of post and rail fencing, 21 houses, a feedmill and storage for 50 tons of hay and straw - all purpose built between 1963 and 1967. The Stud year follows a set pattern, with the breeding season officially beginning on 15th February, and ending with the annual National Stud Fair and Stallion Parade held over the first week in December. Any tour, which will vary depending on the season, takes in the superb Stallion Unit, along with the stallions in residence, Nursery Yards and mares and foals in their paddocks. The helpful, informative tour guides offer a full insight into the workings of a modern stud.

The Stud provides training courses on horse husbandry and stud management for students who wish to make their careers in the thoroughbred breeding industry.

NEWMARKET

On the western edge of Suffolk, Newmarket is home to some 16,000 human and 3,000 equine inhabitants. The historic centre of British racing lives and breathes horses, with 60 training establishments, 50 stud farms, the top annual thoroughbred sales and two racecourses (the only two in Suffolk). Thousands of the population are involved in the trade, and racing art and artefacts fill the shops, galleries and museums; one of the oldest established saddlers even has a preserved horse on display - Robert the Devil, runner-up in the 1880 Derby.

History records that Queen Boadicea of the Iceni, to whom the six-mile Devil's Dyke stands as a memorial, thundered around these parts in her lethal chariot behind her shaggy-haired horses and she is said to have established the first stud here. In medieval times the chalk heathland was a popular arena for riders to display their skills and in 1605 James I paused on a journey north to enjoy a spot of hare coursing. He loved the place and said he would be back; in moving the royal court to his Newmarket headquarters he began the royal patronage which has remained strong down the years. Charles I maintained the royal connection but it was Charles II who really put the place on the map when he, too, moved the royal court to Newmarket in the spring and autumn of each year. He initiated the Town Plate, a race which he himself won twice as a rider and which, in a modified form, still exists.

One of the racecourses, the **Rowley Mile**, takes its name from Old Rowley, a favourite horse of the Merry Monarch. Here the first two classics of the season, the 1,000 and 2,000 Guineas, are run, together with important autumn events including the Cambridgeshire and the Cesarewich. The other is the leafy July Course with its delightful garden-party atmosphere, the venue for all the important summer fixtures.

The visitor to Newmarket can learn almost all there is to know about flat racing and racehorses by making the grand tour of the several establishments which are open to the public (sometimes by appointment only). The **Jockey Club**, which was the first governing body of the sport and until recently the ultimate authority, was formed in the middle of the 18th century and occupies an imposing building which was restored and rebuilt in Georgian style in the 1930s. Originally a social club for rich gentlemen with an interest in the turf, it soon became the all-powerful regulator of British racing, owning all the racing and training land. When holding an enquiry the stewards sit round a horseshoe table and the jockey or trainer under scrutiny faces them on a strip of carpet by the door - hence the expression 'on the mat'.

Next to the Jockey Club in the High Street is the **National Horseracing Museum** (see panel on page 196). Opened by the Queen in 1983, its five galleries chronicle the history of the Sport of Kings from its royal beginnings through to the top trainers and jockeys of today.

Blythburgh Parish Church, Newmarket

Visitors can ride a mechanical horse, try on racing silks, record a race commentary, ask awkward questions and enjoy a snack in the café, whose walls are hung with murals of racing personalities. The chief treasures among the art collection are equine paintings by Alfred Munnings, while the most famous item is probably the skeleton of the mighty Eclipse, whose superiority over his contemporaries gave rise to the saying 'Eclipse first, the rest nowhere'. There are special displays on some of the best-known jockeys, including Fred Archer, the peerless Lester Piggott and Frankie Dettori, and an exhibition of Mrs Shilling's outrageous Ascot hats was a great success in 2001.

A few steps away is **Palace House**, which contains the remains of Charles II's palace; in the same street is **Nell Gwynn's House**, which some say was connected beneath the street to the palace. The diarist John Evelyn spent a night in (or on?) the town during a royal visit and declared the occasion to be "more resembling a luxurious and abandoned rout than a Christian court". The palace is the new location for the Newmarket Tourist Information Centre. Other must-sees on the racing enthusiast's tour are **Tattersalls**, where leading thoroughbred sales take place from April to December; the **British Racing School**, where top jockeys are taught the ropes; the **National Stud**, open from March till August plus race days in September and October (booking essential); and the **Animal Health Trust** based at Lanwades Hall, where a Visitor Centre has recently opened. The National Stud at one time housed no fewer than three Derby winners - Blakeney, Mill Reef and Grundy.

And it is entirely appropriate that the last railway station to employ a horse for shunting wagons (a Suffolk Punch)

should have been at Newmarket. That hardworking one-horse-power shunter retired in 1967.

AROUND NEWMARKET

EXNING

2 miles NW of Newmarket on the A14

A pause is certainly in order at this ancient village, whether on a trip out of Newmarket or arriving from Cambridgeshire on the A14. Anglo-Saxons, Romans, the Iceni and the Normans were all here, and the Domesday Book records the village under the name of Esselinga. The village was stricken by a plague during the Iceni occupation, so its market was moved to the next village. Thus Newmarket acquired its name. Exning's written history begins when Henry II granted the manor to the Count of Boulogne, who divided it between four of his knights. References to them and to subsequent Lords of the Manor are to be found in the little **Church of St Martin**, which might well have been founded by the Burgundian Christian missionary monk St Felix in the 7th century. Water from the well used by that saint to baptise members of the Saxon royal family is still used for similar ceremonies by the current vicar. The A14 is a busy main road, but pulling away from the traffic and spending time around this village will be rewarded by some quiet, pleasant walks.

KENTFORD

5 miles E of Newmarket by the A14

At the old junction of the Newmarket-Bury road stands the grave of a young boy who hanged himself after being accused of sheep-stealing. It was a well-established superstition that suicides should be buried at a crossroads to prevent their spirits from wandering. From time to time flowers are sometimes laid at the Boys Grave by punters hoping for good luck at Newmarket races!

MOULTON
4 miles E of Newmarket on the B1085

This most delightful village lies in wonderful farming country on chalky downland. Its proximity to Newmarket is apparent from the racehorses which are often to be seen on the large green. The River Kennett flows through the green, before running north to the Lark, a tributary of the Ouse. Flint walls are a feature of many of the buildings, but the main point of interest is the 15th century 4-arch **Packhorse Bridge** on the way to the church.

DALHAM
5 miles E of Newmarket on the B1063

Eighty per cent of the buildings are thatched (the highest proportion in Suffolk) and there are many other attractions in this pretty village. Above the village on one of the county's highest spots stands **St Mary's Church**, which dates from the 14th century. Its spire toppled over during the gales which swept the land on the night that Cromwell died, and was replaced by a tower in 1627. Sir Martin Stutteville was the leading light behind this reconstruction and an inscription at the back of the church notes that the cost was £400. That worthy's grandfather was Thomas Stutteville, whose memorial near the altar declares that "he saw the New World with Francis Drake". (Drake did not survive that journey - his third to South America.) Thomas's grandson died in the fullness of his years (62 wasn't bad for those times!) while hosting a jolly party at The Angel Hotel, Bury St Edmunds.

Dalham Hall was constructed in the first years of the 18th century at the order of the Bishop of Ely, who decreed that it should be built up until Ely Cathedral could be seen across the fens on a clear day. That view was sadly cut off in 1957 when a fire shortened the hall to two storeys. Wellington lived here for some years, and much later it was bought by Cecil Rhodes, who unfortunately died before taking up residence. His brother Francis erected the village hall in the adventurer's memory. Cecil is buried in the churchyard.

MILDENHALL
8 miles NE of Newmarket off the A11

On the edge of the Fens and Breckland, Mildenhall was once a port for the hinterland of West Suffolk, though the River Lark has long ceased to be a trade route. Most of the town's heritage is recorded in the excellent **Mildenhall & District Museum** in King Street. Here will be found exhibits of local history (including the distinguished RAF and USAAF base), crafts and domestic skills, the natural history of the Fens and Breckland and, perhaps most famously, the 'Mildenhall Treasure'. This was a cache of 34 pieces of 4th century Roman silverware - dishes, goblets and spoons - found by a ploughman in 1946 at Thistley Green and now on display in the British Museum. There is evidence of much earlier occupation than the Roman era, with flint tools and other artefacts being unearthed in 1988 on the site of an ancient lake.

The parish of Mildenhall is the largest in Suffolk so it is perhaps fitting that it should boast so magnificent a parish church as **St Mary's**, built of Barnack stone; it dominates the heart of the town and indeed its west tower commands the flat surrounding countryside. Above the splendid north porch (the largest in Suffolk) are the arms of Edward the Confessor and of St Edmund. The chancel, dating back to the 13th century,

WOODLANDS STABLES

Holywell Row, Mildenhall, Suffolk IP28 8NB
Tel/Fax: 01638 713825
e-mail: boss@eque-train.co.uk
website: www.eque-train.co.uk

Woodlands Stables in Holywell Row is a flourishing riding school set in the beautiful Suffolk countryside. After many years of running a large stud and training centre in Scotland, owner Doreen Johnstone, known as 'Boss', came south where her children trained and competed to much success. Together with her daughter Lorna, she runs the yard, where they train at all levels. Doreen recently celebrated 50 years of teaching. A perfectionist, she helps all her students reach their full potential. Beginners and experienced riders alike benefit from her expertise in Dressage, Show Jumping and Cross Country.

The secret of Doreen and Lorna's success is the ethos of this fine school: they see each person as an individual, with unique gifts and strengths which they are expert at bringing to the fore. No two riders or horses, are the same, and the Johnstones can explain the influence each rider has and how each horse can be encouraged to give of its best. Woodlands offer a range of clinics on site, and also an e-mail order training service, harnessing the latest technology to provide riders around the world with the benefit of Doreen's vast experience.

CANE AND ABLE ANTIQUES/INTERIORS

The Limes, 22 The Street, Beck Row, Mildenhall, Suffolk IP28 8AD
Tel: 01638 515529 Fax: 01638 583905
e-mail: bob_caneandable2@hotmail.com

They offer a personal, conscientious and comprehensive service which includes caning, rushing, upholstering, fabric supplies, veneering, gilding, carving, joint and wood repairs, wood-turning, desk top leathering, brass fittings and brass casting, marquetry and inlay repairs, and French and wax polishing.

From a workshop situated to the rear of owner Bob Costin's 200-year-old house, Bob painstakingly repairs and restores antique furniture. His expertise has been sought to renovate a caned open-armed chair once belonging to Charles Darwin, a set of eight walnut chairs dating back to the 17th century, a Queen Anne walnut chest on chest circa 1702 and many other priceless

and well-loved chairs and furniture brought to him.

Bob comes from a long line of family chair makers dating back to 1841, when his forebear Henry Costin was a master chair maker in Great Marlow. He is very much still involved in chair design and crafting. He is also happy to undertake furniture sales, search, valuations, and insurance estimates and repairs. Storage and transportation arranged. For expert furniture care and dependable service, look no further.

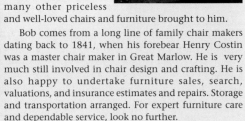

is a marvellous work of architecture, but pride of place goes to the east window, divided into seven vertical lights. Above the nave and aisles is a particularly fine hammerbeam roof whose outstanding feature is the carved angels. Efforts of the Puritans to destroy the angels failed, but traces of buckshot and arrowheads have been found embedded in the woodwork.

Sir Henry North built a manor house on the north side of the church in the 17th century and his successors included a dynasty of the Bunbury family who were Lords of the Manor from 1747 to 1933. Sir Henry Edward Bunbury was the man chosen to let Napoleon Bonaparte know of his exile to St Helena, but the best known member of the family is Sir Thomas, who in 1780 tossed a coin with Lord Derby to see whose name should be borne by a race to be inaugurated at Epsom. Lord Derby won, but Sir Thomas had the satisfaction of winning the first running of the race with his colt Diomed.

BRANDON

9 miles NE of Mildenhall on the A1065

On the edge of Thetford Forest by the Little Ouse, Brandon was long ago a thriving port, but flint is what really put it on the map. The town itself is built mainly of flint, which was mined from early Neolithic times to make arrowheads and other implements and weapons of war. The gun flint industry brought substantial wealth, and a good flint-knapper could produce up to 300 gun flints in an hour. Brandon was the last place in Britain to follow this trade, and when the invention of the percussion cap killed off much of their work they turned to shaping flints for church building and ornamental purposes. The **Heritage Centre**, in a former fire station in George Street, provides visitors with a splendid insight into this industry, while for an even more tangible feel a visit to Grimes

Graves, just over the Norfolk border, reveals an amazing site covering 35 acres and 300 pits.

The whole of this northwest corner of Suffolk, know as Breckland, offers almost unlimited opportunities for touring by car, cycling or walking. A mile south of town on the B1106 is **Brandon Country Park**, a 30-acre landscaped site with a tree and history trail, forest walks, an orienteering course leading into Thetford Forest, a lake, a walled garden, picnic sites and a visitor centre.

ELVEDEN

5 miles S of Brandon on the A11

The road from Brandon leads south through the forest to a historic estate village with some unusual architectural features. Where the three parishes of Elveden, Eriswell and Icklingham meet a tall war memorial in the form of a Corinthian column is a landmark.

Elveden Hall became more remarkable than its builders intended when Prince Duleep Singh, heir to the throne of the Punjab, a noted sportsman and shot, and the man who handed over the Koh-I-Noor diamond to Queen Victoria, arrived on the scene. Exiled to England with a handsome pension, he bought the Georgian house in 1863 and commissioned John Norton to transform it into a palace modelled on those in Lahore and Delhi. Although it is stated that in private Duleep Singh referred to Queen Victoria as "Mrs Fagin......receiver of stolen goods" (the diamond), he kept close contact with the royal household and the Queen became his son's godmother. The Guinness family (Lord Iveagh) later took it over and joined in the fun, adding even more exotic adornments including a replica Taj Mahal, while at the same time creating the largest arable farm in the whole of the country.

North-east Essex has the true feel of East Anglia, particularly around the outstanding villages of the Stour Valley - which has come to be known as Constable Country, shared with its neighbour Suffolk. The inland villages and small towns here are notably historic and picturesque, offering very good touring and walking opportunities. A plethora of half-timbered medieval buildings, farms and churches mark this region out as of particular historical interest. Monuments to engineering feats past and present include Hedingham Castle, Chappel Viaduct and the postmill at Bocking Church Street.

Audley End House & Gardens

Truly lovely villages abound, rewarding any journey to this part of the county. There are also many fine gardens to visit, and the region's principal town, Colchester, is a mine of interesting sights and experiences.

The North Essex Coast has a distinguished history and a strong maritime heritage, as exemplified in towns like Harwich, Manningtree and Mistley. Further examples are the fine Martello Towers - circular brick edifices built to provide a coastal defence against Napoleon's armies - along the Tendring coast at Walton, Clacton, Jaywick and Point Clear. Dating from 1808 to 1812, each is mounted with a gun on the roof.

Epping Forest

The Tendring Peninsula, which takes its name from the old Tendring Hundred (a name coming from the county divisions of Saxon times, of which Tendring was a centre), has a rich and varied heritage ranging from prehistoric remains to medieval churches and elegant Victorian villas. The Tendring Coast contains an interesting mix of extensive tidal inlets, sandy beaches and low cliffs, and the Tendring District Council publishes a series of 'Tendring Trails' beginning at Mistley, Manningtree, Dedham, Ardleigh and other points around the North Essex Coast.

The Stour Estuary, Hamford Water and Colne Estuary are all renowned for seabirds and other wildlife. Many areas are protected nature reserves. The

Manningtree-Ramsey road passes through some of the best coastal scenery in Essex, with some outstanding views of the Suffolk shore.

This is of course also the part of the county known as "the sunshine holiday coast". Resorts, both boisterous and more placid, dot the coastline here: Clacton-on-Sea, Frinton-on-Sea and Walton-on-the-Naze to name but three - and offer many opportunities for relaxation and recreation.

The small northwest Essex towns of Saffron Walden, Thaxted, Great Dunmow and Stansted Mountfichet are some of the most beautiful and interesting in the country. This area is also home to a wealth of picturesque villages boasting weatherboarded houses and pargeting. The quiet country lanes are perfect for walking, cycling or just exploring. This area also retains three beautiful and historic windmills, at Stansted Mountfichet, Aythorpe Roding and Thaxted. Visitors to southwest Essex and the Epping Forest will find a wealth of woodland, nature reserves, superb gardens and rural

Thatched Cottage, Arkesden

delights. Southwest Essex also has major attractions in Audley End House and Waltham Abbey.

Bordering the north bank of the Thames, the borough of Thurrock has long been a gateway to London but also affords easy access to southwest Essex and to Kent. This thriving borough encompasses huge swathes of green belt country, and along its 18 miles of Thames frontage there are many important marshland wildlife habitats. History, too, abounds in this part of the county. Henry VIII built riverside Block Houses at East and West Tilbury, which later became Coalhouse Fort and Tilbury Fort. It was at West Tilbury that Queen Elizabeth I gave the famous speech to her troops, gathered to meet the Spanish Armada threat. Both forts played an important defence role during the two World Wars. At the extreme southeast of the county, Southend is a popular and friendly seaside resort with a wealth of sites and amenities. There are also smaller seaside communities which repay a visit. The area surrounding the Rivers Blackwater and Crouch contains a wealth of ancient woodland and other natural beauty, particularly along the estuaries and the Chelmer and Blackwater Canal. This corner of Essex is ideal for those who enjoy any kind of watersports activities. The island of Northey near Maldon is owned by the National Trust and is a haven for wildlife.

There are hundreds of acres of ancient woodland, much of it coppiced, which is the traditional woodland management technique which encourages a vast array of natural flora and fauna. This stretch of Essex affords some marvellous walking, cycling, birdwatching and other nature pursuits.

LOCATOR MAP

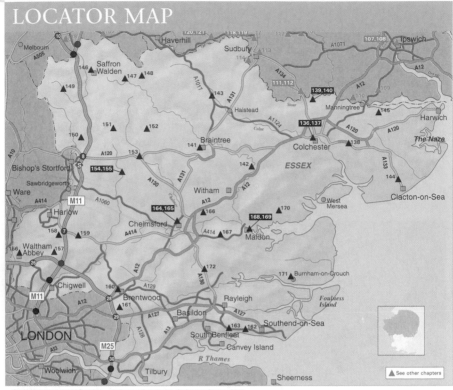

© MAPS IN MINUTES ™ 2001 © Crown Copyright, Ordnance Survey 2001

Advertisers and Places of Interest

COLCHESTER

England's oldest recorded town, Colchester has over 2,000 years of history to discover. During the 1st century, its prime location made it an obvious target for invading Romans, and the Roman Emperor Claudius oversaw the surrender of 11 British Kings in Colchester. In AD 60 Queen Boadicea helped to establish her place in history by taking revenge on the Romans and burning the town to the ground, before going on to destroy London and St Albans. Roman walls - the oldest in Britain - still surround the oldest part of town and Balkerne Gate, west gate of the original Roman town, is the largest surviving Roman gateway in the country. The stretch of ancient wall that runs from the Gate incorporates a quaint little pub called - what else? - the Hole in the Wall.

Today the town is presided over by its lofty Town Hall and enormous Victorian water tower, nicknamed 'Jumbo' after London Zoo's first African elephant, controversially sold to PT Barnum in 1882. The tower has four massive pillars of one and a quarter million bricks, 369 tons of stone and 142 tons of iron, which

COLCHESTER CASTLE

Castle Park, High Street, Colchester
Tel: 01206 282939
website: www.colchestermuseums.co.uk

Colchester Castle is undeniably one of the most important historic buildings in the country, and today, a thousand years after it was built, it is still a living, vibrant place, a potent symbol of Britain's oldest recorded town. Colchester was the first capital of Britain and beneath the Castle's foundations are the remains of one of the most renowned Roman buildings, the Temple of Claudius. To the Romans it was the symbol of their power and success, but to the native Britons it was a symbol of oppression.

The temple became a main target of the rebels led by Queen Boudica (Boadicea) who attacked the Roman town in AD60. The town's citizens barricaded themselves in the temple but after two days they were all killed. It is estimated that as many as 30,000 could have been killed during the sacking of Colchester. After the revolt had been suppressed the town and the temple were rebuilt.

Around 1076 King William I ordered a royal fortress to be built at Colchester, and the great stone base of the now ruined temple was an obvious foundation for the central tower or keep of the new castle. The great size of the temple dictated that of the keep, which was the largest ever built in Britain.

For most of its life the Castle was used as a prison; one of the most infamous episodes in its history occurred in 1645 when Matthew Hopkins, the self-styled Witchfinder General, used the Castle to imprison and interrogate suspected witches. The Castle first opened its doors in the role of Museum in 1860 and today features many hands-on displays to help explain the town-people's experience of Colchester's varying fortunes. Visitors can slip into a toga, feel the weight of Roman armour, try on medieval hats and shoes and see treasures like the Roman bronze statue of Mercury and the Colchester Vase, one of the finest examples of Roman pottery found in Britain.

work to support the 230,000 gallon tank. The elaborate Victorian Town Hall is topped with a statue of St Helena. This good woman, who lived in the 3rd and 4th centuries, was the daughter of King Coel, who built the city that was originally called Camulodunum. Helena fell in love with the leader of the Roman forces, Constantinus Chlorus, and peace was made so that they could marry. She was converted to Christianity and produced a son who became Rome's first Christian Emperor, Constantine the Great.

The town affords plenty to see and explore, which can be done by guided town walks as well as bus tours. A good place to start is **Colchester Castle** itself and its museum (see panel on page 205). The Normans built their castle on the foundations of the Roman temple of Claudius, and since they used many of the Roman bricks in its construction, it boasts the largest Norman keep ever built in Europe - the only part still left standing. The keep houses the Castle Museum, one of the most exciting hands-on historical attractions in the country.

Hollytrees Museum in the High Street is located in a fine Georgian house dating back to 1718. The house belonged to the solicitor and sometime Member of Parliament for Colchester Charles Gray, who put his wealth to the best possible use by devoting much of his money and energy into restoring the Castle, which had sustained great damage during the

Civil War. It is now home to a wonderful collection of toys, costumes, scientific instruments, curios and antiquities, along with a view of Colchester by Pissarro. Also nearby, housed in the former All Saints' Church, is the **Natural History Museum**, with exhibits and many hands-on displays illustrating the natural history of Essex. Around the corner on Trinity Street, another former church, Holy Trinity - the only Saxon building left in Colchester - is home to the **Museum of Social History**, containing displays of rural crafts and country life. An arch opposite this museum leads to **Tymperleys Clock Museum**, the 15th century timber-framed home of William Gilberd, who entertained Elizabeth I with experiments in electricity. Today this fine example of architectural splendour houses a magnificent collection of 18th and 19th century Colchester-made clocks. The Colchester Arts Centre, not far from Balkerne Gate, features a regular programme of visual arts, drama, music, poetry and dance, while the Mercury Theatre is the town's premier site for stage dramas, comedies and musical theatre.

Dutch Protestants arrived in Colchester in the 16th century, fleeing Spanish rule in the Netherlands, and revitalised the local cloth industry. The houses of these Flemish weavers are in the Dutch Quarter, which remains a charming and relatively quiet corner of this bustling town. Close to the railway station are the ruins of St Botolph's Priory, the oldest Augustinian priory in the country, whose remains are a potent reminder of the bitterness of those times.

On Bourne Road, south of the town centre just off the B1025, there's a striking stepped and curved gabled building known as **Bourne Mill**. Built in 1591 from stone taken from the nearby St John's Abbeygate, this delightful restored building near a lovely millpond was originally a fishing lodge, later converted (in the 19th century) into a mill - and still in working order.

Colchester Zoo, just off the A12 outside the town, stands in the 40-acre park of Stanway Hall, with its 16th century mansion and church dating from the 14th century.

Two Colchester specialities are remembered in the annual **Oyster Feast** and **Colchester Rose Show**. Colchester oysters are still cultivated on beds in the lower reaches of the River Colne, which skirts the northern edge of town. A visit to the Oyster Fisheries is a fascinating experience, and the tour includes complimentary fresh oysters and glass of wine.

Just north of the centre of Colchester, **High Woods Country Park** offers 330 acres of woodland, grassland and wetland. A central lake is fed by a small tributary of the River Colne. The land originated as three ancient farms, and forms part of a royal hunting forest. Large numbers of musket balls dating from the Civil War period have been unearthed, indicating that the woods served as a base for the Roundheads.

AROUND COLCHESTER

WIVENHOE
4 miles SE of Colchester off the A133

This riverside town on the banks of the River Colne was once renowned as a smugglers' haunt, and the attractive quayside is steeped in maritime history. There are still strong connections with the sea, with boat-building having replaced fishing as the main industry. The pretty church, with its distinctive cupola atop a sturdy tower, stands on the site of the former Saxon church and retains some impressive 16th century brasses.

The small streets lead into each other and end at the picturesque waterfront, where fishing boats and small sailing craft bob at their moorings. On the Quay visitors will find the **Nottage Institute**, the River Colne's nautical academy; classes here teach students about knots, skippering and even how to build a boat! It is open to visitors on Sundays in summer. The **Wivenhoe Trail**, by the river, is an interesting walk starting at the

MITCHELLS FARM SHOP

Clacton Road, Elmstead, Colchester, Essex CO7 7PE
Tel: 01206 824610 Fax: 01206 824944

Mitchell's Farm Shop is a welcoming family-run shop specialising in the freshest local produce, including a great deal grown on the 600-acre arable farm it is part of. Owners Christine and Ian Mitchell offer a wide range of top-quality vegetables and fruits, together with locally-made ice cream, frozen fish, jams, preserves, pickles, apple juice and much more.

railway station and continuing along the river to Colchester Hythe. Wivenhoe Woods is dotted with grassy glades set with tables, the perfect place for a picnic.

East of the Quay the public footpath takes visitors to the impressive Tidal Surge Barrier, one of only two in the country. Volunteers run a ferry service operating across the River Colne between the Quay at Wivenhoe, Fingringhoe and Rowhedge. Nearby Wivenhoe Park has been the site of the campus for the University of Essex since 1962. Visitors are welcome to stroll around the grounds.

ABBERTON

3 miles S of Colchester off the B1026

Two natural beauties are within reach of this village. **Abberton Reservoir** is a 1,200-acre reservoir and wildlife centre, ideal for birdwatching. The site features a conservation centre, observation room, nature trails and a shop. Four miles further east, **Fingringhoe Wick Nature Reserve** offers visitors 125 acres of woodland and lakes by the Colne estuary.

COPFORD

3½ miles SW of Colchester off the B1022

Copford's crowning glory is the wonderful Norman Church of St Michael & All Angels, with its magnificent 12th century wall paintings, restored after being discovered under layers of whitewash. Many of the paintings show a strong Byzantine influence in design, execution and subject matter.

LAYER MARNEY

6 miles SW of Colchester off the B1022

The mansion, which was planned to rival Hampton Court, was never completed, but its massive eight-storey brick and terra cotta Tudor gatehouse, known as **Layer Marney Tower**, is very impressive. Built between 1515 and 1525, it is the

tallest gatehouse in Britain and one of the most striking examples of 16th century architecture in the land. Its four magnificent towers, in 16th century Italianate design, were built for Lord Marney, Henry VIII's Lord Privy Seal. Only the towers had been built at the time of Lord Marney's death; the work stopped, never to be completed. Lord Marney is buried in the churchyard next to the mansion. As well as spectacular views from the top of the towers, they are surrounded by formal gardens designed at the turn of the century, with lovely roses, yew hedges and herbaceous borders. There is also on site a rare breeds farm, farm shop and tea room, and, new for 2001, an outdoor adventure playground. Special events are held regularly throughout the summer, typified in 2001 by an Easter Egg Quiz, Foolhardy Folk Circus & Workshop; History Days Guided Tours; Craft Fair and Entertainers; and Bicycle Day with organised rides and cycle workshops.

TIPTREE

7 miles SW of Colchester on the B1023

As all true jam-lovers will know, Tiptree is famed as the home of the Wilkin & Sons jam factory, a Victorian establishment which now boasts a fascinating visitors' centre in the grounds of the original factory.

CHAPPEL

5 miles W of Colchester off the A604

Here, on a 4 acre site beside Chappel and Wakes Colne Station, is the **East Anglian Railway Museum**, a comprehensive collection of period railway architecture, engineering and memorabilia in beautifully restored station buildings. For every railway buff, young or old, this is the place to try your hand at being a signalman and admire the handsome restored engines and carriages. Special steam days and other events are held throughout the year. There is also a delightful miniature railway. The dramatic 32-arched Chappel Viaduct standing 75 feet above the Colne Valley and a designated European Monument, was begun in 1846 and opened in 1849.

East Anglian Railway Museum

LAMARSH

9 miles NW of Colchester off the B1087

Paradise Centre on Twinstead Road in Lamarsh is a fun day out for children and grown-ups alike. There are miniature goats, bantams and a play area, while gardeners will find a wide variety of unusual plants, particularly woodland ones, beautifully laid out and for sale.

As with other River Stour communities, there is some superb walking here.

BOXTED

5 miles N of Colchester off the A134

A delightful village skirting the ancient **Essex Way** linking Epping with Harwich. Between here and Great Horkesley is a six-acre site, **Carter's Vineyard**, where visitors can enjoy vineyard and winery

SHEIL NURSERIES

Horkesley Road, Boxted, Colchester, Essex C04 5HS
Tel: 01206 273300 Fax: 01206 272830

The husband and wife team of Dominic and Linda Sheil are partners in the thriving wholesale and retail nursery that bears their name. Both have many years experience in the nursery and allied professions; they ran a wholesale flower business before taking over these premises - an existing nursery - in December 2000, since when they have make significant expansions to the scope and the stock.

Located in three acres just off the A134 Colchester-Sudbury road, the nursery grows perennials and shrubs and seasonal bedding and basket plants. Among the specialities are fuchsias, pelargoniums, with over 100 varieties in stock, and penstemons, with up to 35 varieties available in their season. The

nursery is open from 8.30 to 6 seven days a week, closing only on Christmas Day and Boxing Day. Coach parties from gardening and horticultural clubs and societies are welcome by appointment, and whether alone or in a group visitors can always look forward to a friendly welcome from the owners and a wag of the tail from their black labrador Gunner. Anyone with an interest in gardening will enjoy spending an hour or two at Sheil Nurseries; the countryside in this part of Essex is really delightful, and nearby Colchester, the oldest recorded town in England, is also well worth a visit.

THE COTTAGE GARDEN

Langham Road, Boxted, Essex CO4 5HU
Tel: 01206 272269
website: www.thecottage-garden.co.uk

Three reasons to choose **The Cottage Garden** nursery in Boxted are choice, quality and service. There's an excellent selection of all types of plants and garden furniture, antiques and artefacts. Set in three acres, all plants are home grown with care and attention. With over 20 years experience of growing and selling plants and seeking items to enhance any garden, the friendly staff can offer valuable advice.

tours and wine tastings, and walk the nature trail around lakes and woodland. Power for the enterprise comes from the wind and the sun, and on site is a permanent exhibition of renewable energy ideas.

ARDLEIGH

3 miles NE of Colchester off the A137

Tendring's most western village comprises an attractive group of 16th and 17th century cottages grouped around the fine 15th century **Butterfield Church**. **Spring Valley Mill**, a now privately owned 18th century timber-framed and weatherboarded edifice, was once a working watermill, later adapted to steam. Day and half-day canoeing and sailing lessons can be taken at the Ardleigh Outdoor Education Centre.

DEDHAM

6 miles NE of Colchester off the A14

This is true Constable country, along the border with Suffolk, and the county's prettiest area. The village has several fine old buildings, especially the 15th century flint church, its pinnacled tower familiar from so many Constable paintings. Also here is the school Constable went to, and good walks through the protected riverside meadows of Dedham Vale to Flatford, where Bridge Cottage is a restored thatched 16th century building

housing a display about Constable, who featured this cottage in several of his paintings (his father's mill is across the river lock).

Dedham Vale Family Farm on Mill Street is a 16-acre farm boasting a comprehensive collection of British farm animals, including many different breeds of livestock such as pigs, sheep, cattle, Suffolk horses, goats and poultry. Children may enter certain paddocks to stroke and feed the animals (bags of feed provided).

The **Art and Craft Centre** on Dedham's High Street is well worth a visit, and the **Toy Museum**, also on the High Street, has a fascinating collection of dolls, teddies, toys, games, doll houses and other artefacts of childhoods past.

At Castle House, approximately ¾ of a mile from the village centre on the corner of East Lane and Castle Hill, The **Sir Alfred Munnings Art Museum** is housed in the former home, studios and grounds of the famous painter, who lived here between 1898 and 1920. The museum prides itself on the diversity of paintings and sculptures on view. The house itself, which stands in well-maintained grounds, is a mixture of Tudor and Georgian periods, carefully restored. Munnings' original furniture is still in place.

BRAINTREE

This town and its close neighbour Bocking are sited at the crossing of two Roman roads and were brought together by the cloth industry in the 16th century. Flemish weavers settled here, followed by many Huguenots. One, Samuel Courtauld, set up a silk mill in 1816 and, by 1866, employed over 3,000 Essex inhabitants. The **Working Silk Museum** on South Street features demonstrations of silk production - from start to finish - in a former mill building that has been faithfully restored. The original hand looms, some over 150 years old, are still used to weave silk fabrics for many of the royal houses throughout the world.

The magnificent former Town Hall is another of the many Courtauld legacies. It was built in 1928 with oak-panelled walls, murals by Grieffenhagen showing stirring scenes of local history, and a grand central tower with a five-belled striking clock. A smaller but no less fascinating reminder of Courtauld's generosity is the 1930s bronze fountain, with bay, shell and fish, at the centre of Braintree.

Huguenot names such as Courtauld are connected with international enterprises to this day. Their reason for coming to Britain is a fascinating and poignant tale. Formed in France in 1559 as an organised Protestant group taking direction from Calvin and the Calvinistic Reformation in Geneva, the Huguenots were at first allowed to live and worship freely. However, as political and religious rivalries grew in France, the Catholic majority started to persecute them; a century of war, massacre and bloodshed followed. Finally in 1685 all their rights were stripped. In the chaos that ensued, many died and thousands fled. It was to turn out to be France's loss, for the

BRAINTREE DISTRICT MUSEUM

The Town Hall Centre, Market Place, Braintree, Essex CM7 3YG
Tel: 01376 328868 Fax: 01376 344345
e-mail: jean@bdcmuseum.demon.co.uk
website: www.braintree.gov.uk/museum

In the historic market square (market days Wednesday and Saturday), **Braintree District Museum** is housed in a beautifully converted Victorian school. Visitors are assured of a warm welcome at this award-winning museum, whose elegant exhibition areas are in contrast to the somewhat stern Victorian facade; the exception to this is the faithfully re-created Victorian classroom, where nostalgia lovers will be in their element and where role-play lessons are provided for schools on a daily basis.

Braintree was the centre of the medieval wool trade in north Essex and gained international fame when Courtaulds evolved their revolutionary silk industry in the town. The permanent galleries tell the fascinating story of this industry and also of the development of engineering design - Braintree was also the home of Crittalls. Country crafts such as straw plaiting are featured, along with the rural artists who made their home in Great Barfield and became pivotal in the development of fine and decorative arts in the 1950s and 1960s. John Ray, often considered the father of English natural history, has a dedicated gallery to his ground-breaking research in the 17th century.

A feature of the Museum is the programme of changing exhibitions, often with a craft base such as ceramics, decorative arts and particularly textiles. Friendly staff are pleased to welcome visitors with a free Soundalive audio tour and explain the wide range of craft items available in the shop.

Huguenots were among the most industrious and economically advanced elements in French society. Others gained at France's expense; Huguenots poured into England, and especially East Anglia, where their skills soon made them welcome and valued members of the community.

The **Braintree District Museum** on Manor Street tells the story of Braintree's diverse industrial heritage and traditions (see panel on page 211). The **Town Hall Centre** is a Grade II listed building housing the Tourist Information Centre and the Art Gallery, which boasts a continuous changing programme of exhibitions and works.

AROUND BRAINTREE

CRESSING
4 miles E of Braintree off the B1018

Cressing Temple Barns, set in the centre of an ancient farmstead, are two splendid medieval timber barns commissioned in the 12th century by the Knights Templar. They contain the timber of over 1,000 oak trees; an interpretative exhibition explains to visitors how the barns were made, as a special viewing platform brings visitors up into the roof of the magnificent Wheat Barn for a closer look. There's also a beautiful walled garden re-

creating the Tudor style, with an arbour, fount and physic garden. Special events are held throughout the summer.

FAIRSTEAD
4 miles S of Braintree off the A131

Fairstead (or Fairsted) is an undulating parish about three miles east of the A131, some four miles northwest of Witham. The Church of St Mary and St Peter is an ancient building of flint, in the Norman style, consisting of chancel, nave, north porch and a western tower with a lofty shingled spire with four bells, one of which dates back to before the Reformation. During restoration in the late 1800s various handsome mural paintings were discovered, including, over the chancel arch, Our Lord's Triumphal Entry into Jerusalem, The Last Supper, The Betrayal, Our Lord being Crowned with Thorns, and Incidents on the way to Calvary.

COGGESHALL
5 miles E of Braintree on the A120

This medieval hamlet, a pleasant old cloth and lace town, has some very fine timbered buildings. **Paycocke's House** on West Street, a delightful timber-framed medieval merchant's home dating from about 1500 with unusually rich panelling and wood carvings, is in the care of the National Trust. Inside there's a superb carved ceiling and a display of Coggeshall lace, while outside there's a lovely garden. The National Trust also owns the restored **Coggeshall Grange Barn**, which dates from around 1140 and is the oldest surviving timber-framed barn in Europe. Built for the monks of the nearby Cistercian Abbey, it is a magnificent example of this type of architecture.

Marks Hall Estate began life in Saxon times, and is mentioned in the Domesday Book. In the 15th century, then-owner Sir Thomas Honywood was a leading Parliamentarian who commanded the Essex Regiment during the Civil War. Local legend has it that the two artificial lakes in the grounds were dug by Parliamentary troops during the siege of Colchester in 1648. In 1758, one of his successors, General Philip Honywood, forbade (under the terms of his will) any of his successors to fell timber - thus his lasting legacy of avenues of mature oaks, limes and horse chestnuts, surrounded by one of the largest continuous areas of ancient woodland in the county.

The Estate flourishes with native plants and wildlife, ornamental lakes, a 17th century walled garden, cascades, a coach house and Information Centre. This last is housed in a refurbished 15th century barn, and features informative displays as well as a gift shop and tea room.

An Arboretum is being developed with a collection of trees from all over the world, laid out in geographical themes - Europe, Asia, America, and the southern hemisphere.

KELVEDON
6 miles SE of Braintree off the A12

This village alongside the River Blackwater houses the **Feering and Kelvedon Museum**, which is dedicated to manorial history and houses artefacts from the Roman settlement of Canonium, agricultural tools through the ages and other interesting exhibits.

GREAT SALING
4 miles NW of Braintree off the A120

Saling Hall Garden is a 12 acre site dating from 1698. The small park boasts a marvellous collection of fine trees, particularly pines, and there are water gardens and an extensive collection of unusual plants with an emphasis on trees.

WETHERSFIELD
5 miles NW of Braintree on the B1053

Boydells Dairy Farm is a working farm where visitors are welcome to join in with tasks such as milking, feeding and more. A guided tour mixes fun with education, and all questions are most welcome. From bees to llamas, just about every kind of farm animal can be found here. Goat rides and donkey cart rides, a lovely picnic area and refreshments such

EASTERFORD ANTIQUES

"Millers" Easterford Road, Kelvedon, Essex CO5 9DX
Tel: 01376 570098 Fax: 01376 571022
e-mail: betty@easterford-antiques.fsnet.co.uk

Easterford Antiques is home to a superb range of 17th, 18th and 19th century furniture. Open by appointment only, this superior establishment is located in a former school dating back to 1860, beautifully restored and tastefully decorated to display the many handsome pieces to best advantage. Owner Betty Miller has over 25 years' experience in the antiques business, and can offer expert advice and information.

as "Yoggipops" (sheep's milk yoghurt ice lollies made on-site) make for a perfect family day out. Open to the public April to September.

GREAT BARDFIELD

6 miles NW of Braintree off the B1053

This old market town on a hill above the River Pant is a pleasant mixture of cottages and shops, nicely complemented by the 14th century church of St Mary the Virgin. Perhaps Great Bardfield's most notable feature is, however, a restored **Windmill** that goes by the strange name of 'Gibraltar'.

Here in one of the prettiest villages in all of Essex, **Great Bardfield Museum** occupies a 16th century cottage and features exhibits of mainly 19th and 20th century domestic and farm implements, along with rural crafts such as strawplaiting and corn dollies. Also here is the 19th century village lock-up.

FINCHINGFIELD

6 miles NW of Braintree off the B1053

This charming village is graced with thatched cottages spread generously around a sloping village green that dips to a stream and duck pond at the centre of the village. Nearby stands an attractive

Finchingfield

small windmill. Just up the hill visitors will find the Norman **Church of St John the Baptist** and the **Guildhall** (mentioned in the Domesday book), which has a small museum.

Finchingfield is easily one of the most picturesque and most photographed villages in Essex, featured in many television programmes and the home of the series *Lovejoy*. Here too is the privately owned Tudor stately home, Spains Hall, whose lovely flower garden contains a huge Cedar of Lebanon planted in 1670 and an Adams sundial. Many good roses surround the kitchen garden, which contains an ancient Paulonia tree and a bougainvillea in the greenhouse. The garden is generally open on summer Sunday afternoons.

Finchingfield has an easily followed path along the Finchingfield Brook leading from the village to Great Bardfield, a short distance away.

GOSFIELD

4 miles N of Braintree off the A1017

Gosfield Lake Leisure Resort, the county's largest freshwater lake, lies in the grounds of Gosfield Hall. This Tudor mansion was remodelled in the 19th century by its owner Samuel Courtauld. He also built the attractive mock-Tudor houses in the village.

HALSTEAD

The name 'Halstead' comes from the Anglo-Saxon for Healthy Place. Like Braintree and Coggeshall, Halstead was an important weaving centre. **Townsford Mill** is certainly the most picturesque reminder of Halstead's industrial heritage. Built in the 1700s, it remains one of the most handsome buildings in town. This white, weatherboarded three-storey mill across the River Colne at the Causeway was once a landmark site for the Courtauld empire, producing both the famous funerary crepe and rayon. Today the Mill is an antiques centre.

Though it may now seem somewhat improbable, Halstead's most famous product was once mechanical elephants. Life-sized and weighing half a ton, each one consisted of 9,000 parts and could carry a load of eight adults and four children at speeds of up to 12 miles per hour. Rather less unusual but certainly better remembered is the Tortoise Foundry Company for its warm 'tortoise stoves'.

Castle Hedingham

AROUND HALSTEAD

Castle Hedingham

3 miles NW of Halstead off the B1058

This town is named after its Norman Castle, which dominates the town. One of England's strongest fortresses in the 11th century, even now it is impossible not to sense the power and strength of **Castle Hedingham**. The impressive stone keep is one of the tallest in Europe, with four floors and rising over 100 feet, with 12-ft thick walls, and the banqueting hall and minstrels' gallery can still be seen. The castle was owned by the Earls of

Oxford, the powerful de Vere family, one of whom was among the barons who forced King John to accept the Magna Carta.

The village itself is a maze of narrow streets radiating from **Falcon Square**, named after the half-timbered Falcon Inn. Attractive buildings abound including many Georgian and 15th century houses comfortably vying for space. The **Church of St Nicholas**, built by the de Veres, has avoided Victorian 'restoration' and is virtually completely Norman, with grand masonry and interestingly carved choir seats. There is a working pottery in St James' Street.

At the **Colne Valley Railway and Museum**, a mile of the Colne Valley and Halstead line between Castle Hedingham and Great Yeldham has been restored and

(Continued page 218)

WALK 9

Castle Hedingham and the River Colne

Start	Castle Hedingham
Distance	6 miles (9.7km)
Approximate time	3 hours
Parking	Roadside parking at Castle Hedingham
Refreshments	Pubs and café at Castle Hedingham, pub at Sible Hedingham
Ordnance Survey maps	Landranger 155 (Bury St Edmunds, Sudbury & Stowmarket), Explorer 195 (Braintree & Saffron Walden)

This figure-of-eight walk in the Colne valley starts with a circuit of Castle Park, the wooded parkland surrounding the remains of Hedingham Castle. The rest of the route is across fields and through woodland, including a short but attractive stretch beside the placid River Colne. There are fine views over the valley but some parts of the walk are likely to be muddy and/or overgrown at times.

There are some delightful old houses and cottages in Castle Hedingham, which lies at the foot of the wooded hill occupied by the great castle. The church is an unusually fine and interesting example of an almost complete Norman village church, with a superb late 12th century nave and chancel. At the east end is a rare Norman wheel window.

Hedingham Castle is one of the grandest and best preserved Norman keeps in the country. It was built in 1140 for the powerful De Veres, earls of Oxford, and still stands to its full height of 110ft (33m). Its interior probably gives visitors a better idea of a Norman castle than anywhere else, and the carved stonework and great cross arches in the great hall are normally only seen in the finest cathedrals.

The walk begins in the main street by the Bell Inn and post office. With your back to the inn, turn left, follow the road around a left-hand bend and turn right down Church Lane. Turn right, passing the church, and keep ahead along Crown Street to a T-junction. **A** Take the path ahead – not the parallel drive to the right of it – which passes to the right of Pye Cottage, and this attractive, hedge- and tree-lined path heads gently uphill to a stile. After climbing it, keep

ahead across a field to the end of a hedge, continue uphill alongside the hedge and climb a stile at the top.

Turn right along a winding lane and, at a public footpath sign opposite Rosemary Farm, turn right on to a path which continues between fields. Keep ahead along a narrow enclosed path that heads downhill through woodland bordering Castle Park and pass beside a barrier on to a road. Turn left and look out for steps and a public footpath sign on the right. **B** Climb the steps and walk first along an enclosed path and then along a right-hand field edge to a waymarked post. Turn left, continue across the field towards a farm and head down into a dip, passing to the right of a solitary tree. Do not climb the stile at the bottom of the field but turn right along its left-hand field edge and follow it – there are several twists and turns – to a road.

Cross over, walk along a tarmac track and, soon after passing to the right of Maiden Ley Farm, you join the well-waymarked Hedingham Mills Walk. **C** The track bears left and, where it ends, keep ahead along a rough track to a fork. Take the right-hand enclosed path along the left-hand edge of woodland, which turns right to a stile. Climb it and cross a plank footbridge. Turn left to continue across rough meadowland, bear right through trees to climb a stile and keep ahead to a lane. **D** Turn right, cross a bridge over a disused railway track and, at a public footpath sign, turn left along a track, passing between cottages.

At a waymarked post, turn left to walk along the right-hand edge of a field, follow the edge as it curves first right and then left, pass beside a barrier and continue along a fence-lined path. Keep along the narrow, enclosed path to enter woodland and continue through it to a T-junction. Turn right along a track, at a fork keep ahead along the right-hand track and, at the next fork, take the narrower left-hand path. The path heads gently uphill, re-enters trees and continues up through this most attractive woodland. It then turns right to keep along the left-hand edge of the wood and emerges, via a barrier, on to a lane.

Turn right down this narrow lane and cross a bridge over the disused railway again. Turn right by Hull's Mill, a 19th century rebuilding of an earlier mill, and just after crossing a footbridge over the River Colne by a ford, turn right over a stile. **E** Walk across a field to a hedge corner, keep by the hedge on the left to join the river and continue beside it as far as a field corner. Turn left away from the river, walk along the right-hand edge of fields and, on joining a track, turn right through a hedge gap **F** – here leaving the Hedingham Mills Walk – and follow a track across a field.

Continue along a path by the right-hand edge of the next two fields and, in the corner of the second field, pass through a belt of trees and keep along the right-hand edge of the next field. The path bears right through another belt of trees and curves left to reach a lane in front of Alderford Mill. **G** Turn left along the lane if you want the pub in Sible Hedingham but the route continues to the right to cross a bridge over the Colne. Here you rejoin the Hedingham Mills Walk and follow it back to the start.

Beyond the bridge you temporarily rejoin the outward route and retrace your steps to point **C** just before Maiden Ley Farm. Turn left here off the tarmac track

and walk along a path that keeps along the right-hand edge of a pool. The path then winds through trees and bushes, crosses a plank footbridge and keeps along the right-hand edge of woodland. As you later continue along the left-hand edge of a field, the top of the keep of Hedingham Castle can be seen across the field to the right.

The path eventually reaches a road just to the right of a brick bridge. Turn right and follow it back into Castle Hedingham. ●

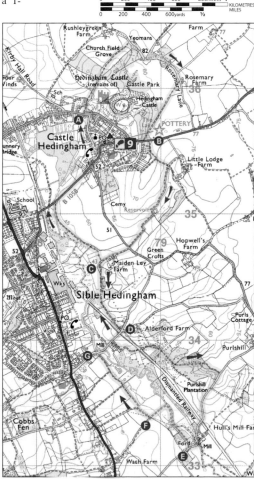

now runs steam trains operated by enthusiasts. The restored Victorian railway buildings house the largest collection of operational heritage rolling stock and steam and diesel locomotives in the county. Steam days are Sundays and Bank Holidays, March-October and Wednesday and Thursday during school holidays. **Colne Valley Farm Park**, set in 30 acres of traditional river meadows, is open from April to September.

SIBLE HEDINGHAM

3 miles NW of Halstead off the A1017

Mentioned in the Domesday Book as the largest parish in England, Sible Hedingham was the birthplace of Sir John Hawkwood, one of the 14th century's most famous soldiers of fortune. He was knighted by Edward III, with whom he fought at Crecy, and subsequently made his fortune as a mercenary in Italy, where he became a General in the Florentine army and married the daughter of the Duke of Milan. He died in Italy and was buried in Florence, from where it is thought that his body was returned to Sible Hedingham. There is an elaborate monument to him in the village church, decorated with hawks and various other beasts.

GESTINGTHORP

5 miles N of Halstead off the A131

The Church of St Mary the Virgin in Gestingthorp is distinctive in many respects. Witness to centuries of Christian worship, the Domesday Book of 1086 tells that 'Ghestingetorp' was held by Ledmer the priest before 1066. The oldest part extant of the existing building is the blocked-up lancet window in the north wall of the chancel, which dates back to the 1200s. Apart from this, most of the chancel, nave and south aisle dates from the 14th century. The tower, constructed in about 1500, is 66 feet high. Of the six

bells hung in the tower, four were cast in 1658-9 by Miles Gray, a Colchester bellfounder. The 16th century fifth and sixth bells were cast in Bury St Edmunds, and recast in 1901. One of the church's handsome memorials commemorates Captain Oates, who died in an attempt to save the lives of his companions on their famous ill-fated expedition to the Antarctic in 1912.

STEEPLE BUMSTEAD

8 miles NW of Halstead off the B1057

In this village on the Suffolk border Edith Cavell, the war heroine, worked as a governess and worshipped at the church. At the crossroads stands the lovely old Moots Hall, with timbered ground floor and overhanging upper storey. Moots were originally held in Saxon times to settle local disputes that weren't worth going to war over, though this hall also saw service as a guildhall and a school.

THE NORTH ESSEX COAST

CLACTON-ON-SEA

16 miles SE of Colchester on the A133

Clacton is a traditional sun-and-sand family resort with a south-facing, long sandy beach, lovely gardens on the seafront and a wide variety of shops and places to explore. It also boasts a wide variety of special events and entertainments taking place throughout the year.

Settled by hunters during the Stone Age, the town grew over the centuries from a small village into a prosperous seaside resort in the 1800s, when the craze for the health benefits of coastal air and bathing was at its peak. **The Pier** was constructed in 1871; at first paddle steamers provided the only mode of transport to the resort, the railway

Gardens, Clacton-on-Sea

Just south of the town, **Jaywick Sands** is a popular spot for a picnic au bord de la mer, boasting one of the finest natural sandy beaches in the county.

LITTLE CLACTON

3 miles NW of Clacton off the A133

Though it shares its name with its near neighbour, this is a town apart. Quiet and secluded, multiple-winner of the Best Kept Village award, Little Clacton features a lovely **Jubilee Oak**, planted to celebrate Victoria's 50th year on the throne. The fine church of St James has been described as one of the most beautiful medieval churches in Essex, and sits at the heart of the village.

Oakwood Crafts Resource Centre in Little Clacton provides an environment for people with learning disabilities to learn and develop work skills, motivation, responsibility, team spirit, self-esteem and confidence through horticulture, woodwork, ceramics, crafts and catering. Set in three acres of land, it opened in 1975 and, as a horticultural

arriving in 1882. The Pier was widened from 30 to over 300 foot in the 1930s and contains all the expected amusements and diversions, both traditional and modern.

On dry land are several arcades and **Clacton Pavilion** and the two main theatres, Princes Theatre and West Cliff. The latter, built in 1928 for summer 'concert party' shows, has been upgraded and turned into an arts centre offering a range of year-round entertainment.

20th-CENTURY CERAMICS

16 The Street, Little Clacton, Essex CO16 9LQ
Tel: 01255 862444 e-mail: enquiries@20th-century-ceramics.com
website: www.20th-century-ceramics.com

Simon Parkes turned a long-time hobby into a full-time business when he opened **20th-Century Ceramics** in March 2000. The two well-lit showrooms hold a notable collection of ceramics, with art deco the speciality. Pieces by Clarice Cliff, Susie Cooper, Carlton Ware, Shelley, Burleigh Ware and Midwinter make up the major part of the display, and there's also a small section devoted to antiques and collectables with a rural theme. Simon attends international antiques fairs and makes extensive use of the internet to locate interesting pieces.

centre, sells a wide range of bedding plants, shrubs and hanging baskets seasonally, along with a selection of wooden garden implements, furnishings and other items, and ceramics. Teas and coffees are available.

HOLLAND-ON-SEA

1½ miles NE of Clacton off the B1032

This attractive community is home to **Holland Haven Country Park**, 100 acres of open space near the seashore, ideal for watching the marine birds and other wildlife of the region. Throughout the area there are a number of attractive walks which take full advantage of the varied coastal scenery

FRINTON-ON-SEA

3 miles NE of Clacton off the B1032

Once a quiet fishing village, this town was developed as a select resort by Sir Richard Cooper, and expanded in the 1880s to the genteel family resort it is today. Situated on a long stretch of sandy beach, Frinton remains peaceful and almost entirely unspoilt. The tree-lined residential avenues sweep elegantly down to the Esplanade and extensive clifftop greensward. Theatre and other open-air events take place throughout the season, and there are also some excellent tennis and golf clubs in the town. The grace and elegance of this sophisticated resort is evidenced all round, as are hints of its distinguished past: Victorian beach huts still dot the extensive beach.

WALTON-ON-THE-NAZE

8 miles NE of Clacton on the B1034

Walton is a traditional, cheerful resort which focuses on the pier and all its attractions, including a ten-pin bowling alley. The gardens at the seafront are colourful and the beach has good sand. **The Backwaters** to the rear of Walton are made up of a series of small harbours and saltings, which lead into Harwich harbour. The charming narrow streets of the town contain numerous shops, restaurants and pubs overlooking the second longest pier in the country. The pier, first built in 1830, was originally constructed of wood and measured 330 feet long. It was extended to its present length of 2,610 feet in 1898, at the same time as the electric train service began.

The wind-blown expanse of **The Naze** just north of Walton is an extensive coastal recreation and picnic area, pleasant for walking, especially out of season when the visitor is likely to have all 150 acres virtually to himself, with great views out over the water. The shape of the Naze is constantly changing, eroded by wind, water and tide.

The year 1796 saw the demise of the ancient church, and somewhere beyond the 800-foot pier lies medieval Walton.

Marina, Walton-on-the-Naze

The sandstone cliffs are internationally important for their shell fossil deposits. Waltonians have been enjoying the bracing sea air since before Neolithic times and flint-shaping instruments have been found here, as well as fossil teeth and the ears of sharks and whales in the Naze's red crag cliffs. The octagonal, brick **Naze Tower** was built in 1720 as a beacon to warn seamen of the West Rocks off shore. A nature trail has been created nearby and the Essex Skipper butterfly and Emperor moth can be seen here.

The **Old Lifeboat House Museum** on East Terrace houses an interpretative museum of local history and development, rural and maritime, covering Walton, Frinton and the Sokens.

Brightlingsea

BRIGHTLINGSEA

7 miles W of Clacton on the B1029

Brightlingsea enjoys a long tradition of shipbuilding and seafaring. In 1347, 51 men and five ships were sent to the siege of Calais. Among the crew members of Sir Francis Drake's fleet which vanquished the Spanish Armada was one William of Brightlingsea. Brightlingsea has the distinction of being the only member of the Cinque Ports outside Kent and Sussex.

The 13th century **Jacobes Hall** in the town centre is one of the oldest occupied buildings in Essex. It is timber-framed with an undulating tile roof and an external staircase. Used as a meeting hall during the reign of Henry III, its name originates from its first owner, Edmund Vicar of Brightlingsea, who was known locally as Jacob le Clerk.

All Saints Church, which occupies the highest point of the town on a hill about a mile from the centre, is mainly 13th century. Here are to be found some Roman brickwork and a frieze of ceramic tiles commemorating local residents whose lives were lost at sea. Its 97 foot tower can be seen from 17 miles out to sea. A light was once placed in the tower to guide the town's fishermen home

Brightlingsea Museum in Duke Street offers an insight into the lives, customs and traditions of the area, housing a collection of exhibits relating to the town's maritime connections and the oyster industry.

There are plenty of superb walks along Brightlingsea Creek and the River Colne, which offer a chance to watch the birdlife on the saltings and the plethora of boats on the water. Today the town is a haven for the yachting fraternity and is the home of national and international sailing championships, with one of the best stretches of sailing on the East Coast.

ELMSTEAD MARKET

6 miles N of Brightlingsea off the A120

Elmstead Market is perhaps best known as the location of **Beth Chatto Gardens**, at

White Barn House, designed and still presided over by the famous gardener herself. Here visitors will find five acres of landscaped gardens including extensive water gardens, shady walks and a Mediterranean-style garden where aromatic drought-loving plants thrive. The adjoining nursery contains a wide variety of plants for sale. Close by is the Rolts Nursery Butterfly Farm.

THORRINGTON

3 miles NW of Brightlingsea off the B1027

Thorrington Tide Mill, built in the early 19th century, is the only remaining Tide Mill in Essex, and one of very few left in East Anglia. It has been fully restored, and although no longer in use the Wheel can be run for guided groups. There is a public footpath, which runs along the creek here.

POINT CLEAR

2 miles SE of Brightlingsea off the B1027

The **East Essex Aviation Museum**, located in the Martello Tower at Point Clear, not only retains its original flooring and roof, but today contains interesting displays of wartime aviation, military and naval photographs, uniforms and other memorabilia with local and US Air Force connections. There are artefacts on show from the crash sites of wartime aircraft in the Tendring area, including the engine and fuselage section of a P51D Mustang fighter piloted by Flight Officer Ray King of 479th Fighter Group. The museum also explores civil and military history from both World Wars. There are very good views from the tower over the Colne Estuary and Brightlingsea.

ST OSYTH

3 miles SE of Brightlingsea off the B1027

This pretty little village has a fascinating history and centres around its Norman church and the ancient ruins of **St Osyth Priory**. The town and Priory were named by Augustinian Canons after St Osytha, martyred daughter of Frithenwald, first Christian King of the East Angles, who was himself beheaded by the Danes in AD 653.

The Priory was founded in the 12th century and built on the site of a nunnery founded by the Princess. Little of the original Priory remains, except for the magnificent late 15th century flint gatehouse, complete with battlements. Heralded as one of the finest monastic buildings in the country, the Priory buildings include a 16th century tithe barn and bishops' lodgings, all set in a landscaped park where deer roam free and peacocks patrol the shady lawns. The grounds are open to the public during the summer months. Within the gatehouse building there is an interesting collection of ceramics and jade. Other attractions include the Fitzwilliam art collection in the Georgian wing, with paintings by Reynolds, Stubbs and Van Dyck.

MERSEA ISLAND

2 miles SW of Brightlingsea off the B1025

Much of this island is a **National Nature Reserve**, home to its teeming shorelife. The island is linked to the mainland by a narrow causeway which is covered over at high tide. The towns of both East and West Mersea have excellent facilities for sailing enthusiasts, and East Mersea is also a haven for birdwatchers.

At Little Wigborough, **Copt Hall Marshes** (National Trust) are part of the Blackwater SSSI (Site of Special Scientific Interest), an area of salt marshes rich in birdlife. The churches at both Little Wigborough and Great Wigborough relate the story of the end of Zeppelin L33, which was shot down in 1916.

HARWICH

Harwich's name probably originates from the time of King Alfred, when *'here'* meant army, and *'wic'* a camp. This attractive old town was built in the 13th century by the Earls of Norfolk to exploit its strategic position on the Stour and Orwell estuary; the town has an important and fascinating maritime history , the legacy of which continues into the present.

During the 14th and 15th century French campaigns it was an important naval base. The famous Elizabethan seafarers Hawkins, Frobisher and Drake sailed from Harwich on various expeditions; in 1561 Queen Elizabeth I visited the town, describing it 'a pretty place and want[ing] for nothing'. Christopher Newport, leader of the

Goodspeed expedition which founded Jamestown, Virginia, in 1607, and Christopher Jones, master of the Pilgrim ship *The Mayflower*, lived in Harwich (the latter just off the quay in Kings Head Street), as did Jones' kinsman John Alden, who sailed to America in 1620. The famous diarist Samuel Pepys was MP for the town in the 1660s, so during this time it was the headquarters of the Kings Navy. Charles II took the first pleasure cruise from Harwich's shores. Other notable visitors included Lord Nelson and Lady Hamilton, who stayed at The Three Cups in Church Street.

Harwich remains popular as a vantage point for watching incoming and outgoing shipping in the harbour and across the waters to Felixstowe. Nowadays, lightships, buoys and miles of strong chain are stored along the front, and passengers arriving on North Sea ferries at Parkeston Quay see the 90 foot high, nine-sided **High Lighthouse** as the first landmark. Now housing the **National Vintage Wireless and Television Museum**, it was built in 1818 along with the Low Lighthouse. When the two lighthouses were in line they could indicate a safe shipping channel into the harbour. Each had replaced earlier wooden structures, and were themselves replaced by cast iron structures (one of which still stands on the front in nearby Dovercourt) in 1863 when the shifting sandbanks altered the channel. Shipping now relies on light buoys to find its way. The Low lighthouse is now the town's **Maritime Museum**, with specialist displays on the Royal Navy and commercial shipping.

Two other interesting museums in the town are the **Lighthouse Museum** off Wellington Road, which contains the last Clacton offshore 34-foot lifeboat and a history of the lifeboat service in Harwich,

Harwich Lighthouse

and the **Ha'penny Pier Visitor Centre** on the Quay, with information on everything in Harwich and a small heritage exhibition.

The **Treadwell Crane** now stands on Harwich Green, but for over 250 years it was sited in the Naval Shipyard. It is worked by two people walking in two 16 foot diameter wheels, and is the only known example of its kind. Amazingly it was operational up until the 1920s. Another fascinating piece of the town's history is the Electric Palace Cinema, built in 1911 and now the oldest unaltered purpose-built cinema in Britain.

The importance of Harwich's port during the 19th century is confirmed by the **Redoubt**, a huge round grey fort built between 1808 and 1810. Its design is an enlarged version of the Martello towers, which dotted the English coast awaiting a Napoleonic invasion which never came (some of these towers of course still exist). Today the Harwich Society has largely restored it and opened it as a museum.

The old town also contains many ancient buildings, including the **Guildhall**, which was rebuilt in 1769 and is located in Church Street. The Council chamber, Mayor's Parlour and other rooms may be viewed. The former gaol contains unique graffiti of ships, probably carved by prisoners, and is well worth putting aside an afternoon to explore.

AROUND HARWICH

DOVERCOURT
1 mile S of Harwich off the A120

This residential and holiday suburb of Harwich has attractive cliffs and beach, and also boasts the Iron Lighthouse or 'Leading Lights' located just off lower Marine Parade. The town has been settled from prehistoric times, as attested to by the late Bronze Age axe-heads found here (now in Colchester Museum). The Romans found the town a useful source of the stone Septaria, taken from the cliffs and used in building. The town that visitors see today developed primarily in Victorian times as a fashionable resort.

MISTLEY
7 miles W of Harwich off the B1352

Here at the gateway to Constable Country, local 18th century landowner, MP and Paymaster General Richard Rigby had grand designs to develop Mistley into a fashionable spa to rival Harrogate and Bath, adopting the swan as its symbol. Sadly, all that remains of Rigby's ambitious scheme are the Swan Fountain, a small number of attractive Georgian houses and **Mistley Towers**, the remains of a church (otherwise demolished in 1870) designed by the flamboyant architect Robert Adams on the south bank of Seafield Bay. From the waterfront, noted for its colony of swans, there are very pleasant views across the estuary to Suffolk.

Mistley Quay Workshops in the High Street feature a pottery workshop, lute/cello maker, harpsichord maker, wood worker, bookbinder, and stained-glass window maker and restorer. There is also a tea-shop on the premises (the key to Mistley Towers can be obtained from the Workshops).

Mistley Place Park Animal Rescue Centre is 25 acres of parkland with animals, country walks, pony rides, wildlife habitats, a lake and great views across the Stour Estuary. The 2,000 rescued animals include horses, rabbits and Vietnamese pigs.

The **Essex Secret Bunker** in Mistley, former county nuclear war headquarters,

ESSEX SECRET BUNKER

Crown Building, Shrubland Road, Mistley,
Essex CO11 1HS
Tel: 01206 392271 Fax: 01206 393847
e-mail: info@essexsecretbunker.com
website: www.essexsecretbunker.com

Follow the **'Secret Bunker'** signs on the B1352 to discover a Cold War operations centre that was the emergency headquarters for the county of Essex in the event of a nuclear war. The 14,000 sq ft concrete bunker was built in 1951, half above ground and half below. The walls are constructed of two feet thick concrete strengthened every few inches with steel mesh; the roof is over three feet thick and the foundations are set in almost ten feet of concrete. Maintained and kept operational for the 40 years of the Cold War, the building lost its original purpose (for which it was thankfully never needed) when the Government decided that the threat of nuclear war had receded sufficiently for the network of bunkers to be decommissioned. In early 1995 the building was renovated and refurbished prior to being opened as a public tourist attraction in time for Easter 1996. Many of the original equipment and fittings have been returned to the site, so the bunker is now a fully authentic exhibition, showing the HQ as it would have been in full readiness for a nuclear attack with the help of sound effects, historically accurate displays, videos and cinemas. The bunker, which is in the care of the Bunker Preservation Trust, is bright and air-conditioned, suitable for all ages, with post Cold War amenities such as a café, gift shop and play area.

Another Cold War bunker, also open to the public, is at Kelvedon Hatch (qv).

is now a public museum offering a fascinating insight into the post-war world of top-secret preparations against nuclear attack. Operational from 1951, it was 'declassified' in 1993 and opened to the public in 1996. Interesting things to see and do, include the giant underground operations room, office and dormitories, telephone exchange communications centre and radio room, powerhouse and filtration plant (see panel above).

MANNINGTREE

9 miles W of Harwich off the B1352

The Walls, on the approach to Manningtree along the B1352, offer unrivalled views of the Stour estuary and the Suffolk coast, and the swans for which the area is famous. Lying on the River Stour amid beautiful rolling countryside, it has often been depicted by artists over the centuries.

Back in Tudor times, Manningtree was the centre of the cloth trade, and later a port busy with barges carrying their various cargoes along the coast to London. Water still dominates today and the town is a centre of leisure sailing.

Manningtree has been a market town since 1238, and is still a busy shopping centre. It is the smallest town in Britain, and a stroll through the streets reveals the variety of its past. There are still traditional (and mainly Georgian) restaurants, pubs and shops, and the views over the river are well known to birdspotters, sailors and ramblers. The town has an intriguing past - as a river crossing, market, smugglers' haven and home of Matthew Hopkins, the reviled and self-styled **Witchfinder General** who struck terror into the local community during the 17th century. Some of his victims were hanged on Manningtree's small village green.

It is believed that the reference in Shakespeare's Henry IV to Falstaff as 'that roasted Manningtree ox' relates to the practice of roasting an entire ox at the town's medieval annual fair.

SAFFRON WALDEN

The town was named after the Saffron crocus, which was grown in the area to make dyestuffs and fulfil a variety of other uses in the Middle Ages. A great part of Saffron Walden's original street plan survives, as do hundreds of fine buildings, many timbered with overhanging upper floors and the decorative plastering known as pargeting. Gog and Magog (or in some versions folk-hero Tom Hickathrift and the Wisbech Giant) battle forever in plaster on the gable of the **Old Sun Inn**, where, legend has it, Oliver Cromwell and General Fairfax both lodged during the Civil War. A typical market town, Saffron Walden's centrepiece is its magnificent **St Mary's Church**, notable for its sheer size, the black marble tomb of Thomas Audley and the 12 bells producing one of the largest peals in the kingdom.

The **Saffron Walden Museum** first opened to the public at its present location in 1835, having been founded 'to gratify the inclination of all who value natural history'. The museum has won numerous awards, including joint winner of the Museum of the Year Award for best museum of Industrial or Social History in 1997. At this friendly, family-sized museum visitors can try their hand at corn grinding with a Romano-British quern, see how a medieval timber house would have been built, admire the displays of Native American and West African embroidery, see the gloves worn by Mary Queen of Scots on the day she died and come face to face with Wallace the Lion, the museum's faithful guardian. The ruins of historic Walden Castle are also here.

On the local Common, once Castle Green, is the largest surviving **Turf Maze** in the country. Only eight ancient turf mazes survive in England, though there were many more in the Middle Ages: if they are not looked after they soon become overgrown and are lost. This one is believed to be some 800 years old.

Henry Winstanley, inventor, engineer and engraver, and designer of the first Eddystone Lighthouse at Plymouth, was born here in 1644. He is said to have held 'lighthouse trials' with a wooden lantern in the lavishly decorated 15th to 16th century church. The Lighthouse, and Winstanley with it, were swept away in a fierce storm in 1703.

The town was also famous for its resident **Cockatrice**, which was hatched from a cock's egg by a toad or serpent and could, it was said, kill its victims with a glance. The Cockatrice was blamed for any inexplicable disaster in the town. Like Perseus and Medusa the Gorgon, a Cockatrice could be destroyed by making it see its own reflection, thereby turning

Saffron Walden

Saffron Walden Parish Church

Rothenstein, who have lived in and around the town as members of the famous artistic community which flourished in and around Great Bardfield. It also exhibits work by many notable 20th century artists who lived and worked in the area before and after the Second World War, as well as contemporary artists working in Essex today. The gallery was purpose designed and opened in 1856 to house the collection of Francis Gibson. The gallery also houses the Lewis George Fry RBA, RWA (1860-1933) Collection, which is exhibited each summer, along with works by Robert Fry (1866-1934) and Anthony Fry.

it to stone. The Saffron Walden Cockatrice's slayer was said to be a knight in a coat of 'cristal glass'.

To the north of the town is Bridge End Gardens, a wonderfully preserved example of an early Victorian garden, complete with the unique Hedge Maze, which is open only by appointment (which can be made at the TIC). Next to the gardens is the **Fry Public Art Gallery**, which has a unique collection of work by artists and designers such as Edward Bawden, Eric Ravilious and Michael

Close to Bridge End is the **Anglo-American War Memorial** dedicated by Field Marshal Viscount Montgomery of Alamein in 1953 to the memory of all the American flyers of the 65th Fighter Wing who lost their lives in the Second World War.

Audley End House was, at one time, home of the first Earl of Suffolk, and at one time home of Charles II. It remains today one of England's most impressive Jacobean mansions, its distinguished

THE GARDEN STUDIO

Lime Tree Court, Saffron Walden, Essex CB10 1HG
Tel: 01799 528072 Fax: 01799 528057
e-mail: catherine@the gardenstudio.co.uk

Catherine Riches, an expert in all aspects of garden design and horticulture, opened the **Garden Studio** in April 2001. Located on two floors of a converted house in the centre of Saffron Walden, her studio stocks an excellent range of French and Italian garden furniture, a selection of unusual pots and planters, terracotta barbecues, high-quality garden tools and numerous garden accessories that are both stylish and practical. Catherine holds a diploma in garden design from Writtle College and an RHS certificate in horticulture.

stone facade set off perfectly by Capability Brown's lake.

The remaining state rooms retain their palatial magnificence and the exquisite state bed in the Neville Room is hung with the original embroidered drapes. The silver, the Doll's House, the Jacobean Screen and Robert Adam's painted Drawing Room are among the many sights to marvel at, and the natural history collection features more than 1,000 stuffed animals and birds.

The collection of paintings includes works by Holbein, Lely and Canaletto. Fascinating introductory talks help visitors get the most from any visit to this, one of the most magnificent houses in England.

In the grounds are the 'Temple of Concord' which Brown dedicated to George III. The organic kitchen garden was recently opened to the public for the first time in 250 years. The gardens are managed by the Henry Doubleday Research Association, who grow and sell a wide range of organic produce in the shop, which also features a restaurant.

The **Audley End Miniature Railway** (separate admission charge) is 1.5 miles long and takes visitors along Lord Braybrooke's private 10¼ inch gauge railway through the beautiful private woods of the house.

Within the rolling parkland of the grounds there are several elegant

outbuildings, some of which were designed by Robert Adam. Among these are an icehouse, a circular temple and a Springwood Column.

AROUND SAFFRON WALDEN

RADWINTER

4 miles E of Saffron Walden off the B1053

Radwinter's **Church of St Mary** boasts a fine old church, which was largely renovated and rebuilt in the 19th century by architect Eden Nesfield. Chief features of the church are a superb Tudor porch with an oversailing room above, and a 16th century Flemish reredos depicting scenes from the life of St Mary. The village also has cottages and almshouses designed by Nesfield.

HADSTOCK

4 miles N of Saffron Walden off the B1052

As well as claiming to have the oldest church door in England, at the parish **Church of St Botolph**, Hadstock also has a macabre tale to tell. The church's north door was once covered with a piece of human skin, now to be seen in Saffron Walden Museum. Local legend says it is a 'Daneskin', from a Viking flayed alive. Lining doors with animal leather was common in the Middle Ages and many so-called 'Daneskins' are just that.

NEWHOUSE FARM

Radwinter, Saffron Walden, Essex CB10 2SP
Tel: 01799 599212 Fax: 01799 599967
e-mail: emmaredcliffe@hotmail.com

Emma and Neil Redcliffe offer top-quality self-catering accommodation in two beautifully restored cottages, The Mews and The Granary. The cottages are situated in the courtyard of a distinguished 16th century farmhouse set in 60 acres of meadowland. Tastefully decorated and furnished to a very high standard, each has three bedrooms (the master rooms with en suite shower) and a family bathroom. The kitchen, dining and sitting areas are equipped with everything needed for a comfortable, come-as-you-please holiday, and both cottages have their own delightful little walled gardens.

However, the skins at Hadstock and at Copford, in northeast Essex, are almost certainly human, the poor wretch at Hadstock undoubtedly having his hide nailed there as a warning to others. The door itself is Saxon, as are the 11th century carvings, windows and arches, rare survivors that predate the Norman Conquest.

BARTLOW

5 miles NE of Saffron Walden off the B1052

Bartlow Hills are reputed to be the largest burial mounds in Europe dating from Roman times. Fifteen metres high, they date back to the 2nd century.

HEMPSTEAD

5 miles E of Saffron Walden off the B1054

The highwayman, **Dick Turpin**, was born here in 1705. His parents kept the Bell Inn, later renamed the Rose and Crown and more recently known as Turpin's Tavern. Gilt letters announce that

It is the Landlord's great desire that no one stands before the fire

over the wide hearth where logs still burn; pictures all around celebrate the infamy of the former innkeeper's son. Turpin trained in London as a butcher but soon embarked, with his gang, on the life of crime for which he is notorious. Sought high and low in his forest hideouts (a special militia was even

recruited), he fled to Yorkshire where, with an assumed name, he continued his nefarious ways. He was eventually captured and hanged at York; he was 34.

Inside the 14th to 15th century village church, an impressively life-like bust carved by Edward Marshall recalls the town's rather worthier son, William Harvey (1578-1657). Harvey was chief physician to Charles I and the discoverer of the circulation of blood, as recorded in his *De Motu Cordis* of 1628. Like many other villages, Hempstead once boasted a village cockpit; its faint outline can still be traced, though the steep banks are now crowned with trees.

WIDDINGTON

4 miles S of Saffron Walden off the B1383

Covering nearly 25 acres, **Mole Hall Wildlife Park** offers visitors the chance to come close to a range of wild and domesticated animals. With the private fully moated 13th century manor house as a backdrop, the wide variety of animals in this excellent park include South American llamas, flamingoes, Formosa Sika deer (which are extinct in the wild), chimpanzees, muntjac, Arctic fox, wallabies, red squirrels and much more. Mole Hall is also home to two species of North American otter: Short-clawed and North American. Domesticated animals such as guinea pigs, rabbits, goats, pigs and sheep can also be seen. The Butterfly

SIMPLY SALMON

Severals Farm, Arkesden, Saffron Walden, Essex CB11 4EY
Tel: 01799 550143 Fax: 01799 550039
e-mail: simplysalmon@cix.co.uk
website: www.simplysalmon.co.uk

Simply Salmon, as its name proudly proclaims, is the home
of traditionally smoked salmon and a range of fine foods that
will tempt every palate. Run by Michael and Sophie Payne,
the company was established in 1991 after Michael was asked
to promote a new brand of smoked salmon called Scottish
Eagle. The traditional process used to smoke this salmon -
where every side of salmon is hung individually in old-fashioned brick kilns and smoked over oak
chippings - produces a uniquely delicious product.

Always keen to respond to customers' requests and expectations for high quality service, customers
are encouraged to design their own distinctive hampers, with a range of tempting products which

includes smoked salmon, prawns, scallops, smoked meats,
award-winning hams, cheeses, pates, preserves, chocolate, etc.,
together with a wide selection of wines, champagnes and ports,
all chosen especially for taste and quality. This fine
establishment offers a mail order service and, in Simply
Delicious, a luxury delicatessen shop on Newport High Street
in Newport, an emporium of all of Simply Salmon's products
as well as new lines including organic ice creams and an exciting
range of home-cooked dishes, frozen ready for the freezer. The
shop is open Tuesday to Friday 8.30 a.m. to 4.30 p.m.; Saturday
8.30 a.m. to 2 p.m. Telephone 01799 541999.

MOUNTFICHET CASTLE & NORMAN VILLAGE
AND THE HOUSE ON THE HILL MUSEUM

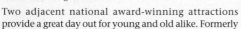

Stansted Mountfichet, Essex CM24 8SP
Tel: 01279 813237 Fax: 01279 816391
e-mail: gold@enta.net
website: www.gold.enta.net

Two adjacent national award-winning attractions
provide a great day out for young and old alike. Formerly

the seat of Baron Mountfichet (one of the 25 Barons who forced King
John to put his seal on Magna Carta), the Castle has been faithfully
reconstructed on the original's ten -acre site, where visitors can gain an
accurate insight into medieval village life, the construction of dwellings
and the defence of the Castle. Next door to the Castle is the House on
the Hill Toy Museum, where since 1991 an ever-growing collection (more
than 70,000 at the last count) of toys, games and books provides
education through entertainment
with the help of sound effects,
animation and hands-on activities.
In 1999 the scope of the Museum
was increased by permanent
displays of film, theatre and
rock'n'roll memorabilia, as well as
an exhibition of vintage end-of-pier
amusements.

Pavilion offers a tropical experience where brilliantly coloured butterflies flit about freely. Within the tropical pavilion you can also find lovebirds and small monkeys, along with a variety of snakes, spiders and insects (safe behind glass). The pools are home to goldfish, toads and terrapins.

Also in Widdington is **Priors Hall Barn**, one of the finest medieval barns in all of southeast England, and owned by English Heritage.

STANSTED MOUNTFICHET

8 miles SW of Saffron Walden off the B1383

Though rather close to Stansted Airport, there are plenty of reasons to visit this village. Certainly pilots approaching the airport may be surprised at the sight of a Norman Village, complete with domestic animals and the reconstructed motte and bailey **Mountfichet Castle**, standing just two miles from the end of the runway. Next door to the Castle is The House on the Hill Toy Museum, where children of

every age are treated to a unique and nostalgic trip back to their childhood (see panel opposite).

Stansted Windmill is one of the best preserved tower mills in the country. Dating back to 1787 and in use until 1910, most of the original machinery has survived. It is open on the first Sunday of each month from April to October; every Sunday in August and on Bank Holiday Mondays.

THAXTED

7 miles SE of Saffron Walden on the B184

This small country town has a recorded history which dates back to before the Domesday book. Originally a Saxon settlement, it developed around a Roman road. It has numerous attractively pargeted and timber-framed houses, and a magnificent Guildhall, built as a meeting-place for cutlers around 1390. The demise of the cutlery industry in this part of Essex in the 1500s led to the Guildhall adopting a new role as the administrative centre of the town. Restored in Georgian times, it became the town's Grammar School, as well as remaining a centre of administration.

The town's famous **Tower Windmill** was built in 1804 by John Webb. In working order until 1907, it fell into disuse and disrepair but has now been returned to full working order. It contains a rural life museum, well worth a visit. Close to the windmill are the town's Almshouses, which provided homes for the elderly even 250 years after they were built for that very purpose.

Thaxted Church stands on a hill and soars cathedral-like over the town's streets. It has been

Thaxted Village

described as the finest parish church in the country and, though many towns may protest long and loud at this claim, it certainly is magnificent. It was also the somewhat unlikely setting for a pitched battle in 1921. The rather colourful vicar and secretary of the Church Socialist League, one Conrad Noel, hoisted the red flag of communism and the Sinn Fein flag in the church. Incensed Cambridge students tore them down and put up the Union Jack; Noel in turn ripped that down and, with his friends, slashed the tyres of the students' cars and motorbikes. A fine bronze in the church celebrates this adventurous man of the cloth.

Conrad Noel's wife is remembered for encouraging Morris dancing in the town. Today, the famous Morris Ring is held annually (usually on the Spring Bank Holiday), attracting over 300 dancers from all over the country who dance through the streets. Dancing can also be seen around the town on most Bank Holiday Mondays, usually in the vicinity of a pub!

Gustav Holst, the composer of the Planets Suite, lived in Thaxted from 1914 to 1925, and often played the church organ. To celebrate his connection with the town, there is a month-long music festival in late June/early July which attracts performers of international repute.

In Park Street, at Aldborough Lodge, the **Thaxted Garden for Butterflies** is an ordinary garden which has been developed with displays depicting the numerous native wild butterfly species which have visited the garden since its opening in 1988.

BROXTED

3 miles SW of Thaxted off the B1051

The parish **Church of St Mary the Virgin** here in the handsome village of Broxted

CHURCH HALL FARM ANTIQUE & CRAFT CENTRE

Church End, Broxted, Great Dunmow, Essex CM6 2BZ
Tel/Fax: 01279 850858

Church Hall Farm Antique & Craft Centre is set in a 15th century listed Essex barn. In this magnificent setting can be found a superb range of antiques, collectables, arts and crafts and books. Tea rooms provide hot and cold homemade dishes. Superior bed and breakfast accommodation is also available adjacent to the Centre, in one of three tasteful, attractive and very comfortable ensuite bedrooms with all modern amenities.

LINDSELL ART GALLERY

Lindsell, nr Dunmow, Essex CM6 3QN
Tel: 01371 870777
website: www.lindsellartgallery.co.uk

Paintings, prints, ceramics, glassware, sculpture and more, created by Essex artists and those from throughout East Anglia, can be found at **Lindsell Art Gallery**. Opened in 1992, this distinguished gallery has become established as an important regional showcase for about 100 East Anglian artists. Regular life drawing classes are held, and the gallery offers a picture-framing service. Open: Thursday to Tuesday 9.30 to 5.30.

has two remarkably lovely stained glass windows commemorating the captivity and release of John McCarthy and the other Beirut hostages, dedicated in January 1993. Though just a few minutes drive from Stansted Airport off the M11, it is a welcoming haven of rural tranquillity.

Church Hall Farm Antique and Craft Centre in Broxted is housed in a magnificent Grade II-listed barn flanked by a willow-lined pond with its own resident ducks! The building itself is a miracle of medieval craftsmanship, located just a few yards from Broxted parish church.

GREAT DUNMOW

13 miles SE of Saffron Walden on the A120

The town is famous for the **'Flitch of Bacon'**, an ancient ceremony which dates back as far as the early 12th century. A prize of a flitch, or side, of bacon was awarded to the local man who "does not repent of his marriage nor quarrel, differ or dispute with his wife within a year and a day after the marriage". Married couples gathered (originally in Little Dunmow) to be interrogated and with great ceremony the winning couple would be seated and presented with their prize. The custom

lapsed on the dissolution of the monasteries, was briefly revived in the 18th century and became established again after 1885. 'Trials' to test the truth are all in good fun, and are carried out every leap year. The successful couple are borne through the streets on chairs and then presented with the Flitch. The ancient 'bacon chair', believed to date from the 13th century, can be seen in Little Dunmow parish church.

Other places of historical interest include the parish church of St Mary at Church End, Great Dunmow, dating back to 1322. The **Clock House**, a private residence built in 15896, was the home of St Anne Line, martyred for sheltering a Jesuit priest. The **Great Dunmow Maltings**, a superb medieval timber-framed building opened to the public in 2000 after complete restoration, is a focal point for local history. IIG Wells lived at Brick House in Great Dunmow, overlooking the Doctor's Pond, where in 1784 Lionel Lukin is reputed to have tested the first unsinkable lifeboat.

Easton Lodge, at Little Easton, has outstanding gardens designed by Harold Peto in 1903 and currently undergoing restoration. Easton Lodge was the home
(Continued page 236)

THE GARDENS OF EASTON LODGE

Easton Lodge, Great Dunmow, Essex CM6 2BB
Tel: 01371 876979
e-mail: enquiries@eastonlodge.co.uk
website: www.eastonlodge.co.uk

The Gardens of Easton Lodge comprise 23 romantic acres designed in 1902 by Harold Peto for Daisy, Countess of Warwick. Abandoned in 1950, they were been gradually restored from 1995. Highlights of a visit include the sunken Italian garden - a delightful suntrap with a 100' balustraded pool; the Glade, formerly Peto's Japanese Garden; the Peto Pavilion; the ruined Shelley Pavilion; the skeleton of the Tree House; and the living sundial with a border featuring every plant mentioned in Shakespeare's plays and sonnets. The 17th century dovecote now houses an exhibition of photography, prints and writings showing the history of Easton Lodge since 1950.

WALK 10

Great Dunmow and Little Easton

Start	Great Dunmow
Distance	5½ miles (8.9km)
Approximate time	2½ hours
Parking	Great Dunmow
Refreshments	Pubs and cafés at Great Dunmow, pubs at Church End
Ordnance Survey maps	Landranger 167 (Chelmsford, Harlow & Bishop's Stortford), Explorer 195 (Braintree & Saffron Walden)

The Flitch Way, a former railway track, is used for the first part of the walk. You then head across fields to the delightful church at Little Easton and continue along tracks and field paths to Great Dunmow's church, over ½ mile (800m) north of the town centre at Church End. The final leg is across meadows beside the River Chelmer.

The walk begins in the Market Place at Great Dunmow by the attractive, half-timbered Elizabethan Old Town Hall. The town is particularly renowned for the ancient custom of the Dunmow Flitch, which consists of awarding a flitch of bacon to a newly married couple who can satisfy the judges that they have managed to live together for a year and a day following the marriage without an argument. The Flitch Trials, revived in the Victorian era, are held every leap year.

Start by turning left along the main street, in the Chelmsford direction, turn right by the war memorial into New Street and at a Flitch Way sign, turn right along a tarmac path. **A** Where the path emerges on to the end of a road, bear right to continue along an enclosed, partially tree-lined path and pass beside a barrier on to a road. Turn left and, where the road turns left, keep ahead to pass beside another barrier and walk along an enclosed tarmac path, passing houses and the end of a road to a stile.

Climb the stile, descend steps to carefully cross the busy A120, ascend steps opposite, go through a kissing-gate and turn right **B** along a tree-lined track. This is the Flitch Way, which follows the line of the former Braintree to Bishop's Stortford Railway. At first the route keeps along the top of an embankment – at one stage there is a boardwalk over a boggy area – later you continue through a cutting, pass under a bridge and keep ahead to a gate. After going through it, turn right along a track, recross the A120 and turn left. At a public bridleway sign, turn right **C** along the left-hand edge of a field, by the side of High Wood, go through a hedge gap in the field corner and keep ahead across the next field. Continue along the right-hand edge of trees and finally walk along a short stretch of enclosed path, curving right to emerge on to a lane by the delightful little church at Little Easton. **D**

The church dates from the Norman period but was partially rebuilt in the

13th and 15th centuries. Inside there are some splendid tombs and monuments, a 12th century wall-painting and some 14th century frescoes. More recent memorials are two stained glass windows that commemorate the 386th United States Bomber Group, which was stationed at Little Easton in the Second World War.

Turn right and, at a public footpath sign just beyond the church, bear right to follow a track across a field, keeping to the left of a group of trees to reach a waymarked post. Continue in the same direction to a T-junction and turn left on to a track that bears right to a house. Cross a tarmac track to the right of the house, walk along the concrete track opposite and, in front of a gate, bear left along a track, by a fence on the right. Bear right to continue along the right-hand edge of a field, go through a kissing-gate and head uphill.

At the top, keep along the right-hand field edge, and the track bears left 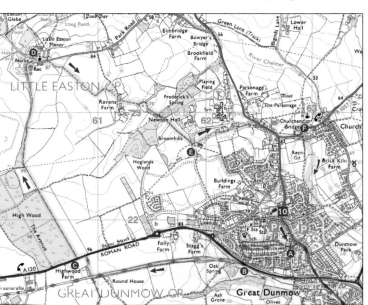 **E** beside trees on the left to a waymarked post. Head across the field to climb a stile, keep ahead by garden fences and hedges on the left and continue across to a stile by another waymarked post. After climbing it, walk along a track and turn right beside a spacious green to reach a road near the Cricketers

pub. Keep ahead and where the main road bends right, turn left, in the Great Bardfield and Finchingfield direction.

The road bends left in front of the Angel and Harp pub to St Mary's, the mainly 14th century parish church of Great Dunmow, but the route continues along a track **F** to the right of the pub. The track bears right in front of a house to a kissing-gate. Go through, bear left across a meadow beside the River Chelmer, pass through a hedge gap and continue across the next meadow to join the river. Keep beside it to a tarmac path by a footbridge and turn right.

At a fork immediately ahead, take the left-hand path, which heads gently uphill to pass beside a barrier. Keep ahead to a road, continue gently uphill to a T-junction and bear right to return to the Market Place.

of the Countess of Warwick, "Darling Daisy", who commissioned spectacular gardens and entertained in lavish style. Her liaison with the Prince of Wales, a frequent guest at Easton, was the talk of the town. In 1895 Daisy abandoned the social whirl and spent the rest of her life supporting good causes and the Labour Party. She died in 1938 surrounded by animals and birds, short of money and living in faded splendour. When war was declared in 1939 the estate was requisitioned by the War Ministry; its wartime uses included billeting of troops rescued from Dunkirk; as an airfield for the use of the USAAF, who flew Marauders and were heavily involved in D-Day; and as an operational base for the RAF. The Ministry handed back the estate to the owners in 1950, since when most of the buildings have been demolished or disposed of - luckily the gardens are being restored to their former glory (see panel on page 233).

LANGTHORNS PLANTERY

Little Canfield, Dunmow,
Essex CM6 1TD
Tel/Fax: 01371 872611

Langthorns Plantery in Little Canfield was created by the present owner Edward Cannon's parents over 20 years ago. Trained at the Cannington College of Horticulture, Edward has worked at wholesale nurseries in Hampshire and The Netherlands, and also as head gardener to West Wratting Park in Cambridgeshire. His experience and conscientious attention to detail are apparent everywhere here at the Plantery, where in addition to the wealth of plants on offer, he can offer garden design advice and quotes on tree surgery work.

The tremendous range of plants, shrubs and specimen trees available, including salvias, penstemons, hostas, viburnum, roses, ornamental trees such as variegated sweet chestnuts, magnolias, and conservatory plants, grasses and bamboos. Plants for hot sunny spots, shade, different soils, ground cover, hedging, winter interest and every colour in the rainbow - in short, for every position, situation and taste - are sold here. The fully trained, knowledgeable and friendly staff are always on hand to give expert advice on all aspects of the plants and gardening. Winner of Silver and Bronze and Floral awards from the Chelsea Flower Show, this excellent nursery is well worth a visit. Open: 7 days a week, 10 am to 5 pm or dusk. Closed Christmas fortnight.

TEAK DIRECT

High Cross Lane, Little Canfield, Essex CM6 1TF
Tel/Fax: 01371 876843

Garden furniture of the highest quality, made from solid teak, is available at **Teak Direct**. Made from teak taken only from sustainable managed forests, the furniture sold here is crafted in simple, classic designs that will enhance any garden. As one of the hardest and most long-lasting woods, teak is ideal for the garden. Each bench, table, chair, lounger, steamer and coffee table is beautifully crafted and finished, and all are sold at affordable prices.

The charming 12th century church in this small village is rich in historic features. Its **Maynard Chapel** features some outstanding marble monuments of the family as well as some famous brasses. The church's oldest treasures are, however, a well-preserved and priceless 12th century wall painting and several 15th century

Lych-gate, Aythorpe Roding Church

frescoes. Two recent additions, two stained glass windows, were unveiled in 1990. The **Window of the Crusaders** and the **Window of Friendship and Peace** are a lasting memorial to the American 386th Bomb Group. Known as 'The Marauders', they were stationed nearby for 13 months and lost over 200 of their number in that short time.

The **Barn Theatre** at Little Easton Manor is located in one of the finest and oldest tithe barns in the country, with magnificent oak timbers and ancient tiled roof. Host to performances by many of the most distinguished actors over the years - including Ellen Terry, Hermione Baddeley, Charlie Chaplin, George Formby and many others - it has been sympathetically restored, enabling it to continue to be used for a host of special events.

HATFIELD BROAD OAK

3 miles SW of Great Dunmow off the B184

This very pretty village has many notable buildings for the visitor to enjoy, including a church dating from Norman times, some delightful 18th century almshouses and several distinctive Georgian houses.

Nearby **Hatfield Forest** to the extreme west of the county is a survivor of a royal hunting forest; many of the features of a medieval forest can still be seen today, including deer, cattle, coppice, pollards, grasslands and rabbit warrens. Once covering a great deal more land, the remaining 400 hectares are now protected by the National Trust and offer splendid woodland walks along with good chases and rides.

AYTHORPE RODING

4 miles SW of Great Dunmow off the B184

Aythorpe Roding Windmill is the largest remaining post mill in Essex. Built on four floors around 1760, it remained in use up until 1935. It was fitted in the 1800s with a fantail which kept the sails pointing into the wind. It is open to the public on the last Sunday afternoon of each month from May to September.

WALTHAM ABBEY

The town of Waltham began as a small Roman settlement on the site of the present-day Market Square. The early Saxon kings maintained a hunting lodge

Waltham Abbey

here; a town formed round this, and the first church was built in the 6th century. By the 8th, during the reign of Cnut (Canute), the town had a stone minster church with a great stone crucifix that had been brought from Somerset, were it had been found buried in land owned by Tovi, a trusted servant of the king. This cross became the focus of pilgrims seeking healing. One of those cured of a serious illness, Harold Godwinsson, built a new church, the third on the site, which was dedicated in 1060 - and it was this self-same Harold who became king and was killed in the battle of Hastings six years on. Harold's body was brought back to Waltham to be buried in his church. The church that exists today was built in the first quarter of the 12th century. It was once three times its present length, and incorporated an Augustinian Abbey, built in 1177 by Henry II. The town became known for the Abbey, which was one of the largest in the country and the last to be the victim of Henry VIII's dissolution of the monasteries, in 1540.

The Abbey's **Crypt Centre** houses an interesting exhibition explaining the history of both the Abbey and the town, highlighting the religious significance of the site. Some visible remains of the Augustinian Abbey include the chapter house and precinct walls, cloister entry and gateway in the surrounding Abbey Gardens. The Abbey Gardens are also host to a Sensory Trail exploring the highlights of hundreds of years of the site's history; there's also a delightful rose garden.

Along the Cornhill Stream, crossed by the impressive stone bridge, the town's Dragonfly Sanctuary is home to over half the native British species of dragonflies and damselflies. It is noted as the best single site for seeing these species for many miles around.

A Tudor timber-framed house forms part of the **Epping Forest District Museum** in Sun Street. The wide range of displays includes exhibits covering the history of the Epping Forest District from the Stone Age to the present day. Tudor and Victorian times are particularly well represented, with some magnificent oak

The Denny Tomb, Waltham Abbey

panelling dating from the reign of Henry VIII, and re-creations of Victorian rooms and shops. There is also an archaeological display and temporary exhibitions covering such subjects as contemporary arts and crafts. The museum has several hands-on displays which help to bring history to life, and features special events and adult workshops throughout the year.

Sun Street is the town's main thoroughfare, now pedestrianised. The Greenwich Meridian (0 degrees longitude) runs through the street, marked out on the pavement and through the Abbey Gardens.

In spite of its proximity to London and more recent development, the town retains a peaceful, traditional character, with its timber-framed buildings and small old-fashioned market which has been held here since the early 12th century (now every Tuesday and Saturday). The whole of the town centre has been designated a conservation area.

To the west of town, the **Lee Navigation Canal** offers opportunities for anglers, walkers, birdwatching and pleasure craft. Once used for transporting corn and other commercial goods to the growing City of London, and having associations with the town's important gunpowder industry for centuries, the canal remains a vital part of town life.

Gunpowder production became established in Waltham as early as the 1660s; by the 19th century the **Royal Gunpowder Mills** employed 500 workers, and production did not cease until 1943, after which time the factory became a research facility. Of the 175 acres the site occupies, approximately 80 have been designated a Site of Special Scientific Interest, and the ecology of the site will offer a rare opportunity for study. With two-thirds of the site a Scheduled Ancient Monument, there are some 21 listed buildings to be found here, some of which date from the Napoleonic Wars. The site also contains some of the finest

ROYAL GUNPOWDER MILLS

Powdermill Lane, Waltham Abbey, Essex EN9 1BN
Tel: 01992 767022 Fax: 01992 710341
website: www.royalgunpowdermills.com

In spring 2001 the **Royal Gunpowder Mills** in Waltham Abbey will be opening its doors to the general public for the first time in its 300 year history. Thanks to funding from the Heritage Lottery Fund and Ministry of Defence, this secret site which was home to gunpowder and explosive production and research for more than three centuries, has been developed to offer visitors a truly unique day out.

Gunpowder production began at Waltham Abbey in the mid 1660's on the site of a late medieval fulling mill. The gunpowder Mills remained in private hands until 1787, when they were purchased by the crown. From this date, the Royal Gunpowder Mills developed into the pre eminent powder works in Britain and one of the most important in Europe.

Set in175 acres of natural parkland and boasting 21 important historic buildings the regenerated site will offer visitors a unique mixture of fascinating history, exciting science and beautiful surroundings. Approximately 70 acres of the site, containing some of the oldest buildings and much of the canal network, will be open for visitors to explore freely. The remaining area of the site including the largest heronry in Essex has been designated as a Site of Special Scientific Interest and will be accessible to the public by way of special guided tours.

examples of industrial archaeology in the world (see panel on page 239).

Lee Valley Regional Park is a leisure area stretching for 26 miles along the River Lea (sometimes also spelled Lee) from East India Dock Basin in east London to Hertfordshire. The Lee Valley is an important area of high biodiversity, sustaining a large range of wildlife and birds. Two hundred species of birds, including internationally important populations of gadwall and shoveller ducks, can be seen each year on the wetlands along the Lea. The Information Centre in the Abbey Gardens provides displays and information on a range of countryside pursuits and interests, sport, leisure and heritage facilities and special events. Of national importance for wintering waterbirds including rare species of bittern and smew, this fine park makes an ideal place for a picnic.

THE ORIENTAL RUG COMPANY

3 Simon Campion Court, High Street, Epping,
Essex CM16 4AU
Tel: 01992 561668 Fax: 01992 570080
website: www.orientalrugco.com

The Oriental Rug Company carries a large, varied and unusual stock of handmade rugs, carpets, kilims and runners from over a dozen countries and also specialises in making carpets to order both in India and Nepal. Valuations and expert cleaning and restoration work undertaken. Open Tuesday to Saturday 9.00 am to 5.30 pm.

WOODLAND PINE & THORNWOOD FIREPLACES

Esgors Farm, High Road, Thornwood Common,
Nr. Epping, Essex CM16 6LY
Tel: 01992 572055 Fax: 01992 573777
e-mail: woodlandpineltd@aol.com

Old buildings on what was previously a dairy farm have been skilfully and attractively converted into showrooms for a thriving business run by Essex born Michael Radley. The rooms, which cover an impressive 7,000 square feet, are crammed full of pine furniture - tables, chairs, cupboards, bookcases, dressers enhanced with pretty pieces of china, stools, wine racks, hi-fi cabinets. Solid pine kitchens are designed, produced and fitted, and the pine pieces bought can be delivered free of charge to the customer.

Michael, who was formerly in the fashion business, started Woodland Pine in 1998, and as well as the huge stock of bespoke pine pieces the well-lit, carpeted showroom space has a large display of fireplaces.

There is ample car parking space at Woodland Pine, which is located on the B1393 between Epping and Harlow, a mile and a half from Junction 7 of the M11. Opening times are 9 am to 5.30 pm 7 days a week. The enterprising Michael Radley also runs Art Nursery at nearby North Weald - see separate panel.

At the southern end of Lee Valley Park, The House Mill, one of two tidal mills still standing at this site, has been restored by the River Lea Tidal Mill Trust. It was built in 1776 in the Dutch style, and was used to grind grain for gin distilling.

Lee Valley Park Farms, along Stubbins Hall Lane, boasts two farms on site. At Hayes Hill Farm visitors can interact with the animals and enjoy a picnic or the children's adventure playground. This traditional farm also boasts old-fashioned tools and equipment, an exhibition in the medieval barn and occasional craft demonstrations. The entry fee to Hayes Hill Farm also covers a visit to Holyfield Hall Farm, a working farm and dairy where visitors can see milking and learn about modern farming methods. Seasonal events such as sheep-shearing and harvesting are held, and there's an attractive farm tea room and a toy shop. Recently a farm trail has been added to this site's attractions, offering wonderful views of the Lee Valley, an expanse of open countryside dotted with lakes and wildflower meadows, attracting a wide range of wildlife including otters, bats, dragonflies, kingfishers, great crested grebes and little ringed plovers. The area is ideal for walking or fishing and the bird hides are open to all at weekends.

Myddleton House Gardens within Lee Valley Park is the place to see the work of the famous plantsman who created them - EA Bowles, the greatest amateur gardener of his time. Breathtaking colours and interesting plantings - such as the National Collection of award-winning bearded iris, the Tulip Terrace and the Lunatic Asylum (home to unusual plants) - are offset by a beautiful carp lake, two conservatories and a rock garden.

AROUND WALTHAM ABBEY

EPPING

4 miles E of Waltham Abbey off the B182

Just off the B1391, on the outskirts of Epping town centre towards Waltham Abbey, this town's handsome **St John's Church** was designed over 100 years ago by GF Bodley.

LOUGHTON

5 miles SE of Waltham Abbey off the A121

Corbett Theatre in Rectory Lane in Loughton is a beautiful Grade I-listed converted medieval tithe barn, where classical, modern and musical theatre productions are performed. The theatre is set in a five-acre site with lovely gardens. Loughton is the burial place of Sarah Martin (1768-1826), who wrote the nursery rhyme *Old Mother Hubbard*.

Loughton borders **Epping Forest**, a magnificent and expansive tract of ancient hornbeam coppice, mainly tucked between the M25 and London. There are miles of leafy walks and rides (horse can be hired locally), with some rough grazing and occasional distant views.

ABRIDGE

7 miles SE of Waltham Abbey off the A113

The **BBC Essex Garden** at Crowther Nurseries, Ongar Road, is a working garden consisting of a vegetable plot, two small greenhouses, and herbaceous and shrub borders. Sheila Chapman, a clematis expert, has 550 varieties of clematis established here. The garden is also home to many farmyard animals which visitors are welcome to see and interact with, and there's a delightful tea shop filled with homemade cakes.

CHINGFORD

6 miles S of Waltham Abbey off the A11

Queen Elizabeth Hunting Lodge in Ranger's Road, Chingford, is a timber-framed hunting grandstand first built for Henry VIII. This unique Tudor-era survivor boasts exceptional carpentry, and is situated in a beautiful part of Epping Forest with ancient oaks and fine views. Photographs of the 1940s and 1950s show that the Lodge and the open spaces around it were a favourite Sunday destination for thousands of Londoners, with massive (and orderly) queues waiting patiently for buses to take them back into the Smoke. The Visitor Centre for the area is located at **High Beach**, near Epping. High Beach (or High Beech) was the home of Alfred, Lord Tennyson between 1837 and 1840. It is recorded

Hunting Lodge, Epping Forest

that the bells of Waltham Abbey, which he could hear from his home, inspired him to write the New Year verses that include 'Ring out the Old, Ring in the New'.

ART NURSERY

Vicarage Lane West, North Weald, Nr. Epping, Essex CM16 6AL
Tel: 01992 523346

Michael Radley, owner of Woodland Pine and Thornwood Fireplaces at Thornwood Common, added another string to his bow at Eastertime 2001, when he took over, **Art Nursery**, which is located close to North Weald Airport and Market. Anyone with an interest in plants and gardening can spend a very happy hour or two pottering round the glasshouses, looking at the impressive array of specimen plants and shrubs along with an equally wide range of garden accessories.

These include handsome wooden troughs and barrels, terracotta pots and planters, hanging baskets, wooden decking, stones for rockeries, gravel and cobbles for paths, garden statues and fountains. To complete the picture there's an extensive choice of durable hardwood garden furniture.

Also on site is the excellent Art Aquatic Centre catering for the needs of anyone wishing to enhance their garden with a pond stocked with exotic fish. Well-informed staff, including members of the Radley family, are always on hand to give advice at this friendly Nursery, which is open seven days a week, from 9 am to 6 pm Monday to Saturday and from 10 am to 4 pm on Sunday.

Broxbourne

5 miles NW of Waltham Abbey off the A10

At Broxbourne **Old Mill and Millpool**, the remains of the old watermill can be seen, the waterwheel of which has been restored to working order. Cruises on the River Lea start from Broxbourne, and motor boats and rowing boats are available for hire.

Hoddesdon

6 miles NW of Waltham Abbey off the A10

Rye House Gatehouse in Rye Road was built by Sir Andre Ogard, a Danish nobleman, in 1443. It is a moated building and a fine example of early English brickwork. It has been restored, and visitors can climb up to the battlements. A permanent exhibition covers the architecture and history of the Rye House Plot of 1683 to assassinate Charles II. Guided tours by prior arrangement. The building lies adjacent to a Royal Society for the Protection of Birds reserve. Other features include an information centre, shop, and circular walks around the site.

Harlow

10 miles NE of Waltham Abbey on the A414

The 'New Town' of Harlow sometimes gets short shrift, but it is in fact a lively and vibrant town with a great deal more than excellent shopping facilities. It has some very good museums and several sites of historic interest. The **Gibberd Collection** in Harlow Town Hall in The High contains a delightful collection of British watercolours, featuring works by Blackadder, Sutherland, Frink, Nash and Sir Frederick Gibberd, Harlow's master planner and the founder of the collection. **Harlow Museum** in Passmores House, Third Avenue, occupies a Georgian manor house set in picturesque gardens which includes a lovely pond

and is home to several species of butterfly. The museum has extensive and important Roman, post-medieval and early 20th century collections, as well as a full programme of temporary exhibitions.

Mark Hall Cycle Museum and Gardens in Muskham Road offers a unique collection of cycles and cycling accessories illustrating the history of the bicycle from 1818 to the present day, including one made of plastic, one that folds, and one where the seat tips forward and throws its rider over the handlebars if the brakes are applied too hard. The museum is housed in a converted stable block within Mark Hall manor. Adjacent to the museum are three period walled gardens.

Gibberd Gardens, on the eastern outskirts of Harlow in Marsh Lane, Gilden Way, reflect the taste of Sir Frederick Gibberd, who designed them on the side of a small valley, with terraces, a wild garden, landscaped vistas, pools and streams and some 80 sculptures.

Harlow Study and Visitors Centre in Netteswellbury Farm is set in a medieval tithe barn and 13th century church. The site has displays outlining the story of Harlow New Town.

Parndon Wood Nature Reserve, Parndon Wood Road, is an ancient woodland with a fine variety of birds, mammals, and insects. Facilities include two nature trails with hides for observing wildlife, and a study centre.

Harlow is the birthplace and burial place of Sarah Flower Adams, who wrote the hymn *Nearer, my God, to Thee*.

Chipping Ongar

8 miles SE of Harlow on the A414

Today firmly gripped in the commuter belt of London, Chipping Ongar began as a Saxon market town ('chipping', or 'cheaping', means market) protected beneath the walls of a Norman castle. The motte and bailey were built by Richard de Lucy in 1155. Only the mound and moat of the castle remain, but the contemporary **Church of St Martin of Tours** still stands. Built in 1080, it has fine Norman flint walls and an anchorite's recess.

There are several other interesting buildings in the town, some dating from Elizabethan times. The children's author Isaac Taylor was pastor here from 1810 until his death in 1829. He is buried in the churchyard, as is his daughter Jane, who wrote the poem *Twinkle, Twinkle Little Star* in a collection she published with her sister Ann.

Explorer David Livingstone was a pupil pastor of the town's 19th century United Reform Church, and lived in Livingstone Cottages before his missionary work in Africa began.

BOBBINGWORTH
2 miles NW of Chipping Ongar off the A414

Blake Hall Gardens at Bobbingworth near Chipping Ongar incorporate a Tropical House, an Ice House, water garden, wild gardens, herbaceous borders, rose garden, sunken garden, duck pond and an ornamental wood. The south wing of the Hall houses the Airscene Aviation WWII Museum run by local RAF enthusiasts.

FYFIELD
2 miles N of Chipping Ongar off the B184

The name 'Fyfield' means five river meadows. Originally a Saxon enclave, the village church of St Nicholas is Norman. There's a beautiful mill house with flood gates in village. Fyfield Hall, opposite the church, is said to be the oldest inhabited timber-framed building in England, dating from around 870.

BEAUCHAMP RODING
3 miles NE of Chipping Ongar off the B184

One of the eight Rodings, it was at Beauchamp Roding that a local farm labourer, Isaac Mead, worked and saved enough to become a farmer himself in 1882. To show his gratitude to the land that made him his fortune, he had a corner of the field consecrated as an eternal resting place for himself and his family. Their graves can still be seen in the undergrowth.

Beauchamp's **Church of St Botolph** stands alone in the fields, marked by a tall 15th century tower and reached by a track off the B184. Inside, the raised pews at the west end have clever space-saving wooden steps, pulled out of slots by means of iron rings.

GOOD EASTER
5 miles NE of Chipping Ongar off the B184

A quiet farming village, now in the commuter belt for London, Good Easter's claim to fame is the making of a world-record daisy chain (6,980 feet 7 inches) in 1985. The village's interesting name is probably derived from 'Easter', the Old English for 'sheepfolds' and 'Good' from a Saxon lady named Godiva.

Close to Good Easter and so named because it stands on higher ground than its neighbour, **High Easter** is a quiet and very picturesque village.

KELVEDON HATCH
4 miles S of Chipping Ongar off the A128

A simple bungalow in the rural Essex village of Kelvedon Hatch is the deceptively simple exterior for the **Kelvedon Secret Nuclear Bunker**, which reaches 100 feet below ground. Built in 1952, it took 40,000 tons of concrete to create a base for up to 600 top Government and civilian personnel in the event of nuclear war. Visitors can explore room after room to see communications equipment, a BBC studio, sick bay, massive kitchens and dormitories, power and filtration plant, government administration room and the scientists' room, where nuclear fall-out patterns would have been measured.

GREENSTED

1½ miles SW of Chipping Ongar off the A414

St Andrew's in Greensted is the country's oldest wooden church, dating from the 9th to the 11th centuries, with a later Tudor chancel. It is famous as the only surviving example of a Saxon log church extant in the world, built from split oak logs held together with dowells. Over the centuries the church has been enlarged and restored; later additions include the simple weatherboarded tower, Norman flint walls, the Tudor tiled roof, Victorian stone coping, porch and stained glass windows. The body of Saint Edmund is known to have been rested here in 1013 on its way back from London to Bury St Edmunds.

The village also has associations with the Tolpuddle 'martyrs', six Dorset farm labourers who were taken to court on a legal technicality because they agitated for better conditions and wages, and formed a Trade Union. After their conviction in 1834 they were condemned to transportation to Australia for seven years. There was a public outcry for their release, and their sentences were commuted in 1837. Unable to return to Dorset, they were granted tenancies in Greensted and High Laver. One of the martyrs, James Brine, of New House Farm (now Tudor Cottage, on Greensted Green), married Elizabeth Standfield, daughter of one of his fellow victims - the record of their marriage in 1839 can be seen in the parish register.

NORTH WEALD

3 miles W of Chipping Ongar off the A414

North Weald Airfield Museum at Ad Astra House, Hurricane Way, North Weald Bassett, is a small, meticulously detailed museum displaying the history of North Weald from 1916 to the present. Collections of photos and artefacts such as uniforms and the detailed records of all flying operations are on display. There is also a video show recounting a day to day account of North Weald history. Guided tours of the airfield can be arranged for large groups. The village itself is dominated by its church, which has a 66' brick tower of 1500. One section of the churchyard is an RAF cemetery.

BRENTWOOD

Brentwood is a thriving shopping and entertainment centre, with quite a distinguished past belying its mainly

modern appearance; the town was a stopping place on the old pilgrim and coaching routes to and from London.

Brentwood Cathedral on Ingrave Road was built in 1991. This classically-styled Roman Catholic church, dedicated to St Mary and St Helen, incorporates part of the original Victorian church that stood on this spot. It was designed by the much-admired architect Quinlan Terry, with roundels by Raphael Maklouf (who also created the relief of the Queen's head used on current coins). **Brentwood Museum** at Cemetery Lode in Lorne Road, in the Warley Hill area of Brentwood, is a small and picturesque cottage museum concentrating on local and social interests during the late 19th and early 20th centuries. It is set in an attractive disused cemetery, which is in itself of great interest.

Brentwood Centre on Doddinghurst Road is one of the top entertainment venues in the UK as well as a comprehensively-equipped sports and leisure centre, while Thorndon Country Park offers the open-air attractions of historic parkland, lakes and woods. The site, formerly a Royal deer park, also features a wildlife exhibition and attractive gift shop.

AROUND BRENTWOOD

MOUNTNESSING

1 mile NE of Brentwood off the A12

This village has a beautifully restored early 19th century windmill as its main landmark, though the isolated church also has a massive beamed belfry. **Mountnessing Post Mill** in Roman Road is open to the public. This traditional weatherboarded mill was built in 1807 and restored to working order in 1983. Visitors can see the huge wooden and iron gears; one pair of stones have been opened up for viewing.

INGATESTONE

3 miles NE of Brentwood off the B1002

Ingatestone Hall on Hall Lane is a 16th century mansion set in 11 acres of grounds. It was built by Sir William Petre, Secretary of State to four Monarchs, whose family continue to reside here. The Hall contains family portraits, furniture and memorabilia accumulated over the centuries, while among the many fine features in the grounds are immaculate lawns, specimen trees, a walled garden, nut walk, lime walk and grass walk. The brick-towered Church of St Edmund and St Mary is replete with memorials to the Petre family, including the superb armour-clad alabaster figure of Sir William himself, at repose with his wife.

BILLERICAY

6 miles E of Brentwood off the A129

There was a settlement here as far back as the Bronze Age, though there is no conclusive explanation of Billericay's name. There is no question about the attraction of the **High Street**, though, with its timber weather-boarding and Georgian brick. The **Chantry House**, built in 1510, was the home of Christopher Martin, treasurer to the Pilgrim Fathers.

The Peasants' Revolt of 1381 saw the massacre of hundreds of rebels just northeast of the town at Norsey Wood. Today this area of ancient woodland is **Norsey Wood Local Nature Reserve**, managed by coppicing (the traditional way of ensuring the timber supply), which also encourages plantlife and birdlife. Guided tours take place in the spring and summer.

Barleylands Farm Museum features a glass-blowing studio, smithy and craft shops and has one of the largest collections of vintage farm machinery in the country. The farm is also home to a wide range of creatures, from honey bees to horses.

GREAT WARLEY

1 mile S of Brentwood on the B186

Warley Place was formerly home to one of the most famous women gardeners, Ellen Willmott, who died in 1934. She introduced to Warley - and to Britain - many exotic plants. A trail takes visitors through what in 1978 became **Warley Place Nature Reserve**, with 16 acres of what was once domesticated garden but has now reverted to woodland. A fascinating selection of trees, shrubs and wildlife make this well worth a visit.

SOUTH WEALD

2 miles W of Brentwood off the A12

This very attractive village has at its

outskirts, **Weald Country Park**, a former estate with medieval deer park, partially landscaped in the 1700s. Featuring lake and woodland, visitors' centre, landscapes exhibition and gift shop, with facilities for fishing and horse-riding, it offers various special events and activities throughout the season.

Old Macdonalds Educational Farm Park in Weald Road is a centre specialising in British farm livestock, with nine breeds of pig, 23 of sheep, six of cattle, 30 of poultry and 30 of rabbit to see and learn about. There are also Shire horses, owls, deer, honey bees and lots more - in short, the largest selection of farm animals and birds and bees in Essex. Guided tours can be booked by appointment. The farm holds daily demonstrations and craft displays; the site also boasts nature trails, an attractive gift shop, playground, classroom facilities and café.

HAZLE CERAMICS

Stallions Yard, Codham Hall, Great Warley, Brentwood, Essex CM13 3JT
Tel: 01277 220892 Fax: 01277 233768
e-mail: hazle@hazle.com website: www.hazle.com

Hazle Ceramics produce an exciting and beautiful range of quality collectible ceramics. Their patented designs are noted for the delicacy of the detail, and each one is hand painted. No two pieces are ever quite the same, and so these miniature architectural masterpieces make unique gifts. Founded in 1990 by Hazle Boyles, who is herself an experienced artist, it now employs craftspeople from all round the region and sells to enthusiasts worldwide. The various delightful ranges include wall plaques, money boxes and pastille burners (the revival of these spice-burning vessels popular in Elizabethan times was innovated by Hazle Ceramics). The 'Nation of Shopkeepers' range of wall plaques has won the award for Best Collectible from the British Craftware Association for its 'originality and value'.

At the Workshop and Visitors' Centre, regular events and craft days are held, with ceramic painting sessions held on Friday and Sunday mornings at 11 am, and Saturdays at 11 am and 2 pm Beginners are welcome, including children aged 8+, as professional ceramic artists guide you in the process of painting plates, tiles, vases, bowls and more. Booking essential.

NORTH THAMES CORRIDOR

GRAYS

12 mils S of Brentwood on the A1089

Thurrock Museum is in the Thamesside Complex in Grays. It collects, conserves and displays items of archaeology and local history from prehistoric times to the end of the 20th century. The archaeological items include flint and metal tools of people who lived in prehistoric Thurrock and pottery, jewellery and coins from the Roman and Saxon period.

WEST THURROCK

1½ miles SW of Grays off the A13

Immortalised by the film *Four Weddings and a Funeral*, little **St Clement's Church** occupies a striking location and is one of a number of picturesque ancient churches in the borough. Although this 12th century church is now deconsecrated, it was in its day a stopping point for pilgrims; visitors can see the remains of its original round tower.

PURFLEET

3 miles W of Grays off the M25

Fans of Bram Stoker's novel *Dracula* will know that in this book the famous vampire buys a house called Carfax in Purfleet. The town's esteemed Royal Hotel is said to have played host to Edward VII, while still Prince of Wales in the 1880s and 1890s, at which time the hotel was called Wingrove's.

The **Purfleet Heritage and Military Centre** is a museum featuring displays of many items of interest and memorabilia in the setting of the No 5 Gunpowder Magazine on Centurion Way.

AVELEY

3 miles NW of Grays off the M25

Belhus Woods Country Park covers approximately 180 acres and contains an interesting variety of habitats, including woodland, two lakes and the remains of a pond designed by "Capability" Brown. The Visitors' Centre to this superb park can be found at the main entrance off Romford Road. Belhus Park Golf Course is a well-established 18-hole course set within this beautiful parkland.

SOUTH OCKENDEN

3 miles N of Grays off the A13

Grangewaters Country Park, managed by Thurrock Environmental and Outdoor Centre, it offers watersports such as water-skiing, windsurfing, sailing and canoeing, as well as mountain biking, climbing and other outdoor pursuits. Brannetts Wood is one of the oldest recorded ancient woodlands in South Essex. It can be reached from the Mardyke Way, or from Stifford Road here in South Ockendon.

The village Church of St Nicholas has one of only six round church towers in Essex. This one was built in the 13th century and used to have a spire, which was sadly destroyed by lightning in the 17th century.

ORSETT

4 miles NE of Grays off the A13

This village was the original seat of local government for the area, and in medieval times the site of one of the palaces of the Bishop of London. The village animal pound and lock-up, the latter last used as a prison in 1848, still exist. **Thurrock Aerodrome**, located between Orsett and Bulphan on the A128, hosts the Orsett Air Fete every year in early August.

HORNDON-ON-THE HILL

6 miles NE of Grays off the B1007

Listed in the Domesday Book as Horninduna, a name which also appears on a Saxon coin of Edward the Confessor (1042-1066), it is said to have once been the site of a Royal Anglo-Saxon mint. The town's 16th century Woolmarket indicates the importance of the wool trade to the region, and is one of the area's historical treasures. The upper room served as Horndon's manor courtroom, while the lower, open area was used for trading in woollen cloth.

The main entrance and visitor centre for **Langdon Nature Reserve** are located off the Lower Dunton Road north of Horndon-on-the-Hill. A bridleway and footpaths lead visitors to meadows, a pond and outstanding ancient woods. Also within the reserve, which is managed by Essex Wildlife Trust, is the Plotlands Museum, housed in an original 1930s plotland bungalow known as the Haven.

LINFORD

3 miles NE of Grays off the A13

Walton Hall Farm Museum on Walton Hall Road has a large collection of historic farm machinery, militaria, household and motoring bygones, a dairy and a nursery, all housed in a 17th century barn. Visitors can watch traditional craftsmen, such as a blacksmith, saddlemaker, printer and wheelwright, at work, and bread is baked most holidays in the old village bakery.

STANFORD-LE-HOPE

4 miles NE of Grays off the A1014

Stanford Marshes is an area to the south of Stanford-le-Hope, next to the Thames, that is home to a variety of wildlife and an ideal location for birdwatching. In Stanford itself, Grove House Wood is a nature reserve managed by Essex Wildlife Trust and the local Girl Guides. A footpath here leads to reed beds, a pond and a brook as well as an area of woodland.

CANVEY ISLAND

10 miles NE of Grays off the A130

Canvey Island is a peaceful and picturesque stretch of land overlooking the Thames estuary with views to neighbouring Kent. The island boasts two unusual museums: **Dutch Cottage Museum** is an early 17th century eight-sided cottage built by Dutch workmen for Dutch workmen and boasting many traditional Flemish features. Castle Point Transport Museum is housed in a 1930s bus garage. It houses a fascinating collection of historic and modern buses and coaches, mainly of East Anglian origin.

WEST TILBURY

3 miles E of Grays off the A1089

West Tilbury was the site chosen for the Camp Royal in 1588, to prepare for the threatened Spanish invasion. Queen Elizabeth I visited the army here, and made her famous speech,

I know I have the body but of a weak and feeble woman: but I have the heart and stomach of a king, and a king of England too.

Hidden away in rural tranquillity overlooking the Thames estuary, West Tilbury remains unspoilt in spite of its proximity to busy, industrial Tilbury. The former local church (now a private dwelling) in this quaint little village is a nautical landmark used for navigation. The list of Rectors of the church, dating from 1279-1978, when the church was disestablished, can be seen in The Kings Head Pub.

EAST TILBURY

5 miles E of Grays off the A13

Coalhouse Fort is considered to be one of the best surviving examples of a Victorian Casement fortress in the country. As such it is a protected Scheduled Ancient Monument. Built between 1861 and 1874 as a first line of defence for the Thames area against invasion, it stands on the site of other defensive works and fortifications dating back to around 1400. Part of the construction work on the Fort was overseen by Gordon of Khartoum. It was designed to be a dedicated Artillery casement fortress, which means that the guns were housed in large vaulted rooms with armour-plated frontages. Beneath these rooms lies an extensive magazine tunnel system to service the artillery. Over the years many alterations were made to the Fort to accommodate new artillery. The Fort was manned during both World Wars, and is now owned by Thurrock Borough Council and administered by The Coalhouse Fort Project, a registered charity manned entirely by volunteers. Open to the public, it contains reconstructions of period guns and other displays, and also houses the **Thamesside Aviation Museum**, with a large collection of local finds and other aviation material. In the two parade grounds visitors will find various artillery pieces and military vehicles. During the year the Fort hosts a range of shows, including an historic artillery rally when various big guns are fired by crews in the uniforms of the period, including a Second World War crew firing a 1940 25-pounder field gun. A guided tour allows visitors to see the magazine tunnels beneath the gun casements and offer a feel for the work and conditions of a Victorian gunner. The tour also takes in the roof of the Fort, from where the view takes in the

two sister forts in Kent and, on a clear day, Southend.

The Fort is set in a lovely riverside park with walks and a children's play area, as well as other items of military history including a Quick Fire Battery and Minefield Control box. You can also follow the old railway tracks, from the Fort to the side of the old jetty, where many of the armaments and supplies for the fort were shipped in.

It is possible that East Tilbury's St Catherine's church occupies the site of one of the first Christian monasteries in the 7th century. Its half-built tower was constructed by the First World War Garrison of Coalhouse Fort.

The **Bata Estate** is a conservation area of architectural and historical interest. Established in 1933, the British Bata Shoe Company was the creation of Czech-born Thomas Bata, who also developed a housing estate for his workforce. This range of uniform flat-roofed houses can still be seen on site.

TILBURY

3 miles SE of Grays off the A1089

Tilbury Fort is a well-preserved and unusual 17th century structure with double moat. The fort affords tremendous views of the Thames estuary. The most violent episode in the fort's history occurred in 1776, during a particularly vociferous cricket match which left three people dead - and we think that today's cricketers sometimes get over-excited! For a small fee visitors to the fort can fire a 1943 3.7mm anti-aircraft gun - a prospect most children and many adults find irresistible. Owned by English Heritage, the site was used for a military Block House during the reign of Henry VIII and was rebuilt in the 17th century. It remains one of Britain's finest examples of a star-shaped bastion fortress. Extensions were made in the 18th and 19th centuries, and the Fort was still being used in the Second World War.

Tilbury Festival is held every year in July in a field near the fort, and features arena events, craft and food stalls and re-enactments of historical events. Tilbury Energy and Environment Centre at Tilbury Power Station provides a nature reserve and study centre for schools and community education. A flat two-mile nature trail leads to and from the Centre.

PITSEA

12 miles NE of Grays off the A13

Wat Tyler Country Park comprises 120 acres of parkland, mainly surrounded by water, operated by Basildon District Council with an emphasis on conservation and natural history. Among the attractions are a marina, miniature railway, historic buildings and the unique **National Motorboat Museum**, illustrating the history and evolution of the motor boat, concentrating on sports and leisure.

SOUTHEND-ON-SEA

Oh! We do like to be beside the Seaside, and at Southend-on-Sea there is always plenty to do and see, and many events throughout the year to ensure its interest and popularity. The town is one of the best loved and friendliest resorts in Britain, featuring the very best ingredients for a break at the seaside.

Southend Pier and Museum brings to life the fascinating past of the longest Pleasure Pier in the world. The Pier itself is 1.3

miles long; visitors can either take a leisurely walk along its length or take advantage of the regular train service that plies up and down the pier.

Central Museum and Planetarium on Victoria Avenue features local history exhibits, while **Sealife Centre** on the Eastern Esplanade employs the most advanced technology to bring visitors incredibly close to the wonders of British marine life. A floral trail guided tour around the parks and gardens will reveal why Southend has won the Britain in Bloom Awards every year since 1993, as well as medals at the Chelsea Flower Show.

The Kursaal indoor entertainment complex is one of the largest in the country, with indoor bowling, synthetic ice and roller rink, a fun casino, children's play area, snooker and pool, arts and crafts, retail units and theme restaurants.

Southend Beach

Prittlewell Priory Park

Traditional entertainment is on hand in the summer and at Christmas at the Cliffs Bandstand, including brass band concerts, afternoon tea dances and evening concerts. Boat trips in summer include occasional outings on a vintage paddle steamer, and ferry trips to Felixstowe are also available from Southend.

The **Southchurch Hall Museum** in Park Lane is a delightful 13th to 14th century timber-framed manor house with Tudor additions. Period room settings are among this museum's many delights.

Prittlewell Priory Museum, slightly north of Southend town centre in Priory Park, is a well-preserved 12th century Cluniac Priory set in lovely grounds and housing collections of the Priory's history, natural history and the Caten collection of radios and communications. The **Beecroft Art Gallery** in Westcliff-on-Sea is one of East Anglia's foremost

galleries and well worth a visit (see panel below).

AROUND SOUTHEND-ON-SEA

OLD LEIGH
½ mile W of Southend off the A13

The unspoilt fishing village of Old Leigh has a long and distinguished history. It is picturesque, with seafront houses and narrow winding alleys, and has also earned its place in history: the pilgrim ship *The Mayflower* restocked here en route to the New World of America in the mid-17th century, and the Dunkirk rescue embarked from here, an event commemorated in a framed poem on the wall of the local pub, The Crooked Billet.

LEIGH-ON-SEA
2 miles W of Southend off the A13

Leigh-on-Sea has a character quite distinct from Southend's, being more intimate and serene, with wood-clad buildings and shrimp boats in the working harbour. The shellfish stall on the harbourside is justly famous. The

---

BEECROFT ART GALLERY

Station Road, Westcliff-on-Sea, Essex SS0 7RA
Tel: 01702 347418 Fax: 01702 347681
website: www.beecroft-art-gallery.co.uk

With fine sea views and a varied collection ranging from 17th century Dutch paintings to contemporary works, as well as a fine exhibition of local views, the **Beecroft Art Gallery** is well worth a visit. The permanent fine art collection is supplemented by a changing

programme of special shows, highlighted by the summer Essex Open Exhibition and the Christmas Show. The Gallery, which is also the venue for numerous art classes, is a charitable trust supported by Southend-on-Sea Borough Council as part of its Leisure Services Department.

Leigh Heritage Centre, housed in a

GREENS HEALTH FOODS

37 Rectory Grove, Leigh-on-Sea, Essex SS9 2HA
Tel/Fax: 01702 475338
e-mail: greenshealthfood@onetel.net.uk
website: www.greenshealthfood.co.uk

Greens Health Foods is the place to shop for wholefoods, offering a wide selection of healthy and tempting foods such as pastas, dried fruits, pulses, dairy products, breads, herbs, spices, juices, chilled and frozen meals, locally-produced honeys and jams, and a full range of herbal remedies and eco-friendly cleaning products, shampoos and soaps. The friendly, knowledgeable staff can assist and advise on all the products sold.

former ancient blacksmith's, now houses historic artefacts.

HADLEIGH

5 miles NW of Southend off the A13

Hadleigh Castle, built originally for Edward III, is owned by English Heritage and once belonged to Anne of Cleves, Catherine of Aragon and Katherine Parr. The ruins, still impressive, were immortalised in a painting by John Constable. Hadleigh Castle Country Park offers a variety of woodland and coastal walks.

HOCKLEY

6 miles NW of Southend off the A129

Hockley Woods is a 280-acre ancient woodland, managed for the benefit of wildlife and the public. Traditional coppice management encourages a diverse array of flora and fauna, including the nationally rare Heath Fritillary butterfly.

RAYLEIGH

6 miles NW of Southend off the A1016

Dutch Cottage at Crown Hill is a traditional Flemish eight-sided cottage based on a 17th century design created by Dutch settlers (it can be visited on Wednesday afternoons by appointment. Rayleigh Mount is a prominent landmark in this part of the county; once a motte and bailey castle built in the 11th century,

it was abandoned some 200 years later. Rayleigh Windmill, in Bellingham Lane close to Rayleigh Mount, was built at the beginning of the 19th century and now houses a fascinating collection of bygones, mostly used in and around Rayleigh.

CHELMSFORD

Roman workmen cutting their great road linking London with Colchester built a fort at what is today called Chelmsford. Then called Caesaromagus, it stands at the confluence of the Rivers Chelmer and Can. The town has always been an important market centre and is now the bustling county town of Essex; it is also directly descended from a new town planned by the Bishop of London in 1199. At its centre are the principal inn, the Royal Saracen's Head, and the elegant Shire Hall of 1791. Three plaques situated high up on the eastern face of the Hall overlooking the High Street represent Wisdom, Justice and Mercy. The building now houses the town's magistrates court.

Chelmsford Cathedral in New Street dates from the 15th century and is built on the site of a church constructed 800 years ago. The cathedral is noted for the harmony and unity of its perpendicular architecture. It was John Johnson, the distinguished local architect who

CHELMSFORD MUSEUM & ESSEX REGIMENT MUSEUM

Oaklands Park, Moulsham Street,
Chelmsford, Essex CVM2 9AQ
Tel: 01245 615100 Fax: 01245 611250
e-mail: oaklands@chelmsfordbc.gov.uk
website: www.chelmsfordbc.gov.uk/leisure/museums

Chelmsford Museum, founded in 1835, has since 1930 been located in a lovely Victorian mansion in a city-centre park. The history of Chelmsford and its people from prehistoric times right up to the present day is told through displays that include geology, natural history (with a live beehive!), costumes and coins. Fine and Decorative Arts are represented by works by Edward Bawden and other regionally based artists, the Tunstall Bequest of 18th century drinking glasses and flamboyant Victorian pieces from Castle Hedingham Pottery.

The Essex Regiment on the same site relates the story of the 44th and 56th Regiments from 1741 to the modern Royal Anglian Regiment. Among the many items on display are a tailcoat of 1785 with Pompadour purple collar and cuffs, a French eagle standard captured in battle in 1812, the Regimental silver and silver drums presented by the people of Essex, medals won by Essex men including four Victoria Cross winners, the Colours of the 44th Foot carried for 102 years, and an Essex Home Guard display. Regularly changing temporary exhibitions supplement the permanent displays at both Museums.

Also under the aegis of Chelmsford Borough Council is a developing Science and Industry project at Sandford Mill, Chelmer Village (Tel/Fax: 01245 475498) with visits by appointment or on open days and science weeks for local schools.

CENTRE OF NATURAL HEALTH

20 New London Road, Chelmsford CM2 0SW
Tel: 01245 350881

Lin Hall MBA DMS LCH - Homoeopath

The Centre of Natural Health can supply a wide range of quality nutritional supplements, special diet foods, weight-training products; friendly, helpful advice. There is also a clinic offering homoeopathy, reflexology, allergy testing, aromatherapy, nutrition, massage, herbalism, Reiki, non-invasive aesthetic treatments (including collagen replacement therapy, skin peels, thread vein and laser hair removal, mineral-based make-up suitable particularly for psoriasis and eczema sufferers).

FURSE RESTORATION

Unit 15, Beechcroft, Damases Lane, Boreham, Chelmsford, Essex CM3 3AL
Tel/Fax: 01245 466744
e-mail: enquiries@furserestoration.co.uk website: www.furserestoration.co.uk
The father and son team of Fred and Andrew Furse run **Furse Restoration**, which is located in a unit of converted farm buildings a short distance northeast of Chelmsford. Fred, in the business for over 40 years, is the man responsible for the expert restoration of antique and period furniture, including hand-finished French polishing. Andrew, a skilled cabinet maker with 15 years experience, undertakes commissions for designing and producing furniture of the highest quality, including oak display cabinets, coffee tables, Victorian-style dining tables, double-door bookcases, TV/video cabinets and chairs in the style of Chippendale and Sheraton.

designed both the Shire Hall and the 18th century Stone Bridge over the River Can, who also rebuilt the Parish Church of St Mary when most of its 15th century tower fell down. The church became a cathedral when the new diocese of Chelmsford was created in 1914; since then it has been enlarged and re-organised inside. The Cathedral boasts memorial windows dedicated to the USAAF airmen who were based in Essex from 1942-5. Chelmsford Cathedral Festival is an annual cultural occasion held each May featuring music, talks, exhibitions and other events.

The Marconi Company, pioneers in the manufacture of wireless equipment, set up the first radio company in the world in Chelmsford in 1899. Exhibits of those pioneering days of wireless can be seen in the **Chelmsford and Essex Museum** in Oaklands Park, as can interesting displays of Roman remains and local history. The **Essex Regiment Museum** is also situated in Oaklands Park. Together these two fine museums exhibit temporary and permanent displays exploring local and social history from prehistoric times up until the present (see panel opposite).

Also in the town, at Parkway, is **Moulsham Mill**, an early 18th century water mill that has been renovated and now houses a variety of craft workshops and businesses. Crafts featured include jewellery, pottery, flowers, lace-making, dolls houses and bears, and découpage work.

Three modern technologies - electrical engineering, radio, and ball and roller bearings - began in Chelmsford. At the **Engine House Project** at Sandford Mill Waterworks, museum collections from the town's unique industrial story provide a fun and fascinating insight into the science of everyday things.

AROUND CHELMSFORD

GREAT BADDOW
1 mile S of Chelmsford off the A130

Baddow Antiques Centre at the Bringy, Church Street, is one of the leading antiques centres in Essex. Here, 20 dealers offer a wide selection of silver, porcelain, glass, furniture, paintings and collectibles. There is also a collection of 300 Victorian brass and iron bedsteads on display.

SANDON
2 miles SE of Chelmsford off the A414

Sandon's village green has produced a notable Spanish **Oak Tree**, the biggest in the country, planted in the centre of the village green. This oak tree is remarkable not so much for its height as for the tremendous horizontal spread of its branches. Around the green are a fine church and a number of attractive old houses, some dating back to the 16th century when Henry VIII's Lord Chancellor, Cardinal Wolsey, was Lord of the Manor of Sandon.

SOUTH HANNINGFIELD
6 miles S of Chelmsford off the A130

The placid waters of nearby **Hanningfield Reservoir** were created by damming Sandford Brook, and transformed the scattered rural settlement of Hanningfield into a lakeside village. Now on the shores of the lake, the 12th century village church's belfry has been a local landmark in the flat Essex countryside for centuries. Some of the timbers in the belfry are said to have come from Spanish galleons, wrecked in the aftermath of Sir Francis Drake's defeat of the Armada.

HIGHWOOD

3 miles SW of Chelmsford off the A414

Hylands House was built in 1728 and is slowly being restored. It is set in beautiful parkland, lawns and formal gardens designed by Humphry Repton and hosts many outdoor events. Rooms open to the public include the entrance hall, blue room, library, drawing room, saloon and boudoir.

Writtle

WRITTLE

2 miles W of Chelmsford off the A414

From a tucked-away corner of St John's Green in this village came Britain's first regular broadcasting service, an experimental 15-minute programme beamed out nightly by Marconi's engineers. Opposite the Green, the Cock and Bell is reputed to be haunted by a young woman who committed suicide on the railway, while further along this street is the Wheatsheaf, one of the smallest pubs in the country. Writtle's parish church of St John features a cross of charred timbers, a reminder of the fire which gutted the chancel in 1974. Ducks swim on the pond of the larger and quite idyllic main village green, which is surrounded by lovely Tudor and Georgian houses.

GREAT LEIGHS

4 miles N of Chelmsford off the A131

The **Great Leighs Great Maze** is one of the most challenging in the world. Set in 8.5 acres of lovely North Essex countryside, it is open every summer. The year 2000 brought further innovations, with extra twists and turns to make this wonderful maze even more of a brain teaser. Ten per cent of all profits go to the Essex Air Ambulance service.

WITHAM

6 miles NE of Chelmsford off the A12/B1018

The River Brain flows through this delightful town; a continuous walk has been created along its length for a distance of about three miles. The settlement dates back to at least the 10th century; remains of a Roman temple have been found at Ivy Chimneys, off Hatfield Road. Witham was for many years the home of Dorothy L Sayers, novelist, theologian and Dante scholar, and the **Dorothy L Sayers Centre** in Newland Street has a reference collection of books by and about her. Blackwater Lane leads to Whetmead, a nature reserve of 25 acres between the rivers Blackwater and Brain.

LITTLE BADDOW

5 miles E of Chelmsford off the A414

Blakes Wood is a designated Site of Special Scientific Interest, an ancient woodland of hornbeam and sweet chestnut renowned for its bluebells. There is a good circular way-marked one-and-a-half mile walk, while cruising along the Chelmer and Blackwater Canal provides the visitor with a unique view of this part of rural Essex.

DANBURY GIFT BASKETS

60 Main Road, Danbury, Essex CM3 4NG
Tel: 01245 222299 Fax: 01245 226865

Situated on the A414 next to the Griffin public house, **Danbury Gift Baskets** is the place to visit when looking for an unusual present. Behind the immaculate black and white facade manager Gill Matthams and her friendly, on-the-ball staff offer a superb range of high-quality, out-of-the-ordinary articles, all colourfully displayed in a setting that is enhanced by the delightful fragrance of aromatic oils and sprays.

Pride of place goes to the wonderful dried and silk flower arrangements made by Pi, a local lady who was previously engaged in graphic design. Also very popular are the Danbury ducks, inspired by the ducks on the village pond and made from straw and real feathers. Hand-painted vases and mirrors, silk scarves, terracotta pots, candles, silver jewellery, china ornaments and découpage clocks are among the other items that make up this unique range, which also includes greetings cards and helium-filled balloons. All goods can be prettily wrapped as gifts, and Gill brightens many a local shop and hotel with bespoke, made-to-order displays.

The village of Danbury, whose attractions also include a fine church with some notable carvings, and excellent walking on the common or in the country park, is located between Chelmsford and Maldon on the A414.

DANBURY

5 miles E of Chelmsford off the A414

This village is said to take its name from the Danes who invaded this part of the country in the Dark Ages. In the fine church, under a rare 13th century carved effigy, a crusader knight was found perfectly preserved, when the tomb was opened in 1779, in the pickle which filled his coffin. Fine carving is also a feature of the bench ends; the oldest among them have inspired modern craftsmen to continue the same style of carving on all the pews. In 1402, 'the devil appeared in the likeness of Firor Minor, who entered the church, raged insolently to the great terror of the parishioners ... the top of the steeple was broken down and half the chancel scattered abroad.' And, in 1941, another bringer of doom, a monster 500lb German bomb, reduced the east end to ruins.

At Danbury Common, acres of gorse flower in a blaze of golden colour for much of the year. To the west, **Danbury Country Park** offers another pleasant stretch of open country boasting woodland, a lake and ornamental gardens. Fishing is available by day permit. Along with Lingwood Common, Danbury Common is at the highest point of the gravel ridge between Maldon and Chelmsford. There is evidence here of Napoleonic defences and old reservoirs. Circular nature trails assist greatly in the exploration of the area.

MALDON

10 miles E of Chelmsford on the A414

The steep, winding streets of the hilltop town of Maldon are full of interesting shops and welcoming inns, and the town's High Street, of which the **Moot Hall** is a distinctive feature, runs right

MALDON

Town Centre Manager, Kings Head Centre,
38 High Street, Maldon, Essex CM9 5PN
Tel: 01621 843984 website: www.maldon.co.uk

Maldon is an historic town with a thousand years of history and a strong maritime tradition, and the range of shops, restaurants, cafés, services and accommodation makes it an excellent place for an extended stay. Visitors should allow plenty of time to stroll around the alleyways leading off the High Street and to see some of the town's many attractions.

The High Street is filled with interesting shops, and on Thursday and Saturday the traditional market adds to the bustle; the farmers market is held on the first Tuesday of each month. At the end of the High Street, Church Street leads down to the Hythe, where visitors

can appreciate Maldon's unique setting at the head of the Blackwater Estuary, home to many of the wonderful old Thames sailing barges.

Maldon has plenty of centrally located hotel and guest house accommodation, including the Benbridge Hotel on the Square, Heybridge; Barges Galore at the Hythe; The Limes, Market Hill; 4 Lodge Road; the Swan Hotel in the High Street; and the Blue Boar Hotel in Silver Street.

HARVEY BROWN LTD

104a High Street, Maldon, Essex CM9 7ET
Tel & Fax: 01621 841770
website: www.harveybrown.co.uk

Harvey Brown, based in Maldon's High Street, produces high-quality new furniture designed in a classical yet simple style. The company, which was founded three years ago, is a small concern able to tailor designs and finishes to individual tastes and requirements while maintaining the highest standards of workmanship. The directors Gary Phipps and Paul Collins have 20 years experience in upholstery, concentrating on traditional methods of restoring antique furniture, so it was a natural progression to produce new pieces with traditional upholstery.

The intention of the company is to produce individual pieces and not a mass-produced collection. The current range comprises a Bridge Chair, Bridge Sofa, Gothic Stool, Dining Chair and Window Seat. Ideas for designs come from a number of sources: the Bridge Chair is a copy of a Georgian chair, originally in mahogany. Light oak gives the Harvey Brown version a more contemporary look, as with the Gothic Stool, which was inspired by a Pugin original. Quarter sawn oak and walnut are the usual choice of wood, and at present the company is investigating the possibility of purchasing wood through the Anglia Woodnet Scheme. New ideas and designs are always forthcoming; these include a large, comfortable sofa and chair, and a large low stool which can be upholstered or have a drop-in cushion top.If clients have a design in mind or a style to match, Harvey Brown offers a bespoke service.

down to the River Blackwater estuary (see panel opposite). The quayside at the Hythe is home to several splendid old Thames barges, which are used for pleasure trips and also take part in races on special days each year.

The Moot Hall was built in the 15th century for the D'Arcy family, and the original spiral brick staircase and 18th century court room are of particular interest, along with remnants of the old borough jail with its exercise yard.

Just outside the town lies the spot where a decisive battle in England's early history took place. At the Battle of Maldon in 991, the English leader, Byrthnoth, was killed by the invading Danes after a fierce three-day struggle. As a result of this defeat the English king, Ethelred the Unready, was obliged to pay an annual tribute to his conquerors. The Danes soon tired of this arrangement, however, and overthrew Ethelred, putting Canute on the throne. In the **Maeldune Heritage Centre** the amazing 42-foot Maldon Embroidery relates the story of the Battle. The Centre is located in the wonderful old Plume Building, which it shares with the Plume Library, the second oldest library in England. Maldon's **Millennium Gardens** are also named in commemoration of the Battle of Maldon, and re-create what a garden would have looked like at the time of this famed event, with a fine variety of herbs - it was originally a monastic herb garden.

Maldon District Museum at 47 Mill Road is a handsome, traditional museum with a range of changing exhibits showcasing a selection of objects associated with the area and the people of the Maldon District. It also tells the story of Maldon salt, produced for generations in the traditional way of letting sea water evaporate naturally, leaving behind just the mineral-rich salt. Famed for its flavour, the salt is sought after by the health-conscious and the gourmet alike. The museum stands adjacent to Promenade Park, an Edwardian park stretching into nearby Hythe Quay. The park comprises a marine lake, amusement centre, mini-golf, boat hire and numerous year-round events. In another open space, Kings Courtyard, stands an intriguing bronze sculpture depicting seven men of Maldon fitted into a waistcoat. This singular item of clothing belonged to one Edward Bright, who when he died in 1750 weighed in at an impressive 44 stone. A wager was struck that 500 men could not fit in Bright's waistcoat; the wager was deemed to have been won when seven men from the local Dengie Hundred fitted into it. Maldon's **Church of All Saints** is notable for its unique triangular tower, a fine Purbeck marble arcade and the Washington window, presented in 1928 by the citizens of Washington, Massachusetts.

Above the town stand the ruins of St Giles the Leper Hospital, founded by King Henry II in the 12th century. As with all monastic buildings, it fell into disuse after Henry VIII's dissolution of the

Thames Barges at Maldon

monasteries, though it retained its roof and was used as a barn until the late 19th century.

LANGFORD

2 miles NW of Maldon off the B1019

The **Museum of Power at Steam Pumping Station**, Hatfield Road, Langford, is an ex-waterworks pumping station which houses a large steam engine and pumps. Many other engines and other interesting artefacts are also on display.

NORTHEY ISLAND

1 mile E of Maldon off the B1026

This small island in the Blackwater Estuary has a large area of undisturbed salt marsh. There are pleasant circular walks along the uneven sea wall. The site is open by appointment with the Warden, who, due to tides which regularly cover the causeway, requires at least 24 hours' notice.

TOLLESBURY

6 miles NE of Maldon off the B1026

Located at the mouth of the River Blackwater, **Tollesbury Marina** has been designed as a leisure centre with a range of on-site activities including two tennis courts, a heated, covered swimming pool, a welcoming bar and a handsome restaurant. The marina is ideally located for exploring the rivers and creeks of the coast - the River Crouch lies south, while the West Mersea and the Rivers Colne, Orwell and Deben are to the North.

HEYBRIDGE BASIN

1 mile E of Maldon off the B1019

The lively boat and barge quay at Heybridge Basin just outside the town offers visitors the best chance to see one of the classic Thames barges with their ox-blood sails in action.

ALTHORNE

6 miles SE of Maldon off the B1010

The church of St Andrews, over 500 years old, has a fine flint and stone tower, built in the perpendicular style. Inside the church is an octagonal font dating from around 1400, which retains its original carvings of saints and angels. A brass plate dated 1508 records that William Hyklott "Paide for the werkemanship of the wall"; an inscription over the west door remembers John Wilson and John Hill, who probably paid for the tower.

To the south, where Station Road meets Burnham Road, stands the villagers' own War Memorial. This solid structure of beams and tiles lends dignity and honour to the tragic roll call of names listed on it. To the north of the village is the golden-thatched, white-walled Huntsman and Hounds, which dates partly from the 14th century.

BURNHAM-ON-CROUCH

9 miles SW of Maldon on the B1012

Burnham-on-Crouch is an attractively old-fashioned yachting station, lively in summer, packed around August Bank Holiday Monday for its regatta. Its nice in wintertime too, with the yachts left to ride at anchor offshore gently rolling, their rigging clacking evocatively.

From the gaily coloured cottages along the quay, the town climbs away from the seashore, its streets lined with a delightful assortment of old cottages and Georgian and Victorian houses and shops. In Tudor times sailing barges thronged the estuary, where now yachts sail to and fro. Seafarers still come ashore to buy provisions, following a tradition that goes right back to medieval times when Burnham was the market centre for the isolated inhabitants of Wallasea and Foulness Islands, who travelled in by ferry from their homes in the estuary.

The whole area was, and still is, famous for its oyster beds.

Burnham-on-Crouch & District Museum at The Quay features agricultural and maritime exhibits relating to the whole of the historic Dengie Hundred. Social history is revealed here too, as well as a good archaeological collection.

Mangapps Farm Railway Museum houses an extensive collection of railway relics of all kinds, including steam and diesel locomotives, carriages and wagons, historic buildings and one of the largest collections of signalling equipment on view anywhere.

St Mary's Church, on the outskirts of town, is constructed of Kentish ragstone which was transported to Burnham by sea. Construction began in the 12th century and was completed in the 14th. The arches and pillars are particularly fine examples of medieval craftsmanship.

MANGAPPS RAILWAY MUSEUM

Southminster Road, Burnham-on-Crouch, Essex CM0 8QQ
Tel: 01621 784898 Fax: 01621 783833
e-mail: mangapps@farmline.com
website: www.mangapps.co.uk

Mangapps Railway Museum in Southminster Road offers an extensive collection of railway memorabilia of all kinds, much of it still in active service here at the museum, including 10 steam and diesel locomotives, over 60 carriages and wagons, historic buildings and one of the largest collections of signalling equipment open to the public. This treasure trove will please railway buffs of all ages, together with anyone with an interest in or fondness for in the quality of workmanship and pride personified by Britain's golden age of steam. This privately owned working museum is set on a 360-acre farm and features a ¾ mile standard gauge passenger carrying line, complete with restored stations, signal boxes and ancillary equipment from various sites throughout East Anglia.

Complementing the working railway, the museum has a fine collection of smaller railway relics of considerable historic and technical interest, such as station signs, notices, posters, station furniture of all kinds, steam engine name plates and silverware - the earliest item being a boundary post from the Stockton & Darlington Railway of 1825 - in one of the largest collections of its kind in the nation. There is also a picnic area on site, a shop, working displays, and light refreshments for sale.

SOUTHMINSTER

3 miles NE of Burnham off the B1021

The old market town of Southminster rises dramatically from the flat and often desolate expanse of the surrounding landscape.

The **Rural Discovery Church of St Lawrence** in Southminster is situated on a hill overlooking the River Blackwater. Exhibitions are held during the summer months, featuring themes with strong local connections, and an art exhibition is staged each September.

BRADWELL-ON-SEA

6 miles NE of Burnham off the B1021

The village of Bradwell-on-Sea, the name of which is derived from the Saxon words 'brad pall', meaning 'broad wall', is home to the famous **Church of St Peter's-on-the-Wall**, said to be the oldest church in England. The first regular inhabitants of this little community at the head of the Dengie Peninsula were the Romans, who built a huge fort here. Little remains of the fort today, as in around AD 650 its bricks, stones and tiles were used to build the church. This was probably the work of the newly appointed Bishop Cedd, who had come south from Lindisfarne to spread Christianity to the Saxon southerners. Cedd returned north for the Synod of Whitby in 664 but died of the plague in that year. In the 14th century the chapel was abandoned and forgotten for 600 years; much of it collapsed, and the nave was used as a barn. Now restored and re-consecrated, it is worth the walk from the car park to reach it.

A visit to Bradwell-on-Sea is well worth the long drive for the sense of being right out on the edge of things - the timeless emptiness is if anything exaggerated by the distant views of the vast modern industrial installations nearby.

St Peter On the Wall, Bradwell-on-Sea

To the south lie the vast and remote marshes of the **Dengie Peninsula**. The salty tang of sea air here, brought inland by the east coast winds, gives an exhilarating flavour to the marshlands. Like the Cambridge and Lincolnshire fens, this once-waterlogged corner of Essex was reclaimed from the sea by 17th century Dutch engineers. The views across the marshes take in great sweeps of countryside, inhabited only by wildfowl, seabirds and cattle grazing on the saltings.

PURLEIGH

3 miles SW of Maldon off the B1010

The first recorded vineyard in Purleigh was planted in the early 12th century, only 400 yards from the 92-acre site of **New Hall Vineyards** in Chelmsford

Road. The first vineyard covered three acres of land next to Purleigh Church, where first US president George Washington's great-great-grandfather was the rector - until the time he was removed from this office for sampling too much of the local brew! Purleigh Vineyard became Crown property in 1163; subsequently the wines produced were taken each year to London to be presented to the King. Free admission to New Hall Vineyards includes a vineyard walk, nature trail and wine tasting in the cellar shop, and guided tours can be arranged by appointment between May and September.

SOUTH WOODHAM FERRERS

5 miles SW of Maldon off the B1012

The empty marshland of the Crouch estuary, a yachtsman's paradise, was chosen by Essex County Council as the site for one of its most attractive new towns schemes. At its centre, this successful 20th century town boasts a traditional market square surrounded by pleasant arcades and terraces built in the old Essex style with brick, tile and weatherboard.

Marsh Farm Country Park in Marsh Farm Road, South Woodham Ferrers, is a working farm and country park adjoining the River Crouch. Sheep, pigs, cattle and hens roam, and among the facilities are an adventure play area, farm trail, visitor centre, gift shop and tea rooms. Guided tours are available by prior arrangement, and special events are held throughout the year.

RETTENDON

6 miles SW of Maldon off the A130

The **Royal Horticultural Society Garden at Hyde Hall** comprises eight acres of year-round hillside colour, with a woodland garden, large rose garden,

RHS GARDEN HYDE HALL

Rettendon, Chelmsford, Essex CM3 8ET
Tel: 01245 400256 Fax: 01245 402100
e-mail: hydehall@rhs.org.uk website: www.rhs.org.uk

RHS Garden Hyde Hall is the proud and impressive result of 40 years of dedication and inspiration, created despite its hilltop setting, heavy clay soil, low rainfall and frequent strong, drying winds. Donated to the Royal Horticultural Society in 1993, a programme of development and improvement has made this delightful and imaginatively planted garden a centre of excellence. Home to the National Plant Collection of Viburnum, the garden is also well known for its superb collection of roses. The colour-themed herbaceous border and new plantings around the lower pond are also

striking examples of garden design. The Farmhouse Garden features a formal design full of bold colour combinations and fascinating plant associations. The Dry Garden displays plants from a variety of arid areas. The Hilltop Garden provides year-round interest with its naturalised spring bulbs and late-flowering tender perennials producing a blaze of autumn colour.

The Visitor Centre offers a wealth of information on many subjects. In the Hyde Hall Garden Library, visitors are welcome to browse through books, journals and CD ROMs exploring a range of topics such as problem places, garden plants, pests and diseases, pruning and more. The Barn Restaurant, Tea Yard and Shop complete this fascinating day out which will delight not just gardeners but anyone with an eye for beauty. Open: every day from 18th March to 10th November. (March to August 10 am to 6 pm and September to November 10 am to 5 pm.)

ornamental ponds with lilies and fish, herbaceous borders, shrubs, trees, and national collections of malus and viburnum. Meals and snacks are available in the attractive thatched barn; there is also a plant centre. Fine views can be had from this attractively landscaped hilltop garden (see panel on page 263).

BATTLESBRIDGE

7 miles SW of Maldon off the A132

Battlesbridge Antiques Centre by the River Crouch at Hawk Hill is the largest in Essex. Housed in five period buildings, more than 70 dealers display and sell their wares. The heart of the Centre is Cromwell House, its ground floor dedicated to specialist dealers with individual units. They will advise, value and give an expert opinion free of charge. They offer a wide variety of old and interesting pieces and collectables.

The Centres' Haybarn Cottages were constructed as dwellings, while, alongside, The Bridgebarn began life as a barn with thatched roof and dates from the 19th century, at which time there were lime kilns nearby. It was converted to its present tiled roof in the 1930s. The building retains some fine oak beamwork, and houses a small 'Penny arcade' with working model roundabout, fortune teller, and "What the Butler Saw" as well as a large collection of antiques for sale.

The Old Granary is nestled on the riverbank and houses five floors of dealers selling collectibles, reproductions, antiques and crafts, including specialists in old phones, clocks, furniture, cigarette cards, jewellery, fireplaces, interior design, dried flowers and much more. There are superb views of the River Crouch from the top floor and the surrounding area. Enjoy them while you take tea in the top-floor coffee shop.

This superb location is also the site of a **Motorcycle Museum**, with displays evoking the history of motorcycling through the ages with some interesting memorabilia. The museum is open on Sundays or by appointment.

Far removed from the hustle and bustle of modern life, the Fens are like a breath of fresh air. Extending over much of Cambridgeshire from the Wash, these flat, Fenland fields contain some of the richest soil in England and surrounding villages such as Soham and small towns such as Ely rise out of the landscape on low hills.

Bridge of Sighs, Cambridge

Before the Fens were drained this was a land of mist, marshes and bogs; of small islands, inhabited by independent folk, their livelihood the fish and waterfowl of this eerie, watery place. Today's landscape is a result of the ingenuity of humanity, with its constant desire to tame the wilderness and create farmland. This fascinating story spans the centuries, from the earliest Roman and Anglo-Saxon times, when the first embankments and drains were constructed to lessen the frequency of flooding. Throughout the Middle Ages large areas were reclaimed, with much of the work being undertaken by the monasteries. The significant influence of the Dutch lives on in some of the architecture and place names of the Fens. Over the years it became necessary to pump rainwater from the fields up into the rivers, and, as in the Netherlands, windmills took on the task. They could not always cope with the height of the lift required, but fortunately the steam engine came along, to be replaced eventually by the electric pumps that can raise thousands of gallons of water a second to protect the land from the ever-present threat of rain and tide. The Fens offer unlimited opportunities for exploring on foot,

View to Riverside, Wansford

by car, bicycle or by boat. Anglers are well catered for, and visitors with an interest in wildlife will be in their element.

Burghley House, Stamford

Southeastern Cambridgeshire covers the area around the city of Cambridge and is rich in history, with a host of archaeological sites and monuments to visit, as well as many important museums. At the heart of it all is Cambridge itself, one of the leading academic centres in the world and a city which deserves plenty of time to explore - on foot, by bicycle or by the gentler, romantic option of a punt.

The old county of Huntingdonshire is the heartland of the rural heritage

Kings Mill and River Cam, Great Shelford

of Cambridgeshire, and the home of Oliver Cromwell beckons with a wealth of history and pleasing landscapes. Many motorists follow the **Cromwell Trail**, which guides tourists around the legacy of buildings and places associated with the great man in the area. The natural start of the Trail is Huntingdon itself, where he was born the son of a country gentleman, and other main stopping places will be covered in this chapter.

The Ouse Valley Way (26 miles) follows the course of the Great Ouse through pretty villages and a variety of natural attractions. A gentle cruise along this stretch of the river can fill a lazy day to perfection, but for those who prefer something more energetic on the water there are excellent, versatile facilities at Grafham Water.

The Nene-Ouse Navigation Link, part of the Fenland Waterway, provides the opportunity for a relaxed look at a lovely part of the region. It travels from Stanground Lock near Peterborough to a lock at the small village of Salters Lode in the east, and the 28-mile journey passes through several Fenland towns and a rich variety of wildlife habitats.

LOCATOR MAP

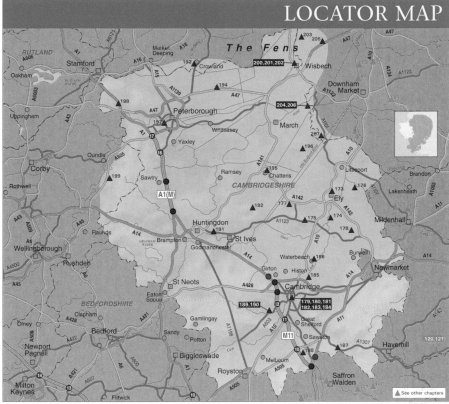

© MAPS IN MINUTES ™ 2001   © Crown Copyright, Ordnance Survey 2001

Advertisers and Places of Interest

ELY

Ely is the jewel in the crown of the Fens, in whose history the majestic Cathedral and the Fens themselves have played major roles. The Fens' influence is apparent even in the name: Ely was once known as Elge or Elig (eel island) because of the large number of eels which lived in the surrounding fenland. Ely owes its existence to St Etheldreda, Queen of Northumbria, who in 673AD founded a monastery on the 'Isle of Ely', where she remained as abbess until her death in 679. It was not until 1081 that work started on the present **Ely Cathedral**, and in 1189 this remarkable example of Romanesque architecture was completed. The most outstanding feature in terms of both scale and beauty is the Octagon, built to replace the original Norman tower, which collapsed in 1322.

Alan of Walsingham was the inspired architect of this massive work, which took 30 years to complete and whose framework weighs an estimated 400 tons. Many other notable components include the 14th century Lady Chapel, the largest in England, the Prior's Door, the painted nave ceiling and St Ovin's cross, the only piece of Saxon stonework in the building. The Cathedral is set within the walls of the monastery, and many of the ancient buildings still stand as a tribute to the incredible skill and craftsmanship of their

Ely Cathedral

designers and builders. Particularly worth visiting among these are the monastic buildings in the College, the Great Hall and Queens Hall. Just beside the Cathedral is the Almonry, in whose 12th century vaulted undercroft visitors can take coffee, lunch or tea - outside in the garden if the weather permits. Two other attractions which should not be missed are the **Brass Rubbing Centre**, where visitors can make their own rubbings from replica brasses, and the **Museum of**

CLOISTERS ANTIQUES

1a Lynn Road, Ely, Cambridgeshire CB7 4EG
Tel: 01353 668558 e-mail: info@cloistersantiques.co.uk

Barry and Joan Lonsdale bid a friendly welcome to the wonderful world of **Cloisters Antiques**, where visitors will find a vast selection of antiques, curios and collectables to suit all tastes and pockets, all on display in bright, cheerful surroundings. Since they purchased the business in September 1999, they have brought their great knowledge of antiques to locals and visitors alike; they welcome single items for purchase, and also offer a valuation service. They have greatly expanded the Book Room, where Octagon Books stock their interesting range of secondhand and antiquarian books. Cloisters Antiques is closed on Tuesday.

Oliver Cromwell's House, Ely

Museum, with nine galleries telling the Ely story from the Ice Age to modern times. The tableaux of the condemned and debtors' cells are particularly fascinating and poignant.

Ely lives not just in the past. The fine architecture and sense of history blend well with the bustle of the streets and the shops and the riverside. That bustle is at its peak on Thursday, when the largest general market in the area is held.

Stained Glass. The latter, housed in the south Triforium of the Cathedral, is the only museum of stained glass in the country and contains over 100 original panels from every period, tracing the complete history of stained glass.

Ely's **Tourist Information Centre** is itself a tourist attraction, since it is housed in a pretty black and white timbered building that was once the home of **Oliver Cromwell**. It is the only remaining house, apart from Hampton Court, where Oliver Cromwell and his family are known to have lived; parts of it trace back to the 13th century, and its varied history includes periods as a public house and, more recently, a vicarage. The Old Gaol, in Market Street, houses **Ely**

AROUND ELY

PRICKWILLOW
4 miles E of Ely on the B1382

On the village's main street is the **Prickwillow Drainage Museum**, which houses a unique collection of large engines associated with the drainage of the Fens. The site had been in continuous use as a pumping station since 1831, and apart from the engines there are displays charting the history of Fens drainage, the effects on land levels and the workings of the modern drainage system.

TWENTY-PENCE GARDEN CENTRE

Twenty-Pence Road, Wilburton, Ely, Cambridgeshire CB6 3RN
Tel: 01353 741024 Fax: 01353 749063
website: www.twentypence.co.uk

Found on the Twenty-Pence Road (B1049), the **Twenty-Pence Garden Centre** in Wilburton can provide the answer to all a gardener's needs, whether for an established garden covering several acres or just a few window-boxes or planters, or whether you are designing your first garden from scratch or are an experienced gardener looking for new ideas.

The centre offers a wide selection of quality plants and produce including ornamental trees, bedding and herbaceous plants, shrubs, roses and trees up to three metres tall, as well as an extensive variety

of house plants. Many of these are grown on-site, including the lovely cyclamens, summer bedding plants and poinsettias. Other garden accoutrements on sale here include a wide selection of paving slabs in a plethora of sizes and styles, Stone Market paving stones, rockery stones and decorative chipping, garden screens, Oriental-style arbours and rose arches, and general garden iron work, ornamental wooden seating plus a range of fencing, trellises, statuary, water features and large garden accessories such as sheds, greenhouses and even conservatories.

Of course you can also find general garden implements and accessories, from tools to Malay terracotta-wear and willow basket-wear to adorn any garden. In summer there is also a range of barbecue equipment. Distinctive gifts include ceramic ornaments, picture frames, dried and fresh-cut flowers, glassware and much, much more.

Run by Andrew and Pandora Povey together with Lesley and Clive Seppings - the centre has been in the Seppings family for 10 years, and Pandora and Clive have been in horticulture during that time as well - this superb centre has expanded over the past two years, and now stretches over 10 acres in total. Andrew Povey says, 'We wanted to bring the business up to date and provide a better service for our customers. The market is constantly growing and we aim to continue to expand to meet that demand. Our website is going well and we're planning to open a coffee shop in the near future.'

The helpful, courteous staff are knowledgeable and can offer expert advice. Open seven days a week: Monday to Saturday 9 am to 5 pm; Sundays 10.30 am to 4 pm Ample car parking. For the widest selection of plants, tools, pots, ornaments, paving, fencing and unusual gifts in the area - all under one roof - look no further.

LITTLEPORT

6 miles N of Ely on the A10

St George's Church, with its very tall 15th century tower, is a notable landmark. Of particular interest are two stained-glass windows depicting St George slaying the dragon. Littleport was the scene of riots in 1861, when labourers from Ely and Littleport, faced with unemployment or low wages, and soaring food prices, attacked houses and people in this area, causing several deaths. Five of the rioters were hanged and buried in a common grave at **St Mary's Church**. A plaque commemorating the event is attached to a wall at the back of the church.

COVENEY

3 miles W of Ely off the A10

A Fenland hamlet on the Bedford Level just above West Fen. Its **Church of St**

Peter-ad-Vincula has several interesting features, including a colourful German screen dating from around 1500 and a painted Danish pulpit. Unusual figures on the bench ends and a fine brass chandelier add to the opulent feel of this atmospheric little church.

SUTTON

6 miles W of Ely off the A142

A very splendid 'pepperpot' tower with octagons, pinnacles and spire tops marks out the grand **Church of St Andrew**. Inside, take time to look at the 15th century font and a fine modern stained-glass window. The reconstruction of the church was largely the work of two Bishops of Ely, whose arms appear on the roof bosses. One of the Bishops was Thomas Arundel, appointed at the age of 21. A mile further west, there's a great family attraction in the **Mepal Outdoor**

SARAH BELLOW - UPHOLSTERY & SOFT FURNISHINGS

Elm Farm, Ely Road, Prickwillow, Ely, Cambridgeshire CB7 4UJ
Tel: 01353 688250

Sarah Bellow adapted former farm buildings on the farm where she was born to set up her Upholstery and Soft Furnishings business. Her credentials are impeccable, including a diploma with honours at the London College of Furniture (with City & Guilds) and spells with an antiques restorer and a firm of upholsterers. She then passed on her knowledge as a teacher for ten years before setting up on the farm in 1984.

She uses the finest materials and traditional techniques and skills in undertaking complete restoration, right from the original (or new) frame to the finished article. Commissions range from a simple drop-in chair seat to a deep-buttoned chesterfield, and quality is the keynote throughout. Sarah can supply a wide range of fabrics, or she will work with materials supplied by the client.

Sarah's other passion is Dales ponies, a tough little breed that were originally used for carrying, among other things, lead for roofing and building. She looks after some of these sturdy little ponies on the farm and is always pleased to introduce them to her clients; she also shows them at local events.

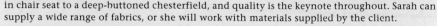

THE GROVE

Sutton Gault, Ely, Cambridgeshire CB6 2BD
Tel: 01353 777196 Fax: 01353 777425

The Grove is a large and impressive Georgian farmhouse with gracious proportions and an atmosphere of relaxed calm. Outside there are attractive gardens and a tennis court. The stone-floored entrance hall leads to the handsome drawing room, dining room and breakfast room. Each of the two guest bedrooms is comfortable and beautifully decorated and furnished. For a taste of real elegance, look no further.

Centre, an outdoor leisure centre with a children's playpark, an adventure play area and boat hire.

HADDENHAM

5 miles SW of Ely on the A1123

More industrial splendour amy be found at **Haddenham Great Mill**, built in 1803 for a certain Daniel Cockle. It is a glorious sight, and one definitely not to be missed. It has four sails and three sets of grinding stones, one of which is working. The mill last worked commercially in 1946 and was restored between 1992 and 1998. Open on the first Sunday of each month and by appointment.

The **Church of St Andrew** stands on a hillside. Look for the stained-glass window depicting two souls entering Heaven, and the memorial (perhaps the work of Grinling Gibbons) to Christopher Wren's sister Anne Brunsell.

STRETHAM

5 miles S of Ely off A10/A1123

The **Stretham Old Engine**, a fine example of a land drainage steam engine, is housed in a restored, tall-chimneyed brick engine house. Dating from 1831, it is one of 90 steam pumping engines installed throughout the Fens to replace 800 windmills. It is the last to survive, having worked until 1925 and still under restoration. During the great floods of 1919 it really earned its keep by working non-stop for 47 days and nights. This unique insight into Fenland history and industrial archaeology is open to the public on summer weekends and on certain dates the engine and its wooden scoop-wheel are rotated (by electricity, alas!). The adjacent stoker's cottage contains period furniture and photographs of fen drainage down the years.

WICKEN

9 miles S of Ely off the A1123

Owned by the National Trust, **Wicken Fen** is the oldest nature reserve in the country, 600 acres of undrained fenland, famous for its rich plant, insect and bird life and a delight for both naturalists and ramblers. Features include boardwalk and nature trails, hides and watchtowers, a cottage with 1930s furnishings, a working windpump (the oldest in the country), a visitor centre and a shop. It is open daily dawn to dusk. **St Lawrence's Church** is well worth a visit, small and secluded among trees. In the churchyard are buried Oliver Cromwell and several members of his family. One of Cromwell's many nicknames was Lord of the Fens; he defended the rights of the Fenmen against those who wanted to drain the land without providing adequate compensation.

SOHAM

6 miles SE of Ely on the A142 bypass

Do not sail past Soham without stopping to look at (or visit if it is a Sunday or Bank Holiday) **Downfield Windmill**. Built in 1726 as a smock mill, it was destroyed by gales and rebuilt in 1890 as an octagonal tower mill. It still grinds corn and produces a range of flours and breads for sale. **St Andrew's Church** is a fine example of the Perpendicular style of English Gothic architecture. Very grand and elaborate, it was built on the site of a 7th century cathedral founded by St Felix of Burgundy. The 15th century west tower has an ornate parapet and two medieval porches. Note, too, the chancel with its panelling and stained glass. A plaque in Soham commemorates engine driver Ben Gimbert and fireman James Nightall, who were taking an ammunition train through the town when a wagon caught fire. They uncoupled it and began to haul it into open country. The wagon exploded, killing the fireman and a signalman.

CAMBRIDGE

There are nearly 30 Cambridges spread around the globe, but this, the original, is the one that the whole world knows as one of the leading university cities. Cambridge was an important town many centuries before the scholars arrived, standing at the point where forest met fen, at the lowest fording point of the river. The Romans took over a site previously settled by an Iron Age Belgic tribe, to be followed in turn by the Saxons and the Normans. Soon after the Norman Conquest William I built a wooden motte and bailey castle and Edward I, a stone replacement: a mound

URSULA GALLOWAY

9 Great Fen Road, Soham Fen, Cambridgeshire CB7 5UQ
Tel: 01353 722435 Fax: 01353 624012

Ursula Galloway is an outstanding wood carver and artist who has been working in her medium since she was in her teens. She undertakes commissions which vary both in scale and complexity. Among her many achievements have been carving the coat of arms for Yehudi Menuhin, beams for St Neot's Church and a number of village signs. She also creates wonderful murals for indoor swimming pools, ceilings, staircases and rooms, paints in watercolours and on silk,

and restores old paintings.

For 20 years and more Ursula has worked from her lovely country cottage, built in the early 19th century, and her studio in the garden. Her work is distinctive and innovative, as she brings a careful eye for detail and the wealth of many years' experience to every piece. She takes part in Cambridge Open Studios every summer and exhibits from time to time. Those interested are welcome to phone and arrange a visit to her fascinating studio and to enquire about specially commissioned designs.

still marks the spot. The town flourished as a market and river trading centre, and in 1209 a group of students fleeing Oxford riots arrived. The first College was Peterhouse, founded by the Bishop of Ely in 1284, and in the next century Clare, Pembroke, Gonville & Caius, Trinity Hall and Corpus Christi followed. The total is now 31, the latest being Robinson College, the gift of self-made millionaire and notable racehorse owner David Robinson.

The Colleges represent various architectural styles, the grandest and most beautiful being King's. Robinson has the look of a fortress; its concrete structure covered with a 'skin' of a million and a quarter handmade red Dorset bricks. The Colleges are all well worth a visit, but places that simply must not be missed include **King's College Chapel** with its breathtaking fan vaulting, glorious stained glass and

Kings College Chapel

Rubens' Adoration of the Magi; Pepys Library, including his diaries, in **Magdalene College**; and Trinity College's wonderful **Great Court**.

A trip by punt along the 'Backs' of the Cam brings a unique view of many of the

THE CONSERVATORY GALLERY

6 Hills Avenue, Cambridge, Cambridgeshire CB1 7XA
Tel: 01223 211311 website: www.businessarts.co.uk
e-mail: pamela.barrell@businessarts.co.uk

A late-Victorian house in a quiet, secluded part of south Cambridge is the setting for Pamela Barrell's **Conservatory Galley**. It was back in 1985 that Pamela, responding to an appeal by an impecunious art-loving friend, was inspired to combine the knowledge gained from an arts degree and an interior design course to provide a service of hiring or buying works of art for company clients. Her talent for finding the right painting for particular spaces at the right price immediately began to benefit both artists and companies, and the corporate art service has never looked back.

The opening of the Conservatory Gallery, with permanent displays and four or five special exhibitions a year, was a natural progression, and Pamela's skills at finding talented artists in all media create exciting exhibitions that are a source of interest and delight to the Gallery's many visitors. The three rooms, the hallway, the conservatory and, in summer, the garden feature paintings, sculpture, ceramics, hand-made jewellery and scarves and a wide selection of artists' cards. Pamela is also a respected maker of hand-stained and polished picture frames, and there is always a wide variety of framing samples to choose from. The Gallery is open from 11 to 5 every Saturday and the first Sunday in each month, with additional Thursday and Friday opening during the special exhibitions. Art classes, led by watercolourist Judith Din, are held in the Gallery on Thursday mornings during term time.

Colleges and passes under six bridges, including the **Bridge of Sighs** (St John's) and the extraordinary wooden **Mathematical Bridge** at Queens'.

Cambridge has nurtured more Nobel Prize winners than most countries - 29 from Trinity alone - and the list of celebrated alumni covers every sphere of human endeavour and achievement: Byron, Tennyson, Milton and Wordsworth; Marlowe and Bacon; Samuel Pepys; Charles Darwin; Charles Babbage: Bertrand Russell and Ludwig Wittgenstein; actors Sir Ian McKellen and Sir Derek Jacobi; Lord Burghley and Harold Abrahams who ran for England; Burgess, Maclean, Philby and Blunt who spied for Russia.

Trinity College Great Court

Many of the Colleges are worth visiting for their gardens alone: fine trees and herbaceous borders in Clare, imposing Cedars of Lebanon in Downing, and in Christ's an ancient mulberry, Indian bean trees and a cypress grown from seed from the tree on Shelley's grave in Rome. The

HOBBS PAVILION

Parker's Piece, Cambridge, Cambridgeshire CB1 1JH
Tel: 01223 367480/505760

Hobbs Pavilion is a superb restaurant set in a former cricket pavilion built in 1950 and named in honour of Cambridge-born Sir Jack Hobbs. Located right in the centre of Cambridge within five acres of the former pitch, there has been a restaurant here since 1971.

This popular and friendly restaurant has earned an enviable reputation for great food and excellent, unobtrusive service, and has been favourably reviewed in The Guardian, FHM magazine and in other respected journals. Here diners are spoilt for choice by the range of expertly prepared and presented dishes which include main courses such as roast duckling, Kashmir lamb, monkfish and sirloin steaks. There are also vegetarian and vegan specials - which live up to Hobbs' claim to be one of the best venues for vegetarian food in Cambridge - and delectable puddings well worth leaving room for.

The decor is modern and comfortable, with wickerwork dining chairs, muted colours and lovely paintings adorning the walls, and daylight streaming in through the French doors. At night the ambience is cosy and welcoming. Open: Monday to Saturday 11 am to 10.30 pm; Sundays 11 am to 4 pm and 6 pm to 10 pm.

University Botanic Garden comprises 40 acres devoted to research and education, a delight to visit at any time of the year. Highlights include a superb collection of native and exotic trees, a tropical glasshouse, an alpine house and a Dry Garden containing 80 species that need no watering.

The Colleges apart, Cambridge is packed with interest for the visitor, with a wealth of grand buildings both religious and secular, and some of the country's leading museums, many of them run by the University. The **Fitzwilliam Museum** is renowned for its art collection, which includes works by Titian, Rembrandt, Gainsborough, Hogarth, Turner, Renoir, Picasso and Cezanne, and for its antiquities from

Botanic Gardens

Egypt, Greece and Rome. **Kettle's Yard** has a permanent display of 20th century art in a house maintained just as it was when the Ede family gave it, with the collection, to the University in 1967. The **Museum of Classical Archaeology** has 500 plaster casts of Greek and Roman

---

KING'S TITHE

13A Camberton Road, Cambridge,
Cambridgeshire CB3 7BA
Tel/Fax: 01223 263610 e-mail: Thornebarton@Lineone.net

King's Tithe is a lovely and spacious family home providing excellent bed and breakfast accommodation. There are two twin bedrooms handsomely furnished and decorated, complete with all amenities. The lounge is attractive and welcoming. The grounds include immaculately kept gardens and a conservatory available for guests. Owners Elisabeth and Cornelius Thorne offer a warm welcome and genuine hospitality to all their guests. 4 Diamonds ETC. No smoking. No children under 8 years and no pets.

FREE PRESS

7 Prospect Row, Cambridge,
Cambridgeshire CB1 1DU
Tel: 01223 368337

One of only six inns in the country to be non-smoking, **Free Press** in Cambridge is a convivial and unspoilt inn, where the excellent food uses the freshest local ingredients. There are always at least four real ales on tap, 12 to 15 malt whiskies, and a good range of other beers, wines and spirits. Dating back to 1840, it was originally a house whose owner, to annoy her tee-total neighbour, began selling gin and beer.

states, and the **University Museum of Archaeology and Anthropology** covers worldwide prehistoric archaeology with special displays relating to Oceania and to the Cambridge area. The **Museum of Technology**, housed in a Victorian sewage pumping station, features an impressive collection of steam, gas and electric pumping engines and examples great and small of local industrial technology. Anyone with an interest in fossils should make tracks for the **Sedgwick Museum of Geology**, while in the same street (Downing) the **Museum of Zoology** offers a comprehensive and spectacular survey of the animal kingdom. The **Whipple Museum of the History of Science** tells about science through instruments; the **Scott Polar Research Institute** has fascinating, often poignant exhibits relating to Arctic and Antarctic exploration; and the **Botanic Gardens** boast a plant collection that rivals those of Kew Gardens and Edinburgh. The work and life of the people of Cambridge and the surrounding area are the subject of the **Cambridge and County Folk**

CAMBRIDGE & COUNTY FOLK MUSEUM

2-3 Castle Street, Cambridge, Cambridgeshire CB3 0AQ
Tel: 01223 355159
website: www.folkmuseum.org.uk

Housed in a late 15th century timber-framed building that was formerly the White Horse Inn, the **Cambridge & County Folk Museum** takes a nostalgic, warm-hearted look at the everyday lives of people from Cambridge and the surrounding area from 1700 onwards. Topics include Crafts & Trades, Town & Gown, Witchbottles, Skating and Eels, and throughout the year themed talks and exhibitions take place. The Museum Shop stocks an interesting range of games and puzzles, books and many other items that make ideal Christmas stocking fillers, all with a nostalgic feel.

Museum, housed in a 15th century building that for 300 years was the White Horse Inn (see panel above). One of the city's greatest treasures is the **University Library**, one of the world's great research libraries with 6 million books, a million maps and 350,000 manuscripts.

Cambridge also has many fine churches, some of them used by the Colleges before they built their own chapels. Among the most notable are St Andrew the Great (note the memorial to Captain Cook); St Andrew the Less; St Bene's (its 11th century tower is the oldest in the county); St Mary the Great, a marvellous example of Late Perpendicular Gothic; and **St Peter Castle Hill**. This last is one of the smallest churches in the

NOMADS

5 Kings Parade, Cambridge, Cambridgeshire CB2 1SJ
Tel: 01223 324588
e-mail: nomads@india.com website: www.nomads.com

Nomads is a fascinating treasure trove of Indian, Asian, African and Afghani rugs, kilims, pottery (including Tibetan singing bowls), fabrics, jewellery and clothing, set in the heart of the city directly opposite King's College. A riot of colour greets customers in this lovely shop, where unique gifts and decorative pieces await them. Owner Phillip Hague is well-travelled and can offer advice and information on his shop's many beautiful wares.

country with a nave measuring just 25ft by 16ft. Originally much larger, the church was largely demolished in 1781 and rebuilt in its present diminished state using the old materials, including flint rubble and Roman bricks. The **Church of the Holy Sepulchre**, always known as the Round Church, is one of only four surviving round churches in England.

AROUND CAMBRIDGE

GIRTON

3 miles NW of Cambridge off the A14

The first Cambridge College for women was founded in 1869 in Hitchin, by Emily Davies. It moved here in 1873 to be "near enough for male lecturers to visit but far enough away to discourage male students from doing the same". The problem went away when Girton became a mixed College in 1983.

RAMPTON

6 miles N of Cambridge off the B1049

A charming village in its own right, with a tree-fringed village green, Rampton is also the site of one of the many archaeological sites in the area. This is **Giant's Hill**, a motte castle with part of an earlier medieval settlement.

MILTON

3 miles N of Cambridge off the A10

Milton is the location of the **College of West Anglia**, formed in 1998 as a result of a merger between Cambridgeshire College of Agriculture and Horticulture, and Norfolk College. This, and another centre in Wisbech, offer many horticultural facilities, including propagation houses for nursery stock and houseplants, nursery standing-out areas and tunnels for growing stock. Also on site are numerous gardens and a large fruit orchard. **Milton Country Park** offers fine walking and exploring among acres of parkland, lakes and woods. There's a visitor centre, a picnic area and a place serving light refreshments.

WATERBEACH

6 miles NE of Cambridge on the b1102

Denny Abbey, easily accessible on the A10, is an English Heritage Grade l-listed Abbey with ancient earthworks. On the same site, and run as a joint attraction, is the **Farmland Museum**. The history of Denny runs from the 12th century, when it was a Benedictine monastery. It was later home to the Knights Templar, Franciscan nuns and the Countess of Pembroke, and from the 16th century was a farmhouse. The old farm buildings have been splendidly renovated and converted to tell the story of village life and

---

CAMBRIDGE GARDEN PLANTS

The Lodge, Clayhithe Road, Horningsea, Cambridge, Cambridgeshire CB5 9JD
Tel: 01223 861370

As featured in The Garden magazine, **Cambridge Garden Plants** specialises in hardy perennials and herbaceous plants and more unusual plants. The nursery has been a thriving concern since 1989; owner Kit Buchdahl's forte is plant associations. He and his staff offer expert advice and a high standard of service and quality. Open: March to October Thursday to Sunday 11-5.30; other times by appointment.

FARMLAND MUSEUM & DENNY ABBEY

Ely Road, Waterbeach, Cambridgeshire CB5 9PQ
Tel/Fax: 01223 860489
e-mail: f.m.denny@tesco.net
website: www.dennyfarmlandmuseum.org.uk

Two thousand years of history are brought fascinatingly to life in a lovely rural setting on the A10 six miles north of Cambridge. The stone-built farmhouse at the heart of the site is actually the remains of a 12th century Benedictine Abbey which at different times was home to Benedictine monks, the Knights Templar and nuns of the Franciscan order, the Poor Clares. The superb Norman interior has been beautifully preserved and restored, and visitors can see the nuns' refectory and the rooms converted for their founder, the Countess of Pembrokeshire. Displays and children's activities tell the story of how Denny has evolved down the centuries.

On the same site, and run by English Heritage as a joint attraction, is the Farmland Museum. Old farm buildings have been splendidly renovated and converted to tell visitors about the rural history of Cambridgeshire from early days to modern times. The Museum is ideal for family visits, with specially designed activities for children, and among the top displays are a village shop, agricultural machinery, a magnificent 17th century stone barn, a traditional farmworker's cottage and the workshops, which include a basket maker and a blacksmith. Special weekend events, from buttermaking demonstrations to traditional building methods, are held regularly at the Museum, which is open from noon to 5pm April to October.

Cambridgeshire farming up to modern times. The museum is ideal for family outings, with plenty of hands-on activities for children, and a play area, gift shop and weekend tearoom (see above).

In the village of **Lode, Anglesey Abbey** was built on the site of a 12th century Augustinian priory, whose ruins were incorporated into a house in about 1600 by a certain livery stable owner called Thomas Hobson. This man had a strict rule that his customers could never make their own choice of which horse to hire but had to accept 'Hobson's Choice'. The house and the 100-acre garden came together triumphantly as a unit thanks to the vision of Huttleston Broughton, the 1st Lord Fairhaven. The garden, created in its present form from the 1930s, is a wonderful place for a stroll, with open lawns,

wide grassy walks, a winter trail, a riverside trail, marvellous trees, a working water mill and one of the finest collections of garden statuary in the country. There's also a plant centre, shop and restaurant. In the house itself is Lord Fairhaven's magnificent collection of

Anglesey Abbey

paintings, sumptuous furnishings, tapestries and clocks.

At nearby **Cottenham**, on the B1049, **All Saints Church** has an unusual tower of yellow and pink Jacobean brick topped with four pinnacles that look like pineapples. The original tower fell down in a gale and this replacement was partially funded by former US President Calvin Coolidge, one of whose ancestors had been living in the village when the tower fell down.

SWAFFHAM PRIOR
8 miles NE of Cambridge on the b1102.

Swaffham Prior gives double value to the visitor, with two churches in the same churchyard and two fine old windmills. The Churches of **St Mary** and **St Cyriac** stand side by side, a remarkable and dramatic sight in the steeply rising churchyard. 13th century St Cyriac was largely rebuilt in the 19th century, but the

Swaffham Prior Windmill

tower is original; St Mary's has an extraordinary tower: square Norman at the base, then octagonal, then three levels of 16 sides, topped by a fibreglass spire. The stained-glass windows depict, among other subjects, Wicken Fen and World War II. One of the mills, a restored 1850s tower mill, still produces flour and can be visited by appointment.

At **Swaffham Bulbeck**, a little way to the south, stands another Church of St Mary, with a 13th century tower and 14th century arcades and chancel. Look for the fascinating carvings on the wooden benches and a 15th century cedarwood chest decorated with biblical scenes.

BURWELL
10 miles NE of Cambridge on the b1102

A village of many attractions with a history going back to Saxon times. **Burwell Museum** reflects many aspects of a village on the edge of the Fens up to the middle of the 20th century. A general store, model farm, local industries and children's toys are among the displays. Next to the museum is the famous **Stephens Windmill**, built in 1820 and extensively restored. The man who designed parts of King's College Chapel, Reginald Ely, is thought to have been responsible for the beautiful **St Mary's Church**, which is built of locally quarried clunch stone and is one of the finest examples of the Perpendicular style. Notable internal features include a 15th century font, a medieval wall painting of St Christopher and roof carvings of elephants, while in the churchyard a gravestone marks the terrible night in 1727 when 78 Burwell folk died in a barn fire while watching a travelling Punch and Judy show. Behind the church are the remains of **Burwell Castle**, started in the 12th century but never properly completed. The **Devil's Dyke** runs through Burwell on its path from Reach to Woodditton. This amazing dyke, 30 yards wide, was built, it is thought, to halt Danish invaders.

REACH

8 miles NE of Cambridge off the A4280

The charming village of Reach is home to the oldest fair in England, which celebrated its 800th anniversary on 1st May, 2000.

LINTON

10 miles SE of Cambridge on the B1052

The village is best known for its zoo, but visitors will also find many handsome old buildings and the Church of St Mary the Virgin, built mainly in Early English style. A world of wildlife set in 16 acres of spectacular gardens, **Linton Zoo** is a major wildlife breeding centre and part of the inter-zoo breeding programme for endangered species. Collections include wild cats, birds, snakes and insects. For children there is a play area and, in summer, pony rides and a bouncy castle.

Some two miles further off the A604, **Bartlow Hills** is the location of the largest Roman burial site to be unearthed in Europe.

STAPLEFORD

5 miles S of Cambridge off the A1307

More great walking and an abundance of history: parkland with traces of an Iron Age hill fort, picnic area, woodland walks

and nature trail. Magog Downs, with the famous **Gog Magog Hills**, is an open area that is perfect for walking and picnics. On top of the hill are the remains of an Iron Age fort. A nearby building is the stable block of a now demolished mansion, beneath whose central arch was buried the Godolphin Arabian, one of the four Arab stallions that are the progenitors of all modern thoroughbred racehorses.

DUXFORD

8 miles S of Cambridge off A505 by J10 of M11

Part of the Imperial War Museum, **Duxford Aviation Museum** is probably the leader in its field in Europe, with an outstanding collection of over 150 historic aircraft from biplanes through Spitfires to supersonic jets (see panel on page 282). The American Air Museum, where aircraft are suspended as if in flight, is part of this terrific place, which was built on a former RAF and US fighter base. Everyone should take time to see this marvellous show - and it should be much more than a flying visit!

At nearby **Hinxton** is another mill: a 17th century water mill that is grinding once more.

GREAT CHISHILL

12 miles S of Cambridge on the B1039

Home to another great windmill, an open-trestle post mill that incorporates

CHILFORD HALL

Linton, Cambridge, Cambridgeshire CB1 6LE
Tel: 01223 895600 Fax: 01223 895605
e-mail: info@chilfordhall.couk
website: www.chilfordhall.co.uk

Established in 1972, **Chilford Hall Vineyard and Winery** is a great day out. This award-winning family business offers wine-tastings, winery tours, a vineyard trail and extended walk. Open daily from 1st March to 23rd December, there's also a Visitor's Centre, the Vineleaf Shop and the Vineleaf Cafe - all well worth a visit. The onsite conference centre caters for up to 1,300.

IMPERIAL WAR MUSEUM DUXFORD

Duxford, Cambridgeshire CB2 4QR
Tel: 01223 835000 Fax: 01223 837267

A branch of the **Imperial War Museum**, Duxford is Europe's premier aviation museum. It was built on a former RAF and USAF fighter base that saw that service throughout the Second World War, and the preserved hangars, a control tower and operations room retain a period atmosphere and from the historic heart of the 85-acre complex.

Over 400,000 visitors come to Duxford each year to see the biplanes and the Spitfires, the Concorde and the Gulf War jets that are among the 180 historic aircraft on show. A major exhibition on the Battle of Britain charts events of 1940, giving an insight into life at the time, and features an RAF Hurricane and a Luftwaffe Messerschmitt 109 that saw action in the Battle. An award-winning modern building designed by Lord Foster houses the American Air Museum with aircraft both on the ground and suspended from the roof as though in flight. Exhibits here range from a U2 Spyplane to a T-10 Tankbuster and the mighty B-52 Stratofortress. Tanks and artillery are on show in the exciting Land Warfare Hall, which houses 50 military vehicles and artillery pieces in a series of realistic and authentic battlefield scenes.

Major attractions are being added each year, and among the latest is an exhibition focusing on Monty and the D-Day landings. Important air shows take place several times each year, featuring resident aircraft, current military aircraft, civilian display teams and solo aerobatic performers. This wonderful museum, which lies south of Cambridge at Junction 10 of the M11, is open throughout the year apart from three days at Christmas.

18th century timbers in its 19th century construction. **Great Chishill Mill** worked until 1951 and was restored in 1966. St Swithin's Church is well worth a visit, and not just on a rainy day. Built of flint, it shows features from many centuries, from the 12th century onwards.

SHEPRETH

8 miles S of Cambridge off A10

A paradise for lovers of nature and gardens and a great starting point for country walks. Shepreth L Moor Nature Reserve is an L-shaped area of wet meadowland - now a rarity - that is home to birds and many rare plants. The nearby **Shepreth Wildlife Sanctuary** at Willersmill began in 1979 as a refuge for injured and orphaned British birds and mammals. Since then, it has spread its wings and grown into one of East Anglia's major places of interest, with a very wide variety of wildlife, from buzzards and barn owls to spur-thighed tortoises and red-eared terrapins, from marmosets and macaques to wolves and wallabies - and of course there are familiar friends like cows and donkeys. The Tropical Pavilion and Reptile House give a taste of the Rain Forest, and to mark the new millennium a new attraction called Waterworld and Bug City was opened, housing the likes of puffer fish, tarantulas and the amazing leaf-cutter ants, who spend their working days building a fungus garden from leaves cut and carried along rope walkways. The Fish Farm by the River Shep (which grows up to become the Cam) has several ponds and a small lake where carp will take food from visitors' fingers.

Around the 18th century **Docwra's Manor**, on Meldreth Road, is a series of enclosed gardens, some wild in appearance, others more formal, that are well worth a visit at any time of the year; a short walk away, **Crossing House and**

Garden, by a level crossing on the Cambridge-Royston railway line, is equally delightful, packing in an estimated 5,000 plants and providing an object lesson in what can be done in a small space. **Fowlmere**, on the other side of the A10, is another important nature reserve, with hides and trails for the serious watcher.

GRANTCHESTER

2 miles SW of Cambridge off the A603

A pleasant walk by the Cam, or a leisurely punt on it, brings visitors from the bustle of Cambridge to the famous village of Grantchester, where Rupert Brooke lived and Byron swam. The walk passes through Paradise Nature Reserve.

Stands the church clock at ten to three
And is there honey still for tea?

The Orchard, with its Brooke connections, is known the world over. Brooke spent two happy years in Grantchester, and immortalised afternoon tea in the Orchard in a poem he wrote while homesick in Berlin. The Orchard remains a wonderful spot for a traditional English tea, under the old fruit trees or in the pavilion warmed by old-fashioned stoves and soothed by the gentle strains of classical music. First planted in 1868, it became a tea garden purely by chance in 1897 when a group of students asked the Orchard's owner, Mrs Stevenson, if she would serve them tea under the fruit trees rather than on the front lawn. Thus started a great Cambridge tradition, and the Orchard soon became a firm favourite with students and visitors to the city, many of them arriving by punt. Time should also be allowed for a look at the **Church of St Andrew and St Mary**, in which the remains of a Norman church have been incorporated into the 1870s main structure.

BARTON

3 miles SW of Cambridge off the A603

Looking south from this pleasant village,

WHITE HORSE

118 High Street, Barton, Cambridgeshire CB3 7BG
Tel: 01223 262327

Built as a family home in the 17th century, **White Horse** is a distinguished restaurant attracting a loyal and growing clientele. People return again and again for the food, ambience and service, which are all second to none. This fine inn has many delightful traditional features, with two cosy bars, one with a handsome inglenook fireplace.

Landlord Richard Ellis, his wife Lyn and their children Joanne and Steven offer a warm and genuine welcome to all their guests. And the home-cooked and home-prepared meals are so popular that the pub is now turning out more than 800 of them a week! Richard and Steven do most of the cooking, creating tempting dishes and snacks for the bar and restaurant, as well as daily specials and a Sunday

carvery. From the mixed grill to lamb, haddock, chicken or salads, there is something to suit every taste. In fine weather guests can enjoy the attractive patio garden area. There are three regular ales on tap, together with changing guest beers.

For those who are keen to explore more of this lovely part of the county and beyond, accommodation is available at the White Horse in a double room and family room, both ensuite.

Burwash Manor Barns

New Road, Barton, Cambridgeshire CB3 7AY
Tel: 01223 263423 Fax: 01223 264567

Michael and Susan Radford run Burwash Manor Farm, where a wide range of unique, interesting shops is located in converted stockyard buildings in the grounds of a moated manor house. It all began in 1986, when the Radfords put an empty barn to good use by filling it with nearly new toys, nursery equipment and clothes. From the success of this first enterprise the site grew, and the attractive farm courtyards are now home to numerous shops and businesses.

The Rocking Horse Toy Shop added new toys to the nearly new, and the toys on sale here are mainly high-quality, traditional, old-fashioned items, from little wooden rattles to dolls houses, wooden farms and rocking horses. The stock also includes books, games and some items of nursery equipment.

The Barn Tea Rooms offer a large selection of cakes and pastries and cooked-to-order lunches with a specials board supplementing the standard menu. It's a cosy, friendly place, with waitress service,

and outside the beamed tea room are an outside seating area and a play area - children are always welcome, and they even have their own menu. On the takeaway front, the Delicatessen has for sale a range of foodstuffs prepared by people who care passionately about the quality of their product. The organic selection includes cheese, ice creams and rare-breed meats, as well as fruit and vegetables; also on offer are seasonal recipe sheets and cooking tips.

The Wine Cellar, in a converted shire horse stable, is a dimly-lit, sawdust-strewn spot where 30 years' experience in the wine trade produce an ever-changing choice of personally chosen, top-quality wines; tastings enable customers to create their own mixed cases.

In the Summer House, an exciting range of textiles and soft furnishings showcases the best of English and Scandinavian styles, with many items designed and made in house. Among the display are top-quality made-to-measure curtains and blinds and items of clothing from jokey wellies to formal evening wear. Persian Tribal Rugs deals in Persian rugs and kelims imported by the owner from nomadic tribes and Iranian villages for the wholesale and retail trade, and there's always an impressive selection on display.

The partners in Providence, located in a converted grain mill, moved to the UK from New England with a mission to spread the word on the Shaker philosophy on cabinets and interiors. Freestanding and built-in cabinets are the speciality, along with a full range of finishing paints, and the stock also includes handmade pottery and New England craft products.

The Christmas Shop - 'Christmas Wonderland in a marquee' - has a beautiful and exciting collection of unusual tree and room decorations and a range of personally selected freshly cut trees. Cambridge Learning is an independent software shop with a mail order catalogue, specialising in selling mainly educational and 'seriously fun' software to schools and homes, and operating a try-before-you-buy policy. The owners always keep an eye open for new products such as a mini-mouse for tiny hands.

Bodyline Health offers various therapies in homely treatment rooms, with fully qualified therapists offering Swedish massage, aromatherapy, reflexology, homeopathy, baby massage classes, head massage and sports and injury therapy.

Burwash Manor Barns are located on bus and cycle routes two miles from Cambridge.

can see the impressive array of radio telescopes that are part of the University's **Mullard Radio Astronomy Observatory.**

ARRINGTON
11 miles SW of Cambridge off the A603

Eighteenth century **Wimpole Hall**, owned by the National Trust, is the largest and probably the most spectacular country mansion in the whole county. The lovely interiors are the work of several celebrated architects, and there's a fine collection of furniture and pictures. Henry Flitcroft designed the gallery and saloon, and the drawing room was the work of Sir John Soane, whose major commissions included the Bank of England, his own house in Lincoln's Inn Fields and the picture gallery at Dulwich College. James Gibbs, best known for his work at St Martin-in-the-Fields, was responsible for the painted library built to house the Harley collection of 50,000 books (these were later sold, and part of the collection became the basis of the British Library). The baroque chapel has a trompe l'oeil ceiling painted by Sir James Thornhill, a historical painter in the service of George I and George II; his work can also be seen at Blenheim, Hampton Court and Chatsworth, and he painted eight scenes

Wimpole Hall

in the dome of St Paul's Cathedral. The magnificent formally laid-out grounds, in whose design Charles Bridgeman, Capability Brown and Humphry Repton all had a hand, include a Victorian parterre, a rose garden and a walled garden. Landscaped **Wimpole Park**, with hills, woodland, lakes and a Chinese bridge, provides miles of wonderful walking and is perfect for anything from a gentle stroll to a strenuous hike. A brilliant attraction for all the family is **Wimpole Home Farm**, a working farm

Chapel in the Hall, Wimpole

that is the largest rare breeds centre in East Anglia. The animals include Bagot goats, Tamworth pigs, Soay sheep and Longhorn cattle, and there's also a pets corner and horse-drawn wagon ride. Children can spend hours with the animals or in the adventure playground. The vast Great Barn houses a collection of farm machinery dating back 200 years.

CAXTON

6 miles W of Cambridge off the A12198/A428

Caxton is home to Britain's oldest surviving **Postmill**, and at nearby Little Gransden another venerable mill has been restored. A scheduled ancient monument, it dates from the early 17th century and was worked into the early years of this century.

MADINGLEY

4 miles W of Cambridge on the A428

The **American Cemetery** is one of the loveliest, most peaceful and most moving places in the region, a place of pilgrimage for the families of the American servicemen who operated from the many wartime bases in the county. The cemetery commemorates 3,800 dead and 5,000 missing in action in the Second World War.

HUNTINGDON

The former county town of Huntingdonshire is ancient, first settled to any extent by the Romans. It boasts many grand Georgian buildings, including the handsome three-storeyed Town Hall.

Oliver Cromwell was born in Huntingdon in 1599 and attended Huntingdon Grammar School. The schoolhouse was originally part of the Hospital of St John the Baptist, founded in the reign of Henry II by David, Earl of Huntingdon. Samuel Pepys was also a pupil here. Cromwell was MP for Huntingdon in the Parliament of 1629, was made a JP in 1630 and moved to St Ives in the following year. Rising to power as an extremely able military commander in the Civil War, he raised troops from the region and made his headquarters in the Falcon Inn. Appointed Lord Protector in 1653, Cromwell was never proclaimed King, though he ran the country until his death in 1658. The school he attended is now the **Cromwell Museum**, located on Huntingdon High Street, housing the only public collection relating specifically to him, with exhibits that reflect many aspects of his political, social and religious life.

All Saints Church, opposite the Cromwell Museum, displays many architectural styles, from medieval to Victorian. One of the two surviving parish churches of Huntingdon, All Saints was considered to be the church of the Hinchingbrooke part of the Cromwell family, though no memorials survive to attest to this. The Cromwell family burial vault is contained within the church, however, and it is here that Oliver's father Robert and his grandfather Sir Henry are buried. The church has a fine

All Saints, Huntingdon

chancel roof, a very lovely organ chamber and a truly impressive stained glass window.

Huntingdon's other church, **St Mary's**, dates from Norman times but was almost completely rebuilt in the 1400s. It boasts a fine Perpendicular west tower, which partially collapsed in 1607. The damage was extensive, and the tower was not completely repaired until 1621. Oliver Cromwell's father Robert contributed to the cost of the repairs, as recorded on the stone plaque fixed to the east wall on the nave, north of the chancel arch.

Cowper House (No 29 High Street) has an impressive early 18th century frontage. A plaque commemorates the fact that the poet William Cowper lived here between 1765 and 1767.

Among Huntingdon's many fine former coaching inns is **The George Hotel**. Although the hotel was badly damaged by fire in 1865, the north and west wings of the 17th century courtyard remain intact, as does its very rare wooden gallery. The inn was one of the most famous of all the posting houses on the old Great North Run. It is reputed that

Dick Turpin used one of the rooms here. The medieval courtyard, gallery and open staircase are the scene of annual productions of Shakespeare.

Along the south side of the Market Square, the **Falcon Inn** dates back in parts to the 1500s. Oliver Cromwell is said to have used this as his headquarters during the Civil War.

About half a mile southwest of town stands **Hinchingbrooke House**, which today is a school but has its origins in the Middle Ages, when it was a nunnery. It was given to the Cromwell family by Henry VIII in 1538, though ghostly nuns are said to still haunt the building. Converted by the Cromwell family in the 16th century, and later extended by the Earls of Sandwich, today's visitors can see examples of every period of English architecture from the 12th to the early 20th century. King James I was a regular visitor, and Oliver Cromwell spent part of his childhood here. The 1st Earl of Sandwich was a central figure in the Civil War and subsequent Restoration, while the 4th Earl (the man who so enjoyed his game of cards that he had to invent the sandwich) was one of the most flamboyant politicians of the 18th century. The remains of the Benedictine nunnery can still be seen. The House is open for guided tours, including lovely cream teas served in the Tudor kitchens.

Hinchingbrooke Country Park covers 180 acres of grassy meadows, mature woodland, ponds and lakes. There is a wide variety of wildlife including woodpeckers, herons, kestrels, butterflies and foxes. The network of paths makes exploring the park easy, and battery-powered wheelchairs are provided for less able visitors. The Visitors Centre serves refreshments at peak times.

Half a mile north, **Spring Common**

offers another chance to enjoy some Cambridgeshire countryside. Covering 13 acres, its name comes from the natural spring which runs constantly and has long been a gathering place. The town developed around rather than within this area of rural tranquillity, which boasts a range of diverse habitats including marsh, grassland, scrub and streams. Plant life abounds, providing food and shelter for a variety of animals, amphibians, birds and invertebrates.

AROUND HUNTINGDON

RAMSEY
9 miles NE of Huntingdon on the B1040

Ramsey is a pleasant market town with a broad main street down which a river once ran.

The medieval **Ramsey Abbey** was founded in 969 by Earl Ailwyn as a Benedictine monastery. The Abbey became one of the most important in England in the 12th and 13th centuries, and as it prospered so did Ramsey, so that by the 13th century it had become a town with a weekly market and an annual three-day festival at the time of the feast of St Benedict. After the Dissolution of the Monasteries in 1539, the Abbey and its lands were sold to Sir Richard Williams, great-grandfather of Oliver Cromwell. Most of the buildings were then demolished, the stones being used to build Caius, Kings and Trinity Colleges at Cambridge, the towers of Ramsey, Godmanchester and Holywell churches, the gate at Hinchingbrooke House and several local properties.

In 1938 the house was converted for use as a school, which it remains to this day. To the northwest are the ruins of the once magnificent stone gatehouse of the late 15th century - only the porter's lodge

remains, but inside can be seen an unusual large carved effigy made of Purbeck marble and dating back to the 14th century. It is said to represent Earl Ailwyn, founder of the Abbey. The gatehouse, now in the care of the National Trust, can be visited daily from April to October.

The church of St Thomas à Becket of Canterbury forms an impressive vista at the end of the High Street. Dating back to about 1180, it is thought to have been built as a hospital or guesthouse for the Abbey. It was converted to a church to accommodate the many pilgrims who flocked to Ramsey in the 13th century. The church has what is reputed to be the finest nave in Huntingdonshire, dating back to the 12th century and consisting of seven bays. The church's other treasure is a 15th century carved oak lectern, thought to have come from the Abbey.

Most of **Ramsey Rural Museum** is housed in an 18th century farm building and several barns set in open countryside. Among the many fascinating things to see are a Victorian home and school; a village store; and restored farm equipment, machinery, carts and wagons. The wealth of traditional implements used by local craftsmen such as the farrier, wheelwright, thatcher, dairyman, animal husbandman and cobbler offer an insight into bygone days.

The unusual **Ramsey War Memorial** is a listed Grade II memorial consisting of a fine bronze statue of St George slaying the dragon atop a tall, octagonal pillar crafted of Portland stone.

SAWTRY
8 miles NW of Huntingdon on the A1

The main point of interest has no point! **All Saints Church**, built in 1880, lacks tower and steeple, and is topped by a bellcote. Inside are marvellous brasses and pieces from ancient Sawtry Abbey.

Just south of Sawtry, Aversley Wood is a conservation area with abundant birdlife and plants.

STILTON

12 miles NW of Huntingdon off A1

An interesting high street with many fine buildings and a good choice for the hungry or thirsty visitor, as it has been since the heyday of horse-drawn travel. Journeys were a little more dangerous then, and Dick Turpin is said to have hidden at the famous Bell Inn.

Blue Stilton - "the King of English cheeses" - is a rare example of an English cheese that has won fame and favour overseas. It was never actually made in Stilton, but was sold from the Bell Inn to coach travellers pausing on their journey along the Great North Road. The landlord of the Bell in the early 18th century was married to a daughter of Elizabeth Scarbrow, housekeeper at Quenby Hall near Leicester. This lady was renowned for her cheese and another of her daughters acquired the recipe and supplied the cheese, traditionally made with milk from Shorthorn cows, to the Bell. It is now made in a dozen dairies in Leicestershire, Nottinghamshire and Derbyshire.

ELLINGTON

4 miles W of Huntingdon off the A14

A quiet village just south of the A14 and about a mile north of Grafham Water. Both Cromwell and Pepys visited, having relatives living in the village, and it was in Ellington that Pepys' sister Paulina found a husband, much to the relief of the diarist, who had written:

We must find her one, for she grows old and ugly.

All Saints Church is magnificent, like so many in the area, and among many fine features are the 15th century oak roof and the rich carvings in the nave and the aisles. The church and its tower were built independently.

BRAMPTON

2 miles SW of Huntingdon off the A1

Brampton is where **Huntingdon Racecourse** is situated. An average of 18 meetings (all jumping) are scheduled every year, including Bank Holiday fixtures (extra-special deals for families). Its big day is in November, when the Grade 2 Peterborough Chase is the feature race. Brampton's less speculative attractions include the 13th century Church of St Mary, and **Pepys House**, the home of the great diarist Samuel's uncle. This person was a cousin of Lord Sandwich, who got Samuel his job at the Admiralty. Samuel was born in London and educated at Huntingdon School, St Paul's in London and Magdalene College, Cambridge. He was a frequent visitor to Brampton, including a spell in 1665 when any citizen who had the means avoided London like the plague.

GRAFHAM

5 miles SW of Huntingdon on the B661

Created in the mid-1960s as a reservoir, **Grafham Water** offers a wide range of outdoor activities for visitors of all ages, with 1,500 acres of beautiful countryside, including the lake itself. A ten-mile perimeter track is great for jogging or cycling, and there's excellent sailing, windsurfing and fly fishing.

The area is a Site of Special Scientific Interest, and an ample nature reserve at the western edge is run jointly by Anglian Water and the Wildlife Trust. There are nature trails, information boards, a wildlife garden and a dragonfly pond. Many species of waterfowl stay here at various times of the year, and bird-watchers have the use of six hides, three of them accessible by wheelchair.

An exhibition centre has displays and video presentations of the reservoir's history, a gift shop and a café.

KIMBOLTON

8 miles SW of Huntingdon on the B645

There is history aplenty here, and a lengthy pause is in order to look at all the interesting buildings. St Andrew's Church would head the list were it not for **Kimbolton Castle**, which along with its gatehouse dominates the village. Parts of the original Tudor building are still to be seen, but the appearance of the castle today owes much to the major remodelling carried out by Vanbrugh and Nicholas Hawksmoor in the first decade of the 18th century. The gatehouse was added by Robert Adam in 1764. Henry VIII's first wife Catherine of Aragon spent the last 18 months of her life imprisoned here, where she died in 1536. The castle is now a school, but can be visited on certain days in the summer (don't miss the Pellegrini murals).

BUCKDEN

4 miles SW of Huntingdon on the A1

This historic village was an important coaching stop on the old Great North Road. It is known particularly as the site of **Buckden Towers**, the great palace built for the Bishops of Lincoln. In the splendid grounds are the 15th century gatehouse and the tower where Henry VIII imprisoned his first wife, Catherine of Aragon, in 1533.

ST NEOTS

10 miles SE of Huntingdon off the A1

St Neots, named after the Cornish saint whose remains were interred here some time before the Norman Conquest, dates back to the founding of a Saxon Priory, built on the outskirts of Eynesbury, in 974. Partially destroyed by the Danes in 1010, it was re-established as a Benedictine Priory in about 1081 by St Anselm, Abbot of Bec and later Archbishop of Canterbury. For the next two centuries the town and the Priory flourished, and charters were granted by Henry I to hold fairs and markets. The Priory was demolished at the time of the Dissolution of the Monasteries, and in the next century the area by the town bridge was the site of a battle between the Royalists and Roundheads - an event sometimes re-enacted by Sealed Knot societies, as on the 350th anniversary in July 1998.

St Neots repays a visit on foot, since there are many interesting sites and old buildings tucked away. The famous **Market Square** is one of the largest and most ancient in the country, and a market has been held there every Thursday since the 12th century. The magnificent parish **Church of St Mary the Virgin** is a very fine edifice, known locally as the "Cathedral of Huntingdonshire". It is an outstanding example of Late Medieval Architecture. The gracious interior complements the 130-foot Somerset-style tower, with a finely carved oak alter, excellent

Riverside Walk, St Neots

Victorian stained glass and a Holdich organ, built in 1855.

St Neots Museum - opened in 1995 - tells the story of the town and the surrounding area. Housed in the former magistrates court and police station, it still has the original cells. Eye-catching displays trace local history from prehistoric times to the present day.

Less than three miles north of St Neots at Little Paxton is **Paxton Nature Reserve**. Created alongside gravel workings, the Reserve attracts thousands of water birds for visitors to observe from hides. The wealth of wildlife means that the area is an SSSI (Site of Special Scientific Interest) and ensures a plethora of colour and activity all year round. The site also features nature trails and a visitor centre. It has thousands of visiting waterfowl, including one of the largest colonies of cormorants, and is particularly noted for its wintering wildfowl, nightingales in late spring and kingfishers. There are about four miles of walks, some suitable for wheelchairs. Spring and summer also bring a feast of wildflowers, butterflies and dragonflies.

EYNESBURY
1 mile S of St Neots on the A428

Eynesbury is actually part of St Neots, with only a little stream separating the two. Note the 12th century **Church of St Mary** with its Norman tower. Rebuilt in the Early English period, it retains some well preserved, locally sculpted, 14th century oak benches.

History has touched this quiet and lovely village from time to time: it was the home of the famous giant James Toller, who is buried in the middle aisle of the church in 1818. Only 21 when he died, he measured some 8 feet tall - it is said he was buried here to escape the attentions of body snatchers, whose activities were widespread at the time.

Eynesbury was also the birthplace of the Miles' Quads, the first ever surviving quadruplets in Britain.

BUSHMEAD
6 miles W of St Neots off the B660

The remains of **Bushmead Abbey**, once a thriving Augustinian community, are well worth a detour. The garden setting is delightful, and the surviving bits include some interesting stained glass.

GODMANCHESTER
2 miles SW of Huntingdon off the A1

Godmanchester is linked to Huntingdon by a 14th century bridge across the Ouse. It was a Roman settlement and one that continued in importance down the years, as the number of handsome buildings testifies. One such is **Island Hall**, a mid-18th century mansion built for John Jackson, the Receiver General for Huntingdon; it contains many interesting artefacts. This family home has lovely Georgian rooms, with fine period detail and fascinating possessions relating to the owners' ancestors since their first occupation of the house in 1800. The tranquil riverside setting and formal gardens add to the peace and splendour - the house takes its name from the ornamental island that forms part of the grounds. Octavia Hill was sometimes a guest, and wrote effusively to her sister that Island Hall was "the loveliest, dearest old house, I never was in such a one before."

Wood Green Animal Shelter at Kings Bush Farm, Godmanchester is a purpose-built, 50-acre centre open to the public all year round. Cats, dogs, horses, donkeys, farm animals, guinea pigs, rabbits, llamas, wildfowl and pot-bellied pigs are among the many animals for visitors to see, and there is a specially adapted nature trail and restaurant.

St Mary's Church is Perpendicular in style, though not totally in age, as the tower is a 17th century replacement of the 13th century original. A footpath leads from the famous Chinese Bridge (1827) to **Port Holme Meadow**, which at 225 acres is one of the largest in England and the site of Roman remains. It is a Site of Special Scientific Interest, with a huge diversity of botanical and bird species. Huntingdon racecourse was once situated here, and it was a training airfield during the First World War. Another site of considerable natural activity is **Godmanchester Pits**, accessed along the Ouse Valley Way and home to a great diversity of flora and fauna.

PAPWORTH EVERARD

6 miles S of Huntingdon on the A1198

One of the most recent of the region's churches, St Peter's dates mainly from the mid-19th century. Neighbouring Papworth St Agnes has an older church in St John's, though parts of that, too, are Victorian. Just up the road, on the green in the middle of the village of Hilton, is the famous **Hilton Turf Maze**, cut in 1660 to a popular medieval design. In the centre is an obelisk with inscriptions relating to the designer of the Maze, William Sparrow.

THE GREAT OUSE VALLEY

HEMINGFORD ABBOTS

3 miles SE of Huntingdon off the A14

Once part of the Ramsey Abbey Estate, Hemingford Abbots is set around the 13th century Church of St Margaret, along the banks of the Great Ouse. Opportunities for angling and boating facilities, including rowing boats for hire, swimming, country walks, golf and a recreation centre are all within a couple of miles. The village hosts a flower festival every two years.

Just to the east is **Hemingford Grey**, with its church on the banks of the Ouse. The manor at Hemingford Grey is reputedly the oldest continuously inhabited house in England, built around 1130, and visits (by appointment only) will reveal all the treasures in the house and garden. The garden was the work of the last owner of the house, Lucy Boston, the distinguished writer of children's books.

FENSTANTON

7 miles SE of Huntingdon off the A14 bypass

Lancelot 'Capability' Brown (1716-1783) was Lord of the Manor from 1768, and he, his wife and his son are buried in the graveyard of the medieval church. Born in Northumberland, Brown started his working life as a gardener's boy before moving on to Stowe, where he worked under William Kent. When Kent died, Lancelot Brown set up as a garden designer and soon became the leading improver of grounds in England, known for the natural, unplanned appearance that he brought to his designs. He acquired the nickname "Capability" from his habit of saying that a place had "capabilities".

WYTON

2 miles E of Huntingdon off the A1123

Wyton is mentioned in the Domesday Book, and is thought to have been founded in the 8th century. It is a popular tourist destination thanks to its proximity to **Houghton Mill** (see panel opposite) and opportunities for riverside walks, as well as its charming thatched buildings and shops.

HOUGHTON

5 miles E of Huntingdon on the A1123

Houghton Meadows is a Site of Special Scientific Interest with an abundance of hay meadow species. One of the most popular walks in the whole area links Houghton with St Ives.

St Ives

6 miles E of Huntingdon off the A1123

An ancient town on the banks of the Great Ouse which once held a huge annual fair and is named after St Ivo, said to be a Persian bishop who came here in the Dark Ages to spread a little light. In the Middle Ages, kings bought cloth for their households at great wool fairs and markets, and a market is still held every Monday. The Bank Holiday Monday markets are particularly lively affairs, and the Michaelmas fair fills the town centre for three days. Seagoing barges once navigated up to the famous six-arched bridge that was built in the 15th century and has a most unusual two-storey chapel in its middle. Oliver Cromwell lived in St Ives in the 1630s and the statue of him

St Ives Bridge and River Ouse

on Market Hill, with its splendid hat, is one of the most familiar landmarks. It was made in bronze, with a Portland stone base, and was erected in 1901. It was originally designed for Huntingdon, but they wouldn't accept it!

The beautiful parish church in its churchyard beside the river is well worth a visit. The quayside provides a tranquil mooring for holidaymakers and there are

Houghton Mill

Houghton, Huntingdon,
Cambridgeshire PE28 2AZ
Tel: 01480 301494 Fax: 01480 469641
website: www.nationaltrust.org.uk/
 houghtonmill

The National Trust-owned **Houghton Mill** deserves its reputation as a popular tourist attraction. There has been a mill on this site for some 1,000 years. The present mill dates from the 18th century. This impressive five story brick and clapboard structure stands on a tributary of the River Ouse midway between Huntingdon and St Ives.

The mill is one of the last and the most complete to survive in the area. As such it is the most important of the very few remaining mills. It has recently had its wheel restored, as part of a 1.2 million pound restoration project and is fully operational. This has provided improved facilities for visitors. Open days during the summer months offer visitors the chance to see the mill in action, and to appreciate the different forms of sustainable energy - a water turbine which generates electricity for the site and for other National Trust properties, and the waterwheel at work to produce stoneground flour. Milling takes place on Sundays and Bank Holiday Mondays, and the site also contains an art gallery, miniature millstones to turn by hand, and a tea room. In addition, the area to the north of the mill is an unusual survival of undeveloped Ouse riverbank, which the Trust intends to protect for its ecological interest and landscape value as an appropriate setting for this fine mill.

wonderful walks by the riverside.

Clive Sinclair developed his tiny TVs and pocket calculators in the town, and a famous son of St Ives was the great Victorian rower John Goldie, whose name is remembered each year by the second Cambridge boat in the Boat Race.

The **Norris Museum**, in a delightful setting by the river, tells the story of Huntingdonshire for the past 175 million years or so, with anything from fossils, mammoth tusks and models of the great historic reptiles through flint tools, Roman artefacts and Civil War armour to lace-making and ice-skating displays, and contemporary works of art. A truly fascinating place that is open throughout the year and is admission free. Exhibitions include a life-size replica of a 160 million year old Ichthyosaur. There are remains of Mammoths from the Ice Ages, tools and pottery from the Stone Age to Roman times and relics from the medieval castles and abbeys. Also on show are toys and models made by prisoners of the Napoleonic Wars.

As I was going to St Ives I met a man with seven wives.

Each wife had seven sacks, each sack had seven cats, each cat had seven kits.

Kits, cats, sacks and wives, how many were going to St Ives?

None, of course, but today's visitors are certain to have a good time while they are here.

Just outside St Ives are **Wilthorn Meadow**, a Site of Natural History Interest where Canada geese are often to be seen, and **Holt Island Nature Reserve**, where high-quality willow is being grown to re-introduce the traditional craft of basket-making. Spot the butterflies, dragonflies and kingfishers.

EARITH
4 miles E of St Ives on the A1123

The **Ouse Washes**, a special protection area, runs northeast from the village to Earith Pits, a well-known habitat for birds and crawling creatures. Some of the pits are used for fishing. The Washes are a wetland of major international importance supporting such birds as ruffs, Bewick and Whooper swans, and hen harriers. The average bird population is around 20,000. Some of the meadows flood in winter, and ice-skating is popular when the temperature really drops. There's a great tradition of ice skating in the Fens, and the Fenmen were the national champions until the 1930s.

SOMERSHAM
4 miles NE of St Ives on the B1040/B1060

The **Raptor Foundation** is found here, a major attraction, where owls and other birds of prey find refuge. There are regular flying displays and falconry demonstrations. Somersham once had a

PARKHALL NURSERIES & GARDEN CENTRE

Parkhall Road, Somersham, Cambridgeshire PE28 3HW
Tel: 01487 840397 Fax: 01487 741311

Quality, value and variety are the watchwords at **Parkhall Nurseries & Garden Centre**, which John Rigby runs with his parents and an excellent team of friendly, well-informed staff. Open every day from 9 o'clock till 6, the centre stocks the *biggest and best* retail selection of trees and bamboos in Cambridgeshire, and an impressive range of pots and planters, rockery stone, chinese granite lanterns and statuary is also on display. Other specialities include specimen shrubs, Japanese maples, native and imported bonsai trees, cacti, grasses, alpines and unusual topiary. This site is a "must see" for anyone mad about plants.

palace for the Bishops of Ely, and its splendid Church of St John would have done them proud.

PETERBOROUGH

The second city of Cambridgeshire has a long and interesting history that traces back to the Bronze Age, as can be seen in the archaeological site at **Flag Fen**. Although a cathedral city, it is also a New Town (designated in 1967), so modern development and expansion have vastly increased its facilities while retaining the quality of its historic heart. Its crowning glory is, of course, the Romanesque **Cathedral**, built in the 12th and 13th centuries on a site

Lock on the River Nene

that had seen Christian worship since 655AD. Henry VIII made the church a cathedral, and his first queen, Catherine of Aragon, is buried here, as for a while was Mary Queen of Scots after her execution at Fotheringay. Features to note are the huge (85 foot) arches of the West Front, the unique painted wooden nave ceiling, some exquisite late-15th century fan vaulting, and the tomb of Catherine. Though the best known of the city's landmarks, the Cathedral is by no means the only one. The **Peterborough Museum and Art Gallery** covers all aspects of the history of Peterborough from the Jurassic period to Victorian times..

There are twin attractions for railway enthusiasts in the shape of **Railworld**, a hands-on exhibition dealing with modern rail travel, and the wonderful **Nene Valley Railway**, which operates 15-mile steam-hauled trips between Peterborough and its headquarters and museum at Wansford. Thomas, an engine which used to work at a local sugar beet factory, is the children's favourite, but there are many locomotives from British Railways days, including Bullied Pacific 34081 *92 Squadron*, and many from overseas. The line operates every Sunday,

Peterborough Cathedral

Saturdays from April to October, Wednesdays from May to August and on certain other days. **Nene Park**, by Ferry Meadows Station, is a popular stooping-off place with play areas, picnic sites, a miniature railway and cycle and nature trails. A feature on the main railway line at Peterborough is the historic Iron Bridge, part of the old Great Northern Railway and still virtually as built by Lewis Cubitt in 1852.

Just outside the city, by the river Nene, is **Thorpe Meadows Sculpture Park**, one of several open spaces in and around the city with absorbing collections of modern sculpture.

AROUND PETERBOROUGH

PEAKIRK

7 miles N of Peterborough off the A15

A charming little village, somewhat off the beaten track, with two important attractions. In the wetland to the east of the village are the **Peakirk Waterfowl Gardens**, 20 acres of gardens and waterways that are home to hundreds of birds from all over the world. The village church is of Norman origin and is the only one in the country dedicated to **St Pega**, the remains of whose hermit cell can still be seen.

CROWLAND

10 miles NE of Peterborough off the A1073

It is hard to imagine that this whole area was once entirely wetland and marshland, dotted with inhospitable islands. Crowland was one such island, then known as Croyland, and on it was established a small church and hermitage back in the 7th century, which was later to become one of the nation's most important monasteries. The town's impressive parish church was just part of the great edifice which once stood on the site. A wonderful exhibition can be found in **Crowland Abbey**, open all year round. The remains cover a third of the Abbey's original extent.

Crowland's second gem is the unique **Trinity Bridge** - set in the centre of town on dry land! Built in the 14th century, it has three arches built over one over-arching structure. Before the draining of the Fens, this bridge crossed the point where the River Welland divided into two streams.

THORNEY

8 miles E of Peterborough on the A47

Thorney Abbey, the church of St Mary and St Botolph, is the dominating presence even though what now stands is but a small part of what was once one of the greatest of the Benedictine Abbeys. Gravestones in the churchyard are

ROCKINGHAM FENDER SEATS

Grange Farm, Thorney, Peterborough, Cambridgeshire PE6 0PJ
Tel: 01733 270233 Fax: 01733 270512
e-mail: clubfenders@rockingham-fenderseats.com
website: www.rockingham-fenderseats.com

Practical and decorative, fender seats are enjoying a revival today. **Rockingham Fender Seats** in Thorney offers a showroom where various styles are on display in settings around fireplaces. Fender seats guard the fire and add distinction and comfort to any fireside area. Please telephone in advance and staff will be happy to show you around. A colour brochure is available on request.

evidence of a Huguenot colony settling here after fleeing from France in the wake of the St Bartholomew's Day massacre of 1572. The **Thorney Heritage Museum** is a small, independently run museum of great fascination, describing the development of the village from a Saxon monastery, via Benedictine Abbey to a model village built in the 19th century by the Dukes of Bedford. The main innovation was a 10,000-gallon water tank that supplied the whole village; other villages had to use unfiltered river water.

WHITTLESEY

5 miles E of Peterborough off the A605

The market town of Whittlesey lies close to the western edge of the Fens and is part of one of the last tracts to be drained. Brick-making was a local speciality, and 180-ft brick chimneys stand as a reminder of a flourishing industry. The **Church of St Andrews** is mainly 14th century, with a 16th century tower, and the chancel, chancel chapels and naves still have their original roofs. A walk round this charming town reveals an interesting variety of buildings: brick, of course, and also some stone, thatch on timber frames, and rare thatched mud boundary walls.

A highlight of Whittlesey's year is the **Straw Bear Procession** that is part of the four-day January festival. A man clad in a suit of straw dances and prances through the streets, calling at houses and pubs to entertain the townspeople. The origins are obscure: perhaps it stems from pagan times when corn gods were invoked to produce a good harvest; perhaps it is linked with the wicker idols used by the Druids; perhaps it derives from the performing bears which toured the villages until the 17th century. What is certain is that at the end of the jollities the straw suit is ceremoniously burnt. Whittlesey is the birthplace of the writer LP Hartley (*The Go-Between*) and the soldier Sir Harry Smith, hero of many 19th century Indian campaigns. He died in 1860, and the south chapel off St Mary's Church (note the beautiful spire) was restored and named after him.

FLAG FEN

6 miles E of Peterborough signposted from the A47 and A1139

Flag Fen Bronze Age Excavations comprise massive 3,000-year-old timbers that were part of a major settlement and have been preserved in peaty mud. The site includes a Roman road with its original surface, re-creations of a Bronze Age settlement, a museum of artefacts, rare breed animals and a visitor centre with a shop and restaurants. Ongoing excavations, open to the public, make this one of the most important and exciting sites of its kind.

Flag Fen

MARCH

14 miles E of Peterborough off the A141

March once occupied the second largest 'island' in the great level of Fens, and as the land was drained the town grew as a trading and religious centre, and in more recent times as a market town and major railway hub. **March and District Museum**, in the High Street, tells the story of the people and the history of March and the surrounding area, and includes a working forge and a reconstruction of a turn-of-the-century home. **St Wendreda's** uniquely dedicated church, at Town End, is notable for its magnificent timber roof, a double hammerbeam with 120 carved angels, a fine font and some impressive gargoyles. John Betjeman declared the church to be "worth cycling 40 miles into a headwind to see".

The **Nene-Ouse Navigation Link** runs through the town, affording many attractive riverside walks, and just outside

D.J.'s Gardeners Dream

134 London Road, Chatteris, Cambridgeshire PE16 6SG
Tel: 01354 693937 Fax: 01354 695536
e-mail: d.j.white4@virgin.com

Just outside Chatteris on the B1050 road to Somersham, **D.J.'s Gardeners Dream** is a family-run nursery that really does help to make gardeners' dreams come true. The White family specialise in producing a large proportion of their own quality plants, including bedding plants, plants for hanging baskets and tubs, a large selection of perennials, alpines, herbs and trees. House plants are on display in a separate heated greenhouse, and in the shop a wide range of garden tools and sundries is always in stock.

A large area is devoted to paving, walling and fencing products, along with models of some of the wide selection of sheds, greenhouses and conservatories. Garden consultations are undertaken by the centre's Kew-trained staff, who are always on hand with helpful advice and guidance on any gardening problems.

Also on site is an aquatic centre with a shop and a large show pond with specimen fish. Everyone is welcome at D.J.'s, a member of the Horticultural Trades Association, and senior citizens can enjoy coach trips, workshops and discount shopping on Wednesdays. D.J.'s is open from 9 am to 5.30 pm Monday to Saturday and from 10 am to 4.30 pm on Sunday.

THYME HOUSE NURSERY

22 High Street, Manea, March,
Cambridgeshire PE15 0JA
Tel/Fax: 01354 680412

Specialising in both traditional and more unusual plants, **Thyme House Nursery** offers trees, bedding plants and more for garden, patio and conservatory. Because they are growers, they can offer plants at wholesale prices. Among the more unusual plants for sale are hardy ferns, tree ferns, palms, ornamental grasses and bamboos. There is also a very good garden planning and design service.

the town, off the B1099, is **Dunhams Wood**, four acres of woodland set among the fens. The site contains an enormous variety of trees, along with sculptures and a miniature railway. Also on the outskirts, signposted from the A141 and B1101, is **Stagsholt Farm Park and Stud**, home to many horses (including the superb Suffolk Punch) and housing a fascinating array of farming and rural bygones.

STONEA

3 miles SE of March off the B1098

Stonea Camp is the lowest 'hill' fort in Britain, built in the Iron Age and unsuccessful against the Romans. It is a scheduled ancient monument whose banks and ditches were restored after excavations in 1991. The site is also an increasingly important habitat for wildlife.

CHATTERIS

8 miles S of March off the A141

A friendly little market town with a museum that has recently moved into modern town-centre premises. The Church of St Peter and St Paul has some 14th century features but is mostly more modern in appearance, having been substantially restored in 1909.

LONGTHORPE

2 miles W of Peterborough off the A47

Longthorpe Tower, part of a fortified

manor house, is graced by some of the very finest 14th century domestic wall paintings in Europe, featuring scenes both sacred and secular: the Nativity, the Wheel of Life, King David, the Labours of the Months. The paintings were discovered during renovations after the Second World War. Here, too, is **Thorpe Hall**, home of the Sue Ryder Centre (see panel on page 300).

ELTON

6 miles W of Peterborough on the B671

Elton is a village on the river Nene, with stone-built houses and thatched roofs. **Elton Hall** is a mixture of styles, with a 15th century tower and chapel, and a major Gothic influence. The grandeur is slightly deceptive, as some of the battlements and turrets were built of wood to save money. The hall's sumptuous rooms are filled with art treasures (Gainsborough, Reynolds, Constable) and the library has a wonderful collection of books. The recently restored grounds feature yew and hornbeam hedges, an old-fashioned knot herb garden, an arboretum, a Victorian rose garden and a sunken garden with a lily pond.

THORNHAUGH

8 miles W of Peterborough off the A1/A47

Hidden away in a quiet valley is **Sacrewell Farm and Country Centre**, whose centrepiece is a working watermill.

SUE RYDER CARE CENTRE THORPE HALL

Thorpe Road, Longthorpe, Peterborough,
Cambridgeshire PE3 6LW
Tel: 01733 330060 Fax: 01733 269078
website: www.sueryffercare.org

Thorpe Hall is a splendid example of a Cromwellian mansion - the only one in the United Kingdom still standing in its own grounds. The Hall was built for Oliver St John, a member of Oliver Cromwell's cabinet, in 1652. The fact that Oliver St John was married to Cromwell's favourite niece, Elizabeth, perhaps helps to explain why this building is so special. The beautifully restored gardens at Thorpe Hall are open to the public and, during the summer months especially, they attract people from all over the United Kingdom and overseas. The ground floor of the Hall can be viewed by appointment and it's well worth taking time to admire the gorgeous wood carving in the Chapel, the magnificent Great Hall and the more intimate Parlour.

Since 1991 Thorpe Hall has been a Sue Ryder Care Centre providing specialist palliative care for local people with life-limiting diseases such as cancer. As well as a 24-bed hospice, Thorpe Hall also offers day care to over 60 people with chronic neurological illnesses. The south-facing courtyard at Thorpe Hall doubles as a sun trap and picnic area. Enjoying a picnic lunch with the scent of lavender wafting on the warm breeze on a sunny day is just one of the delights of Thorpe Hall. Just along the courtyard from the picnic area is the local Sue Ryder charity shop. It sells all sorts of recycled goods, including clothes, books, bric-a-brac, records, jigsaws, etc and has a reputation for being one of the best charity shops in the area. The shop is open every day, including Saturdays and Sundays, from 12 noon till 4pm and is staffed by volunteers. The shop manager can be phoned on 01733 264361.

Thorpe Hall workshop and display areas are situated in the old courtyard between the charity shop and the plant centre. Renato Antonelli is a real craftsman who creates beautiful furniture and many other items using natural materials gathered locally through conservation and recycling. Some of Rennie's work has been displayed in the Sculpture Garden at Burghley House, Stamford and his bog oak carvings at Flag Fen, Peterborough. Contact Renato Antonelli at www.eco-art.co.uk or on 01733 263389.

Situated in the old walled kitchen garden, the Thorpe Hall Plant Centre and Herb Nursery is open every day between 9.30am and 4.30pm. It is stocked with good-quality plants and herbs in season plus a variety of trees, shrubs, terracotta and garden stoneware. At present there are no public catering facilities near the Plant Centre. Visitors are advised to seek out the Butterfly Hotel or the Boat House Restaurant just down the road. Contact the Plant Centre on 01733 334443.

The Peterborough branch of the Society of Model Engineers has its headquarters at Thorpe Hall. Every Sunday afternoon between Easter and October children and adults enjoy rides on the miniature railway. The track has been laid out - complete with footbridge and tunnel - in what was Thorpe Hall's orchard. The ticket office and refreshments area can be found just inside the gate which is entered from the old courtyard, across from the Plant Centre.

SACREWELL FARM AND COUNTRY CENTRE

Thornhaugh, Peterborough, Cambridgeshire PE8 6HJ
Tel/Fax: 01780 782254

Built around a working 18th century water mill, **Sacrewell Farm and Country Centre**, run by a charitable organisation devoted to agricultural improvement, research and education, offers fascinating collections of farming implements from a bygone age and a range of farm animals, together with nature trails, play area, gift shop, restaurant serving light refreshments and facilities for camping and caravanning. Special events are held throughout the year such as lambing weekends and steam rallies.

LILFORD LODGE FARM

Barnwell Oundle, Peterborough, Cambridgeshire PE8 5SA
Tel/Fax: 01832 272230
e-mail: trudy@lilford-lodge.demon.co.uk

Trudy and Dolf Dijksterhuis welcome guests to their 300-acre mixed farm set in the attractive Nene Valley. Bed & Breakfast guests stay in the recently converted 19th century farmhouse, where the comfortably appointed accommodation consists of a double room, two twins, two singles and a family unit. All the bedrooms have en suite facilities, with central heating, tv and tea-makers, and the breakfast room and lounge are available for guests' use throughout the day. The farm has fishing rights on a single bank stretch of the River Nene.

All kinds of farming equipment are on display, and there's a collection of farm animals, along with gardens, nature and general interest trails, play areas, a gift shop and a restaurant serving light refreshments.

which face each other across the river. The finest of all the properties is undoubtedly **Peckover House**, a redbrick dwelling built in 1722 and bought at the end of the 18th century by Jonathan Peckover, a member of the Quaker banking family. The family gave the

WISBECH

One of the largest of the Fenland towns, Wisbech was a port in medieval times and still enjoying shipping trade with Europe. Somewhere along the navigable channel to the sea King John lost his jewels. Wisbech is at the centre of a thriving agricultural region and the 18th century in particular saw the building of rows of handsome houses, notably in North Brink and South Brink,

Museum Square, Wisbech

ELGOOD'S BREWERY & GARDENS

North Brink, Wisbech,
Cambridgeshire PE12 1LN
Tel: 01945 583160
Fax: 01945 587711

Elgood's Brewery is a 200-year-old classic Georgian brewery situated on the bank of the River Nene. This friendly and relaxing place is set amid true rural splendour.

The brewery was established in 1795, and was one of the first in this style to be built outside London. It is a lively and welcoming establishment, the perfect setting in which to savour a pint of one of their famous award-winning ales, enjoy a range of delicious snacks and home-made cakes in the cafe, or stroll around the gardens. Visitors can also enjoy observing traditional brewing methods, which use original open copper vessels - and can then sample a selection of real ales.

Famous locally and further afield for its welcoming hospitality and classic ales, Elgood's is not just for real ale enthusiasts - though there's plenty here to delight them as well. Behind the brewery is a four-acre garden with 150-year-old specimen trees, herbaceous borders, a lake, rockery, water features, exotics house, rose and herb gardens, and boasting many original Georgian and Victorian features. Beyond the walled gardens, there are lawns leading to the Millennium Maze, planted in the winter of 1992/93 - photographs of its progress are in the Visitors' Centre. The resident team of gardeners are happy to answer any questions. There is no 'formal route' to follow; visitors are welcome to roam at will, enjoying this marvellous garden, as have the Elgoods for many years.

This family-owned business is still run by the Elgoods: Nigel, his wife Anne and their three daughters. Belinda Sutton and Jennifer Everall are responsible for the Brewery and Claire Simpson,

who is qualified in garden design, has re-landscaped and planted the garden. Other amenities and attractions to delight the visitor include the café and licensed bar, gift and plant shop. The staff are helpful and friendly; in the garden shop they are happy to offer advice.

Gardens open: May to September, Wednesday to Friday, Sundays and Bank Holiday Mondays 1 pm - 5 pm; brewery tours Wednesday to Friday 2 pm. Please phone for more details.

building to the National Trust in 1948. Behind its elegant facade are splendid panelled rooms, Georgian fireplaces with richly carved overmantels, and ornate plaster decorations. At the back of the house is a beautiful walled garden with summerhouses and an orangery.

No 1 South Brink is the birthplace of Octavia Hill (1838-1912), co-founder of the National Trust and a tireless worker for the cause of the poor, particularly in the sphere of housing. The house is now the **Octavia Hill Museum** with displays and exhibits commemorating her work. More Georgian splendour is evident in the area where the Norman castle stood. The castle was replaced by a bishop's palace in 1478 and in the 17th century by a mansion built for Cromwell's Secretary of State John Thurloe. Local builder Joseph Medworth built the present Regency villa in 1816, and of the Thurloe mansion only the gate piers remain. The

Georgian Crescent, Wisbech

Wisbech and Fenland Museum is one of the oldest purpose-built museums in the country, and in charming Victorian surroundings visitors can view displays of porcelain, coins, rare rocks, Egyptian tomb treasures and several items of national importance, including the manuscript of Charles Dickens' *Great Expectations*, Napoleon's Sèvres breakfast

HUGGABLES TEDDY BEAR SHOP

4 Market Place, Wisbech, Cambridgeshire PE13 1DT
Tel: 01945 466100 Fax: 01945 466106
website: www.huggables.com

Belinda Bowen's love affair with teddy bears had already lasted many years when she opened **Huggables** in September 1998. Starting in very small premises elsewhere in Wisbech, she and her partner Tony Holmes have expanded the business into one of the largest and best-stocked teddy bear shops in Britain.

Behind the bow-windowed frontage of a tall Georgian building, the ground floor is a paradise for lovers of teddy bears, with bears of all colours and sizes and prices looking for new owners. At the top end of the market are the famous Steiff bears, aristocrats of the breed, and other notable manufacturers include Merrythought and Deans. Boyds Bears, newer to the market, are becoming very popular, and

as collectors items are still very reasonably priced. Bears are not the only inhabitants of this splendid shop on the market place. They are happy to share the well-lit display space with all kinds of dolls, from classic baby dolls to porcelain bride dolls and vinyl fashion dolls, each individually numbered, with a wide range of clothes and accessories to build up a fashion wardrobe.

Wisbech, one of the largest and most important of the Fenland towns, offers a wide variety of things to see and do, but for many visitors Huggables is a place they simply can't bear to miss!

SMART PROPERTIES

2A South Brink Place, Wisbech, Cambridgeshire PE13 1JB
Tel: 01945 583125 Fax: 01945 475109
(evenings 01945 583852)
website: www.thisiswisbech.co.uk/tiw/ac/smartproperties.htm

A lovely holiday cottage awaits guests in historic Wisbech, capital of the Fens. **Smart Properties** has a fully modernised and charming 17th century cottage to accommodate a family of four. There is a handsome beamed lounge, fully fitted kitchen with every modern amenity, dining area overlooking an enclosed courtyard, two spacious bedrooms and a bathroom and utility area with washing machine and tumble dryer.

WALPOLE WATER GARDENS

Chalk Road, Walpole St Peter, Wisbech,
Cambridgeshire PE14 7PH
Mobile: 0771 874 5935
website: www.walpolewatergardens.com

Admission is free to **Walpole Water Gardens**, an unusual place with over 20 kinds of eucalyptus, as well as palms, banana trees, bamboos, cannas, grasses and much more. Relaxing and welcoming, the picturesque grounds also include an art gallery featuring paintings and limited edition prints of wildlife and landscapes, a very good tea room, and shop selling exotic plants and Koi carp. Guided tours available.

ORGANIC CONNECTIONS

Riverdale, Town Street, Upwell, Wisbech, Cambridgeshire PE14 9AF
Tel: 01945 773374 Fax: 01945 773033
e-mail: sales@organic-connections.co.uk
website: www.organic-connections.co.uk

Organic Connections is a family-run business that puts a premium on top-quality produce grown without the use of artificial pesticides or fertilisers. Edwin and Karen Broad have been involved in Organics for ten years, and cater for the growing number of consumers who are worried about the links established between illness and allergies and the regular intake of pesticide residues. The site at Upwell is 100% organic, and Organic Connections work with local growers to supply the widest range and continuity from the UK. All the produce and growers are inspected annually by the Soil Association.

The main outlet for individual customers is through the Organic Box Scheme, which delivers boxes of produce to the customer in the shortest possible time. The standard boxes range from the Value Fruit and Veg Box at £7.50 to a Family Box at £25. Other options include a Barbecue Box, Mediterranean Box and a Pasta Box with organic pasta, chopped and puréed tomatoes and a selection of appropriate vegetables. Add-on Boxes of individual fruits and vegetables are available, and there are even boxes for cats and dogs. Organic Connections also offer a wonderful range of breads and rolls. Every product is produced to Soil Association Organic standards; grain syrups and fruit juices are the only sweeteners, and no hydrogenated fat is used.

set captured at Waterloo, and an ivory chess set that belonged to Louis XIV.

Wisbech is the stage for East Anglia's premier **Church Flower Festival**, with flowers in four churches, strawberry teas, crafts, bric-a-brac, plants and a parade of floats. The event takes place at the beginning of July. The most important of the churches is the Church of St Peter and St Paul, with two naves under one roof, and an independent tower with a peal of ten bells. Note the royal arms of James I and the 17th century wall monuments in the chancel. Other sights to see in Wisbech include **Elgoods Brewery**, a classic 200-year-old brewery at North Brink on the banks of the River Nene. Visitors can enjoy a pint and a snack, see the way beer is traditionally brewed and take a stroll round the gardens, which include a Millennium Maze (see panel on page 302). A prominent sight in town is the impressive 68 foot limestone memorial to Thomas Clarkson, one of the earliest leaders of the movement to abolish slavery. The monument was designed by Sir Giles Gilbert Scott in Gothic style.

THE FENS AROUND WISBECH

WEST WALTON AND WALTON HIGHWAY
3 miles NE of Wisbech off the A47/B198

There are several attractions here, notably the **Church of St Mary the Virgin** with its magnificent 13th century detached tower that dominates the landscape. West Walton is home to the **Fenland and West Norfolk Aviation Museum**, whose exhibits include Rolls-Royce Merlin engines, a Lightning jet, a Vampire and a Jumbo jet cockpit simulator. The museum is open at weekends in the summer.

GRASMERE PLANTS

School Road, Terrington St John, Wisbech, Cambridgeshire PE14 7SE
Tel: 01945 880514 e-mail: fleming@tstjohn.freeserve.co.uk

Shrubs and plants of all kinds are on display and for sale at **Grasmere Plants**, a charming little nursery started by Angela Fleming some 20 years ago. A wide variety of unusual shrubs, perennials, grasses and ornamental conifers are in stock at the nursery, which is open daily from April to October. Angela also opens her own delightful 1-acre garden to visitors on Thursday, Friday and Sunday afternoons, or by appointment. It contains lawns, trees, shrubs, herbaceous borders and seats for the weary.

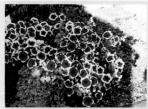

C & I D MARTIN

Mulberry House, 62 St Peter's Road, Upwell, Wisbech, Cambridgeshire PE14 9EJ
Tel: 01945 772239

Established in 1963 by Charles Martin's father in 1963, **C & I D Martin** is the one-stop outlet for every gardening need. As commercial producers of high-quality plants and nursery stock, the Martins grow all the plants in their own nurseries, so visitors can see the plants in various stages of growth, from seedlings to the final product. A side of the business that is growing all the time is the making up of planted bowls, baskets and patio containers, either to the customer's specification or left to the expertise of the staff, who are always ready with advice and tips for gardeners.

LEVERINGTON

1 mile NW of Wisbech off the A1101

The tower and spire of the **Church of St Leonard** date from the 13th and 14th centuries. The most exceptional feature of an exceptionally interesting church is the 15th century stained-glass Jesse window in the north aisle. There are many fine memorials in the churchyard. Oliver Goldsmith wrote *She Stoops to Conquer* while staying in Leverington.

PARSON DROVE

6 miles W of Wisbech on the B1187

Parson Drove is a Fenland village which Samuel Pepys visited in 1663. He stayed at the village's Swan Inn and mentions it in his diaries. It was a centre of the woad industry until 1914, when the last remaining woad mill was established. Parson Drove is most certainly not the "heathen place" once described by Pepys!

The **Parson Drove Visitors Centre** is set in the old Victorian lock-up on the village green, a building with an unusual 170-year history. Photographs and documents trace the story of this lovely Fens village.

WELNEY

12 miles S of Wisbech off the A1101

The **Wildfowl & Wetland Trust Welney** is a 900-acre site supporting an ever-changing variety of wildlife and birdlife on the borders of the meadows. There are hides for bird-watchers, a visitor centre and a tearoom. Teal, wigeon and various sorts of goose abound, but the most spectacular sight occurs at dusk from early November, when up to 5,000 yellow-nebbed Bewick's swans splash down to claim their roosting sites (see below).

THE WILDFOWL & WETLANDS TRUST

Hundred Foot Bank, Welney, Wisbech, Cambridgeshire PE14 9TN
Tel/Fax: 01353 860711
e-mail: welney@wwt.org.uk website: wwt.org.uk

The **Wildfowl & Wetland Trust Welney** is a wetland paradise of international importance with something to offer whatever the season. In winter, enjoy the magic of hundreds of Whooper and Bewick's Swans accompanied by flocks of thousands of ducks. During the day, carpets of Wigeon graze this precious wetland, while flocks of Pintail, Teal, Gadwall and Shoveler dabble in the pools and lagoons. Late afternoon is a special time as flocks of swans flight-in to claim their night roosting sites. Summer brings an atmosphere of peace and tranquillity broken only by the piping calls of waders, drumming Snipe and the chatter of warblers. Lush meadows are bordered by a dazzling display of Purple Loosestrife, Great Willowherb and Marsh Woundwort. Visitors can stroll along the boardwalks through rustling reedbeds, and spend a while pond-dipping for water beasts. The Visitor Centre houses displays, educational facilities and a well-stocked gift shop. WWT Welney also runs a packed programme of special events throughout the year.

TOURIST INFORMATION CENTRES

CAMBRIDGESHIRE

CAMBRIDGE

Wheeler Street
Cambridge
Cambridgeshire
CB2 3QB

Tel: 01223 322640
Fax: 01223 457588

Open all year
Open Bank Holidays

ELY

Oliver Cromwell's House
29 St Mary's Street
Ely
Cambridgeshire
CB7 4HF

Tel: 01353 662062
Fax: 01353 668518

Open all year
Open Bank Holidays

HUNTINGDON

The Library
Princes Street
Huntingdon
Cambridgeshire
PE18 6PH

Tel: 01480 388588
Fax: 01480 388591

Open all year
Closed Bank Holidays

PETERBOROUGH

45 Bridge Street
Peterborough
Cambridgeshire
PE1 1HA

Tel: 01733 452336
Fax: 01733 452353

Open all year
Open Bank Holidays

ST NEOTS

The Old Court
8 New Street
St Neots
Cambridgeshire
PE19 1AE

Tel: 01480 388788
Fax: 01480 388791

Open all year
Closed Bank Holidays

WISBECH

2-3 Bridge Street
Wisbech
Cambridgeshire
PE13 1EW

Tel: 01945 583263
Fax: 01945 463078

Open all year
Closed Bank Holidays

WITHERNSEA

Pier Towers
Withernsea
HU19 2JS

Tel: 01964 615683
Fax: 01964 615683

Not open all year
Open Bank Holidays

ESSEX

BRAINTREE

Town Hall Centre
Market Place
Braintree
Essex
CM7 3YG

Tel: 01376 550066
Fax: 01376 344345

Open all year
Closed Bank Holidays

BRENTWOOD

Pepperell House
44 High Street
Brentwood
Essex
CM14 4AJ

Tel: 01277 200300/201111
Fax: 01277 202375

Open all year
Closed Bank Holidays

CHELMSFORD

County Hall
Market Road
Chelmsford
Essex
CM1 1GG

Tel: 01245 283400
Fax: 01245 430705

Open all year
Closed Bank Holidays

CLACTON-ON-SEA

23 Pier Avenue
Clacton-on-Sea
Essex
CO15 1QD

Tel: 01255 423400
Fax: 01255 430906

Open all year
Open Bank Holidays

COLCHESTER

Visitor Information Centre
1 Queen Street
Colchester
Essex
CO1 2PG

Tel: 01206 282920
Fax: 01206 282924

Open all year
Open Bank Holidays

FLATFORD

Flatford Lane
Flatford, East Bergholt
Colchester
Essex
CO7 6UL

Tel: 01206 299460
Not open all year
Open Bank Holidays

HARWICH

Essex County Council
Iconfield Park, Parkeston
Harwich
Essex
CO12 4EN

Tel: 01255 506139
Fax: 01255 240570

Open all year
Open Bank Holidays

MALDON

Coach Lane
Maldon
Essex
CM9 4UH

Tel: 01621 856503
Fax: 01621 875873

Open all year
Open Bank Holidays

SAFFRON WALDEN

1 Market Place
Market Square
Saffron Walden
Essex
CB10 1HR

Tel: 01799 510444
Fax: 01799 510445

Open all year
Closed Bank Holidays

SOUTHEND-ON-SEA

19 High Street
Southend-on-Sea
Essex
SS1 1JE

Tel: 01702 215120
Fax: 01702 431449

Open all year
Open Bank Holidays

THURROCK

Granada Motorway Service Area
M25 Thurrock
Grays
Essex
RM16 3BG

Tel: 01708 863733
Fax: 01708 862440

Open all year
Open Bank Holidays

WALTHAM ABBEY

4 Highbridge Street
Waltham Abbey
Essex
EN9 1DG

Tel: 01992 652295
Fax: 01992 716234

Open all year
Open Bank Holidays

NORFOLK

AYLSHAM

Bure Valley Railway Station
Norwich Road
Aylsham
Norfolk
NR11 6BW

Tel: 01263 733903
Fax: 01263 733814

Open all year
Open Bank Holidays

CROMER

Prince of Wales Road
Cromer
Norfolk
NR27 9HS

Tel: 01263 512497
Fax: 01263 513613

Open all year
Open Bank Holidays

DISS

Meres Mouth
Mere Street
Diss
Norfolk
IP22 3AG

Tel: 01379 650523
Fax: 01379 650838

Open all year
Open Bank Holidays

FAKENHAM

Red Lion House
Market Place
Fakenham
Norfolk
NR21 9BY

Tel: 01328 851981

Not open all year
Open Bank Holidays

GREAT YARMOUTH

Marine Parade
Great Yarmouth
Norfolk
NR31 8NE

Tel: 01493 842195
Accom. No.: 01493 842195
Fax: 01493 846221

Not open all year
Open Bank Holidays

HOVETON

Station Road
Hoveton
Norfolk
NR12 8UR

Tel: 01603 782281
Accom. No.: 01603 782281
Fax: 01603 782281

Not open all year
Open Bank Holidays

HUNSTANTON

Town Hall
The Green
Hunstanton
Norfolk
PE36 6BQ

Tel: 01485 532610
Fax: 01485 533972

Open all year
Open Bank Holidays

KING'S LYNN

The Custom House
Purfleet Quay
King's Lynn
Norfolk
PE30 1HP

Tel: 01553 763044
Accom. No.: 01553 763044
Fax: 01553 777281

Open all year
Open Bank Holidays

MUNDESLEY

2 Station Road
Mundesley
Norfolk
NR11 8JH

Tel: 01263 721070

Not open all year
Open Bank Holidays

NORWICH

The Guildhall
Gaol Hill
Norwich
Norfolk
NR2 1NF

Tel: 01603 666071
Fax: 01603 765389

Open all year
Open Bank Holidays

SHERINGHAM

Station Approach
Sheringham
Norfolk
NR26 8RA

Tel: 01263 824329
Fax: 01263 321663

Not open all year
Open Bank Holidays

WELLS-NEXT-THE-SEA

Staithe Street
Wells-next-the-Sea
Norfolk
NR23 1AN

Tel: 01328 710885
Fax: 01328 711405

Not open all year
Open Bank Holidays

SUFFOLK

ALDEBURGH

The Cinema
51 High Street
Aldeburgh
Suffolk
IP15 5AU

Tel: 01728 453637
Fax: 01728 453637

Open all year
Open Bank Holidays

BECCLES

The Quay
Fen Lane
Beccles
Suffolk
NR34 9BH

Tel: 01502 713196
Accom. No.: 01502 2713196
Fax: 01502 713196

Not open all year
Open Bank Holidays

BURY ST EDMUNDS

6 Angel Hill
Bury St Edmunds
Suffolk
IP33 1UZ

Tel: 01284 764667
Fax: 01284 757084

Open all year
Open Bank Holidays

FELIXSTOWE

The Seafront
Felixstowe
Suffolk
IP11 8AB

Tel: 01394 276770
Fax: 01394 277456

Open all year
Open Bank Holidays

IPSWICH

St Stephens Church
St Stephens Lane
Ipswich
Suffolk
IP1 1DP

Tel: 01473 258070
Fax: 01473 258072

Open all year
Open Bank Holidays

LAVENHAM

Lady Street
Lavenham
Suffolk
CO10 9RA

Tel: 01787 248207

Not open all year
Open Bank Holidays

LOWESTOFT

East Point Pavilion
Royal Plain
Lowestoft
Suffolk
NR33 OAP

Tel: 01502 523000
Fax: 01502 539023

Open all year
Open Bank Holidays

NEWMARKET

Palace House
Palace Street
Newmarket
Suffolk
CB8 8EP

Tel: 01638 667200
Fax: 01638 660394

Open all year
Closed Bank Holidays

SOUTHWOLD

Town Hall
Market Place
Southwold
Suffolk
IP18 6EF

Tel: 01502 724729
Fax: 01502 722978

Not open all year
Open Bank Holidays

STOWMARKET

Wilkes Way
Stowmarket
Suffolk
IP14 1DE

Tel: 01449 676800
Fax: 01449 614691

Open all year
Open Bank Holidays

SUDBURY

Town Hall
Market Hill
Sudbury
Suffolk
CO10 1TL

Tel: 01787 881320

Open all year
Open Bank Holidays

WOODBRIDGE

Station Buildings
Woodbridge
Suffolk
IP12 4AJ

Tel: 01394 382240
Fax: 01394 382240

Open all year
Open Bank Holidays

INDEX OF ADVERTISERS

INDEX OF WALKS

Travel Publishing

Regional and National guides to the less well-known places of interest and places to eat, stay and drink

Regional guides to traditional pubs and inns throughout the United Kingdom

Regional and National guides to 18 hole golf courses and local places to stay, eat and drink

COUNTRY LIVING
M A G A Z I N E
RURAL GUIDES

Regional and National guides to the traditional countryside of Britain and Ireland with easy to read facts on places to visit, stay, eat, drink and shop

For more information:

Phone: 0118 981 7777   e-mail: travel_publishing@msn.com
website: www.travelpublishing.co.uk

Easy-to-use, Informative
Travel Guides on the British Isles

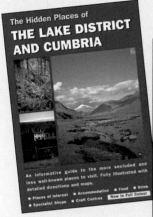

The Hidden Places of
**THE LAKE DISTRICT
AND CUMBRIA**

An informative guide to the more secluded and
less well-known places to visit. Fully illustrated with
detailed directions and maps.

● Places of Interest ● Accommodation ● Food ● Drink
● Specialist Shops ● Craft Centres **Now In Full Colour**

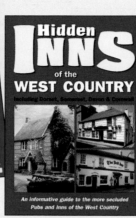

**Hidden
INNS**
of the
WEST COUNTRY
Including Dorset, Somerset, Devon & Cornwall

An informative guide to the more secluded
Pubs and Inns of the West Country

The Hidden Places of
SCOTLAND

● Food
● Drink
● Accommodation
● Places of Interest

An informative guide to the more
secluded and less well-known places
to visit in Scotland. Fully illustrated
with detailed directions and maps

Now in Full Colour

COUNTRY LIVING
**GUIDE TO
RURAL
ENGLAND
THE SOUTH**

● Where to go ● What to see ● What to do
● Where to stay ● Where to eat ● Where to buy
Fully illustrated with detailed directions and maps

**THE GOLFERS GUIDE
to Ireland**

Packed with information on Golf Courses and where to stay, eat and drink

Dermot Gilleece

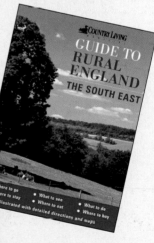

COUNTRY LIVING
**GUIDE TO
RURAL
ENGLAND
THE SOUTH EAST**

Where to go ● What to see ● What to do
Where to stay ● Where to eat ● Where to buy
illustrated with detailed directions and maps

Travel Publishing Limited

7a Apollo House ● Calleva Park ● Aldermaston ● Berkshire RG7 8TN

ORDER FORM

To order any of our publications just fill in the payment details below and complete the order form. For orders of less than 4 copies please add £1 per book for postage and packing. Orders over 4 copies are P & P free.

Please Complete Either:

I enclose a cheque for £ [   ] made payable to Travel Publishing Ltd

Or:

Card No: [   ] Expiry Date: [   ]

Signature: [   ]

NAME: [   ]

ADDRESS: [   ]

TEL NO: [   ]

Please either send, telephone, fax or e-mail your order to:

Travel Publishing Ltd, 7a Apollo House, Calleva Park, Aldermaston, Berkshire RG7 8TN
Tel: 0118 981 7777   Fax: 0118 982 0077 e-mail: karen@travelpublishing.co.uk

	Price	Quantity		Price	Quantity
Hidden Places Regional Titles			**Hidden Places National Titles**		
Cambs & Lincolnshire	£7.99	....	England	£11.99	....
Chilterns	£8.99	....	Ireland	£11.99	....
Cornwall	£8.99	....	Scotland	£11.99	....
Derbyshire	£7.99	....	Wales	£11.99	....
Devon	£8.99	....			
Dorset, Hants & Isle of Wight	£8.99	....	**Hidden Inns Titles**		
East Anglia	£8.99	....	Heart of England	£5.99	....
Gloucestershire & Wiltshire	£7.99	....	Lancashire & Cheshire	£5.99	....
Heart of England	£7.99	....	South	£5.99	....
Hereford, Worcs & Shropshire	£7.99	....	South East	£5.99	....
Highlands & Islands	£7.99	....	South and Central Scotland	£5.99	....
Kent	£8.99	....	Wales	£5.99	....
Lake District & Cumbria	£8.99	....	Welsh Borders	£5.99	....
Lancashire & Cheshire	£8.99	....	West Country	£5.99	....
Lincolnshire & Nottinghamshire	£8.99	....			
Northumberland & Durham	£8.99	....	**Country Living Guides to Rural England**		
Somerset	£7.99	....	East Anglia	£9.99	....
Sussex	£7.99	....	South of England	£9.99	....
Thames Valley	£7.99	....	South East of England	£9.99	....
Yorkshire	£7.99	....	West Country	£9.99	....

Total Quantity [   ]   **Total Value** [   ]

READER REACTION FORM

The *Travel Publishing* research team would like to receive reader's comments on any visitor attractions or places reviewed in the book and also recommendations for suitable entries to be included in the next edition. This will help ensure that the *Country Living series of Rural Guides* continues to provide its readers with useful information on the more interesting, unusual or unique features of each attraction or place ensuring that their visit to the local area is an enjoyable and stimulating experience. To provide your comments or recommendations would you please complete the forms below and overleaf as indicated and send to:

The Research Department, Travel Publishing Ltd,

7a Apollo House, Calleva Park, Aldermaston, Reading, RG7 8TN.

Your Name:

Your Address:

Your Telephone Number:

Please tick as appropriate: Comments ☐ Recommendation ☐

Name of Establishment:

Address:

Telephone Number:

Name of Contact:

READER REACTION FORM

Comment or Reason for Recommendation:

....

....

....

....

....

....

....

....

....

....

....

INDEX TO TOWNS & PLACES OF INTEREST

I